GRANDPARENTS IN CULTURAL CONTEXT

Grandparents in Cultural Context provides a long overdue global view of the changing roles of grandparents. The 11 main chapters are by experts on grandparenthood in the Americas, Europe, Russia, Asia, Africa and the Middle East, and the editors integrate findings from these cutting-edge chapters with past work to formulate an agenda for future international research. Rather than statistically dense research reports, each chapter provides a thought-provoking and integrative review of research, real-life case stories, cultural/historical backgrounds, predictions for the future, and applied implications for grandparenthood across and within societies.

Calling special attention to the roles of grandfathers, and of societies seldom represented in the literature, this book cites hundreds of references to work previously unavailable in English-language publications. It also includes learning features (including maps, demographic tables, discussion questions, and web resources) that make it suitable as a text for upper division under graduate or graduate level courses in the behavioral, social, and family sciences. It is relevant to psychology, gerontology, family studies, anthropology, family/comparative sociology, education, social work, gender studies, ethnic studies, psychiatry, and international studies. Practitioners, service providers, policymakers, and internationally minded grandparents will also enjoy this book.

David W. Shwalb (Ph.D., University of Michigan, Developmental Psychology) is Professor of Psychology at Southern Utah University. Co-editor of six previous books including *Fathers in Cultural Context* (2013, Routledge), he is a former Society for Cross-Cultural Research president and Fulbright awardee.

Ziarat Hossain (Ph.D., Syracuse University, Child and Family Studies) is a Professor of Family and Child Studies and Regents' Lecturer at the University of New Mexico. He is a former Society for Cross-Cultural Research president and Fulbright Scholar.

GRANDPARENTS IN CULTURAL CONTEXT

Edited by
David W. Shwalb
Ziarat Hossain

Routledge
Taylor & Francis Group

NEW YORK AND LONDON

First published 2018
by Routledge
711 Third Avenue, New York, NY 10017

and by Routledge
2 Park Square, Milton Park, Abingdon, Oxon, OX14 4RN

Routledge is an imprint of the Taylor & Francis Group, an informa business

© 2018 Taylor & Francis

Library of Congress Cataloging-in-Publication Data
Names: Shwalb, David W., author. | Hossain, Ziarat, author.
Title: Grandparents in cultural context / David W. Shwalb, Ziarat Hossain.
Description: 1st Edition. | New York : Routledge, 2018. |
Includes bibliographical references and indexes.
Identifiers: LCCN 2017006867| ISBN 9781138125780 (hb : alk. paper) |
ISBN 9781138188501 (pb : alk. paper) | ISBN 9781315642284 (ebook)
Subjects: LCSH: Grandparents–Cross-cultural studies. |
Grandparenting–Cross-cultural studies.
Classification: LCC HQ759.9 .S549 2017 | DDC 306.874/5–dc23
LC record available at https://lccn.loc.gov/2017006867

ISBN: 978-1-138-12578-0 (hbk)
ISBN: 978-1-138-18850-1 (pbk)
ISBN: 978-1-315-64228-4 (ebk)

Typeset in Bembo
by Out of House Publishing

Visit the eResources website: www.routledge.com/9781138188501

David W. Shwalb

To my grandparents,

- Harry (Hersch) and Lena Newman Shwalb. Harry (Figure D.1) emigrated from Berestechko (now in Ukraine) to the US in 1906. As the only Shwalb to leave the Old World, Harry saved the Shwalb name from the Holocaust, passing on the family line to their only child, Richard, and four grandchildren.
- Solomon and Martha (Figure D.2) Landberg Greenwald. Immigrants from Nesvizh (now in Belarus) in the 1890s, they worked seven days a week as shopkeepers to provide a better life in America for their three children, Sidney, Shirley, and Sylvia, and six grandchildren.

And to my wife, colleague, better-half, and role model as a grandparent:

- Barbara J. Shwalb (Figure D.3). Barbara is an active, involved, loving, and passionate grandmother who treasures each of her grandchildren and great-grandchildren.

FIGURE D.1 Harry Shwalb with grandson Gene

FIGURE D.2 Martha Greenwald with granddaughter Edie

FIGURE D.3 Barbara Shwalb with granddaughter Courtney

Source: Courtesy of David W. Shwalb.

Ziarat Hossain

To my grandparents,

- Adalat Bepari and Saleha Khatun, who were born and raised in Dhaka, Bangladesh. They had one daughter, three sons, and 28 grandchildren. My father, Zainul, was their fourth child.
- Alhaj Safatullah Khan (Figure D.4) and Shakhina Khatun (Figure D.5), who were also born and raised in Dhaka. They had nine children (four sons and five daughters) and 68 grandchildren. My mother, Saira, was their fourth child. I was the first of their grandchildren to arrive in the U.S., in 1989.

FIGURE D.4 Alhaj Safatullah Khan

FIGURE D.5 Shakhina Khatun with grandson Sunny

CONTENTS

CONTRIBUTORS

Yasser Abdelazim, Department of Geography and GIS, Assiut University, Assiut City, Egypt

Rosa Azambuja, Postgraduate Program on Family in Contemporary Society, Catholic University of Salvador, Salvador, Brazil

Nandita Babu, Department of Psychology, University of Delhi, Delhi, India

Ana Cecília Bastos, Postgraduate Program on Family in Contemporary Society, Catholic University of Salvador, Salvador, Brazil

Ann Buchanan, Department of Social Policy and Intervention, University of Oxford, Oxford, UK

Cristina Dias, Center of Biological Sciences and Health, Catholic University of Pernambuco, Recife, Brazil

Mogeda El-Keshky, Department of Psychology, King Abdul-Aziz University, Jeddah, Saudi Arabia

Mahmoud Emam, Department of Psychology, Sultan Qaboos University, Muscat, Oman

Heribert Engstler, German Centre of Gerontology, Berlin, Germany

Regina Fanjul de Marsicovetere, Unidad de Bienestar Estudiantil, Universidad del Valle Guatemala, Guatemala City, Guatemala

Christine A. Fruhauf, Department of Human Development and Family Studies, Colorado State University, Fort Collins, CO, USA

Judith L. Gibbons, Department of Psychology, Saint Louis University, St. Louis, MO, USA

Ntombizonke A. Gumede, Human and Social Development, Human Sciences Research Council, Pretoria, South Africa

Bert Hayslip Jr., Department of Psychology, University of North Texas, Denton, TX, USA

Ziarat Hossain, Department of Individual, Family and Community Education, University of New Mexico, Albuquerque, NM, USA

Jung-Hwan Hyun, Department of Childcare & Education, Seoul Theological University, Buchon City, South Korea

Stan Ingman, Applied Gerontology Program, University of North Texas, Denton, TX, USA

Daniela Klaus, German Centre of Gerontology, Berlin, Germany

Pei-Chun Ko, Asia Research Institute & Center for Family and Population Research, National University of Singapore, Singapore

Katharina Mahne, German Centre of Gerontology, Berlin, Germany

Monde Makiwane, Human and Social Development, Human Science Research Council, Pretoria, South Africa & North–West University, Mafikeng, South Africa

Mzolisi Makiwane, Department of Education, Government of South Africa, Pietermaritzburg, South Africa

Ami Moore, Department of Sociology, University of North Texas, Denton, TX, USA

Jessica E. Morales, Department of Individual, Family and Community Education, University of New Mexico, Albuquerque, NM, USA

Elias Mpofu, Discipline of Rehabilitation Counselling, University of Sydney, Sydney, Australia; & Educational Psychology and Inclusive Education, University of Johannesburg, Johannesburg, South Africa

Magen Mhaka-Mutepfa, International Health Program, University of Sydney, Sydney, Australia

Jun Nakazawa, Department of Developmental Science, Chiba University, Chiba, Japan

Elaine Rabinovich, Postgraduate Program on the Family in Contemporary Society, Catholic University of Salvador, Salvador, Brazil

David W. Shwalb, Department of Psychology, Southern Utah University, Cedar City, UT, USA

Maximiliane E. Szinovacz, Department of Gerontology, University of Massachusetts Boston, Boston, MA, USA

Jennifer Utrata, Department of Sociology and Anthropology, University of Puget Sound, Tacoma, WA, USA

Shivani Vij, Department of Psychology, Aryabhatta College, University of Delhi, Delhi, India

FOREWORD

As I outlined in the introduction to the *Handbook on Grandparenthood* (Szinovacz, 1998), there has been substantial progress in grandparenting research since the middle of the 20th century, and this progress has continued during the past two decades. Yet significant gaps in research on grandparenthood remain. One of these gaps is without doubt insufficient knowledge of or attention to contextuality. Grandparenthood is a universal status, yet its experience and meaning vary considerably across societies, cultures, and different population subgroups. This diversity in grandparenting experiences and meanings evolves, at least in part, from the contexts in which grandparenthood is embedded, ranging from societal structures (e.g., historical, cultural, or socioeconomic) to subcultural value patterns and norms, or gender roles.

This gap can be attributed to several limitations in past research. First, research on grandparenthood in many countries is either non-existent or in its very beginnings. We thus have in-depth knowledge about grandparenthood in some (mainly Western and developed) nations, but lack information on grandparenthood in many other less developed societies (e.g., in Africa). However, research on grandparents in diverse cultures, at different stages of development, is essential both for theory construction and to inform social policy. For example, extended family structures often serve to bring grandparents and grandchildren together, free mothers to pursue farm work or gainful employment while grandparents care for their children, and serve as safety nets for aging grandparents. Modernization in some countries (e.g., in Asia) has been accompanied by a transition from extended to more nuclear family structures. More research on grandparenting in countries undergoing modernization could indicate whether and when during the modernization process families become more nuclear and which factors hasten, hinder, or altogether counteract such transitions in family structure. Such insights are essential to establish both the extent and timing for developing institutionalized social supports for child and elder care.

A second limitation in past research is the lack of comparative cross-national, cross-cultural, and cross-subcultural studies. Such comparative studies can help disentangle the complex interplay of diverse factors on grandparental roles and behaviors. For instance, the widespread predominance of grandmothers in the care of grandchildren has been mainly attributed to gender norms that emphasize women's roles as caregivers and kin keepers. However, selected historical or socio-economic contexts may further strengthen or lessen this normative mandate. Male absence in families either due to wars (Russia, Africa) or to single parenthood, violence, or crime may engrain matrifocal grandparenting, whereas reliance on female employment for family support may promote more egalitarian gender roles and thus more participation of grandfathers in the care of grandchildren (some African-American families, urban middle-class families in numerous countries).

Yet another limitation in past research is the reliance on cross-sectional studies and thus on specific stages in the grandparenting experience. From a life course perspective, it is essential to follow the development of grandparent roles over time and to assess how grandparent roles and meanings change as grandchildren and grandparents age. For example, much of the literature focuses on grandparents' care for grandchildren, but such care is not needed once the grandchildren have reached adulthood. In contrast, we know very little about grandparent–grandchild relations once grandparents become frail and approach death, although the handful of studies suggest that parental care for grandparents can have a profound influence on the grandchildren (Szinovacz, 2008; see also Chapter 6, this volume).

Another focus of the life course perspective is the timing of life events. Current literature stresses that increased longevity and declining fertility are leading to fundamental changes in family structures, namely a shift from horizontally extended families (many same-generation relatives, but few co-existing generations) to so-called beanpole families (Bengtson, Rosenthal, & Burton, 1990) with few same-generation relatives but considerable vertical extension (e.g., grandparents live into grandchildren's adulthood, great-grandparents). This concept presumes that vertical extension of families is based foremost on increases in longevity. However, it also depends, according to some research (Matthews & Sun, 2006), on the timing of childbearing. Trends toward delayed fertility in some cultures and subcultures will thus lead to wide variations in the onset of grandparenthood. In addition, the timing between births and the number of births will determine whether grandparents simultaneously have several grandchildren of similar age or grandchildren ranging from babies to adults. If the spread between births is large enough generations may even overlap. For example, Queen Elizabeth II has a 5-year-old great-grandchild (Prince George, the son of her grandson Prince William, and a 9-year-old grandson, James, Viscount Severn, the son of her son Prince Edward). As shown in the introduction to the 1998 *Handbook*, both longevity, timing of fertility, and fertility rates vary widely across nations, which thus leads to considerable variation in the onset of grandparenthood and its duration. These variations are likely to have profound effects on how grandparents enact their role. For example, a 40-year-old grandmother is likely to engage in very different activities with her grandchildren than a 65-year-old grandmother. Furthermore, the young grandmother may experience inter-role conflict with employment, whereas the older grandmother may be faced with simultaneous grandchild and parent care responsibilities.

Insufficient attention has also been paid to the dual role of gender in grandparenting. On the one hand, we know very little about grandfathers; on the other hand much of the research does not differentiate between paternal and maternal grandparents. To close this gap, it is essential to conduct research that includes both grandmothers and grandfathers and studies that compare the roles and activities of paternal and maternal grandparents. The chapters in this volume demonstrate that hands-on care is nearly universally grandmothers' domain, although grandfathers have started to participate in such care in some Western countries as well as in select urban middle-class families in other regions. Patrilineal family systems such as those in Asia or in the Middle East (with the exception of Jewish families) tend to favor close relations and co-residence with paternal grandparents, whereas the bilateral kinship systems in much of Europe and the US promote closer relationships between grandchildren and maternal grandparents, primarily through strong mother–daughter ties (Rossi & Rossi, 1990).

In view of these limitations, and the list is certainly not exhaustive, a volume addressing grandparenthood in many different societies and cultures was long overdue. This book offers not only insights into the diversity of grandparent experiences across various cultures and societies, but also demonstrates biases in current (mainly Western) research, which includes the lack of attention to grandfathers or lack of differentiation between maternal and paternal grandparents. The laudable emphasis on inclusion of material on grandfathers in all chapters indicates that although grandfathers may play a relatively marginal role in some societies (e.g., Russia), they can serve important functions as transmitters of culture and family authority figures in other countries (e.g., Arabic countries).

Comparisons across cultures also allow identification of factors associated with specific grandparent roles and their influence on grandparents' and grandchildren's well-being. For example, skipped-generation households (due to wars in the Middle East, the AIDS pandemic in Africa, and outmigration in China) seem to be universally burdensome for grandparents. The only exception is, perhaps, fostering of grandchildren with the specific purpose of providing support and companionship to grandparents, as is the case in Ghana. Other grandparenting structures have more diverse outcomes, depending on whether or not they are normative and voluntary. For example, the traditional extended families in Asia or the Middle East were typically seen as normative and seemed to provide benefits to grandparents, parents (despite some conflicts between grandmothers and their daughters-in-law), and grandchildren, whereas the mainly non-normative and involuntary extension of households to care for frail or dying grandparents can place a heavy burden on the parents and the grandchildren (Szinovacz, 2008; Zarit, 2004). Similarly, research in Western countries suggests that grandparents play a marginal role in the financial support of families, whereas such support seems to be quite commonplace in some African and Asian countries.

Another important aspect of this volume is the coverage of pertinent old age and family policies. These sections demonstrate which policies empower grandparents to fulfill their responsibilities and to maintain contacts with grandchildren (e.g., visitation rights in some Western countries), and which policies exacerbate grandparents' plight (e.g., China's household registration system, which often forces migrant workers to leave their children behind in their rural homes under the care of the grandparents). They also demonstrate vividly the lack of family support in many countries, which can result in heavy financial burdens for grandparents.

We still have much to learn about grandparenthood in all cultures but especially in developing and non-Western societies. This volume provides an important first step toward a cross-cultural understanding of grandparenthood and toward insights into the diverse contexts that shape grandparents' roles and functions. Given the important support that grandparents provide for families and that families offer grandparents, more comparative research is needed not only to expand our knowledge base but also to inform policies.

Maximiliane E. Szinovacz

References

Bengtson, V. L., Rosenthal, C., & Burton, L. (1990). Families and aging: Diversity and heterogeneity. In R. H. Binstock & L. K. George (Eds.), *Handbook of aging and the social sciences* (3rd ed., pp. 263–287). New York: Academic Press.

Matthews, S., & Sun, R. (2006). Incidence of four-generation family lineages: Is timing of fertility or mortality a better explanation?. *Journals of Gerontology B: Psychological and Social Sciences, 61*(2), S99–S106. doi:10.1093/geronb/61.2.S99

Rossi, A. S., & Rossi, P. H. (1990). *Of human bonding: Parent–child relations across the life course.* New York: Aldine de Gruyte.

Szinovacz, M. E. (1998). Grandparent research: Past, present, and future. In M. E. Szinovacz (Ed.), *Handbook on grandparenthood* (pp. 1–20). Westport, CT: Greenwood Press.

Szinovacz, M. E. (2008). Children in caregiving families. In M. E. Szinovacz & A. Davey (Eds.), *Caregiving contexts: Cultural, familial, and societal implications* (pp. 161–190). New York: Springer.

Zarit, S. H. (2004). Family care and burden at the end of life. *Canadian Medical Association Journal, 770*, 1811–1812.

PREFACE

Grandparents in Cultural Context documents the contexts and practices of grand-parents across a wide variety of societies. This exploration will indicate that there is vast diversity and commonality in their roles between and within societies and regions. Previous scholarship on grandparents (reviewed in Chapter 1) has sug-gested the worldwide significance and involvement of grandparents within fami-lies, but research documentation has been scant in most countries outside Western Europe and North America. We edited this volume to fill the geographical gaps in the literature, and hope the insights within the 11 main chapters stimulate new discussions about research and theories. Meanwhile, work on this book caused us to reflect about our own grandparents; we hope that many readers may also gain a deeper personal understanding of their own grandparents as we uncover the con-textual nature of grandparenthood.

As fellow past-presidents of the Society for Cross-Cultural Research (SCCR), we had organized various sessions on fathering and families for SCCR confer-ences, and following the success of *Fathers in Cultural Context* (Shwalb, Shwalb, & Lamb, 2013, Routledge) we decided at the SCCR's 2015 annual meeting in Albuquerque to propose a similar international volume on grandparents, who seemed to be even more neglected than fathers in the cross-cultural literature. As developmental psychologists with a shared cross-cultural perspective, our previous respective research endeavors had focused on fathering, parenting, and child devel-opment. Our past work made it obvious to us that today's parents are very much a product of what they learned from today's grandparents, and that parents and grandparents are influenced by many of the same contextual and cultural factors. Thus, our focus on grandparents in this volume was a natural extension of our past work on parents and families.

For the sake of readability and cross-chapter comparisons, each of the 11 main chapters has a similar structure, and they share at least three important features. First, all chapter contributors discuss the research literature within the sociocultural context of grandparents in a particular society or region. Second, we insisted that every chapter contain at least a brief section on grandfathers, who are too often omitted from research studies of grandparents. Third, every chapter includes a discussion of policy or legal issues with implications for grandparents. These three features are articulated within the contexts of societal norms and values, globalization, technological changes, migration, and health issues. Rather than technical or statistically dense research reports, each chapter provides a thought-provoking, comprehensive, and integrative review of empirical data, real-life examples, cultural influences, and applied implications for grandparenthood across and within societies.

Designed first as a resource for scholars and students, this volume is also suitable as a textbook or supplemental reader for upper division undergraduate or graduate level courses in the behavioral, social, and family sciences. It is highly relevant to the disciplines of psychology, gerontology, family studies, anthropology, family/comparative sociology, education, social work, gender studies, ethnic studies, psychiatry, and international studies. Practitioners, service providers, and policymakers interested in grandparents may also find this book useful.

Multidisciplinary scholarship on grandparents is a growing specialization. The findings presented in this book, overall and chapter-by-chapter, present a compelling case that changes in longevity, socioeconomic conditions, and cultural practices will make the study of grandparents even more important in the future. In addition to making the case for more international studies of grandparents, this book reveals across societies the need to study how to care for the growing numbers of grandparents worldwide. We sincerely hope that this book will stimulate research that will help people everywhere to better understand, support, and repay our grandparents, and to build international bridges between cultures, scholars, and grandparents.

David W. Shwalb and Ziarat Hossain

ACKNOWLEDGMENTS

We thank Georgette Enriquez, Brian Eschrich, Rachel Severinovsky, Mhairi Bennett, and Debra Riegert of Routledge/Taylor & Francis for their encouragement and expert guidance, along with Emma Harder, Liz Davey (Out of House Publishing) and Anny Mortada. We express our deepest gratitude to the authors of the 11 main chapters for their patience with our editing and requests for multiple drafts of their contributions, and to Maximiliane Szinovacz for writing an authoritative Foreword. Geographer Paul R. Larson of the Southern Utah University (SUU) Department of Physical Science customized five maps to help readers understand the relationship between grandparenting and "place," and SUU's Rohn Solomon designed the front cover of this book with excellence. We sincerely thank Hadeel Al-Essa and Andrea Jaquish at the University of New Mexico (UNM) for their work on the Indexes. Appreciation is also due to Twyla Hill and other (anonymous) reviewers of our book prospectus.

(David Shwalb) – Appreciation is also due to the SUU Psychology Department (Britt Mace, Chair; and Joan Young) and the SUU College of Humanities & Social Sciences (James McDonald, Dean). Special thanks are extended to SUU President Scott Wyatt and Provost Bradley J. Cook for granting a 2015–2016 sabbatical to enable work on this volume, and to co-editor Ziarat Hossain for his characteristic patience, insights, and friendship. Our amount of work as co-editors was equal. Most importantly, I thank Barbara J. Shwalb, who first suggested that we study grandparents, for her career-long wise and excellent scholarship, collaboration, and encouragement. I (along with Barbara) acknowledge our own grandchildren and great-grandchildren, with love: Alexis, Benjamin, Boris, Brantley, Caden, Corbin, Courtney, Davy, Elijah, Elizabeth, Havah, Jenny, Kayla, Kelty, Lucy, Lumen, Meagan, Rachel, Sam, Tommy, Zanna, and Zoe. Finally, we are indebted to our children, Lori, Connie, Becky, David, and Debbie, who have encouraged us to be active grandparents.

(Ziarat Hossain) – I thank my UNM colleagues, Jay Parkes (Department Chair), Hector Ochoa (College of Education Dean), and Carol Parker (Senior Vice-Provost) for approving a 2016 sabbatical to enable work on this book. I also acknowledge the assistance I received from my department staff and students. I am grateful to David Shwalb for offering me the opportunity to co-edit this book with him, and to Jaipaul Roopnarine (Syracuse University) for providing academic mentorship throughout my professional life. I am indebted to my wife (Rozy Akhter) and three wonderful children (Razine, Ryan, and Ziana) for allowing me to work long hours on the book. Finally, my parents (Zainul Abedeen and Saira Khatun) and grandparents deserve special thanks for raising me with great care and love.

PART I
Introduction

1

INTRODUCTION

David W. Shwalb and Ziarat Hossain

The roles of grandparents have changed throughout human history and have varied across cultures. For example, grandfathers were revered as symbols of absolute family patriarchy in many societies; men (including grandfathers) enjoyed authority over women in ancient Chinese, Roman, and Greek civilizations, and early in the histories of the Hindu, Judaic, Christian, and Islamic religions (Falk & Falk, 2002). Grandmothers and grandfathers within all of these traditions have transmitted values and rituals as socialization agents for their children and grandchildren. Meanwhile, religions and indigenous practices have often idealized the authority role of grandfathers. Despite our knowledge of the importance of grandparents in these ancient traditions, social scientists have only recently begun to study grandparents across modern cultural communities.

In fact, 25 years after *The Psychology of Grandparenthood: An International Perspective* (Smith, 1991) showed the need for global studies of grandparenthood, grandparents remain under-studied in most countries (as was also emphasized in the Foreword, this volume). This is despite recognition of the contemporary importance of grandparents by specialists in gerontology, sociology, psychology, family studies, and other disciplines (Szinovacz, 1998). Meanwhile, rapid and varied demographic and social changes in many societies have called attention to changes in the nature of grandparents' roles. Specifically, in some societies grandparents now have longer lifespans than previously in history and comprise a growing proportion of the overall population. Additionally, families have more generations alive, and there are fewer siblings, aunts, uncles, and other relatives within each generation (Harper, 2005). We know that such trends influence the lives of grandparents and their families, as mediated by numerous contextual variables.

Grandparenting research has typically been uncommon in developing countries. This particular gap in documentation is unfortunate because grandparents may have traditionally had an especially strong role as authorities in non-Western and traditional societies. This concentration of research in developed societies is also ironic because grandparental involvement is often stronger in developing societies than in Western societies, where most grandparenting research takes place (Pope Edwards, Ren, & Brown, 2015). In some affluent societies the concept of grandparental "non-interference" (see also Chapter 6 on the UK) asserts that grandparents should not interfere with parental authority over children. Yet there has been notable scientific research on grandparents in many developing societies in the 21st century, evidenced by the studies reported in this book and other recent volumes (e.g., Arber & Timonen, 2012; Mehta & Thang, 2012; Buchanan & Rotkirch, 2017).

Our book introduces the reader to several hundred recent research studies on grandparents that were previously only accessible in non-English-language publications. It includes findings from five continents and from countries and regions inhabited by a majority of the world's population. Experts on grandparents and family relations in 11 diverse societies (or regions) discuss cultural, economic, and historical influences, the social science research literature on grandparents, variations between and within cultures, comparisons between grandmothers and grandfathers, and social policies relevant to grandparenting. We do not claim that the 11 main chapters represent all grandparents in any of these societies or regions, or that the research literatures cumulatively generalize to a majority of the world's population. Rather, the book was planned to provide diverse geographic coverage, to give readers various perspectives on grandparenting across many population groups worldwide.

In this book we distinguish between "grandparents" (the people), "grandparenting" (their behavior), and "grandparenthood" (conceptualizations of grandparents and their behavior). Another distinction is made between "cultures" (patterns of thoughts, feelings, and behaviors transmitted between generations, which vary within each society), "societies" (social groups or communities that live in common geographic regions), and "nations" (or countries, consisting of large and numerous groups who share political/geographical boundaries and a government).

Geographical and Population Coverage

Figure 1.1 shows the geographical coverage of this book, and Table 1.1 provides recent demographic data from each of the 11 main chapters. We hope that readers will refer to Table 1.1 often to understand and compare the demographic contexts of countries portrayed in each chapter.

Chapter Structure and Contents

As editors, we asked all chapter contributors to follow a common framework. We thought this approach would make our book more readable for newcomers to

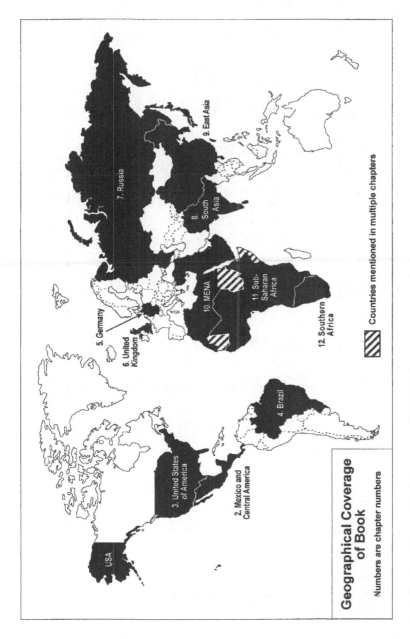

FIGURE 1.1 Geographical Coverage of This Book

Source: Courtesy of Paul R. Larson.

TABLE 1.1 Sociodemographic Characteristics of Selected Countries in Different Regions

Chapter	Country	Total Population (in millions)	Pop. Density (per sq. km)	Median Age	% Pop. > 65	Age at 1st Marriage (Female)	Fertility Rate	% in Poverty	% Urban	% Literate (M)	% Literate (F)	Life Expectancy (M)	Life Expectancy (F)	Per Capita Income (US$/year)
2	Mexico	127	65	27.6	6.8	23.0	2.3	53.2	79.2	96.2	94.2	72.9	78.6	9,710
2	Guatemala	16.3	153	21.4	4.4	21.6	2.9	59.3	51.6	87.4	76.3	70.1	74.1	7,700
3	USA	321.4	269	37.8	15.3	26.9	1.9	15.1	81.6	N/A	92.9	77.3	82.0	55,800
4	Brazil	207.8	25	31.6	8.1	29.7	1.8	21.4	85.7	92.2		70.0	77.3	15,600
5	Germany	81.4	234	46.8	21.8	31.7	1.4	15.5	75.3	N/A		78.3	83.0	46,900
6	UK	65.1	269	40.4	18.1	31.7	1.9	15.0	82.6	N/A		78.4	82.8	41,200
7	Russia	144.1	9	39.1	13.9	24.4	1.6	11.2	74	99.7	99.6	64.7	76.6	25,400
8	Bangladesh	169	1,237	26.3	5.9	18.6	2.4	31.5	34.3	64.6	58.5	69.0	72.9	1,097
8	India	1,311.1	441	19.9	6.1	20.2	2.5	29.8	32.7	81.3	60.6	67.0	69.4	6,200
8	Pakistan	188.9	245	23	4.4	22.7	2.8	29.5	38.8	69.5	45.8	65.5	69.4	5,000
9	Japan	127	348	46.5	26.9	29.7	1.4	16.1	93.5	N/A		81.4	88.3	38,100
9	S. Korea	50.6	519	40.8	13	28.8	1.3	14.6	82.5	N/A		77.0	83.3	36,500
9	China	1,371.2	146	37.1	10.4	24.7	1.6	6.1	55.6	98.2	94.5	73.4	77.7	14,100
10	Egypt	91.5	92	23.8	4.2	22.7	2.8	25.2	43.1	82.2	65.4	71.1	76.5	11,800
10	Israel	8.4	387	29.6	11.1	26.2	2.7	22.0	92.1	98.7	96.8	80.4	84.4	33,700
11	Nigeria	182.2	200	18.2	3.1	21.6	5.2	70.0	47.8	69.2	49.7	52.0	54.1	6,100
12	S. Africa	55.0	45	26.5	5.5	30.6	2.3	35.9	64.8	95.5	93.1	60.8	63.9	13,200

Adapted from *The World Fact Book* (retrieved from https://www.cia.gov/library/publications/resources/the-world-factbook/).

this field and make comparisons of grandparents between societies and regions more manageable. The chapter structure/framework includes the following elements:

1. Proverbs – Placed at the beginning of each chapter, proverbs (Hwang, Sigel, & Lamb, 1996) are a window into a society's beliefs and values, including its traditional or contemporary view of grandparents. Brief explanations of the proverbs are provided in an Appendix before the References section of each chapter, which encourages readers to interpret each proverb before seeing the author's explanations.
2. A case story – Placed before the introductory section of each chapter, the contributor supplies a brief story of a grandparent or grandparents and their grandchild or grandchildren, which exemplifies important aspects of grand- parenting or lifestyles in their society/region. No case story "represents" an entire society; rather, the case stories demonstrate that every grandparent is unique and yet is also a product of his/her culture.
3. Contextual background – As the book's title suggests, we strongly empha- size contextual influences. Each chapter discusses how cultural, historical, social, economic, and/or demographic backgrounds affect grandparents, e.g., divorce, immigration, religion, political systems, economic disparities, social- structural issues, etc.
4. Theoretical approach(es) – Many theories have been employed to understand grandparenthood (Szinovacz, 1998), and each contributor supplies examples of the theoretical orientations she/he believes are most helpful to understand grandparenthood in their society/region. Although grandparenting research is often atheoretical, it was interesting to see what theories the various chap- ter writers chose as most useful. Some theories (intergenerational solidar- ity model, Erikson's psychosocial theory, etc.) were cited in several chapters, while other theories were referenced only in one chapter (e.g., social con- structionist theories of gender, structural lag theory, etc.).
5. Research literature – Every chapter reviews quantitative and/or qualitative research on grandparents in the target region or society; in some cases, the literature is supplemented by anecdotal evidence. We asked authors to avoid the use of figures and tables, and their chapters are thought-provoking and integrative rather than heavy on statistics. Depth and breadth of research lit- erature vary widely between chapters, which reflects a robust field of inquiry in some countries and minimal activity elsewhere.
6. Grandfathers – We requested a specific sub-section about grandfathers for each chapter, because grandfathers have been neglected by researchers and are under-represented in most previous books and articles on grandpar- enting (Buchanan & Rotkirch, 2017; United Nations, 2011). Inclusion of this chapter element assured grandfatherhood a prominent place in this volume.

7. Subcultural variations – Every chapter includes information on diversity. This section discusses indigenous groups, subcultures, geography, and other contextual variables, and heterogeneity of grandparents even within sub-populations. The amount of emphasis on diversity in each chapter depends on the nature of its population(s) and the availability of information about such variability.

8. Social policy issues – Policy or legal issues related to grandparenting are featured in all chapters, but in some countries/regions little information on policies or laws was available.

9. Comparisons and predictions – We asked contributors to make comparisons of grandparents across societies, between the multiple societies represented in regional chapters, and with depictions of grandparents from other chapters of this book. Authors were also encouraged to offer personal comments and opinions about grandparents and the future of grandparenthood, even where objective evidence was absent.

10. Appendix – After the explanations of the proverbs, each chapter concludes with a short list of websites relevant to grandparenting, and with three discussion/essay questions to encourage critical thinking by student readers.

Chapter Previews

We divided the main chapters of this book into four geographical sections: the Americas, Europe/Russia, Asia, and Africa/Middle East. Each of these sections, and indeed each chapter, discusses a unique combination of contextual backgrounds, research literature, and social policies. Highlights from the 11 main chapters are as follows: From the Americas we learn about the key role of extended families in Mexico and Central America (Chapter 2), diverse circumstances including surrogate parents and LGB grandparents in the US (Chapter 3), and grandparents who raise grandchildren in the contexts of changing matriarchy and patriarchy in Brazil (Chapter 4). In the Europe/Russia section, Germany (Chapter 5) provides an especially rich consideration of theoretical and conceptual issues, the UK (Chapter 6) presents the emergence of "new grandfathers," and the Russia author (Chapter 7) explains the prominent position of grandmothers rather than grandfathers in the context of a matrifocal family system. Next, two regional Asian chapters emphasize such issues as income disparities and urban/rural differences within the massive Indian Sub-Continent of South Asia (Chapter 8) and the impacts on grandparental roles of the different social-economic systems of Japan, Korea, and China within East Asia (Chapter 9). A chapter on grandparents in Southeast Asia had been planned for this volume but sadly had to be cancelled due to the chapter authors' personal circumstances. Finally, there are three chapters on Africa and the Middle East, the most under-represented geographical areas in past books about grandparents. We read about the impact of historical changes of Islam on the traditional role of grandparents in the MENA (Middle East/Northern Africa) region (Chapter 10); research findings from Israel are also cited in this chapter. In sub-Saharan Africa (Chapter 11) the emphasis is on grandparents as "carers" in the context of the AIDS pandemic. Lastly, we learn about how health and work conditions affect the traditional and contemporary roles of both grandmothers and grandfathers in Southern African communities (Chapter 12).

Theoretical Orientations

Szinovacz (1998) has previously categorized and elaborated an array of theoretical approaches to grandparenthood, and Arber and Timonen (2012) updated these perspectives. Unfortunately, theoretical development on grandparenthood remains quite limited. We sought to illuminate the many ecological systems in which grandparental roles are embedded, and Bronfenbrenner's bioecological model was our impetus to publish a book that emphasizes contextual and background factors (Bronfenbrenner & Morris, 2006). As cross-cultural developmental psychologists who focus our scholarship on family relations, we both have also been particularly influenced by psychosocial theory. Work on this volume opened our eyes to many other theoretical perspectives from the fields of gerontology, sociology, and anthropology, which are explained and illustrated within the 11 main chapters. These include:

- family sociology approaches (Parsons, 1943) – Chapter 2, including role theories such as role strain versus role enhancement hypotheses (Goode, 1960; Marks, 1977) and disengagement versus activity theories (Cumming & Henry, 1961; Hochschild, 1975); the intergenerational solidarity model – Chapters 2, 4, 9, 10, 12, and intergenerational conflict theory – Chapters 4, 12; other frameworks that describe the grandparental role (e.g., Pinazo Hernandis, 1999) – Chapters 2, 3, 6, 7, 9, 10; social exchange theory, and the altruism model – Chapter 8; and a "corporate model" – Chapter 9;
- evolutionary approaches (Coall, Hilbrand, Sear, & Hertwig, 2016; Hawkes, O'Connell, Jones, Alvarez, & Charnov, 1998; Voland, Chasiotis, & Schiefenhovel, 2005) such as the "grandmother hypothesis" – Chapters 3, 8, 9;
- developmental theories including developmental contextual theory (Glaser et al., 2013; Harkness, Mavridis, Liu, & Super, 2015; Lerner, 2002) – Chapters 3, 5; psychosocial theory (Erikson, 1963) – Chapters 5, 6, 8; and lifespan developmental theory (Baltes, 1997) – Chapter 5;
- social constructionist theories of gender (Krekula, 2007) – Chapter 4;
- generational stake hypothesis (Bengston & Kuypers, 1971 – Chapter 6;
- sociocultural theory (Vygotsky, 1978) – Chapter 9;
- structural lag theory (Baker, Silverstein, & Putney, 2008) – Chapter 11.

Beyond the critique of grandparenting research as often atheoretical, another issue raised by Szinovacz (1998, p. 261) was that grandparenting researchers must be more cognizant of analysis at the societal, family, dyadic, and individual "levels." Our chapter contributors seldom refer to which level(s) were the focus of their research literatures, and such analysis is seldom reported in most individual research studies. Suffice it to say that the lack of discussion of theories or levels of analysis makes it difficult to compare or integrate studies within and between societies. This problem is compounded for one who seeks to integrate research on an international basis, and this problem is not at all unique to research on grandparents. Szinovacz (Foreword, this volume, xvi) further notes that grandparenting research has been deficient in consideration of the "timing of life events" and over-reliant on cross-sectional research designs. Although this volume addresses some of the geographical limitations in the international literature, and pays special attention to the roles of grandfathers (another deficit identified in the Foreword), the literature reviews in the 11 main chapters indeed illustrate all the conceptual and methodological deficiencies identified by Szinovacz.

Previous International Volumes on Grandparenthood

We are indebted to several scholars who have also published internationally minded books about grandparents. Most of their anthologies included authors from a wide variety of societies and academic disciplines, and all of these volumes are recommended to the reader.

Szinovacz's *Handbook on Grandparenthood* (1998), a multidisciplinary handbook primarily from the field of gerontology, features an incisive methodological, theoretical, and conceptual treatment of grandparenthood, although its coverage of diversity is mainly limited to a section on "Variations in Grandparenting Experiences" among American ethnic groups (African-Americans, Hispanics, Asian-Americans), and a cross-cultural chapter based on analysis of data from the Human Relations Area Files.

Arber and Timonen's *Contemporary Grandparenting: Changing Family Relationships in Global Contexts* (2012) was written mainly from the perspectives of sociology, social work, and social policy, and is notable for its up-to-date historical overviews of scholarship on grandparenting, including the international field. It emphasizes cultural contexts and its geographical coverage is primarily Europe, the US, China, Hong Kong, and Singapore.

Experiencing Grandparenthood: An Asian Perspective, was edited by Mehta and Thang (2012). This book (co-authored by a gerontologist and a socio-cultural anthropologist) provides good cultural coverage of grandparenting and focuses on Asian populations: Japan, China, Singapore, Thailand, Malaysia, and Hong Kong. As a well-integrated anthology of empirical studies in a diverse, wide-ranging, and previously under-studied region, it illuminates social policies and the future of Asian grandparenting.

Buchanan and Rotkirch's (2017) *Grandfathers: Global Perspectives* provides up-to-date references, an emphasis on grandfathers, and geographical coverage of the US, UK, North America, Denmark, New Zealand, Asia, and South Africa.

Grandparenthood, by Bengston and Robertson (1985), limited its cultural coverage mainly to diversity within the US. Specifically it presents data from five European-American ethnic groups and African-American grandmothers, and also reports an anthropological study of white Californian grandparents. Kornhaber's (1995) *Contemporary Grandparenting* included only one chapter on "Cultural and Historical Variations." Finally, Smith (1991) was a groundbreaking volume in its "international" subtitle and perspective, but its geographical coverage is limited to Europe and North America.

Looking Ahead

In Chapter 13 (Chapter Themes, Highlights, and Recommendations) we recap seven themes that appear in the main chapters of this book. Aware that it is problematic to generalize about diverse populations within any society and region (or to compare national groups and regions), we attempt nonetheless to draw some comparisons between the chapters that stood out to us as we completed work on this volume. We note differences and similarities in the portrayals between and across chapters, offer our opinions about the future of grandparenthood from an international standpoint, and make recommendations about how to build a more valid international database on grandparenting. Finally, we added a final case story written just before this book went to press, to draw attention to both the individuality and shared humanity of grandparents everywhere. We offer our informed opinions and interpretations of the overall view that emerges from this volume, but urge scholars, practitioners, policymakers, grandparents, and parents alike to draw their own conclusions. We hope that this book will contribute to the further internationalization of scholarship on grandparenthood, especially through its emphasis on historical and contextual factors, updated and extensive reference citations, and inclusion of findings from societies that were previously inaccessible and under-represented in the grandparenthood literature.

Appendix

Additional Resources

Corporation for National & Community Service – Foster Grandparents Program (www.nationalservice.gov/programs/senior-corps/foster-grandparents)

This website includes information about the Foster Grandparent Program. It outlines where Foster Grandparent volunteers often serve and the parameters to qualify as a volunteer.

American Grandparents Association (Grandparents.com)
This national organization provides information and support to grandparents of all ages. Its topics include fostering positive relationships with grandchildren, grandchildren and development, intergenerational family relationships, divorce, and health and well-being.

Mehr Generationen Haeuser (www.mehrgenerationenhaeuser.de; in German only) Multi-generational housing is a government-funded concept allowing people to meet across generations. Spaces are created for the public to engage in common activities, with elderly helping the young and the young helping the elderly.

Discussion Questions

1. This chapter suggests that grandparents *may* be more involved in developing societies, yet grandparents are more often studied by researchers in developed societies. What do you think would be the reasons for this discrepancy?
2. Why do you think it was only in the 21st century that international (non-Western) studies of grandparents became common and international books on grandparents began to appear?
3. This chapter lists a very wide variety of theories relevant to grandparenting. What are the advantages and disadvantages of having such a range of theoretical approaches?

References

Arber, S., & Timonen, V. (2012). *Contemporary grandparenting: Changing family relationships in global contexts.* Bristol, UK: Policy Press.

Baker, L. A., Silverstein, M., & Putney, N. M. (2008). Grandparents raising grandchildren in the United States: Changing family forms, stagnant social policies. *Journal of Social Policy, 7,* 53–69.

Baltes, P., B. (1997). On the incomplete architecture of human ontogeny: Selection, optimization, and compensation as foundations of developmental theory. *American Psychologist, 52,* 366–380.

Bengston, V. L. & Kuypers, J. A. (1971). Generational difference and the developmental stake. *Aging & Human Development, 2,* 249–260.

Bengston, V., & Robertson, J. (Eds.). (1985). *Grandparenthood.* Beverly Hills, CA: Sage.

Bronfenbrenner, U., & Morris, P. A. (2006). The bioecological model of human development. In W. Damon & R. M. Lerner (Eds.), *Handbook of child psychology: Vol. 1. Theoretical models of human development* (pp. 793–828). New York: Wiley.

Buchanan, A., & Rotkirch, A. (2017). *Grandfathers: Global perspectives.* London, UK: Palgrave Macmillan.

Coall, D., Hilbrand, S. Sear, R., & Hertwig, R. (2016). A new niche? The theory of grandfather involvement. In A. Buchanan & A. Rotkirch (Eds.), *Grandfathers: Global perspectives* (pp. 21–44). London, UK: Palgrave Macmillan.

Cumming, E., & Henry, W. E. (1961). *Growing old, the process of disengagement.* New York: Basic Books.

Erikson, E. (1963). *Childhood and society* (2nd ed.). New York: Norton.

Falk, U., A., & Falk, G. (2002). *Grandparents: A new look at the supporting generation.* Amherst, NY: Proetheus Books.

Glaser, K., Price, D, di Gessa, G., Ribe, E., Stuchbury, R. & Tinker, A. (2013) *Grandparenting in Europe: Family policy and grandparents' role in providing childcare.* London: Grandparents Plus.

Goode, W. (1960). A theory of role strain. *American Sociological Review, 25,* 483–496.

Harkness, S., Mavridis, C. J., Liu, J. J., & Super, C. M. (2015). Parental ethnotheories and the development of family relationships in early and middle childhood. In L. A. Jensen (Ed.), *The Oxford handbook of human development and culture: An interdisciplinary approach* (pp. 271–291). New York: Oxford University Press.

Harper, S. (2005). Grandparenthood. In M. L. Johnson (Ed.), *The Cambridge handbook of age and ageing* (pp. 422–428). Cambridge: Cambridge University Press.

Hawkes, K., O'Connell, J. F., Jones, N. G., Alvarez, H., & Charnov, E. L. (1998). Grandmothering menopause, and the evolution of human histories. *Proceedings of the National Academy of Science of the United States of America, 95,* 1336–1339.

Hochschild, A. (1975). Disengagement theory: A critique and proposal. *American Sociological Review, 40,* 553–569.

Hwang, C. P., Lamb, M. E., & Sigel, I. E. (Eds.). (1996). *Images of childhood.* Hove, UK: Psychology Press.

Kornhaber, A. (1995). *Contemporary grandparenting.* Thousand Oaks, CA: Sage.

Krekula, C. (2007). The intersection of age and gender: Reworking gender theory and social gerontology. *Current Sociology, 55,* 155–171.

Lerner, R.M. (2002). *Concepts and theories of human development* (3rd ed.). Mahwah, NJ: Erlbaum.

Marks, S. (1977). Multiple roles and role strain: Some notes on human energy, time, and commitment. *American Sociological Review, 42,* 921–936.

Mehta, K. K., & Thang, L. L. (2012). *Experiencing grandparenthood: An Asian perspective.* New York: Springer.

Parsons, T. (1943). The kinship system of the contemporary United States. *American Anthropologist, 45*(1), 22–38.

Pinazo Hernandis, S. (1999). Social significance of the grandparent role. *Revista Multidiciplinar de Gerontología, 9,* 169–176.

Pope Edwards, C., Ren, L., & Brown, J. (2015). Early contexts of learning: Family and community socialization during infancy and toddlerhood. In L. A. Jensen (Ed.), *The Oxford handbook of human development and culture: An interdisciplinary approach* (pp. 165–181). New York: Oxford University Press.

Smith, P. K. (1991). *The psychology of grandparenthood: An international perspective.* New York: Routledge.

Szinovacz, M. E. (1998). *Handbook on grandparenthood.* New York: Greenwood Press.

United Nations. (2011). *Men in families and family policy in a changing world.* Retrieved from www.un.org/esa/socdev/family/docs/men-in-families.pdf

Voland, E., Chasiotis, A., & Schiefenhovel, W. (2005). *Grandmotherhood: The evolutionary significance of the second half of female life.* New Brunswick, NJ: Rutgers University Press.

Vygotsky, L. S. (1978). Mind in society: Development of higher psychological processes. (M. Cole, V. John-Steiner, S. Scribner, & E. Souberman, Eds.). Cambridge, MA: Harvard University Press.

PART II
The Americas

2

GRANDPARENTING IN MEXICO AND CENTRAL AMERICA

"Time and Attention"

Judith L. Gibbons and Regina Fanjul de Marsicovetere

AUTHOR NOTE

The authors would like to thank Katelyn E. Poelker for her kindness and unflagging efforts to track down and format references, as well as Margarita, Margie, Celestino, and Manuela for sharing their stories of grandparenting. This chapter is dedicated to the memory of Domingo, a kind and caring grandfather to 24 grandchildren.

PROVERBS FROM MEXICO

1. "The grandparent is not synonymous with old age, but with love." (*El abuelo no es sinónimo de vejez, sino de amor*)
2. "The parents to raise, the grandparents to spoil." (*Para criar, los padres, para malcriar, los abuelos*)

(see p. 34 for interpretations of proverbs)

CASE STORIES

We visited Domingo (85) and his wife Margarita (86) in their home, a one-room mud-floor adobe house near San Martin Jilotepeque, Guatemala. Their first language is Kaqchikel, but Domingo had learned a great deal of Spanish so he could contribute more to the conversation which was conducted in that language. Half of the room was occupied by an altar, and the other half by a simple bed on which Domingo was sitting. Present were the two authors, a granddaughter (Gloria, 25) and daughter-in-law Felipa. Domingo passed away about one month after the interview.

Domingo and Margarita had six children, 24 grandchildren, and nine great-grandchildren. Almost all lived within walking distance and enjoyed family celebrations. Everyone agreed that "you have to take care of your family." It was the responsibility of sons, daughters, and grandchildren to visit the grandfather, and they had the "right" to take care of his needs: bring him fruit, a cup of water, or wash his clothes. When the grandchildren were young, grandparents would play with them, tell stories of working in the coffee farms on the coast, and, when needed, provide food. Domingo taught his grandchildren values such as respect for other people and the importance of hard work. He had the right to discipline and care for them. The main themes of the conversation were love and affection: "I love my grandchildren." "I enjoy everything about being a grandfather." Margarita said, "I love my grand-children. When they fight among themselves or their mother hits them, ay Dios, it hurts my heart."

In Guatemala City, we met with Margie, a homemaker, wife of businessman Julio. They have two sons and three grandchildren: 6-year-old triplets. The grand-children visit and stay over almost every Friday night. She feels "super close" to them: "The grandchildren count on me to solve every little problem." "When I play with them I find my inner child; with one I play soccer, another loves to do experiments…and the girl loves costumes." Their grandfather invents stories that fascinate them. Margie wants her grandchildren to be true to themselves, to discern what is best for them. She teaches them those values by not forcing them to do many things. There are only three rules in the house: take off your shoes, don't fight with each other, and be polite. "What I can give my grandchildren is lots of time and attention. When they are here I give them 100% of my time. They give me unconditional love, trust, and affection." But not all grandparents are like that, Margie claims; some are simply not interested and others are too busy. Margie reflected that compared to the past, grandchildren have fewer constraints today; they are allowed to question "why" and we explain.

We also briefly interviewed Celestino, a chauffeur living in Antigua Guatemala, who has 11 children, 27 grandchildren, and one great-grandchild. When the grand-children were little he took them to the fields to work; they learned how to care for crops and helped him in agriculture. The whole family often gets together for celebrations. He enjoys being with his grandchildren, but at those gatherings, their mothers take care of discipline. Celestino's thoughts and life are guided by his commitment to Christianity: he said that "grandchildren are the crown of the grandparent," referring to the Bible, Proverbs 17:6. Most important to him is that his grandchildren follow a righteous path, work hard, and not become drug addicts or thieves.

Manuela, of Mayan descent, was born in the Western highlands but now lives in Guatemala City. She has one adult son and is the grandmother of three girls, ages 1 through 9. She has a close relationship with her granddaughters and sees them every week when she takes them swimming. She sees her major role as a grandparent as being to support and guide their overall health: physical, emotional, and spiritual. She also is part of an organization, a "circle of grandparents," that aims to improve

the health of Mother Earth and its inhabitants. She worries about the future: "when
I think of the kind of life that my grandchildren are going to live, I feel some uncer-
tainty; they will require greater strength than I needed, especially in terms of climate,
water, violence, and alienation."

Although all of these grandparents grew up and live in Guatemala, within
100 miles of the capital city, they reflect a diversity of ideas and experiences as
grandparents.

This chapter draws from published literature and the preceding case stories to
explore commonalities of grandparenting in the countries of Central America and
Mexico, and diversity rooted in culture, gender, ethnicity, and socioeconomic conditions. We employ the framework of Pinazo Hernandis (1999) to describe mutual
help and support between grandparents and grandchildren, and grandparents' roles
as sources of identity, role models, caregivers, socialization agents, and transmitters
of culture. We also include evidence of influences which are both negative and
positive for grandparents as well as their grandchildren, and describe unique features that influence grandparenting in this region.

Cultural, Historical, Social, Economic, and Demographic Background

Mexico and the seven countries of Central America – Guatemala, Honduras, El
Salvador, Nicaragua, Belize, Panama, and Costa Rica (see regional map, Figure 2.1) –
are enormously diverse both geographically and culturally. From a geographic
perspective, this region includes hot and humid coastlines along the Atlantic and
Pacific coasts, inland lowland jungles, dryer and more temperate deserts, high pla-
teaus, and mountainous rainforests, as well as a myriad of sub-climates with diverse
landscapes (New World Encyclopedia, 2013). In cultural terms, Panama, Costa
Rica, Nicaragua, Honduras, El Salvador, Guatemala, Belize, and Mexico encompass
a great number of diverse ethnic groups, which vary in their proportions of the
total population in each country (Central Intelligence Agency [CIA], 2016a). The
majority of the population in all of these countries is made up of *mestizos* (known
as *Ladinos* in Guatemala), who are descended from both indigenous peoples and
European immigrants. The second largest group in most of these countries (except
Belize) is either indigenous or white. Within-country diversity is also profound.
For example, about 40% of Guatemalans are of indigenous Mayan descent and
speak one of the 22 Mayan languages (Programa de las Naciones Unidas para el
Desarrollo [PNUD], 2005). Despite this diversity, the grandparenting context in
this geographical area seems to reflect some common features. Colonization by
Spain is part of the history of most of the region, with Spanish remaining as the
most common language and Christianity as the most common religion.

In recent history, several countries of the region, including Guatemala,
Nicaragua, and El Salvador, have emerged as post-conflict societies (Luciak, 2011).

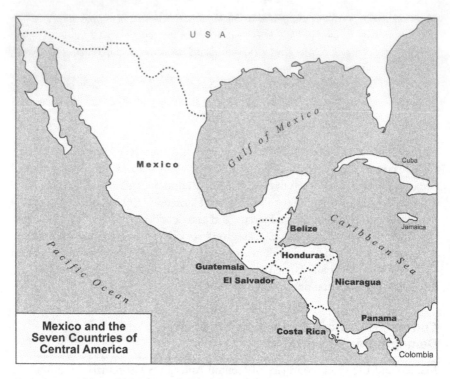

FIGURE 2.1 Map of Mexico and Central America

Source: Courtesy of Paul Larson.

Grandparents are likely to have lived during the conflicts and may transmit inter-generational trauma to their children and grandchildren. The region has also experienced a great deal of out-migration (emigration) for economic and other reasons (Brick, Challinor, & Rosenblum, 2011). When parents migrate, grandparents may become the primary caregivers of their grandchildren (see, e.g., Estrada Iguíniz, 2009; Montes de Oca Zavala, 2010).

The inhabitants of these countries also share some cultural characteristics. According to Hofstede's classic study of cultural values, the majority of Latin American societies are high in collectivism, a sense of duty and obligation to the in-group or extended family. Countries in the region also score high in uncertainty-avoidance, a value that is evidenced by strict norms and a plethora of rules and regulations (Hofstede, 2011). Most, including Guatemala, Mexico, Panama, and El Salvador, but excluding Costa Rica, are also high in power-distance, the acceptance of hierarchical relationships and unequal distribution of power in society (Hofstede, 2011). Another important cultural value is familism. In describing the central features of Mexican culture, Díaz-Guerrero (1972) pointed to the centrality of the family, as well as distinct roles for women, men, and children.

FIGURE 2.2 Domingo, the bedridden grandfather of 24, is visited and comforted by Gloria, his granddaughter. Behind is seated his wife, Margarita, and lower on the bed is Felipa, his adult daughter-in-law. Domingo said that his grandchildren had the right to attend to his needs.

Source: Courtesy of Judith Gibbons.

The countries of Central America and Mexico are also economically diverse. The countries differ in terms of gross national income (GNI) per capita (from less than US$2,000 per year in Nicaragua to more than US$10,000 per year in Costa Rica and Panama; World Bank, 2016b). Overall, there are high rates of poverty and high economic disparity. The percentage of the population living on less than US$1.90 per day ranges from 1.7% in Costa Rica to 18.9% in Honduras (World Bank, 2016c). GINI ratios (a measure of economic inequality) are all above those of North America and Western Europe (World Bank, 2016a). The implications of these data for grandparenting are that many families may struggle to secure basic necessities and that all members of the family may be expected to contribute to the economic well-being of the family.

The populations of this region are younger than those in most of the world. About 8% of the world's population is over 65 (and growing because of a demographic shift; National Institute on Aging, 2011), whereas 43% of the world's population is under 25 (United Nations Population Fund [UNFPA], 2011). Central America and Mexico have relatively low percentages of older adults (ranging from 3.7% in Belize to 8.0% in Panama) and high numbers of young people (ranging from 40% in Costa Rica to 58% in Guatemala; CIA, 2016c). These demographics reflect a high proportion of youth compared to the proportion of elderly in this region.

Theoretical Perspectives

According to Bates and Taylor (2013), most research on grandparenting is atheoretical and fragmentary. A classic theory that may aid in understanding the issues that grandparents encounter is developmental theory. According to Erikson (1950, 1982), the psychosocial crisis that individuals face during middle adulthood is that of generativity versus stagnation (about ages 40–64). At 65 and later they may also address the issue of integrity, coming to terms with the meaning of life.

We may think of grandparents as very old, but often this is not the case. The mean age for becoming a mother in Central America and Mexico ranges from 19.7 to 21.3 years of age (CIA, 2016b). Thus, people become parents significantly earlier than in the global north; for example, the mean age in the US is 25, and in Spain almost 30 (CIA, 2016b). The consequence is that people in Mexico and Central America tend to become grandparents at a young age. Extrapolating from the parenting statistics, individuals first become grandparents at age 40–45. According to a newspaper account, the average age of becoming a grandparent in Mexico is 43, confirming the relative youth of grandparents (El Heraldo de Chihuahua, 2015). Psychosocial theory would suggest that grandparents see their primary task as contributing something to society, and especially to succeeding generations. Through their direct influence on their grandchildren, grandparents can leave a legacy. To the extent that they contribute to the family's welfare, through financial support, physical caregiving, and emotional support, they also enact generativity.

A descriptive framework to understand grandparenting is provided by Pinazo Hernandis (1999). According to this schema, grandparents can influence the lives of their grandchildren in five ways: they can provide help or support, socialize or teach their grandchildren, serve as role models, provide the impetus (through aging and death) for reflection on the meaning of life, and sometimes have a negative impact. All of these influences are affected by the ages of grandparents and their grandchildren, their geographic distance and frequency of contact, the nature of their shared activities, and the perceptions of the grandchildren. Another factor would be culture or shared values and beliefs.

A more limited theory about the nature of intergenerational relationships is the generational stake hypothesis, which argues that the older generation feels closer to younger generations than the younger generations do to them (Bengston & Kuypers, 1971). This is often explained in terms of developmental theory, that older generations have a "stake" in young people, but the young people's task is to differentiate themselves from the older generation. Although the generational stake hypothesis has been supported by a great deal of research, a study of Mexican immigrants to the US revealed some contradictory results. In that study, grandsons reported more affection and closeness for their grandfathers than their grandfathers did for them (Giarrusso, Feng, Silverstein, & Bengston, 2001).

Another factor may also be important in the relations of Mexican American grandparents and grandchildren: acculturation. Silverstein and Chen (1999) found that more acculturated adult grandchildren reported less frequent interaction with their grandparents and declines in affection over time. These studies showed that (1) research on diverse grandparents may be used to evaluate the universality of theories, and (2) cultural context (e.g., acculturation) is essential to understanding grandparenting. Of these theories, the descriptive framework of Pinazo Hernandis (1999) may be most useful to structure the research findings; however, it needs to be supplemented by developmental and cultural theories to be more comprehensive.

Literature on Grandparenting in Central America and Mexico

The centrality of the extended family in the cultural values of Mexico and Central America cannot be overstated. The family serves as the basic unit of social organization and the lens through which individuals view the world. This was illustrated by a study of the ideal persons of adolescents in 21 countries in which extended family members figured prominently in the drawings and photographs of adolescents from Guatemala, compared to those from other countries (Gibbons & Stiles, 2004). Describing the cultural premises of Mexican culture, Díaz-Guerrero (1972) identified 22 assumptions about life; 13 of these addressed family roles. Examples of such assumptions included: "A person should always obey his/her father," "The man should wear the pants in the family," and "A good wife should always be faithful to her husband" (p. 244). This view of the family reflects a patriarchal and hierarchal structure that may extend to the roles of senior family members such as grandparents. Based on the limited literature about grandparenting in the region, we may organize the roles of grandparents in the family, according to the schema of Pinazo Hernandis (1999), as follows: help and support, socialization, role model, reflection on meaning of life, and negative impact.

Help and Support

The mutual support of family members is unmistakable in the regional literature. Montes de Oca Zavala (2009) termed this "generational reciprocity," whereby family members from all generations work together for the well-being of the family, related to the cultural value of *familismo*. For example, families develop strategies, including migration of one or more members, to satisfy the needs of the family in the face of poverty, illness, and hunger (Montes de Oca Zavala, 2009). When the father of the family migrates, others, including grandparents, siblings, mother, and close neighbors, engage in activities formerly assigned to the father (Estrada Iguíniz, 2009). They provide not only material help, but also close affective bonds.

In one study of people over 60 years of age in Mexico, Cervantes (2013) found that grandparents both give and receive help from their children and grandchildren. Those younger than 70 years old give more than they receive. After age 70, grandparents receive more help than they give, but even at age 90 and above they still contribute. Grandchildren overall receive more help than they give. Reciprocity in the relation between grandparents and their grandchildren was evident in our opening case story of Domingo and Margarita, who both gave and received food and aid from grandchildren, depending on developmental stage and need.

Grandparents may receive not only physical help and support from their grandchildren, but also less tangible benefits. Among Mayans in Mexico, Villagómez Valdés and Sánchez González (2014) found that grandchildren provided emotional support and were a source of affection, company, empathy, recognition, and attentive listening. In the case story interview above, Margie echoed those findings in saying, "They give me unconditional love, trust, and affection....it is something magic."

Grandmothers of Jalisco, Mexico often care for their grandchildren (Partidas, 2004). "The grandmother is the perfect substitute for the mother" (Partidas, 2004, p. 71), and her caregiving is an expression of family solidarity. One of Partidas' interviewees, Dolores, left her 4-year-old son with her mother for weeks at a time while she worked in another city. Another mother, Mónica, shared activities with her son during the day, and then left him with her mother while she worked the evening shift. She was grateful to her mother for this help that enabled her to earn money to support her son. In this and related studies, grandmothers most often cared for the children of their daughters (Garay Villegas, Montes de Oca Zavala, & Guillén, 2014; Jiménez Pelcastre, 2012).

When children have special needs, grandmothers can be a consistent source of support, as shown in a Panamanian study (Gardner, Scherman, Efthimiadis, & Shultz, 2004). Grandmothers provided caregiving, economic support, and help with schooling, recreation, and spiritual needs. Rather than dwelling on the negative, they showed patience, understanding, affection, and respect in their interactions with their grandchild.

In a study of the illustrations in first and second grade textbooks used in Mexico, Margarito Gaspar (2012) noted that grandparents were portrayed as an integral part of the family. One illustration showed a grandfather taking his granddaughter to school. Most grandparents were depicted as living with, visiting, or caring for their grandchildren. Frequent contact with grandchildren was mentioned by all the interviewee grandparents in our opening case stories, including Domingo, Margie, Celestino, and Manuela.

Grandparents' Roles in Socialization and Transmission of Culture

The term *abuelos* is often used to denote ancestors in Central America and Mexico, especially among indigenous communities (see, e.g., Falla Sánchez, 2013).

Therefore, poems and prayers may invoke the term *abuelos* metaphorically to represent those who have gone before, and to express respect for the wisdom of ancestors and one's spiritual heritage (Deuss, 2007). In Manuela's case story, her organization used the title of grandparents in this metaphorical sense, as protectors of the environment.

Among the Maya, actual biological grandparents are considered the main figures of authority; they maintain the social structure as they transmit, reinforce, and monitor cultural values and practices for the benefit of the younger generations. Because of their wisdom and lifelong experience, they are recognized by their communities as prominent examples of how to practice respect for moral principles and norms of coexistence (Car, Eder, & Garcia Pú, 2005).

Traditions among the Garífuna ethnic group of Honduras, Nicaragua, and Guatemala are similar (Meza Márquez, 2012). Grandmothers, in particular, are responsible for transmission of the culture and identity of their people. The grandmother of the Garífuna poem "Grani" provides warmth, joy, and a sense of celebration in the daily life of the grandchildren, which strengthens their self-esteem and identity (Meza Márquez, 2012).

Likewise, indigenous heritage is transmitted by grandparents and senior family members among the Nocutzepo community in Mexico (Urrieta, 2013). Children and youth acquire *saberes* (knowings) such as a sense of responsibility, through participation in community life. The knowledge acquired includes not only specific skills, but also ways of viewing the world. In one example, three generations of family members, from the 83-year-old grandfather to a 4-year-old grandchild, were observed cutting up pumpkins to remove the seeds. The children learned to contribute to the family and community, as well as a specific skill. These ways of imparting knowledge are consistent with research findings by Rogoff and her colleagues – that the primary way of learning in indigenous heritage families and communities is by observation and pitching in (Rogoff, Mejía-Arauz, & Correa-Chávez, 2015). This way of learning was illustrated by Celestino's case story when he took his grandchildren to the fields to help him sow and harvest crops.

Despite the important roles of grandparents in transmitting traditional values, grandparents and their traditions sometimes provide paths that may not foster the well-being of the younger generation. The life story of Irma Alicia (recounted in Falla Sánchez, 2013) is one example. This woman was abused physically and psychologically by her husband for years. When she finally decided to leave him, she worried that she was ignoring the wisdom of her grandmothers, who would advise her to carry her cross and endure the abuse.

Grandparents as Role Models and Sources of Identity

Beyond transmission of cultural values, grandparents may be role models and sources of identity. In a study of marginalized youth in Mexico, students described two kinds of people who helped them persist in school: those who pushed them through support and those who pulled them through example (Silas Casillas, 2008). Grandparents could serve both of those functions, especially by being models for hard work and persistence.

In some communities, children and youth are defined by their family line and ancestors (Urrieta, 2013). For example, a child in the Mexican community of Nocutzepo identified himself as "Juanito el de María de Inés." In other words, he was the little Juan from his grandmother, María de Inés.

Negative Influences and Effects

Under some conditions, co-residence with grandparents may be associated with detrimental consequences (Marks, 2007). A 32-country study of student performance in reading, science, and mathematics (OECD's 2000 Program for International Student Assessment [PISA] Study) revealed that 15-year-old students who lived with their grandparents had significantly lower scores than students who did not (also participating in the PISA study and covered by other chapters of this book were Brazil, Germany, Japan, Korea, Russia, the UK, and the US). For example, the mean reading score for Mexican students who lived with grandparents was 389; for those who did not reside with grandparents it was 434. Although socioeconomic factors partially accounted for this difference, the detrimental effects of living with grandparents persisted after controlling for socioeconomic status. Marks speculated that co-residence with a grandparent may sometimes reflect other disruptions in the household, such as a migrating parent or a recent divorce (Marks, 2007).

A more mixed influence of grandparents is depicted in the life story of Thelma Lucía (Falla Sánchez, 2013) from Honduras. She moved in with her grandparents to attend school, but her grandfather was an alcoholic and mistreated her grandmother and other family members. The grandmother insisted that Thelma Lucía leave the house when he arrived home, so that she would not see what transpired. So although she was able to get an education through co-residence with grandparents, Thelma was also exposed to an alcoholic and abusive grandfather.

Sometimes the relationship with grandchildren can also be deleterious for grandparents (Jiménez Pelcastre, 2012). For example, caretaker grandmothers in rural Hidalgo, Mexico expressed feelings of resignation about caring for their grandchildren. They saw these advantages: economic help from their children, satisfaction from seeing their grandchildren's development, and the affection and company of their grandchildren. However, they were physically exhausted because the job often entailed long hours, especially when caring for babies or sick children. Childcare also kept them from obtaining paid work, and made them economically dependent on their children. Psychologically, they often found themselves anxious and concerned for their grandchildren, especially as the grandchildren entered adolescence; some took drugs, dropped out of school, or insulted, intimidated, stole from, or denigrated their grandmothers. Jiménez Pelcastre named the problem, *síndrome de la abuela esclava* [syndrome of the enslaved grandmother]. There was no evidence of negative or abusive relationships among our interviewees, but ours was not a representative sample and rather consisted of acquaintances who were interested in talking about grandparenting.

Other Factors that Influence the Relationship

As mentioned earlier in our discussion of the descriptive framework of Pinazo Hernandis (1999), the ages of grandparents and their grandchildren, geographic distance and frequency of contact, nature of their shared activities, and grandchildren's perceptions all impact relations between grandparents and their grandchildren.

The ages of both the grandparents and the grandchildren affect how they spend time together. As Margie said in her case story, speaking about her 6½-year-old grandchild, "I find my inner child." Teenagers, on the other hand, may pose challenges for custodial grandparents (Jiménez Pelcastre, 2012). Adult grandchildren in Mexican American families experienced less closeness and less frequent interaction with their grandparents, especially if the adult grandchildren were highly acculturated to US culture (Silverstein & Chen, 1999). The age of the grandparents also affects the relationship, as witnessed by Celestino, who no longer works in the fields with his grandchildren as he did when he was younger.

The geographical distance between grandparents and their grandchildren undoubtedly influences their relationship (Gardner et al., 2004; Pinazo Hernandis, 1999). In Mexico and two Central American countries for which there are data, the percentages of children who live in households with adults other than their parents (which likely indicates co-residence with grandparents) are relatively high: Nicaragua at 55%, Costa Rica at 41%, and Mexico at 45%. In comparison, the rate for the US is 27% (Scott, Wilcox, Ryberg, & DeRose, 2015). Looking at the statistics from the other direction, in Mexico 46% of adults over 60 live with extended family, 40% with a spouse only, and 12% live alone. Of people over 60 in Mexico, about 30% live with young children, who are most likely their grandchildren (Instituto Nacional de Estadística y Geografía [INEGI], 2010). While extended family structure may be more common in Central America than elsewhere, many grandparents do not live with their grandchildren. This was the case with the four families described in the case stories; although all of the Guatemalan grandparents lived near their grandchildren, none resided with them.

There is not much qualitative or quantitative research focused on how grandparents and grandchildren in Central America and Mexico spend time together. However, in one study Guatemalan and Salvadorean grandchildren reported that their favorite grandparent often watched television, listened to music, or played with them; took care of their needs; explained things; told them stories; and took them to school (González Bernal, González Santos, Ortiz Oria, & González Bernal, 2010). Some of those same activities were mentioned

FIGURE 2.3 A 6-year-old girl and her grandparents play cooking soup. They had constructed a grill over pieces of firewood and had added water, leaves, and artificial grapes. Guatemalan grandparents often spend a lot of time with their grandchildren, engaging in real or pretend daily chores.

Source: Courtesy of Judith Gibbons.

by the grandparents interviewed for the case stories of this chapter. Domingo and Celestino described family celebrations with all the grandchildren. Margie described how she plays soccer, does experiments, and dresses up with her grandchildren. In Figure 2.3, the grandparents are "playing house" with their granddaughter, helping her to prepare a fictive soup on a toy grill. All these activities involve grandparents who accommodate the children's interests and needs.

The perceptions of the grandchildren, although less often studied, are also important in the relationship. In a study of children in Guatemala and El Salvador (González Bernal et al., 2010), the favorite grandparent was most often the maternal grandmother, who was very important to the grandchildren and contributed greatly to their well-being. Grandchildren spent time with her several times a week or even daily and saw her as an important provider of care, understanding, love, pampering, and material things.

Overall, the research literature about grandparents in Mexico and Central America is primarily anecdotal and limited in scope. More comprehensive studies, both quantitative and qualitative, would greatly add to knowledge about the nature of the relationships. Particularly lacking are data on the perspectives of grandchildren. How do they see their relationships with grandfathers and with grandmothers as fostering their development?

Grandfathers in Central America and Mexico

There is little specific information on the role of grandfathers and their relationships with grandchildren in Mexico and Central America. In the information available, there is variability between urban and rural settings, and among different ethnic groups and subcultures.

Because there is insufficient research data available specifically about grandfathers, we need to review some literature on men's roles in general in the region (e.g., Gibbons & Luna, 2015). A major organizing construct is *machismo*, an extreme masculinity, often associated with aggression, hyper-sexuality, patriarchy, and misogyny. Expressions of *machismo* from the scale of Mexican premises developed by Díaz-Guerrero (1972) include, "Men are by nature superior to women," and "The father should always be the head of the household." *Machismo* as an ideology and family structure is widespread within the region (Fernández Poncela, 1999–2000; Gibbons & Luna, 2015). Recent conceptualizations of *machismo* have revealed a second dimension to the concept; along with traditional *machismo* represented by hypermasculinity, aggression, and domination of women, there is a gentler *machismo*, termed *caballerismo* (Arciniega, Anderson, Tover-Blank, & Travey, 2008) *Caballerismo* can be translated as "gentlemanliness," or "knightliness" and focuses on nurturance and protection of the family.

Both aspects of *machismo* can be seen in descriptions of grandfathering in the region. A brusque and aloof type of grandfather was revealed in rural Latin America (Sánchez Salgado, Orozco Mares, & Oneto Piaze, 2010). Grandfathers were seen as less heroic, tender or loving than their female counterparts, perhaps because of a lifelong habit of evading household problems by going out for a drink with friends when things get difficult. That traditional, patriarchal, and stern grandfather was also described by González Bernal et al. (2010) in a study of the grandparent–grandchild relationships in Guatemala and El Salvador. On the other hand, in some urban settings grandfathers were seen as being favored by their grandchildren because they imposed discipline less often (Sánchez Salgado et al., 2010). The mellower, indulgent urban grandfather is congruent with that portrayed by the Mexican author Fuentes Aguirre (2007). This author labeled grandfatherhood as a God-given blessing and poetically idealizes the special moments spent with his grandchildren from their birth through adolescence. Both of the case story grandfathers, Domingo and Celestino, expressed similar ideas. Domingo's assertion that "you have to take care of your family" is the central axiom of *caballerismo*.

Although patriarchy is prevalent in the region, in some Central American subcultural groups, such as garífuna communities, women tend to take the lead role and make the important decisions (De Corró, 2013; Kerns, 1997; Hobson, 2006). In matrilineal societies (sometimes mislabeled as "matriarchal"), fathers and grandfathers play minimal roles in children's lives; usually the mother's brother is a more important figure (Schneider, 1961).

In sum, it seems that throughout Central America and Mexico grandfathers may have highly variable levels of involvement, and they may be less directly involved in caregiving of grandchildren compared to grandmothers (De la Fuente Anuncibay, González Bernal, González Santos, & González Bernal, 2014), which is a finding consistent throughout most of the other chapters of this volume.

Variations in Grandparenting

As noted above, grandparenting varies according to economic conditions, rural/urban residence, culture, and age. Three specific phenomena may affect the relations between grandparents and grandchildren in Central America and Mexico: religion (Pew Research Center, 2014), the growth of youth gangs (Portillo, 2012; Seelke, 2014), and the migration of members of the parent generation (Montes de Oca Zavala, 2010). As in Brazil (see Chapter 4), the majority of the population of the region is Christian, traditionally Catholic with increasing levels of conversion to Protestantism. Religious beliefs may support traditional family structure, including patriarchy, as reflected in the comments of Celestino, who saw his role as grandfather to be governed by his religious beliefs.

The appearance of youth gangs in poverty-stricken neighborhoods has been the result of many factors, which include the culture of violence spawned by long-lasting civil wars; rapid urban growth; lack of education, job opportunities, and community infrastructure; and the presence of illegal drugs, all combined with problems within the family. Especially in Guatemala, Honduras, and El Salvador, gangs have replaced grandparents and parents as a dominant influence in the lives of many young people (Castillo Berthier, 2013; Cruz, 2005). This is what Celestino may have been alluding to when he mentioned his hope that his grandchildren "not become drug addicts or thieves." In marginalized neighborhoods, some grandparents fear their own grandchildren, who may become violent and attack them; in recent years, newspapers have reported a number of cases of grandmothers killed by grandsons in Central America (González, 2013; La Prensa Gráfica, 2015).

A third specific issue for many families in Mexico and Central America is the migration of one or both parents, usually undertaken to increase the well-being of the family through financial remittances (Mohr de Collado, 2007; Montes de Oca Zavala, 2009). A number of advantages may accrue to the family. For example, remittances may allow younger children in the family to stay in school (Magazine & Ramírez Sánchez, 2007). However, the remaining family may face new challenges even if they receive enough to cover basic expenses. Often grand-parents are called upon to be the custodians of their grandchildren, and to play the roles of parents in terms of caregiving and guidance (Estrada Iguíniz, 2009). Although grandparents often report positive aspects to that role, they may also suffer health consequences, including stress (Jiménez Pelcastre, 2012), as well as the diversion of funds from their own health needs to those of their grandchil-dren (Scott, 2012). If they care for a large number of grandchildren – up to nine in the case of one 80-year-old Belizean grandmother (Tout, 1994) – they may not be able to provide the attention and care needed (Mohr de Collado, 2007). Even when grandparents migrate with their children and grandchildren to the US, half of them end up living in overcrowded housing, in less than ideal conditions, and with major responsibility for the care of their grandchildren (Fuller-Thomson & Minkler, 2007); see Chapter 3, on the US, for related research findings on Mexican American grandparents.

Social Policies and Governmental Influences on Grandparents

Grandparents' legal rights and representation in the bodies of law vary greatly from country to country in this region. According to Nicaragua's Código de Familia (2014), for instance, grandparents may be legally considered to be head of a household and are specifically included in the definition of family; accord-ingly, they may object legally to the adoption of a grandchild and may become guardians of their grandchildren under certain circumstances. Meanwhile, in Belize's Families and Children Act (2003) there is no mention of grandparents, nor any special rights for them.

In Honduras' Código de Familia (2007) grandparents are included with chil-dren and spouses as recipients of pension and maintenance from the head of the household, when they cannot fend for themselves. Mexico has a different civil code for every state, 31 in total (Chávez Asencio, n.d.). In Costa Rica (Código de Familia, 1997) and Guatemala (Sigüeza Sigüeza, 2010), grandparents, parents, and grandchildren are mutually responsible for providing support, care, and nourish-ment for each other, when one of the parties is unable to fend for him or herself due to disability and the immediately responsible member of the family (usually the parent) is unable to provide for dependent minors or older adults.

In most countries of the region (Costa Rica, El Salvador, Guatemala, Mexico, Nicaragua, and Panama), grandparents are next in line after the parents to become legal guardians for their minor grandchildren, or adult grandchildren who have disabilities or are unable to fend for themselves, and may be named a legal guard-ian or "tutor." (Codigo Civil para el Distrito Federal, 1928 in Mexico; Código Civil de la República de Panamá, 1912; Código de Familia, 1993 in El Salvador; Código de Familia, 1997 in Costa Rica; Código de Familia, 2014 in Nicaragua; Sigüeza Sigüeza, 2010 in Guatemala). In Honduras, (Código de Familia, 2007) an order of priority is specified to determine which grandparent obtains legal guardianship: first the paternal grandfather, then the maternal grandfather, then the paternal grandmother, and lastly the maternal grandmother. In Guatemala, on the other hand, both paternal grandparents have priority over maternal grandparents, regardless of which family is better able to provide for the needs of the child (Galvez Mazariegos, 2010).

In Costa Rica (Código de Familia, 1997), El Salvador (Código de Familia, 1993), and Nicaragua (Código de Familia, 2014) grandparents are legally obligated to support their dependent grandchildren to the best of their abilities, when the parents are absent or can no longer do so.

In cases of parents' divorce, in Costa Rica (Código de Familia, 1997) and El Salvador (Código de Familia, 1993), grandparents have the right to visit and continue communications with their grandchildren. Although there are no specific laws in any of these countries that mention the state's or society's responsibilities toward grandparents, there is a binding treaty of international law that addresses the rights of older adults (Organization of American States [OAS], 1988). It includes protection of individuals from the consequences of old age and disability through a social security system, and a gradual coverage of food and specialized medical care for elderly persons who may no longer be able to provide for themselves.

Based on this treaty, most countries have developed a set of laws and some have even created a government agency specifically designed to guarantee the rights of older adults (Villareal Martinez, 2005). However, most of these laws lack mechanisms to enforce them and in reality governments have not been able to provide their intended benefits (such as social security, adequate housing, medical care, food, recreation, and other resources). As a result, living conditions for many grandparents in this region are far from ideal (Alvarado Pérez & González Conteras, 2008, in El Salvador; Mejía et al., 2014 in Honduras; and Mora Jiménez, 2009–2010 in Costa Rica).

Although efforts have been made to create adequate policies to protect the rights of grandparents in the region, the difficulty of enforcing these laws has resulted in their having minimal impact on the lives of grandparents and grandchildren alike.

Conclusions and Speculation

In Mexico and Central America, grandparents are recognized as integral members of the family; they provide support and when needed act as the primary caregivers for grandchildren. Intergenerational solidarity is fostered by a strong tradition of allegiance to one's extended family, and a united and integrated family contributes to happiness. In the case story, Margarita said, "when the grandchildren fight among themselves or their mother hits them, it hurts my heart." In many families grandparents are not only held in high esteem, but they are expected to pass on cultural values to their grandchildren. Domingo wants his grandchildren to be respectful and hardworking. Margie wants her grandchildren to be true to themselves. Celestino wants his grandchildren to be hardworking, proper, and law-abiding.

Manuela would like her grandchildren to be healthy in the physical, emotional, and spiritual domains.

Grandparents love and value their grandchildren as the "crown of the aged," a perspective that reflects their emphasis on generativity. Through their grandchildren, traditions and values are carried forward. Four countries of the region – Honduras, Mexico, Nicaragua, and Panama – have established official holidays celebrating grandparents: *Día de los Abuelos* (Day of the Grandparents), Costa Rica celebrates the Day of the Older Adult. In these countries, where the extended family may be the center of every important celebration, grandparents are the pillars that support traditions and affective bonds that bind together different generations.

What might the future hold for the next generations of grandparents in Central America and Mexico? Globalization, leading to increased rural-to-urban migration and mechanization of agriculture, is likely to change the lifestyle of many families. Future grandparents will be less likely to live like Domingo and Margarita, engaged in manual labor agriculture and residing in close proximity to their children and grandchildren. Large family gatherings will be less frequent and families more scattered and less integrated. The trend toward fewer households of extended family members and more households of nuclear families may continue.

Technological advances are likely to have multiple consequences for the lives of grandparents and their grandchildren. The physical dispersion of families may be mitigated by increased reliance on technology for communication. There are already more cell phones in Guatemala than there are people (International Telecommunications Union, 2014). With increasing access to the internet, video calling may become available to large segments of the population, which will open further avenues for family communication and integration. On the other hand, youth more than elders may have expertise in the new technologies, propelling the region into a pre-figurative culture. Defined by Mead (1973), a pre-figurative culture is one in which younger generations teach the older ones, instead of the other way around. This was evident in the case story interview of Margie, who pointed out that her 6-year-old grandchildren proudly teach her how to use applications on their electronic devices.

Other trends in Central America and Mexico consist of increasing levels of violence, especially in Honduras, Guatemala, and El Salvador, along with population growth, low funding for education, and political and economic problems. If these trends continue, there is likely to be further emigration and more economic dependence on remittances from family members who work abroad. Another consequence of these trends is that grandparents would be increasingly called upon to care for their grandchildren. Of course, there is the possibility that this trajectory may be reversed, given sufficient investments in crime prevention, education, strengthening of families, rehabilitation of gang members, and anti-corruption efforts. Whether the current trends continue or are thwarted, the next few generations are likely to see substantial changes in family relationships, including those between grandparents and their grandchildren.

Summary

The roles of grandparents in Central America and Mexico have been influenced by the region's colonial history, social conflict, economic disparity, high rates of poverty, migration to other countries, overwhelmingly Christian beliefs, proliferation of gangs, as well as by ethnic and cultural diversity. Despite their differences, there are some common threads shared by grandparents across this region. Central American and Mexican grandparents tend to be younger than in other regions of the world. They express love, affection, and support for their grandchildren. They transmit cultural values to the younger generations, and, when needed, fill in as caregivers. For the most part, they are an essential part of the family, sharing the same household, or visiting frequently. Grandparents can become overburdened by the responsibility of caring for grandchildren, especially when the parents move to another country. In most cases the maternal grandmother is the favorite and closest grandparent. However, many grandfathers are influenced by *caballerismo* (knightliness or gentlemanliness), and prioritize their roles of support and protection of the family. The roles of grandparents in the region are most closely linked to cultural values of family unity and to the developmental task of generativity for adults and elders.

Appendix

Meaning of Proverbs

"The grandparent is not synonymous with old age, but with love."

Grandparents need not be old, but instead fairly young, particularly in this region where it is uncommon for each generation of women to become mothers as teenagers. Most grandparents in this region enjoy and love their grandchildren, so they are frequently identified with love.

"The parents to raise, the grandparents to spoil."

Except in cases where the parents are absent and grandparents assume a parenting role, grandparents do not usually discipline, set limits, or do the hard work of educating children; grandparents tend to spend more pleasant time with children, providing love and affection without the responsibility for raising them.

Additional Resources

Hernandez Ramos, J. (n.d.). *Family in Latin America*. (www.difi.org.qa/app/media/660)

Through a speech written about Mexican families, Hernandez Ramos highlights the changes and challenges facing them in the 21st century. Although his conclusions are drawn from data in Mexico, the extent to which these conclusions could be generalized to families in Central American countries merits discussion.

Fauné, M. A. (1995). *Central America's family and women: What does reality say?* (www.envio.org.ni/articulo/1874 (in Spanish only))

In this article, Fauné provides a comprehensive profile of Central American families, while dispelling commonly perpetuated stereotypes. Although much of the content still applies 20 years later, a point for discussion may be to consider how the impact of remittances, migration, and transnational families may contribute to the ever-evolving picture of Central American families.

Shepard, W. (n.d.) *Grandparents raise children in Latin America.* (www.vagabond-journey.com/grandparents-raise-children-in-latin-america//)

Although this short article represents the casual observations of an insightful tourist, it points out the widespread practice around the world of shared caregiving. What Shepard might have missed, however, was that older siblings also take care of young children.

Discussion Questions

1. Based on your reading of this chapter, should grandparents be responsible to take care of young children when the parents have to emigrate to find jobs in other countries? What are the benefits, challenges, and risks of grandparents caring for grandchildren?
2. When the parents are present, what can grandparents contribute to the lives of their grandchildren (in Central America and Mexico) that parents cannot?
3. How is grandparenting in Mexico and Central America similar or different from grandparenting in other regions of the world?

References

Alvarado Pérez, E. G., & González Contreras, A. C. (2008). *The effectiveness of public health programs for the elderly implemented by the National Council on Comprehensive Care.* (Unpublished thesis). University of El Salvador, San Salvador, El Salvador.

Arciniega, G. M., Anderson, T. C., Tover-Blank, Z. G., & Tracey, T. J. G. (2008). Toward a fuller conception of machismo: Development of a traditional machismo and caballerismo scale. *Journal of Counseling Psychology, 55,* 19–33. doi: 10.1037/0022-0167.55.1.19

Bates, J. S., & Taylor, A. C. (2013). Taking stock of theory in grandparent studies. In M. A. Fine & F. D. Fincham (Eds.), *Handbook of family theories: A content-based approach* (pp. 51–70). New York: Routledge.

Bengston, V. L., & Kuypers, J. A. (1971). Generational difference and the developmental stake. *Aging & Human Development, 2*, 249–260. doi:10.2190/AG.2.4.b

Brick, K., Challinor, A. E., & Rosenblum, M. R. (2011). *Mexican and Central American immigrants in the United States.* Retrieved from www.migrationpolicy.org/research/mexican-and-central-american-immigrants-united-states

Car, G., Eder, K., & Garcia Pú, M. (2005). *The heritage of the grandmothers and grandfathers.* Retrieved from http://asecsaguatemala.org/Descargas/Investigacion%20Herencia%20de%20las%20Abuelas%20y%20los%20abuelos.pdf

Castillo Berthier, H. (2013, September 1). Gangs, youth, and violence. *México Social.* Retrieved from http://mexicosocial.org/index.php/secciones/especial/item/351-pandillas-jóvenes-y-violencia

Central Intelligence Agency (CIA). (2016a). *The world factbook.* Retrieved from www.cia.gov/library/publications/the-world-factbook/

Central Intelligence Agency (CIA). (2016b). *The world factbook: Mother's mean age at first birth.* Retrieved from www.cia.gov/library/publications/the-world-factbook/fields/2256.html

Central Intelligence Agency (CIA). (2016c). *The world factbook: Age structure.* Retrieved from www.cia.gov/library/publications/the-world-factbook/geos/gt.html

Cervantes, L. (2013). Supports in homes with at least one elderly person in the State of Mexico. *Papeles de Población, 19*(75), 1–30.

Chávez Asencio, M. F. (n.d.). *The family in Mexican legislation.* Retrieved from www.juridicas.unam.mx/publica/librev/rev/jurid/cont/23/pr/pr22.pdf

Código Civil de la República de Panamá [Civil Code of the Republic of Panama]. (1912). 2 la República de Panamá §47.

Codigo Civil para el Distrito Federal [Civil Code for the Federal District]. (1928). Asamblea Legislativa del Distrito Federal, IV Legislatura. Retrieved from www.ssp.df.gob.mx/TransparenciaSSP/sitio_sspdf/art_14/fraccion_i/normatividad_aplicable/59.1.pdf

Código de Familia [Family Code]. (1993). 677, la Asamblea Legislativa de la Republica de El Salvador §217 §219 §221 §291.

Código de Familia [Family Code]. (1997). 5467, la Asamblea Legislativa de la Republica de Costa Rica §101, §152 §169 § 177.

Código de Familia [Family Code]. (2007). 76–84, Corte Suprema de Justicia República de Honduras § 217.

Código de Familia [Family Code]. (2014). 807, Nicaragua Asamblea Nacional §37, §234, §256 §357 §379.

Cruz, J. M. (2005). Factors associated with youth gangs in Central America. *ECA: Estudios centroamericanos*, 685–686, 1155–1182.

De Corró, M. M. (2013). Panamanian culture: A hot hybrid. ReVista Harvard Review of Latin America. Retrieved from http://revista.drclas.harvard.edu/book/panamanian-culture

De la Fuente Anuncibay, R., González Bernal, J., González Santos, J., & Gonzaléz Bernal, E. (2014). Joint activities and the image grandchildren have about the grandparent–grandchild relationship: An intercultural perspective. *CADMO, 22*, 57–68. doi:10.3280/CAD2014-001007

Deuss, K. (2007). *Shamans, witches, and Maya priests: Native religion and ritual in highland Guatemala.* London: The Guatemala Maya Centre.

Díaz-Guerrero, R. (1972). A factorial scale of historico-sociocultural premises of the Mexican family. *Revista Interamericana de Psicología, 6*, 235–244.

El Heraldo de Chihuahua. (2015, August 19). El abuelo no es sinónimo de vejez, sino de amor [Grandparent is not synonymous with old age, but with love]. *El Heraldo de Chihuahua.* Retrieved from www.oem.com.mx/elheraldodechihuahua/notas/n3920038.htm

Erikson, E. H. (1950). *Childhood and society.* New York: W. W. Norton & Company.

Erikson, E. H. (1982). *The life cycle completed.* New York: W. W. Norton & Company.

Estrada Iguíniz, M. (2009). Enacting parental roles in the context of emigration between Mexico and the United States. *Revista de Antropología Social, 18,* 221–234.

Falla Sánchez, R. (2013). Testimonies: Original peoples in contemporary Central America. *Anuario de Estudios Centroamericanos, Universidad de Costa Rica, 39,* 413–458.

Families and Children Act. (2003). 173. The Subsidiary Laws of Belize. Retrieved from www.oas.org/dil/Families_and_Children_Subsidiary_Act_Belize.pdf

Fernández Poncela, A. M. (1999–2000) Family arrangements and disarrangements (Central America and Nicaragua). *Revista Chilena de Antropología, 15,* 131–144.

Fuentes Aguirre, A. S. (2007). *Of grandmothers, grandfathers, and other blessed angels.* Mexico, D. F.: Diana (Grupo Planeta).

Fuller-Thomson, E., & Minkler, M. (2007). Central American grandparents raising grandchildren. *Hispanic Journal of Behavioral Sciences,* 29(1), 5–18. doi:10.1177/0739986306293680

Galvez Mazariegos, J. J. (2010). Legal study of article 216 of the civil code as to the priority of the paternal grandparents in the recognition of a minor in the event of disability or death of parents. (Unpublished thesis). University of San Carlos de Guatemala, Guatemala City, Guatemala.

Garay Villegas, S. Montes de Oca Zavala, V., & Guillén, J. (2014). Social support and social networks among the elderly in Mexico. *Journal of Population Ageing, 7,* 143–159. doi: 10.1007/s12062-014-9099-2

Gardner, J. E., Scherman, A., Efthimiadis, M. S., & Shultz, S. K. (2004). Panamanian grandmothers' family relationships and adjustment to having a grandchild with a disability. *Aging and Human Development, 59*(4), 305–320. doi:10.2190/L60R-MF1N-98AV-TMV3

Giarrusso, R., Feng, D., Silverstein, M., & Bengston, V. L. (2001). Grandparent–adult grandchild affection and consensus: Cross-generational and cross-ethnic comparisons. *Journal of Family Issues, 22,* 456–477. doi:10.1177/019251301022004004

Gibbons, J. L., & Luna, S. (2015). For men life is hard, for women life is harder: Gender roles in Central America. In S. Safdar & N. Kosakowska-Berezecka, (Eds.), *The psychology of gender & culture* (pp. 307–325). New York: Springer.

Gibbons, J. L., & Stiles, D. A. (2004). *The thoughts of youth: An international perspective on adolescents' ideal persons.* Greenwich, CT: Information Age Publishing.

González, O. (2013, September 6). Grandson had participated in a crime against his grandmother and her granddaughter in Jutiapa. *Prensa Libre.* Retrieved from www.prensalibre.com/jutiapa/abuela_y_nieta-jutiapa-menor_capturado-crimen_en_jutiapa_0_988101325.html

González Bernal, J. J., González Santos, J., Ortiz Oria, V., & González Bernal, E. (2010). The relation between grandparents and grandchildren from an intercultural perspective. *International Journal of Developmental and Educational Psychology, 2*(1), 669–676.

Hobson, L. (2006). "Sexual magic" and money: Strategies of Miskita women in the global economy. *Wani revista del Caribe Nicaragüense, 46,* 62–72. Retrieved from http://revistas.bicu.edu.ni/index.php/wani/article/view/69

Hofstede, G. (2011). Dimensionalizing cultures: The Hofstede model in context. *Online Readings in Psychology and Culture, 2*(1). Retrieved from http://scholarworks.gvsu.edu/orpc/vol2/iss1/8

Instituto Nacional de Estadística y Geografía (INEGI). (2010). *Sociodemographic profile of older adults.* Retrieved from http://internet.contenidos.inegi.org.mx/contenidos/productos/prod_serv/contenidos/espanol/bvinegi/productos/censos/poblacion/2010/perfil_socio/adultos/702825056643.pdf

International Telecommunication Union (2014). *Percentage of individuals using the internet.* Retrieved from www.itu.int/en/ITU-D/Statistics/Pages/stat/default.aspx

Jiménez Pelcastre, A. (2012). Violence in old age: the case of grandmothers who care for their grandchildren in a rural locale in the state of Hidalgo. *El Cotidiano, 174,* 19–32.

Kerns, V. (1997). *Women and the ancestors: Black Carib kinship and ritual* (2nd ed.). Urbana, IL: University of Illinois Press.

Luciak, I. (2011). *After the revolution: Gender and democracy in El Salvador, Nicaragua, and Guatemala.* Baltimore, MD: Johns Hopkins University Press.

Magazine, R., & Ramírez Sánchez, M. A. (2007). Continuity and change in San Pedro Tlalcuapan, Mexico: Childhood, social reproduction, and transnational migration (pp. 52–73). In J. Cole & D. Durham (Eds.), *Generations and globalization: Youth, age, and family in the new world economy* (pp. 52–73). Bloomington, IN: Indiana University Press.

Margarito Gaspar, M. (2012). Everyday Mexican life as portrayed in the images of textbooks. *Revista Iberoamericana de las Ciencias Sociales y Humanísticas, 1*(1). Retrieved from https://dialnet.unirioja.es/servlet/articulo?codigo=5056002

Marks, G. N. (2007). Detrimental effects of living with a grandparent: Cross-national evidence. *Journal of Comparative Family Studies, 38*(1), 169–177.

Mead, M. (1973). Prefigurative cultures and unknown children. In P. K. Manning (Ed.), *Youth: Divergent perspectives* (pp. 193–206). New York: John Wiley and Sons.

Mejía, M. A., Rivera, P. M., Urbina, M., Alger, J., Maradiaga, E., Flores, S., & Sierra, L. (2014, June–December). Disability in the elderly: Characteristics and relevant factors. *Revista de la Facultad de Ciencias Médicas,* 27–33.

Meza Márquez, C. (2012). Literary discourse of the Garífuna poets of the Central American Caribbean: Honduras, Nicaragua, and Guatemala. *Latinoamérica: Revista de Estudios Latinoamericanos, 55,* 245–278.

Mohr de Collado, M. (2007). The Garínagu in Central America and other places: Identities of an Afro-Caribbean population between tradition and modernity. *Indiana, 24,* 67–86.

Montes de Oca Zavala, V. (2009). Families and intergenerational solidarity in Mexico: Challenges and opportunities. In Family Support Networks and Population Aging, (pp. 107–111). Retrieved from www.unfpa.org/sites/default/files/pub-pdf/family_support_networks2009.pdf

Montes de Oca Zavala, V. (2010). Migration in Mexico, transnational families and social support networks for women and men older adults. *Ageing Horizons, 9,* 59–75.

Mora Jiménez, M. (2009–2010). Are the human rights of the elderly being protected? The legal discourse. *Revista Ciencias Sociales,* 126–127, 123–134. doi:10.15517/rcs.v0i126-127.8779

National Institute on Aging. (2011). *Global health and aging.* Retrieved from https://d2cauhfh6h4x0p.cloudfront.net/s3fs-public/global_health_and_aging.pdf?q.52VK49USX58EJwZ3BjLl.yphsH2T_

New World Encyclopedia. (2013). Central America. Retrieved from http://www.newworldencyclopedia.org/entry/Central_America

Organization of American States (OAS). (1988). *Additional protocol to the American convention on human rights in the area of economic, social, and cultural rights "protocol of San Salvador."* Retrieved from www.oas.org/juridico/english/treaties/a-52.html

Partidas, R. (2004). Workers in the electrical plant in Jalisco: Grandmothers as providers of childcare. *El Cotidiano, 19*(125), 68–77.

Pew Research Center (2014). *Religion in Latin America: Widespread change in a historically Catholic region.* Retrieved from www.pewforum.org/files/2014/11/Religion-in-Latin-America-11-12-PM-full-PDF.pdf

Pinazo Hernandis, S. (1999). Social significance of the grandparent role. *Revista Multidiciplinar de Gerontología, 9,* 169–176.

Portillo, N. (2012). Studies on youth gangs in El Salvador and Central America: A review of their participatory nature. *Apuntes de Psicología, 30*(1–3), 397–407.

Programa de las Naciones Unidas para el Desarrollo (PNUD). (2005). *Ethnic-cultural diversity: Citizenship in a plural state.* Guatemala City, Guatemala: PNUD.

Rogoff, B., Mejía-Arauz, R., & Correa-Chávez, M. (2015). A cultural paradigm: Learning by observing and pitching in. In M. Correa-Chávez, R. Mejía-Arauz, & B. Rogoff (Eds.), *Advances in child development and behavior: Children learn by observing and contributing to family and community endeavors: A cultural paradigm* (pp. 1–22). New York: Elsevier.

Sánchez Salgado, C. D., Orozco Mares, I., & Oneto Piaze, L. (2010). Analysis and perspectives of the social construction of old age in rural/urban areas of Mexico, Chile, and Puerto Rico. *Ageing Horizons, 9,* 3–18.

Schneider, D. M. (1961). Introduction: The distinctive features of matrilineal descent groups. In D. M. Schneider & K. Gough (Eds.), *Matrilineal kinship* (pp. 1–29), Berkeley, CA: University of California Press.

Scott, M. A. (2012). Paying down the care deficit: The health consequences for grandmothers caring for grandchildren in a Mexican migrant community of origin. *Anthropology & Aging Quarterly, 33*(4), 142–151.

Scott, M. E., Wilcox, W. B., Ryberg, R., & DeRose, L. (2015). *World family map 2015: Mapping family change and child well-being outcomes.* Retrieved from http://worldfamilymap.ifstudies.org/2015/wp-content/themes/WorldFamilyMap/WFM-2015-ForWeb.pdf

Seelke, C. R. (2014). *Gangs in Central America.* Congressional Research Service. Washington, DC: The Library of Congress.

Sigüeza Sigüeza, G. A. (2010). *Civil code decree law number 106.* Retrieved from http://biblio3.url.edu.gt/Libros/2011/codigo.pdf

Silas Casillas, J. C. (2008). Why does Miriam go to school? Resilience in basic Mexican education. *Revista Mexicana de Investigación Educativa, 13*(39), 1255–1279.

Silverstein, M., & Chen, X. (1999). The impact of acculturation in Mexican American families on the quality of adult grandchild–grandparent relationships. *Journal of Marriage and Family, 61,* 188–198. doi:10.2307/353893

Tout, K. (1994). Grandparents as parents in developing countries. *Ageing International, 21*(1), 19–23. doi:10.1007/BF02681175

La Prensa Gráfica. (2015, January 8). Un joven asesina a puñaladas a su abuela en El Salvador [A young killer stabbed his grandmother to death in El Salvador]. *La Prensa Gráfica.* Retrieved from www.laprensagrafica.com/2015/01/08/un-joven-asesina-a-pualadas-a-su-abuela-en-el-salvador

United Nations Population Fund (UNFPA). (2011). *State of world population 2011.* Retrieved from www.unfpa.org/sites/default/files/pub-pdf/EN-SWOP2011-FINAL.pdf

Urrieta, L., Jr. (2013). Familia and comunidad-based saberes: Learning in an indigenous heritage community. *Anthropology & Education Quarterly, 44*(3), 320–335. doi:10.1111/aeq.12028

Villagómez Valdés, G., & Sánchez González, M. C. (2014). Mayan women: Aging, poverty, and vulnerability. *Península, 9*(2), 75–98.

Villareal Martinez, M. (2005). Legislation on behalf of the elderly in Latin America and the Caribbean. Santiago, Chile: United Nations. Retrieved from http://repositorio.cepal.org/bitstream/handle/11362/7206/S0501092_es.pdf;jsessionid=64AD80E4866C2F7F4F72A78DEDD79114?sequence=1

World Bank. (2016a). *GINI index.* Retrieved from http://data.worldbank.org/indicator/SI.POV.GINI

World Bank. (2016b). *GNI per capita, Atlas method.* Retrieved from http://data.worldbank.org/indicator/NY.GNP.PCAP.CD

World Bank. (2016c). *Poverty headcount ratio at $1.90 a day.* Retrieved from http://data.worldbank.org/indicator/SI.POV.DDAY

3

GRANDPARENTING IN THE UNITED STATES

Cultural and Subcultural Diversity

Bert Hayslip Jr. and Christine A. Fruhauf

PROVERBS

    1. "If nothing is going well, call your grandmother."
    2. "Perfect love sometimes does not come till the first grandchild."

(see p. 54 for interpretations)

CASE STORIES

Our first case story depicts a fairly typical grandparental experience, with grandparents who maintain contact with their grandchildren despite life changes such as retirement or relocation.

> *Bob and Mary have been grandparents for six years. Their granddaughter is 6 years old and their grandson has just turned 3. They eagerly anticipated the births of each grandchild and were present when each was born. When their son and his wife lived close by, they were able to regularly visit and hold their granddaughter, kiss her, make eye contact with her, talk to her, feed her, and especially cuddle her. But when their son's family moved approximately 100 miles south, they were still able to make monthly visits to their granddaughter, and, later, to their grandson, attending birthday parties and family gatherings whenever possible. Bob and Mary retired two years later and moved to the beach approximately 1,000 miles away. Despite this distance, they regularly Skype and talk to their grandchildren, send them presents, and fly back for birthdays, recitals, and during school vacations. Although separated by distance, they have found ways to stay close to their grandchildren, and hope to move back part time to be able to see them more often and to be closer to them.*

A second case story exemplifies the experience of a grandmother who was raising her grandchild. This is an increasingly common phenomenon in middle and later life for many grandparents who not only raise their grandchildren, but also take care of an ill family member.

> *Nora has raised her granddaughter since the girl was quite young, due to her son's drug abuse. Complicating matters, her granddaughter has experienced emotional difficulties and school problems that have required counseling and medication. During the early years of raising her granddaughter, her husband was diagnosed with Lou Gehrig's disease and declined steadily until his death five years ago. During this time, she cared for him, held a part-time job, and dealt with the difficulties her granddaughter was experiencing. His death caused her much grief and the demands of raising a grandchild isolated her from her friends. She began to experience depression, which required personal counseling and medication. In addition, she attended a support group which she found very helpful. Her granddaughter has since graduated from high school and is now out on her own. This has enabled Nora to find full-time work and to begin to live her life more fully.*

Cultural, Historical, Social, Economic, and Demographic Influences on Grandparents

The Nature of Grandparenting in the United States

Becoming a grandparent is a common experience for many adults in the US. As life expectancy increased (and has now stabilized, see Table 1.1), so have the chances of becoming a grandparent (Uhlenberg, 2009). Seventy-five percent of those born in 2000 will have at least one grandparent still living when they reach age 30; nearly 60% of older adults have at least one grandchild, and 80% of middle-aged and older adults are grandparents (American Association of Retired Persons, 2002).

Many aspects of grandparenthood in the US reflect the *diversity* along demographic, financial, social, and educational parameters that characterizes American families (see Walsh, 2012). This diversity influences how grandparents define their roles, a key dimension of which is to transmit cultural and personal values to a grandchild (Pratt, Norris, Hebblethwaite, & Arnold, 2008). Grandparents also can serve as a support for that child and his/her family in times of crisis (Moore & Rosenthal, 2015), wherein they may also buffer the effects of their parents' divorce on grandchildren (Henderson, Hayslip, Sanders, & Louden, 2009). Grandparents who are more highly educated can positively impact their grandchildren's academic abilities as well as their emotional development (Jaeger, 2012), and greater emotional/financial involvement by grandparents longitudinally predicts grandchildren's prosocial behavior and school involvement (Yorgason, Padilla-Walker, & Jackson, 2011). Not surprisingly, greater emotional closeness to a grandparent is linked to fewer adjustment difficulties among adolescents (Attar-Schwartz, 2015). Alternatively, grandchildren can help familiarize their grandparents with matters of contemporary culture (e.g., using technology, school violence, music, fashion, drug use, sexuality). Grandparenthood can also lessen one's fears about isolation, loneliness, or dying, as shown by Friedman, Hechter, and Kreager's (2008) finding that grandparents who invested themselves more fully into the grandparent role had reduced uncertainty about their end of life. Finally, grandparents who are actively involved have better cognitive performance over time, better emotional health, and greater longevity (Christensen, 2014; Gurn & Beneke, 2015).

While grandparents can accurately predict the nature of their roles (Somary & Stricker, 1998), grandparenting is nevertheless *counter-transitional* (Hagestad, 1988), i.e., it depends upon the actions of others (chiefly one's son or daughter). This is important because people may have to define themselves as grandparents at a time in their lives when they are not ready to enter the role – such grandparents see themselves as either too young or too old to be grandparents. Whether one is a first-time "off-time" or "on-time" grandparent impacts one's relationships with a grandchild, and for some individuals off-time grandparenting, especially if one is younger, may disrupt life plans and careers (Hayslip & Montoro-Rodriguez, 2015). Older off-time grandparents may fear that they may not live long enough to enjoy a relationship with their grandchildren or that poor health may undermine the quantity and quality of such interactions.

Theoretical Approaches to Grandparenting

Perhaps the most well-known theoretical approach to grandparenting is Erikson's (1963) psychosocial theory, which emphasizes the psychosocial crisis of *generativity versus stagnation*. To be generative is to generate or produce something of enduring value, or to create a legacy, based on the awareness of one's own mortality. The most direct expression of generativity is to have children and grandchildren. Thus, in transmitting family values and cultural traditions, and in influencing grandchildren in ways that will reflect one's transcendent influence on them, grandparents can derive meaning and satisfaction from their roles (Newton & Baltys, 2014). They may also re-experience earlier feelings attached to raising their own children. Failing in these respects, people may become self-absorbed and stagnate.

Developmental contextual theory (Lerner, 2002) can also be helpful. A contextual view of grandparenting (as highlighted by the title of this book) recognizes the complexity of human relationships, wherein people influence and are influenced by others. Grandparents and grandchildren are best thought of in *dyadic* terms; their influence on one another is *dynamic* and *bidirectional,* in that the *developmental trajectories* of both grandparents and their grandchildren coexist and are superimposed upon one another (Combrinck-Graham, 1985). Importantly, in *systemic* terms (Silverstein, Giarrusso, & Bengtson, 2003) the nature and extent of grandparents' contact with their grandchildren is primarily *mediated* by the quality of the grandparent's relationship to the grandchild's parent, where the adult child serves as a *gatekeeper* who influences the amount and nature of contact with grandchildren (Connidis, 2010).

Lifespan developmental theory emphasizes multiple antecedents of developmental change (Baltes, 1997). Grandparent–grandchild dyads can be understood in *normative age-related* terms, where roles and relationships evolve over time, consistent with changes in physical and social emotional functioning experienced by both members of this dyad. The influence of *cohort-specificity* in each generation's influence upon the other is also essential, as each generation is uniquely shaped by the historical context in which they grew up. Additionally, recognition of *non-normative* variations on typical grandparent–grandchild interactions is also important for understanding such relationships. It follows that each generation's influence on the other is largely *unique* to each grandparent–grandchild dyad.

Quantitative and Qualitative Research on Grandparenting in the US

Whether grandparents believe they are important in the lives of their grandchildren influences how they define their roles as central or peripheral, and this perception lays the groundwork for how (and if) they will assist in their grandchild's development as well as how (and if) they will influence the family as a whole. Thus, the *meaning* one assigns to the grandparental role influences the *style* of grandparenting one adopts, i.e., the behaviors one displays in expression of this meaning (Hayslip & Page, 2012). In this respect, responsibility for child discipline, financial assistance, visitation, advice to the parent, sharing of religious faith, and support of the parents in decision-making must be negotiated between grandparents, their adult children, and their adult children's partners (see Hayslip, Maiden, Page, & Dolbin-MacNab, 2015).

Influences on Grandparent–Grandchild Contact

Contact with a grandchild sets the tone for the extent to which one can be influential in that child's life; in the US most grandparents (68%) see their grandchildren every one or two weeks, and the vast majority (89%) believe they play at least a somewhat important role in their grandchildren's lives (Lampkin, 2012). Not surprisingly, as in our opening case story, *geographic/physical proximity* best predicts the extent of grandparent–grandchild contact (Reitzes & Mutran, 2004), and grandparents who are geographically distant may need to be proactive to maintain contact with their grandchildren.

Age also impacts the nature and extent of the contact grandparents have with their grandchildren, in that the grandparent–grandchild relationship is likely to be different when grandchildren are young and grandparents are in good health to when grandchildren are adults and grandparents are older, ill, or frail. When grandchildren are young the focus is primarily on play and childcare, while during adolescence grandparents' roles often involve acting as a listener, support, and family historian (Michels, Albert, & Ferring, 2011). Indeed, grandparents in poorer health may be viewed differently by grandchildren who expect grandparents to be physically active or have the resources to travel. Yet, older grandparents can still provide emotional support or offer advice to grandchildren, buffer stressful parental relationships, and be a role model/financial advisor to the child (see Connidis, 2010; Smith & Drew, 2002). *Gender* also affects contact with grandchildren, whereby grandmothers anticipate the role earlier and get involved sooner (Smith & Drew, 2002); generally speaking, American children tend to favor grandmothers over grandfathers (see Connidis, 2010). The *number of grandchildren* one has also influences contact; a greater number of grandchildren decreases the frequency of contact given to each grandchild (Uhlenberg & Hammill, 1998). *Marital status* also affects contact with grandchildren, especially for grandfathers (Uhlenberg & Hammill, 1998), i.e., divorced older men have far less contact. Widowed grandfathers may also have less contact with their grandchildren than married ones because they lack a wife to facilitate the maintenance of family ties. Not surprisingly, when parents divorce grandparent–grandchild contact lessens, and the quality of the grandparent–grandchild relationship suffers (Drew & Silverstein, 2007).

Grandfathers in Cultural Context

In American culture, the generalization that grandfathers are less central than grandmothers (Hayslip, Shore, & Henderson, 2000) is influenced by the fact that there is little published research on this topic. Indeed, Mann (2007a) argues that this perception may reflect a feminized view of grandfathers, whereas the experiences of grandmothers are emphasized. At least some grandfathers' roles are likely shaped by culture; for example, among Hispanic and African families the construct of *familism* (see Chapter 2, this volume) predicts greater involvement by grandfathers, born of their identity as active contributors to the family as a whole. Such families may be better able to cope with the stresses of living in poverty (Keene, Prokos, & Hein, 2012). Grandfathers and grandmothers may communicate a given family's cultural heritage and are expected to do so by their grandchildren (Wiscott & Kopera-Frye, 2000). Alternatively, grandfathers who define themselves as more traditional may be less involved in the above respects. Unfortunately, little empirical work has been produced to substantiate these perspectives.

Grandfathers can be sources of wisdom and role models for those not regularly exposed to male family members; Mann, Kahn, and Leeson (2013) found that grandsons aged 12 and over saw their paternal grandfathers in the most positive terms. Indeed, despite having worked full time when they were younger, men derive much meaning and satisfaction from caring for a grandchild (St. George & Fletcher, 2014). Such men, who tend to be older, express satisfaction with grandparenting, have had active relationships with their young grandchildren, and are happy with their involvement in the tasks of child-rearing. In addition, Roberto, Allen, and Blieszner (2001) showed that despite a lack of geographic proximity, grandfathers in crisis situations became more actively involved and were quite able to transcend a male-oriented remote style of grandparenting to form close and loving grandchild relationships; this proactivity reflects the construct of *generative grandfathering* (Bates, 2009).

FIGURE 3.1 A grandfather and his granddaughter have a tea party together, an activity this granddaughter loves. Being meaningfully involved in his granddaughter's life is very important to the grandfather, as it is for the granddaughter to receive her grandfather's love and attention. Such connections are vital to the development of both the grandfather and the granddaughter.

Source: Courtesy of Generations United.

Grandfathers, more than grandmothers, offer instrumental support to their children whose child has died when they perform tasks and offer financial assistance; engagement in work as a means to help with their grief recovery is more common among grandfathers than grandmothers (Hayslip & White, 2008). Interestingly, male grandchildren's stories about their grandfathers emphasize the importance of work and recreation, with grandmothers playing supportive roles, while adult granddaughters' stories suggest that their grandmothers must make up for the deficiencies of their grandfathers (Goodsell, Bates, & Behnke, 2011).

Consistent with the lack of focus on grandfathers, virtually nothing is known about the impact of raising grandchildren on grandfathers, although among African American but not among Hispanic grandparent caregivers (some of whom are grandfathers), poorer health is associated with co-residence with a grandchild (Chen, Mair, Bao, & Yang, 2015). Health concerns, depression, and feelings of powerlessness in child-rearing sometimes characterize men's responses to parenting a grandchild (Hayslip, Kaminski, & Earnheart, 2006). Clearly, there is a need to study the issue of culture as it bears on grandfathers' roles and involvement with their grandchildren.

Subcultural Variations in Grandparenting

Related to cultural change as a factor in understanding grandparenting is the influence of culture *per se*. Culture reflects internalized shared norms and mores as well as values transmitted across generations (Cole, 1999).This perspective reflects the view of grandparents as mentors for younger parents, transmitters of cultural values and heritage, or as agents of socialization and influence for their grandchildren.Whether one's cultural or ethnic background uniquely defines grandparenting depends upon whether this role is a valued one. In this respect, Sandel, Cho, Miller, and Wang (2006) found differences in the meaning of the grandparent role between Taiwanese and Euro-American grandmothers. Studies of the cultural context in which grandparenting occurs also stress race and ethnicity as influences on grandparenting, whereby grandparents may serve the roles of the family historian, or living ancestor who teaches the grandchild ethnic traditions, culture, and history (Strom, Carter, & Schmidt, 2004). For example, African American grandparents have almost twice the degree of involvement with their grandchildren compared with White grandparents (see Szinovacz, 1998), though co-residence may undermine this effect (see Chen et al., 2015). Mexican Americans have larger, more multigenerational families, report higher satisfaction relating to their grandchildren, and have more intergenerational contact (Toledo, Hayslip, Emick, Toledo, & Henderson, 2000). Saxena and Sanders (2009) found that role importance, geographic distance, and to an extent, acculturation predicted grandparent relationship quality among Asian Indian immigrant grandchildren in the US.

Although the literature on grandparenting in cultural context is quite limited and for the most part dated, one key to understanding it is whether *familism* – a construct central to the lives of African American and Hispanic/Latino grandparents – is a valued attribute in people's lives, (see Hayslip, 2009). The degree of intergenerational support (typically more common among minority families), extent of acculturation and immigration status, whether the grandparent speaks English, and the co-residence of grandparents and grandchildren – which also characterizes African American and Hispanic/Latino grandfamilies (Generations United, 2015) – all influence the grandparent's relationship with the grandchild, the nature of help and support provided to grandchildren, and the socialization of the grandchild into the dominant culture.

Race and ethnicity clearly do influence grandparenthood. For example, African American grandparents report being invested in their grandchildren's education and provide financial support to them and their parents. These grandparents involve grandchildren to build a sense of community and often fill in as parents when biological parents are unavailable or unable to be present (Gibson, 2005). African American grandparents assume a teacher role (particularly among grandmothers) and serve as role models to grandchildren (Strom, Heeder, & Strom, 2005). Given their status as role models, African American grandparents are often considered a *significant other*, e.g., someone whose behaviors and attitudes are held in high regard (Mann, 2007b). Finally, African American grandparents influence their grandchildren's feelings about religion and spirituality, and their religious beliefs (Gutierrez, Goodwin, Kirkinis, & Mattis, 2014).

Silverstein and Chen (1999) found that gaps in cultural beliefs and values reduced social interaction between generations among Mexican American families; language barriers contributed to this finding although it was not the sole reason. Further, researchers who examined Chinese cultural values among immigrant Chinese American women revealed that grandmothers believe they spent much of their grandmothering role teaching grandchildren to have good character and to behave properly, especially when around their elders (Nagata, Cheng, & Tsai-Chae, 2010). This was achieved by high frequency of contact and in some cases co-residence, which is common among immigrant Chinese families. Finally, both South Asian and East Asian American grandparents display a high degree of involvement with grandchildren, particularly among younger grandparents and those with no disability, and grandmothers often parent grandchildren (Phua & Kaufman, 2008). Participants in these studies included some grandparents who emigrated from other countries, or perhaps are now considered "Americanized" grandparents. What is then important for researchers to consider are the similarities and differences among such cultural groups, e.g., Chinese grandparents versus Chinese American grandparents, etc.

FIGURE 3.2 These grandchildren and their grandmother are attending a rally that celebrates grandparents who raise their grandchildren. Their attendance reflects the commitment grandparents make in seeing to the physical, social, and emotional welfare of the grandchildren they raise. Grandchildren are proud to be raised by their grandparents, and the grandparents gain satisfaction in being role models that enrich their grandchildren's lives.

Source: Courtesy of Generations United.

Grandparents as Caregivers to their Grandchildren

In the US, grandparents who raise their grandchildren are quite prevalent. In 2006, 6.1 million grandparents lived with their grandchildren, and approximately 2.4 million of these grandparents were raising their grandchildren (Statistical Abstract of the United States, 2008). The number of caregiver grandparents rose as a result of the recession of 2008/2009 (Pew Foundation, 2010). Culture also influences the absolute incidence of grandparent caregiving, which is higher for Whites; the odds that one will assume a caregiver role are, however, greater for Hispanic and African American grandparents (US Census Bureau, 2000). Grandparent care-givers tend to be younger, the mother's parents, in worse health, more socially isolated, poorer, less highly educated, and raising boys, all relative to noncustodial grandparents (Generations United, 2015). In some cases, grandparent caregiving exists in a *skipped generation* household (see also Chapter 9, this volume), i.e., where the adult parent is absent. Even when the grandparent and adult child co-reside, the grandparent may still have primary responsibility for caring for the grand-child. Co-parenting is more common, relative to Caucasians, among Hispanics and African Americans (Fuller-Thomson & Minkler, 2001). Generally speaking, grandparents in skipped-generation households tend to fare worse physically and emotionally (Generations United, 2015), and this effect is more pronounced among African Americans than among Hispanics (Chen et al., 2015).

Grandparent caregiving is usually linked to the divorce, drug use, incarceration, job loss, teenage pregnancy, or death of the adult child, as well as to the abandon-ment or abuse of the grandchild. These circumstances often stigmatize and isolate grandparents from needed social-emotional support (Hayslip, Glover, & Pollard, 2015). Thus, it is not surprising that grandparent caregivers often feel overloaded and confused about their roles as parents and grandparents (see Hayslip, Shore, Henderson, & Lambert, 1998). Importantly, the impact of grandmothers' distress on grandchildren's adjustment is mediated by dysfunctional parenting (Smith, Palmieri, Hancock, & Richardson, 2008), and may be exacerbated by the grand-parent's negative attitudes toward child-rearing, as well as the tendency of some grandparents to rely on their grandchildren for emotional support (Kaminski, Hayslip, Wilson, & Casto, 2008). It is important to point out that many grandpar-ent caregivers display resilience in response to the challenges they face (Hayslip & Smith, 2013).

LGB Grandparents

Many of today's older lesbian, gay, or bisexual (LGB) adults had children through previous heterosexual relationships, and as younger cohorts of LGB individu-als continue to have biological or adoptive children, LGB grandparenting may become more prominent (Stelle, Fruhauf, Orel, & Landry-Meyer, 2010). It is well known that the middle generation provides opportunities and mediates connections between grandparents and grandchildren (Uhlenberg & Hammill, 1998), and this effect may be amplified for LGB grandparents. For example, management of disclosure about sexual orientation to grandchildren is a primary issue for LGB grandparents, and adult children assume a significant role in the coming-out process (Fruhauf, Orel, & Jenkins, 2009; Orel & Fruhauf, 2006). In most families, adult children assisted LGB grandparents in coming out to grandchildren by answering the grandchildren's questions; however, when the middle generation does not accept their parent's sexual orientation, the grandparent–grandchild relationship often is nonexistent (Fruhauf et al., 2009; Orel & Fruhauf, 2006) and LGB grandparents may not be able to engage as they had wished in their grandparent role. Finally, as reflected by the lack of references to LGB grandparents in any other chapter of the present volume, it is important to note that to our knowledge no studies have been published which examine LGB grandparents from other countries. Research on this population would greatly benefit from further exploration of health, well-being, and family dynamics of intergenerational relationships among US and international LGB grandparents and their grandchildren.

Social Policy and Grandparents

Unlike the approaches in other countries, particularly those with "cradle to grave" healthcare programs and services, a traditional view in social policy in the US is that families provide a safety net for older adults (Estes, 2001) and vice versa. In part due to the economic recession in 2008/2009, more multigenerational families have been created by economic necessity, with Hispanic grandparents more likely than African American or White grandparents (Luo, LaPierre, Hughes, & Waite, 2012) to be living in multigenerational homes. Increasingly, grandparents are also asked to assist their adult children with the care for grandchildren with special needs; this is a special burden and stress for grandparents who are disabled or do not live nearby (Mitchell, 2006). In addition, balance between work and family responsibilities is no longer an issue only faced by parents, and Meyer's (2014) research addressed how non-custodial grandmothers (ages 51–70) who work for pay and provide unpaid childcare for their grandchildren manage work and grandchild care. The grandmothers in Meyer's study rearranged their work schedules, used vacation time and/or sick days, and often brought work home so they could assist their adult children with care needs (Meyer, 2014). In addition, a few grandmothers changed jobs to better accommodate their grandchild care, which resulted for some grandmothers in higher wages and more flexibility, while other individuals experienced greater financial burdens (Meyer, 2014). These differences and the variability of grandparents' experiences reflect both the cultural norms of family support in the US and the contextual factors which influence the middle-generation's need for assistance from grandparents (Cox, Brooks, & Valcarcel, 2000).

Despite the focus on family members who provide care for each other, social policies related to aging emerged not only after the 1935 Social Security Act but again in 1965 when the Older Americans Act (OAA) was passed (see Wacker & Roberto, 2014). As previously described in this chapter, grandparents are increasingly asked by child welfare agencies to provide care to grandchildren when parents are unable to do so (Geen, 2004). As a result, a number of social policies in the US have been implemented to assist in support for custodial grandparents. For example, the National Family Caregiver Support Program was established in 2000 as an amendment to the OAA. Through this program, state Units on Aging and county Area Agencies on Aging are required to expand their provision of information, referrals, social services, and respite care to meet the needs of custodial grandparents (Feinberg & Newman, 2006). In 2003, the Living Equitably: Grandparents Aiding Children and Youth Act was passed; it is an additional federal law that aims to support the housing needs of grandparent-headed families. But all too often there are barriers that prevent many older grandparents from finding affordable living arrangements that meet both their needs and their grandchildren's needs (Bertera & Crewe, 2013). Finally, the Affordable Care Act aids grandparents and grandchildren by providing financial relief for their medical expenses (Bertera & Crewe, 2013). These various 21st century federal laws and social policies have decreased some of the burden faced by grandfamilies while grass-roots and community initiatives also have assisted grandparents with additional needs (Fruhauf & Hayslip, 2013).

In addition to grandparents who raise grandchildren, older adults (those aged 60 and older) who are in financial need may qualify to participate in the Foster Grandparent Program (FGP), regardless of whether they are biological grandparents. FGP is a national program under which adults engage in weekly volunteer experiences with children under the age of 21 with special needs and are often assigned to volunteer schools, pediatric hospital wards, and public homes for orphans or children (Wacker & Roberto, 2014). It not only provides a small stipend to older adults, it also provides older Americans with social and psychological benefits (Nash & Bradley, 2006). As a result of the positive outcomes of the FGP, federal social policy introduced the Retired Senior Volunteer Program in 1969 to reach older adults who could volunteer regardless of financial need, as they do not receive a stipend (Nash & Bradley, 2006). In the US, all of these laws and social policies increasingly provide protection for older adults, including grandparent caregivers, from burdens, costs, and social/psychological strain.

Conclusions and Predictions on the Future of Grandparenting

In this chapter, we have characterized the experiences of grandparents in the US along a number of dimensions, which reflected the theme of diversity in American families. Indeed, this emphasis on diversity should challenge our notions regarding what is typical grandparenting. There are many advantages to both generations when grandparents are involved in their grandchildren's lives. These can be viewed in the context of several theoretical frameworks within which grandparenting can be understood, as we stress the dynamic nature of grandparent–grandchild relationships. It is important to understand how further social policies can be applied to grandparents in the context of diversity.

Families have clearly changed over the last two decades (Connidis, 2010), and increasing numbers of families are *verticalized*, i.e., multigenerational (Hagestad, 1988) This will change the experience of future grandparenthood in many ways. For example, it will increase the likelihood of care for an older grandparent, but it will also increase the odds of having a grandparent, given the likely cohort-related differences in grandparenting as a function of shifts in life expectancy and the decline of birthrates (Statistical Abstract of the United States, 2008). It is also likely that future cohorts of grandparents will be in the grandparent role for a longer period of time, be more highly educated, be in better health, have fewer grandchildren (which decreases the competition between grandchildren for a grandparent's time), and be more likely to be retired (Uhlenberg, 2009). Thus, future generations of grandparents may be able to make even more meaningful investments into their grandchildren's lives due to their greater longevity and the greater availability of programs and services for older adults (see Wacker & Roberto, 2014). In the context of the growing emphasis on diversity in American culture, we expect that many assumptions about grandparenting, given the likely increase in Latino and African American grandparents relative to White grandparents, will need to be revised in concert with greater knowledge about grandparents of different races and ethnicities. We also expect that there will be more research focus on grandfathers, and on grandparents with non-traditional sexual orientations and identities.

It is interesting to speculate about how grandparents in the US may differ from those of different nations. Given the ethnic and cultural diversity, and the influx of immigrants into the US, it could be that American grandparents would be characterized by greater adherence to their particular cultural, subcultural, and country of origin customs, identities, and attitudes. In these respects, issues of conflict between the customs, attitudes, and beliefs of one's country of origin versus those of American culture are likely, whereby older generations are likely to adhere to the former and younger generations would likely adapt to the latter. Consequently, values reflecting the importance assigned to familism versus individualism, born of intergenerational conflict as a function of differential degrees of acculturation, may quite likely be unique to American culture.

Given the aging of the US population, interest in and information regarding great-grandparents, about whom researchers know relatively little, is likely to increase. In this respect, countries such as Japan or China, whose aging populations are also growing rapidly, might also be eventually characterized by a more widespread interest in both grandparents and great-grandparents (as confirmed by Chapter 9). In addition, given the prevalence of divorce, abuse, and drug abuse as they pertain to younger generations unable or unwilling to raise their children, the salience of grandparent caregiving will likely remain a center-piece of family life in the US relative to cultures where grandparents still retain a more traditional or even symbolic role and are unlikely at present to take on grandchild-rearing on a full-time basis. In contrast, in some Eastern cultures grandparents who do care for their grandchildren do so as an extension of their relationship to their adult children who have left small villages to find work in larger cities.

One issue that is not represented in the literature concerning US grandparents, although it is addressed in other cultures (see Chapters 10, 11, and 12), is the importance of grandparenting in war-torn areas. This focus might include the important role grandparents have during active wars or when individuals and families become refugees. It also should include attention to the grief grandparents experience when they lose children and grandchildren to war-related violence. Finally, future research is needed on US grandparenting when parents are deployed to serve in the military; this is not addressed in the literature. A focus on grandparents in the context of war would be consistent with the attention that must be given to what commonalities grandparents share and what differentiates them across cultures.

Summary

This chapter presented an overview of grandparenting in the US, with particular attention to the diversity among grandparents along several parameters. Framing grandparenting in the context of such diversity are several theories (e.g., Erikson's psychosocial theory, lifespan developmental theory, developmental contextualism). We examined both quantitative and qualitative research on grandparenting in the US, with special emphasis upon grandparent–grandchild relationships. In addition, topics speaking to the diversity among grandparents were addressed in terms of: (1) grandfathers, who are best understood in the context of cultural influences on their roles, (2) subcultural variations in grandparenting, where variation related to race and ethnicity is examined, (3) grandparents who are raising their grandchildren, and (4) lesbian, gay, and bisexual grandparents. Consistent with an emphasis on context, the chapter addressed social policy as it pertains to grandparents, wherein attention to cultural and subcultural variation is critical and attention to both the quality of intergenerational relationships and to the unique needs of grandparents who are full-time caregivers to their grandchildren is necessary. Further, our discussion was tempered by the existence of programs designed to meet such grandparents' needs and the accessibility of related services to such persons. The chapter concluded with predictions regarding the future of grandparenting in the US, and a discussion of possible differences from grandparents in other cultures.

Appendix
Meaning of Proverbs

> "If nothing is going well, call your grandmother."
> "Perfect love sometimes does not come till the first grandchild."

These proverbs speak to the special bonds between grandparents and grandchildren, wherein each contributes to the lives of the other. Grandchildren often turn to their grandparents for help and support, and grandparents experience true joy in the birth of their grandchildren, which contributes to the meaningfulness of the grandparent role.

Additional Resources

Administration on Aging & Administration for Community Living – National Family Caregiver Support Program (www.aoa.acl.gov/AoA_Programs/HCLTC/Caregiver/)

This website includes detailed information about the National Family Caregiver Support Program (Older Americans Act, Title IIIE). It includes the purpose of the program, eligible program participants (including grandparents raising grandchildren), data on its services, funding history, caregiver stories, and additional resources and weblinks.

The Brookdale Foundation Group – Relatives as Parents Program (www.brookdalefoundation.org/RAPP/rapp.html)

The Brookdale Foundation Group has provided continued funding for local and statewide initiatives and programs related to grandparents raising grandchildren since 1991. It was in 1996 that it established the Relatives as Parents Program to support relative caregivers and the children outside of the foster care system. This website includes useful information from their newsletter, publications, and multimedia sessions, and national and state weblinks.

Generations United (www.gu.org)

This very proactive organization seeks to improve the lives of children and older people through intergenerational collaboration, public policies, and the development of programs to serve all. Their mission in this respect is to bring persons of different generations together to define common agendas as well as to give each generation a unique voice.

Discussion Questions

1. Please describe the current aging policies in the US as related to grandparenting. In your answer, use the theories described in this chapter to frame your

answer and provide three suggestions for future changes to aging policy to support older adults and their families.

2. Describe the major tenets of Erikson's psychosocial theory, contextual theory, and lifespan theory as each relates to grandparents. What do these different approaches have in common? What differentiates them?

3. What factors have led to our relative lack of knowledge about grandfathers? What aspects of grandparenting do they share with grandmothers? In what respects do grandfathers play a unique role in their grandchildren's lives?

References

American Association for Retired Persons. (2002). The grandparent study 2002 report. Washington, DC: American Association for Retired Persons.

Attar-Schwartz, S. (2015). Emotional closeness to parents and grandparents: A moderated mediation model predicting adolescent adjustment. *American Journal of Orthopsychiaty, 85,* 495–503.

Baltes, P. B. (1997). On the incomplete architecture of human ontogeny: Selection, optimization, and compensation as foundations of developmental theory. *American Psychologist, 52,* 366–380.

Bates, J. S. (2009). Generative grandfathering: A conceptual framework for nurturing grandchildren. *Marriage and Family Review, 45,* 331–352.

Bertera, E. M., & Crewe, S. E. (2013). Parenthood in the twenty-first century: African American grandparents as surrogate parents. *Journal of Human Behavior in the Social Environment, 23,* 178–192. doi:10.1080/10911359.2013.747348

Chen, F., Mair, C., Bao, G., & Yang, Y. (2015). Race/ethnic differentials in the health consequences of caring for grandchildren for grandparents. *Journals of Gerontology: Psychological and Social Sciences, 70B,* 793–803.

Christensen, S.G. (2014). The association between grandparenthood and mortality. *Social Science and Medicine, 118,* 89–96.

Cole, M. (1999). Culture in development. In M. Bornstein & M. Lamb (Eds.), *Developmental psychology: An advanced textbook* (pp. 73–124). Mahwah, NJ: Lawrence Erlbaum.

Combrinck-Graham, L. (1985). A developmental model for family systems. *Family Process, 24,* 139–150. doi:10.1111/j.1545-5300.1985.00139.x

Connidis, I. A. (2010). *Family ties and aging.* Thousand Oaks, CA: Pine Forge Press.

Cox, C. B., Brooks, L. R., & Valcarcel, C. (2000). Culture and caregiving: A study of Latino grandparents. In C. B. Cox (Ed.), *To grandmother's house we go and stay: Perspectives on custodial grandparenting* (pp. 218–232). New York: Springer.

Drew, L. M., & Silverstein, M. (2007). Grandparents' psychological well-being after loss of contact with their grandchildren. *Journal of Family Psychology, 21,* 372–379. doi:10.1037/0893-3200.21.3.372

Erikson, E. (1963). *Childhood and society* (2nd ed.). New York: Norton.

Estes, C. (2001). *Social policy and aging: A critical perspective.* Thousand Oaks, CA: Sage.

Feinberg, L. F., & Newman, S. L. (2006). Preliminary experiences of the States in implementing the national family caregiver support program: A 50-state study. In F. G. Caro (Ed.), *Family and aging policy* (pp. 95–113). New York: Haworth.

Friedman, D., Hechter, M., & Kreager, D. (2008). A theory of the value of grandchildren. *Rationality and Society, 20,* 31–63. doi:10.1177/1043463107085436

Fruhauf, C. A., & Hayslip, B. Jr. (2013). Understanding collaborative efforts to assist grand-parent caregivers: A multileveled perspective. *Journal of Family Social Work, 16*, 382–391. doi:10.1080/10522158.2013.832462

Fruhauf, C. A., Orel, N. A., & Jenkins, D. (2009). The coming-out process of gay grandfa-thers: Perceptions of their adult children's influence. *Journal of GLBT Family Studies, 5*, 99–118. doi:10.1080/15504280802595402

Fuller-Thomson, E., & Minkler, M. (2001). American grandparents providing extensive child care to their grandchildren: Prevalence and profile. *The Gerontologist, 41*, 201–209. doi:10.1093/geront/41.2.201

Geen, R. (2004). The evolution of kinship care policy and practice. *Children, Families and Foster Care, 14*, 131–139.

Generations United (2015). *The state of grandfamilies in America.* Washington, DC: Generations United.

Gibson, P. A. (2005). Intergenerational parenting from the perspective of African American grandmothers. *Family Relations, 54*, 280–297.

Goodsell, T., Bates, J., & Behnke, A. (2011). Fatherhood stories: Grandparents, grandchil-dren, and gender differences. *Journal of Social and Personal Relationships, 28,* 134–154.

Gurn, K., & Beneke, C. (2015). Grandparenthood predicts late-life cognition: Results from the Women's Healthy Ageing Project. *Maturitas, 81*, 317–322.

Gutierrez, I. A., Goodwin, L. J., Kirkinis, K., & Mattis, J. S. (2014). Religious socialization in African American families: The relative influence of parents, grandparents, and siblings. *Journal of Family Psychology, 28*, 779–789. doi:10.1037/a0035732

Hagestad, G. O. (1988). Demographic change and the life course: Some emerging trends in the family realm. *Family Relations, 37*, 405–410. doi:10.2307/58411

Hayslip, B. (2009). Ethnic and cross cultural perspectives on custodial grandparenting. In J. Sokolovsky (Ed.), *The cultural context of aging: Worldwide perspectives* (3rd ed., pp. 346–356). Westport, CT: Greenwood Publishing.

Hayslip, B. & Montoro-Rodriguez, J. (2015, November). *First-time grandparenthood: Effects of on-timeness and off-timeness.* Paper presented at the Annual Scientific Meeting of the Gerontological Society of America. Orlando, FL.

Hayslip, B. Jr., & Page, K. S. (2012). Grandparenthood: Grandchild and great-grandchild relationships. In R. Blieszner & V. H. Bedford (Eds.), *Handbook of families and aging* (2nd ed., pp. 183–212). Santa Barbara, CA: Praeger.

Hayslip, B., & Smith, G. (2013). *Resilient grandparent caregivers: A strengths-based perspective.* New York: Routledge.

Hayslip, B., & White, D. (2008). Grandparents as grievers. In M. S. Stroebe, R. O. Hansson, W. Stroebe, & H. Schut (Eds.), *Handbook of bereavement research* (3rd ed.). Washington, DC: American Psychological Association.

Hayslip, B., Glover, R., & Pollard, S. (2015). Noncaregiving grandparent peers' perceptions of custodial grandparents: Extent of life disruption, needs for social support, and social and mental health services. In M. H. Meyer (Ed.), *Grandparenting in the US* (pp. 207–225). Amityville, NY: Baywood.

Hayslip, B., Kaminski, P., & Earnheart, K. (2006). Gender differences among custodial grandparents. In B. Hayslip & J. Hicks-Patrick (Eds.), *Custodial grandparents: Individual, cultural, and ethnic diversity* (pp.151–168). New York: Springer.

Hayslip, B., Shore, R. J., & Henderson, C. (2000). Perceptions of grandparents' influ-ence in the lives of their grandchildren. In B. Hayslip & R. Goldberg-Glen (Eds.), *Grandparents raising grandchildren: Theoretical, empirical, and clinical perspectives* (pp. 35–46). New York: Springer.

Hayslip, B., Maiden, R., Page, K., & Dolbin-MacNab, M. (2015). Grandparenting. In P. Lichtenberg, B. Mast, B. Carpenter, & J. Wetherell (Eds.), *APA handbook of clinical geropsychology* (pp. 497–512). Washington, DC: American Psychological Association.

Hayslip, B., Shore, R. J., Henderson, C. E., & Lambert, P. L. (1998). Custodial grandparenting and grandchildren with problems: Their impact on role satisfaction and role meaning. *Journal of Gerontology: Social Sciences, 53B,* S164–S174. doi:10.1093/geronb/53B 3.S164

Henderson, C., Hayslip, B., Sanders, L., & Louden, L. (2009). Grandmother–grandchild relationship quality predicts psychological adjustment among youth from divorced families. *Journal of Family Issues, 30,* 1245–1264.

Jaeger, M. M. (2012). The extended family and children's educational success. *American Sociological Review, 77,* 903–922. doi:10.1177/0003122412464040

Kaminski, P., Hayslip, B., Wilson, J., & Casto, L. (2008). Parenting attitudes and adjustment among custodial grandparents. *Journal of Intergenerational Relationships, 6,* 263–284. doi:10.1080/1535077080215773

Keene, J., Prokos, A., & Hein, B. (2012). Grandfather caregivers: Race and ethnic differences in poverty. *Sociological Inquiry, 82,* 49–77.

Lampkin, C. L. (2012). *Insights and spending habits of modern grandparents.* Washington, DC: American Association of Retired Persons.

Lerner, R. M. (2002). *Concepts and theories of human development* (3rd ed.). Mahwah, NJ: Lawrence Erlbaum.

Luo, Y., LaPierre, T. A., Hughes, M. E., & Waite, L. J. (2012). Grandparents providing care to grandchildren: A population-based study of continuity and change. *Journal of Family Issues, 33,* 1143–1167.

Mann, R. (2007a). Out of the shadows? Grandfatherhood, age, and masculinities. *Journal of Aging Studies, 21,* 281–291.

Mann, W. (2007b). The significant other: Type and mode of influence in the lives of Black families. In H. P. McAdoo (Ed.), *Black families* (4th ed., pp. 184–200). Thousand Oaks, CA: Sage.

Mann, R., Kahn, H., & Leeson, G. (2013). Variations in grandchildren's perceptions of their grandfathers and grandmothers: Dynamics of age and gender. *Journal Of Intergenerational Relationships, 11*(4), 380–395. doi:10.1080/15350770.2013.839326

Meyer, M. H. (2014). *Grandmothers at work: Juggling families and jobs.* New York: New York University Press.

Michels, T., Albert, I., & Ferring, D. (2011). Emotional relationships with grandparents: The adolescent view. *Journal of Intergenerational Relationships, 9,* 264–280. doi:10.1080/15350770.2011.593435

Mitchell, W. (2006). The role of grandparents in intergenerational support for families with disabled children: A review of the literature. *Child and Family Social Work, 12,* 94–101. doi: 10.1111/j.1365-2206.2006.00421.x

Moore, S. M., & Rosenthal, D. (2015). Presonal growth, grandmother engagement, and satisfaction among non-custodial grandmothers. *Aging and Mental Health, 19,* 136–143.

Nagata, D. K., Cheng, W. J. Y., & Tsai-Chae, A. H. (2010). Chinese American grandmothering: A qualitative exploration. *Asian American Journal of Psychology, 1,* 151–161.

Nash, B. Jr., & Bradley, D. B. (2006). Federal policies and local realities: The case of Appalachian senior programs. *Educational Gerontology, 32,* 351–365. doi:10.1080/03601270600564104

Newton, N., & Baltys, I. (2014). Parent status and generativity within the context of race. *International Journal of Aging and Human Development, 78,* 171–195.

Orel, N. A., & Fruhauf, C. A. (2006). Lesbian and bisexual grandmothers' perceptions of the grandparent–grandchild relationship. *Journal of GLBT Family Studies, 2*, 42–70. doi:10.1300/J461v02n01_03

Pew Foundation. (2010). *Since the start of the great recession, more children raised by grandparents.* Retrieved from http://pewresearch.org/pubs/1724

Phua, V. C., & Kaufman, G. (2008). Grandparenting responsibility among elderly Asian Americans. *Journal of Intergenerational Relationships, 6*, 41–59. doi:10.1300/J194v06n01_04

Pratt, N., Norris, J. E., Hebblethwaite, S., & Arnold, M. (2008). Intergenerational transmission of values: Family generativity and adolescents' narratives of parent and grandparent value teaching. *Journal of Personality, 76*, 171–198. doi:10.1111/j.1467 6494.2007.00483.x

Reitzes, D. C., & Mutran, E. J. (2004). Grandparenthood: Factors influencing frequency of grandparent–grandchild contact and grandparent role satisfaction. *Journal of Gerontology: Social Sciences, 59B*, S9–S16. doi:10.1093/geronb/59.1.S9

Roberto, K. A., Allen, K., & Blieszner, R. (2001). Grandfathers' perceptions and expectations of relationships with their adult grandchildren. *Journal of Family Issues, 22*, 407–426. doi:10.1177/019251301022004002

Sandel, T., Cho, G., Miller, P., & Wang, S. (2006). What it means to be a grandmother: A cross-cultural study of Taiwanese and Euro-American grandmothers' beliefs. *Journal of Family Communication, 64*, 255–278. doi:10.1207/s15327698jfc0604

Saxena, D., & Sanders, G. F. (2009). Quality of grandparent–grandchild relationships in Asian-Indian immigrant families. *International Journal of Aging and Human Development, 68*, 321–338. doi:10.2190/AG.68.4.c

Silverstein, M., & Chen, X. (1999). The impact of acculturation in Mexican American families on the quality of adult grandchild–grandparent relationships. *Journal of Marriage and the Family, 61*, 188–198.

Silverstein, M., Giarrusso, R., & Bengtson, V. L. (2003). Grandparents and grandchildren in family systems: A socio-developmental perspective. In V. L. Bengtson & A. Lowenstein (Eds.), *Global aging and challenges to families* (pp. 75–102). New York: Aldine de Gruyter.

Smith, P. K., & Drew, L. M. (2002). Grandparenthood. In M. Bornstein (Ed.), *Handbook of parenting* (Vol. 3, pp. 141–172). Mahwah, NJ: Lawrence Erlbaum.

Smith, G. C., Palmieri, P., Hancock, G., & Richardson, R. (2008). Custodial grandmothers' psychological distress, dysfunctional parenting, and grandchildren's adjustment. *International Journal of Aging and Human Development, 67*, 327–358. doi:10.2190 /AG.67.4.c

Somary, K., & Stricker, G. (1998). Becoming a grandparent: A longitudinal study of expectations and early experiences as a function of age and lineage. *The Gerontologist, 38*, 53–61. doi:10.1093/geront/38.1.53

St. George, J., & Fletcher, R. (2014). Men's experiences of grandfatherhood: A welcome surprise. *International Journal of Aging and Human Development, 78*, 351–378.

Statistical Abstract of the United States. (2008). Births and birth rates. Washington, DC: US Census Bureau, American Community Survey.

Stelle, C., Fruhauf, C. A., Orel, N., & Landry-Meyer, L. (2010). Grandparenting in the 21st Century: Issues of diversity in grandparent–grandchild relationships. *Journal of Gerontological Social Work, 53*, 682–701.

Strom, R. D., Carter, T., & Schmidt, K. (2004). African-Americans in senior settings: On the need for educating grandparents. *Educational Gerontology, 30*, 287–304. doi:10.1080 /03601270490278821

Strom, R. D., Heeder, S. D., & Strom, P. S. (2005). Performance of Black grandmothers: Perceptions of three generations of females. *Educational Gerontology, 31,* 187–205.

Szinovacz, M. E. (1998). Grandparent research: Past, present, and future. In M. Szinovacz (Ed.), *Handbook of grandparenthood* (pp. 1–22). Westport, CT: Greenwood.

Toledo, R., Hayslip, B., Emick, M., Toledo, C., & Henderson, C. (2000). Cross-cultural differences in custodial grandparenting. In B. Hayslip & R. Goldberg-Glen (Eds.), *Grandparents raising grandchildren: Theoretical, empirical and clinical perspectives* (pp. 107– 124). New York: Springer.

Uhlenberg, P. (2009). Children in an aging society. *Journal of Gerontology: Social Sciences, 64B,* S489–S496. doi:10.1093/geronb/gbp001

Uhlenberg, P., & Hammill, B. (1998). Frequency of grandparent contact with grandchild sets: Six factors that make a difference. *The Gerontologist, 38,* 276–285. doi:10.1093/ geront /38.3.276

US Census Bureau. (2000). Current population survey. Washington, DC: Government Printing Office.

Wacker, R. R., & Roberto, K. A. (2014). *Community resources for older adults: Programs and services in an era of change* (4th ed.). Los Angeles, CA: Sage.

Walsh, F. (2012). *Normal family processes: Growing diversity and complexity.* New York: Guilford.

Wiscott, R., & Kopera-Frye, K. (2000). Sharing the culture: Adult grandchildren's perceptions of intergenerational relations. *International Journal of Aging and Human Development, 51,* 199–215.

Yorgason, J., Padilla-Walker, L., & Jackson, J. (2013). Nonresidential grandparents emotional and financial involvement in relation to early adolescent grandchild outcomes. *Journal of Research on Adolescence, 21,* 552–558.

4

GRANDPARENTS IN BRAZIL

The Contexts of Care and Economic Support for Grandchildren

Cristina Dias, Rosa Azambuja, Elaine Rabinovich, and Ana Cecília Bastos

PROVERBS

1. "The parents educate and the grandparents do the opposite." (*Os pais educam, os avós deseducam*)
2. "The grandmother is twice a mother." (*Avó é mãe duas vezes*)

(see p. 75 for interpretations)

CASE STORY: THE WISDOM OF THE GRANDMOTHERS

Daniel Munduruku belongs to the Munduruku Indian ethnic group. He has learned from his grandmothers that every elderly Munduruku woman is called a grand-mother. They are like "radar" in the community because they know how to watch, listen to, and advise all people. One day, Daniel asked for his grandmother's advice after he had a fight with his best friend. She told him that friends sometimes make mistakes and that only he could work this out with his friend. She said: "If you don't want to do that it's OK, but remember that's the way we show courage. And courage is not only fighting tigers, snakes, wild animals, or spirits of the forests. Courage is looking within and being able to make the best decisions to live well" (Munduruku, 2006, p. 24). Daniel then met his friend, hugged him, and they went to play together by the river.

Historical, Social, Demographic, and Economic Backgrounds of Grandparenthood

Brazil was colonized by the Portuguese who arrived in 1500 to find five million native indigenous people with about 1,000 ethnicities (Maggi, 2014). The original cultural context of this land inspired us to start this chapter with the case story of an Indian grandmother. Brazil later declared freedom for its four million slaves from Africa (IBGE, 2010), and this is why we chose a picture (Figure 4.2) showing women of African descent to depict grandmotherhood. Such historical events and sources of diversity are fundamental to the study of Brazilian relationships between grandparents, especially grandmothers, and their grandchildren. Family relationship dynamics are also influenced by the establishment of extended families and primarily linked to a rural lifestyle. In addition, notable rural–urban migration processes in the 1950s and 1960s added more complexity to intergenerational relationships and grandparental roles in Brazilian society.

Throughout our history there have been important changes in the roles played by grandparents. The specifics of these changes are related to gender, social class, and regional differences that are typical of a country with continental dimensions. It is possible that grandparents who are not as busy acquiring competency as caregivers as young parents, and in most cases are not absorbed by the demands of a professional career, can better see to the future of their grandchildren and pass on their cultural legacy. Figure 4.1 illustrates a typical party in a city near Salvador, Bahia. The grandparents are introducing their grandchildren to a ritual that dates back to 1888 and the celebration of the abolition of slavery in Brazil. The scene depicted in this photograph also highlights the horizon, symbolizing the hopeful future grandparents wish to transmit to their grandchildren. Brazilian grandmothers are often matriarchs and authorities in their families. The power of grandmothers is reinforced by the fact that many of them have economic resources based on their retirement benefits (Camarano, 2003). These resources strengthen mothers and matrilineal bonds and marginalize men's roles in the family, in the context of high divorce rates and normative maternal custody of children.

About 87% of the 205 million Brazilians reside in cities and metropolitan areas. The number of people older than 40 now exceeds 76 million, many of whom are grandparents (PNAD, 2013). Over 13% (23.5 million) of Brazil's current population are elderly (65 years and older), and this number will increase to about 30% by 2050 (IBGE, 2012). In addition, life expectancy has grown considerably in recent decades. At the beginning of the 20th century, Brazilians on average lived for only 33 years, but by the 1990s average life expectancy was 66.9 years; in 2010 it was 74.0 years for males and 77.7 for females. As elsewhere, gender differences in life expectancy are due to deaths from car accidents, homicides, and alcohol abuse, which affect more men than women (IBGE, 2010). Men are generally less careful with their health, and neglect periodic physical exams and treatment of chronic diseases. The data also reflect differences in the quality of men's health compared to that of women of the same age, as males and females age differently.

Changes in the Brazilian population and in the organization of socioeconomic groups vary by region and are mainly due to distinct temporal impacts of the modernization process on its national territory. According to the National Household Sampling Research (PNAD, 2013), changes in the composition and characteristics

FIGURE 4.1 The Brazilian Northeast State of Bahia is well known for its black/African cultural influence, as seen in musique, dance, candomblé, and capoeira. The photo, taken during a religious ceremony by the sea, represents the strong presence and influence of black Brazilian women as mothers and spiritual leaders.

Source: Courtesy of Mário Vítor Bastos.

of family arrangements tend to occur first in regions with higher socioeconomic dynamism, which leads to the incorporation of new values and habits into the process of social reproduction of Brazilian families from the South and Southeast (IBGE, 2012). Aging of the population and the increase of women's participation in the labor market are now causing a revolutionary change in Brazilian families. Data from the Institute of Applied Economic Research suggest that an increase in the proportion of women, elderly people of both genders, and elderly heads of households are all notable phenomena (PNAD, 2013). According to this research, 13.8 million elderly Brazilians led families, and among those who were 60 or older 56% were women. Of the 23.8% of the elderly who were in the category of "spouse," 81.4% were women. In about 6.2 million households the elderly person was the household head or spouse, and resided with adult sons and daughters; 2.3 million of these households included grandchildren. In the last decade, the number of grandchildren and great-grandchildren raised by grandparents and great-grandparents has grown to over 1.7 million. The role of Brazilian grandparents as care providers has been highlighted by many authors (e.g., Araújo & Dias, 2002; Cardoso, 2011; Peixoto, 2004). Unemployment, divorce, and widowhood, as well as sons and daughters who never leave their parents' home, are major reasons that older and younger generations live together, especially in the so-called "popular families" in Brazil (Peixoto, 2004).

The preceding social and demographic changes have encouraged scholars to pay more attention to research on grandparents in Brazil. This chapter is an attempt to analyze the socioeconomic and cultural contexts of grandparenting within Brazilian society. First, we present a framework of changes felt in the roles and images of grandparents over time. Second, we examine the main variables that describe relationships between grandparents, parents, and sons/daughters. Finally, we focus on those grandparents who raise their grandchildren. We can see that most grandparenting research in Brazil has focused on grandmothers, which is explained by women's higher longevity and intense participation in the care of other family members. We will also discuss the commitments and interests of grandfathers in Brazil.

Theoretical Approaches

In Brazil, research on grandparents and aging is relatively new and descriptive in nature. In fact, there are no recognizable academic efforts to employ theoretical frameworks to understand grandparenting in our country. In view of the strong presence of grandparents in the family, grandparents' financial and care support for grandchildren, and grandparent–grandchild relationship dynamics over time, both bioecological systems (Bronfenbrenner, 1989) and life course (Bengtson & Allen, 1993) theories are well suited to interpreting Brazilian grandparenthood. Specifically, the interaction dynamics of grandparents evolve over time, and a host of personal and environmental factors (e.g., divorce and migration of adult children – factors which are studied worldwide, as evidenced throughout this book) influence grandparents' role in the family. At the same time, physiological changes and abilities influence the cultural meaning of grandparenthood and grandparents' role expectations in Brazilian society. Brazilians acknowledge that "giving grandparents" will need help in the future as they become older. The cultural notion of reciprocity ensures that adult children or grandchildren would care for their aged grandparents when needed. Overall, in our opinion, bioecological systems and life course theories explain how the interplay of ecological, physiological, cultural, and other environmental factors explain grandparenting in Brazil. Yet there has simply been no application of these theories in Brazil by those who study grandparents.

Research Literature on Grandparents

Grandparenthood in Brazil is a very complex reality because of our country's heterogeneous ecologies, regionally based cultural differences, and diversity as related to social class and gender. Today's grandparents are different from those in the past and from what they will probably be in the future, because of changes in social and professional activities, technologies to communicate with grandchildren, and globalization. In particular, the recent trend to use technological innovations and tools facilitates new communicative approaches and styles that have implications for more frequent and effective interactions between generations.

The results of a recent study of the experiences of grandchildren who live with their grandparents in urban families showed the major use of technology for personal communication (Ramos, 2014). According to this study, grandparents and grandchildren maintained frequent contacts through phone conversations, emails, and text messages. Social media and social networking were also cited by Ramos as a frequent communication tool. Another study investigated the growth of relationships between grandparents and their grandchildren through Skype and other internet tools that function as phones and webcams (Rocha, 2013). Rocha found that the use of technology, although it lacked the kinesthetic qualities of direct physical touch or a hug or cuddle, triggered emotions and connections by sight and vocal sounds via Skype. Grandparents reported that affection, affinity, and love between them and their grandchildren strengthened after their internet-assisted contacts. They appreciated the benefits of technology that helped them contact and communicate with grandchildren in a timely and speedy manner, and reported that their relationships became closer and stronger.

As also depicted in most of the other chapters of this volume, the traditional role of Brazilian grandparents was to transmit family history, values, and cultural heritage to younger generations. They provided the link between the past and present, and cared for and monitored the growth of grandchildren from a certain distance. Their contemporary role included responsibilities such as following their grandchildren's school performance, guiding their behavior, manners, and peer relationships, and providing care. The case story of Daniel illustrates how one grandmother encouraged her grandchild to successfully negotiate a positive outcome in peer interactions. Furthermore, contemporary grandparents are often their grandchildren's confidantes and companions. This role helps them to establish a connection between generations and mediate the relationship between their own children and their grandchildren (Cardoso, 2011; Gerondo, 2006; Ramos, 2011). Therefore, the past image of Brazilian grandparents has been transformed. Grandparents were traditionally represented as bent-over and gray-haired people who were limited to playing with their grandchildren, cuddling with them or telling stories. Nowadays, as in many other countries described in this book, we observe young or mature grandparents with full physical vitality who are committed to their own projects and interests. They tend to relate well to their grandchildren in leisure and fun activities. Although increased contacts facilitate mutual interests and influences including learning experiences and shared care, contemporary grandparents and grandchildren also have a need to negotiate tension and conflicts (Dias & Silva, 1999).

A host of personal, family, environmental, cultural, and sociodemographic factors influence the way grandparents perform their family roles. Whereas some factors may facilitate a harmonious relationship between grandparents and grandchildren, some factors may bring about the context for difficult interactions. For example, unemployed grandparents with limited economic resources may not be able to provide effective financial support and/or buy plenty of gifts for their grandchildren. Unlike parents, many grandparents are not obligated to care for the grandchildren. However, there is a social expectation and consensus that grandparents should be in the position of caregivers and advisors to parents, especially when asked to do so. This keeps the balance between conferring affection on their grandchildren without spoiling them, and helping their sons and daughters without pushing them or undermining their authority (Aratangy & Posternak, 2005; Dias & Silva, 1999). It is important to keep in mind that the caregiving and involvement activities have implications for the quality of intergenerational relationships that may vary by age and socioeconomic groups.

Relationships between Grandparents and Grandchildren

There is a huge range in the ages of grandparents in modern Brazil. Available data suggest that the age at which a person becomes a grandparent in Brazil varies between ages 35 and 70 (Cardoso, 2011). One study indicated that Brazilian college students viewed their grandparents as a source of knowledge and experience and that they found their interactions to be useful for their lives (Dias & Silva, 2003). These college-age grandchildren also acknowledged that interactions such as shared activities, talks, visits, and stories influenced the formation of their personal character. Likewise, adult and married grandchildren from middle-class backgrounds responded that grandparents were still very important people in their lives (Oliveira, 2015). Through quality interactions, grandparents had an impact on their professional, religious, moral, emotional, and psychosocial behaviors and values. However, geographical distance and the grandparents' own needs (e.g., leisure and occupational) sometimes precluded them from interactions with their grandparents on a regular basis. Results from another study, conducted on 8–10-year-old grandchildren from low-income families, showed that the nature of relationships between grandparents and grandchildren was influenced by affinities and roles performed by grandfathers and grandmothers (Ramos, 2006). These grandchildren felt very close to their maternal grandparents, and they spent significant time and often co-resided with these grandparents. Elsewhere, educated, young (average age = 42), and high-income grandparents reportedly showed supportive behaviors toward their pregnant teenage grandchildren (Dias, Viana, & Aguiar, 2003). In this latter study, grandparents apparently came to understand that the expectant and/or new mother and father needed help. The findings of Dias et al. suggest that contemporary grandparents realize that family support for their grandchildren is vital for the maintenance of values, reciprocity, and interdependent relationships.

Many grandparents, especially in poor communities, raise their own grandchildren (Oliveira, 1999). In such cases parents are unable to attend to their children, and with time and commitment these grandparents transition well to a parenting role. As is often mentioned elsewhere in this book (especially in Chapters 11 and 12, this volume), grandparents often transfer material assets and transmit symbolic values and a heritage to their grandchildren. In line with Brazilian cultural norms, these interactions strengthen generational reciprocity and the moral virtue of gratitude. In addition, grandparents often take the initiative to raise grandchildren, as they are committed to the well-being of their family members (Araújo & Dias, 2010). Other studies suggest that even before they take over the task of raising grandchildren, grandmothers in low-income families are already involved in care for the children (Mainetti & Wanderbrooke, 2013). In some situations, the grandchildren themselves preferred to live with their grandparents. The main reasons for the grandparents to assume their care were issues of mental illness or chemical dependence, lack of knowledge about the identity of the father, and negligence or child abuse by the parents. Although their reasons may be culture-specific, the phenomenon of grandparents as primary caregivers is reminiscent of the same theme mentioned in the previous Americas chapters (Chapters 2 and 3) and several other chapters in this book.

Brazilian elderly grandmothers keep an especially active interest in and relationship with their grandchildren when the grandchildren are very young (Oliveira, Gomes, Tavares, & Cárdenas, 2009). For example, one study reported that the young grandparents were much more available to their grandchildren than the older grandparents (Rabinovich & Azevedo, 2012), i.e., the relationship is particularly strong between younger grandparents and younger grandchildren. This is perhaps due to the strong physical condition of young grandparents, who have the strength to follow the grandchildren around and play with them. Women's employment in the paid labor market and the lack of daycare institutions also create a demand for grandparents, especially grandmothers, to be actively involved with young grandchildren (not unlike the situation in East Asia described in Chapter 9). Limited findings from rural communities indicate that many grandparents tend to adopt and care for their first-born grandchild (Santos, Silva, & Pontes, 2011). In these communities, women's caregiving and men's provisioning responsibilities are still the dominant expression of gender roles, which results in a need for grandparents' love, care, and support for their grandchildren.

Overall, available empirical findings suggest that there are positive relations between grandparents and grandchildren across age groups, socioeconomic classes, and generations. Grandparents, especially in poor neighborhoods, are also often direct caregivers for their grandchildren. However, there is a lack of research on relationships between grandparents and grandchildren in rural communities (Santos et al., 2011). More research is needed to study grandparenting in remote rural communities in Brazil, and about the health and psychological implications for grandparents when they raise grandchildren.

Gender Roles and Family Relations

Ramos (2011) conducted research on middle- and upper-middle-class Brazilian families to understand how young grandchildren describe gender relations between generations. Her results showed that relationships between grandparents and grandchildren were influenced by affinities, the quality of family relationships, family lineage, and the interactive styles of grandparents. In another study, generational differences more than gender differences determined the way grandchildren perceived the role relations of fathers, mothers, siblings, and grandparents within the family (Carvalho, Moreira, & Rabinovich, 2010).

The context of gender and the lineage of grandparents are still paramount forces that determine levels of grandparental involvement in care for grandchildren. Maternal grandmothers, regardless of their residential arrangements, reportedly participate more intensively in the care of the grandchildren than others in the family (Rabinovich & Azevedo, 2012). Although paternal grandmothers in their study were less involved with grandchildren than maternal grandmothers, paternal grandmothers were more involved than grandfathers from both sides of the family. Clearly, these grandmothers play a much more vigorous role in grandchildren's care and socialization than grandfathers, and the maternal side does it substantially more than the paternal side. This is possibly because of residential proximity and the fact that the mother trusts her own mother (i.e., the maternal grandmother) with the care and socialization of her children. These findings may be somewhat different than what has been observed in Chinese families, where the paternal side more often plays a significant role in young children's care and socialization (Li & Lamb, 2015; see Chapter 9).

In line with cultural norms and expectations, maternal grandmothers are an important source of care for the grandchildren in Brazil, and they are often called upon to help the family (Araújo & Dias, 2010; Rabinovich & Azevedo, 2012). However, in the general framework of traditions and changes in Brazilian society, grandparents including grandfathers are regarded as loving and caring toward grandchildren (Pedrosa, 2006).

Grandfathers in Cultural Context

Matriarchy is well recognized in Brazil, yet the tradition of patriarchy guides the grandfather to transmit to male children the importance of procreation and provisioning roles for men (Aratangy & Posternak, 2005. The status and actions of the grandfather also influence gender relations in the family. While grandparents influence grandchildren in various developmental areas (social, moral, cognitive, health, emotional, etc.), grandfathers express their influence primarily through play and leisurely interactions. Older grandchildren, however, receive advice from them about life skills, work, and finances. Grandparents' involvement in direct care for grandchildren is noticeably limited for this age group (Dias & Silva, 1999).

FIGURE 4.2 A 60-year-old grandfather and his 1-year-old grandchild smile through a playhouse window. This photo symbolizes how contemporary Brazilian grandfathers are more involved and share more play activities with their grandchildren than in past generations.

Source: Courtesy of Mário Vítor Bastos.

Limited available findings of empirical research on Brazilian grandfathers suggest that they take pride in their grandchildren. Grandfathers consider a grandchild to be like an additional child who continues and expands the family line (Pedrosa, 2006). It appears that compared to fathers (Bastos, Volkmer-Pontes, Brasilieiro, & Serra, 2013), grandfathers are more available to grandchildren since grandfathers do not have to go to work as providers. The guardianship role of the grandfather becomes very important, especially in female-headed single parent households. Here the grandfather may compensate for the roles and responsibilities of an absent and/or uninvolved father. These grandfathers also provide economic support and discipline children (Aratangy & Posternak, 2005). In fact, the mere presence of the grandfather inspires children to behave well in the family and in public. However, grandfathers are apparently not as much involved in grandchildren's care and education, generally, as are grandmothers in Brazilian society.

Grandparents as Caregivers

In Brazil, grandmothers work as primary caregivers for grandchildren in cases of teenage pregnancy, parental divorce, mother's employment outside the home, handicapped children, drug abuse, parents' or child's major illnesses (e.g., AIDS), and death of the parents (Dias, Costa, & Rangel, 2005). Specifically, grandmothers usually feed, clean, and play with their young grandchildren. When needed, they also take grandchildren to school. Further, grandparents assume total responsibility for grandchildren when their parents migrate to another location for employment. Because of the global economy and job opportunities, many parents leave home to find work, even in another country, similar to the situation described for South Asia in Chapter 8, and elsewhere. The issue of migration-related childcare has become more common nowadays than it was decades ago. Grandparents step in to fill the vacuum and take care of grandchildren, sometimes for years (Gerondo, 2006; Schuler, 2015).

Some grandparents take care of their grandchildren part time and others who do it as their main activity. Part-time and full-time involvement in care activities have differential levels and types of implications for grandparents. Many full-time caregiver grandparents report higher levels of stress and tiredness from raising their grandchildren. Other grandparents become less involved in care to avoid authority conflicts between them and their sons and daughters. To provide for the new generation, caregiver grandparents express satisfaction in life, feel a sense of personal renovation and accomplishment, adore the company of the grandchildren, ameliorate feelings of loneliness, and enjoy the sense of usefulness and dynamism that taking care of grandchildren provides (Dias & Costa, 2006). On the other hand, grandparental care can decrease the quality of their physical and mental health, challenge social and family life, increase financial overload and stress levels, diminish personal time, and lead to health problems or conflicts with the parents (Cardoso, 2011; Dias, Hora, & Aguiar, 2010). These findings suggest that Brazilian grandparents who are actively involved in childcare demonstrate ambivalence, in that they care deeply about the well-being of their grandchildren and may also feel overloaded with care responsibilities (Dias, Costa, & Rangel, 2005).

Teenage Pregnancy

Teenage pregnancy is a significant concern for Brazilian parents and professionals (Dias, Hora, & Aguiar, 2010). The birth rate among teenagers (ages 15–19) in Brazil is comparatively high. About 12% of 14 million teenagers had at least one child in 2010 (IBGE, 2012), and as a consequence many parents become grandparents at an early age. Often these pregnancies and births are unplanned, and teenage mothers require family support to adapt to this life transition. It is usually the grandmother who steps in to support teenage parents.

There are striking regional differences in how teenagers engage themselves in childcare and other family chores. According to one study, teenagers in rural families assumed childcare and other family responsibilities, whereas urban teenagers stayed with their parents and received childcare support from other family members including grandparents (Fonseca & Bastos, 2001). It is interesting to note that teenage mothers in urban families tended to receive more family support than teenage mothers in rural communities. Although urban grandmothers in Brasilia criticized their granddaughters for early pregnancy, and sometimes advised them to have an abortion, they supported and approved of the mothering skills of their granddaughters (Silva & Salomão, 2003). Grandmothers and teenage mothers jointly raise children, as most urban teenage mothers co-reside with their parents.

Divorce

Parental separation and divorce are additional reasons for Brazilian grandparents to take responsibility for raising grandchildren (Araújo & Dias, 2010; Dias, Costa, & Rangel, 2005; Dias & Costa, 2006). In 2004, Brazil documented 130,500 divorces, and this number went up to 314,100 in 2014, an increase of 162% (IBGE, 2015). This growing number of divorces is one cause of a gradual change in Brazilian family dynamics. Marriage dissolution is increasingly acceptable, and such a change in social norms leads grandparents to help with childcare. In many cases, divorced fathers obtain custody of the child, and they desperately seek help from their parents (especially their mothers) to care for the child (Portal Brasil, 2015). It is also not uncommon for fathers to receive help from both sides of the extended family.

Empirical data further suggest that divorced or separated sons and daughters received mainly emotional support such as advice, transmission of information about the family, and phone messages from their parents (Araújo & Dias, 2002). Researchers also observed that there was a decrease in the grandparental visits to their grandchildren, mainly due to the fact that grandchildren and their custodial parent (usually the mother) move into the grandparents' house after the separation or divorce. In the long run, however, grandparents became actively engaged in care of these resident grandchildren.

Parents' Work

A pregnant daughter usually anticipates that her mother will be available with childcare when the baby is born. Such a cultural mindset clearly reflects that grandparents are already committed to taking care of the grandchildren during the pregnancy of their daughters (Atalla, 1996). Whereas some Brazilian grandmothers studied by Atalla felt pressured to decide to care for their grandchildren as a duty and did it reluctantly, others gladly expected and accepted this responsibility. Atalla's findings further suggested that their feelings were ambivalent, i.e., fatigue and fear of losing their privacy mixed with accomplishment, renewal, pride, and satisfaction. At the same time, grandmothers' involvement in care demonstrated health, love, work, and a feeling of usefulness.

Cardoso interviewed 12 middle-class grandmothers (ages 51–82) who cared for their grandchildren, all residents in the cities of Rio de Janeiro and Niterói in southeast Brazil. In particular, grandmothers were readily available to care for grandchildren of employed parents (Cardoso, 2011). Although this study also showed that many grandmothers found it difficult to constantly deal with this assignment, each grandmother found the best possible way to add the caregiver responsibility to her own personal tasks and other family chores. Overall, caregiver grandmothers provide practical support for their sons and daughters who are parents, and affective support for their grandchildren. This involvement indicates a supportive caregiving environment and strong family relationships (Cardoso, 2011).

Migration of Parents

As mentioned earlier, many South American parents migrate to other countries for employment. Like grandparents in Mexico and Central America (see Chapter 2), Brazilian grandparents and especially grandmothers take full childcare responsibility for grandchildren when parents emigrate to other countries. Just as we have mentioned for grandparents of teenage parents, grandparents as primary caregivers of their grandchildren express mixed feelings about these emigration-related experiences. Grandparents were happy with the presence of the grandchild in their daily lives, yet they felt overloaded by care responsibilities (Silva, Coelho, Oliveira, Borges, & Oliveira, 2010). Despite the commitment and love grandparents showed for their grandchildren, they were reportedly tired and overwhelmed by the full-time care involvement. These grandparents struggled and faced additional challenges when the grandchildren reached adolescence (Schuler, 2015).

Sick or Disabled Grandchildren

Grandmothers often take care of their grandchildren who are ill and hospitalized for an extended period of time. These grandmothers have reported happiness and a sense of being protective when they take care of their hospitalized grandchildren (Gerondo, 2006). This involvement is one more way for grandmothers to offer family support to their adult children and grandchildren. The findings of Gerondo also showed that some grandmothers even accepted legal custody to provide unabated care for their sick grandchildren. Another study sought to explore the experiences of people responsible for children or adolescents who were not living with their parents and who were enrolled in the APAE center in Poços de Caldas, in central Brazil, and who were responsible for children and adolescents with disabilities (Couto, 2010). These children suffered from parental neglect, abuse, abandonment, and rejection. Couto studied the choices, expectations, feelings, and routines of taking on such care. The grandparents were the closest family members responsible for taking care of these children. Her research attempted to understand caregiver grandparents' choices, expectations, feelings, and routines of care, and found that grandmothers were the main care providers for neglected children. As a part of the family network, these grandmothers revealed a deep sense of attachment, responsibility, and duty toward their grandchildren. Yet these caregiver grandmothers expressed ambivalent feelings because they were overburdened (Couto, 2010).

It is common for grandparents to extend their support to the parents who give birth to a child with special needs. Brazilians understand that this is an instance where family support can relieve the parental stress related to children with disabilities and childcare. One study on this topic showed that grandparental support coupled with music therapy resulted in significant health benefits for young grandchildren (ages 10–27 months) with disabilities (Mariano & Fiamenghi Jr., 2011). This support also strengthens family and intergenerational relationships between grandparents and grandchildren. Grandparents are well aware of any family shortcomings, and protection of the grandchild from situations of abandonment or neglect was a fundamental reason for grandparents to have assumed responsibility. Other reasons for grandparents' involvement in care included their sense of family responsibility, moral duty, and feelings of affection for their grandchildren. Brazilian grandparents, especially in low-income families, believe it is their duty to take care of their grandchildren since the family is seen as a network where each one has responsibilities and obligations toward the other. This tendency is very much like that expressed about grandparents in Mexico and Central America (see Chapter 2,) and the chapters from Africa.

The Significance of Caring for Grandparents Who Act as Caregivers

Research evidence clearly indicates that factors such as health, financial situation, and relationships with sons/daughters or daughters/sons-in-law are central to understanding whether grandparents' involvement in childcare has a positive or negative implication for grandparents and/or the family system (Dias, Costa, & Rangel, 2005). Social changes in recent decades have brought about new family arrangements in Brazilian urban contexts, whereby several generations co-habit in the home space. Through the practice of care for their grandchildren, grandparents become important in the transmission of material goods and inheritance. Also guided by moral obligations between kin or social networks, grandparents establish material, affective, and symbolic exchanges between generations.

Research on grandmothers and grandfathers who raised their grandchildren in the poor area north of Aracaju (northeast Brazil) has reported that despite feeling overwhelmed with childcare responsibilities, grandparents grew in self-esteem and gained the respect and admiration of other family members (Silva, 2012). Likewise, grandparents in northeast Brazil took care of and supported their grandchildren regardless of the presence or absence of the parents in the family (Alves, 2013). Findings from these studies clearly indicate the desire and conviction of grandparents to take care of their grandchildren. This care and socialization also allows a Brazilian grandparent to instill values, morality, and social norms in their grandchildren, which enables grandparents to shape the personality of a grandchild. Most Brazilian grandparents believe that caring for a grandchild is a family custom and is a much-needed resource for the parents. They also support the notion that the tradition of the grandparents' role in childcare must be maintained in the contexts of modernization and changing social values that impinge on their social, family, and personal life (Dias, Costa, & Rangel, 2005). It is also important to recognize that in addition to the grandparental role, some grandparents are keen to keep one or more grandchildren with them in order to still feel what it is like to exercise parental functions at an older age.

Subcultural Variations: Research in Other Latin-American Countries

One study of Uruguayan grandparents and grandchildren showed that 73% of grandchildren reported that their relationships with grandparents brought them much happiness; 54% regularly visited their maternal grandparents, and only 33% visited their paternal grandparents (Prato, Hernández, Techera, & Rivas, 2012). These results indicated a remarkable closeness between maternal grandparents and grandchildren in Uruguay (which borders Brazil), which is similar to the findings of research on grandchildren in Brazil. Furthermore, 98% of Uruguayan grandparents in the study by Prato et al. stated that their quality of life improved due to the company of their grandchildren. It is worth noting that only a minority of both Uruguayan and Brazilian grandparents who were responsible for childcare have reported the role of grandparent to be a burden.

Grandparents in Argentina (which also borders Brazil) who took care of grandchildren at least nine hours a week for at least two years, reportedly participated in childcare because of the parents' work and their desire to teach their grandchildren to be productive citizens (Weisbrot & Giraudo, 2012). Similar to findings in Brazil, many Argentinian grandmothers expressed ambivalent feelings that combined personal satisfaction and fatigue, physical exertion, and lack of time to care for themselves. Overall, Argentinian grandmothers in this study thought that grandparenting was a socially expected role; this theme reverberates across South American societies.

Elsewhere, in Apiao on the archipelago of Chiloe (Chile) an unmarried woman who becomes pregnant does not normally marry the father of her child. The biological father of the child or any other relatives who do not want to take care of the child are usually separated from the child's life and lineage. The absence of the father and even of the mother is not considered abandonment because the child becomes the primary charge of society. In particular, elderly Chilean people may ask for a grandson or granddaughter to live with them. Thus, the children call their parents by their names and grandparents are called "father" or "mother." In this cultural community, grandparents' care of grandchildren is valued as productive work (Bacchiddu, 2012).

After the end of the military dictatorship in the 1970s, a number of Argentinian grandmothers were aided by feminist scholars to start a movement called "Grandmothers of the Plaza de Mayo" (Koike, 2013). The primary goal of this movement was to locate and regain the grandchildren who were abducted by the previous military junta. Their efforts showed that Argentinian grandmothers took an active interest in locating the whereabouts of their lost grandchildren, who were victims of military and political oppression for decades. Likewise, through a movement called "Black Us," Colombian grandmothers of African descent (known as *abuela* or *aguéla*) started to socialize their grandchildren with African ancestry and values (Palmeira, 2012). Again, it was the grandmothers who led the younger generations to create a link to their families and heritage.

Another significant aspect of grandparenthood in rural Brazil is that grandparents often use their retirement benefits to support their grandchildren's schooling (Albuquerque, Lobo, & Raymundo, 1999). This investment strengthens the efforts to build human capital and reduces child labor in the country. Overall, grandparents, especially grandmothers, across Latin-American societies (including Brazil) are highly involved with their grandchildren. The finding of the predominance of the grandmaternal role here is somewhat similar to that reported for grandmothers' involvement with grandchildren in Russia (see Chapter 7).

Speculation, the Future, and Conclusions

Our findings from the limited available literature suggest that Brazilian grandparents, especially grandmothers, play a significant caregiver and socialization role for their grandchildren. Fortunately, there is now a renewed interdisciplinary interest in this topic, in the fields of anthropology, psychology, nursing, social work, education, and gerontology in Brazil. There are an increasing number of dissertations, theses, and books which focus on relations between grandparents and grandchildren in Brazil.

As we have seen in this chapter, there are numerous variations in the grandparental role in Brazil. This diversity is based on gender differences, health status and age, geographical variations, types of family structures, and socioeconomic status. Given the regional and cultural variability, it is necessary for more research to be conducted to explore the complexity of relationships between grandparents and grandchildren. For example, we envision that scholars will focus on the causes and consequences of grandparents raising grandchildren, and their policy implications in the context of changing demographics and childcare options in Brazil (Camarano, 2003). In addition, an interdisciplinary approach to grandparenthood will inform health professionals, educators, psychologists, demographers, and therapists to examine the impact of sociocultural and economic changes on the elderly in Brazil.

We predict that more Brazilians than ever will assume the roles of grandparents and great-grandparents as life expectancy increases for the population. This will offer an opportunity to the young generation to harness the affection, care, knowledge, and experience of grandparents. However, this also may lead to increased conflicts and tensions between generations, mainly due to the modernization process that changes values and lifestyles over time. Therefore, it will be necessary not only to focus on research, interventions, and programs that facilitate the relationship between the various generations in the family, but also to offer resources for health care, education, and mental health services to help grandparents cope with these challenges. The current literature suggests that either grandchildren prefer their maternal grandparents to interact with or maternal grandparents are more involved with their grandchildren than paternal grandparents. However, future grandparents will more likely be called to balance the attention and care they provide for their paternal and maternal grandchildren. With declining birth rates, future grandparents will have fewer grandchildren in their lives, albeit for a longer period of time. In view of the rapid modernization of Brazil, future research should focus on the nature of socioeconomic and emotional relationships between grandparents and grandchildren in rural, urban, and indigenous families.

Summary

This chapter highlighted the sociodemographic and cultural contexts of grandparents in Brazil. An increase of life expectancy has contributed to the growth of the elderly population, and accordingly more people now experience the roles of grandparents and great-grandparents and live with the younger generations for an extended period of time. The image and roles of Brazilian grandparents typically varies by age, socioeconomic status, family lineage, and gender of grandparents. For instance, maternal grandparents are reportedly more involved with their grandchildren than paternal grandparents. In addition, grandmothers provide basic care for grandchildren, whereas grandfathers usually discipline and play with grandchildren. It was also shown in this chapter that grandmothers raise grandchildren due to reasons such as teen pregnancy, divorce, work and migration of parents, and illness or disability of the grandchildren. Finally, this chapter reported that grandparents provide remarkable economic support for their grandchildren who come from low-income and female-headed single parent families.

Appendix

Meaning of Proverbs

"The parents educate, the grandparents do the opposite."

This Brazilian proverb means that parents are responsible for children's education. However, grandparents may interfere with parents' strict learning process when they affectionately relieve some parental pressure on children. This proverb may not apply to all contemporary grandparents, because many of them are in charge of their grandchildren.

"The grandmother is twice a mother."

This frequently used proverb indicates that a grandmother is more than a mother because she is the mother of her own child and the mother of her child's children. Therefore, a grandmother plays the role of a mother in two ways. This proverb underscores the fact that the grandmother is very important in family dynamics; in many circumstances a grandmother is called "mother" in Brazil and in other South American countries.

Additional Resources

Programa de Avós de Pampilhosa da Serra – Program Grandparents Conversations (www.cm-pampilhosadaserra.pt/pages/273 (in Portuguese only))
   The Program Grandparents Conversations is a social intervention program started by the Social Service of the Municipality of Pampilhosa da Serra in 2012. This program provides activities and benefits for the non-institutionalized elderly population to promote well-being, self-esteem, leisure and entertainment, and active aging.

Associação dos Idosos do Brasil – Association of Brazilian Elderly (Aibgyn. com.br (in Portuguese only))
   The Association of Brazilian Elderly, based in Goiania, Goias, is an NGO founded in 1989. Its goal is to promote the achievement of a just social policy for the elderly, and to work for better quality of life for the elderly. It has more than 1,200 members and promotes various activities, such as gymnastics, yoga, courses, occupational therapy, choreography, literacy classes, English, Spanish, dance evening, and music therapy.

Associaçao dos avós exlcludos – Association for Excluded Grandparents (https://www.facebook.com/Associacao-dos-avos-excluidos-434816206558101/)
   The association deals with emotional and legal problems through relevant legislation, on behalf of grandparents who are excluded from visitation or contact with their grandchildren due to interference from their children or sons/daughters-in-law.

Discussion Questions

1. How do grandparents and their roles compare between Brazilian and other South American countries?
2. How do Brazilian grandmothers play important roles in their grandchildren's life?
3. Do you still have living grandparents? If so, please describe your relationship with them and how this relationship is different from what we described as the grandparent–grandchild relationships in Brazilian families.

References

Albuquerque, F., B., Lobo, A., & Raymundo, J., S. (1999). Analysis of the psychosocial repercussions due to the concession of rural benefits. *Psicologia, Reflexão e Crítica, 12*(2), 503–519.

Alves, S. M. M. (2013). *To care or to be responsible? An analysis of the relationship between generations between grandparent and grandchild.* (Master's thesis). Social Studies Center Applied, State University of Ceará, Fortaleza.

Aratangy, L. R., & Posternak, R. (2005). *The book of grandparents: At grandparents' home is it always Sunday?* Sao Paulo: Artemeios.

Araújo, C. P., & Dias, C. M. de S. B. (2010). Low income guardian grandparents. *Pesquisas e Práticas Psicossociais, 4*(2), 229–237.

Araújo, M. R. G. L., & Dias, C. M. S. B. (2002). Role of grandparents: support offered to grandchildren in situations of separation/divorce of parents. *Estudos de Psicologia (Natal), 7*(1), 91–102. doi:10.1590/S1413-294X2002000100010

Atalla, M. M. A. (1996). Grandchildren through grannies' eyes: Experiences of grandparents who care for their grandchildren. (Master's thesis). Institute of Psychology, University of São Paulo, São Paulo.

Bacchiddu, G. (2012). Reluctant mothers, maternal grandparents and forgotten fathers: The undoing of kinship relations in Apion, Chiloé. *Tellus, 12*(23), 35–53.

Bastos, A. C., Volkmer-Pontes, V., Brasilieiro, P. G., & Serra, H. M. (2013). Fathering in Brazil: A diverse and unknown reality. In D. Shwalb, B. Shwalb, & M. Lamb (Eds.), *Fathering in cultural context* (pp. 228–249). New York: Routledge.

Bengtson, V. L., & Allen, K. R. (1993). The life course perspective applied to families over time. In P. G. Bass (Ed.), *Sourcebook of family theories and methods: A contextual approach* (pp. 469–499). New York: Plenum.

Bronfenbrenner, U. (1989). Ecological system theory. *Annals of Child Development, 6*, 187–249.

Camarano, A. A. (2003). Elderly woman: family support or agent of change? *Estudos Avançados, 17*(49), 35–63.

Cardoso, A. R. (2011). *The twenty-first century grandparents, mutations and rearrangements in contemporary family.* Curitiba: Juruá.

Carvalho, A. M., Moreira, L. V. C., & Rabinovich, E. P. (2010). Children's views about family: A quantitative approach. *Psicologia: Teoria e Pesquisa, 26*(3), 417–426.

Couto, F. P. (2010). Shared lives: Grandmothers and handicapped grandchildren in situations of violence and abandonment. (Doctoral dissertation). Faculty of Medical Sciences, State University of Campinas.

Dias, C. M. S. B., & Costa, J. M. (2006). A study of the grandmother guardian in Recife. In M. C. L. A. Amazonas, A. O. Lima, & C. M. S. B. Dias (Eds.), *Women and family: Various speeches* (pp. 127–138). Workshop Publisher Book, São Paulo.

Dias, C. M. S. B. & Silva, D. V. (1999). Role of grandparents: A literature review of the last three decades. In T. Féres-Carneiro (Ed.), *Couple and family, between tradition and transformation* (pp. 118–149). Rio de Janeiro: Nau.

Dias, C. M. S. B., & Silva, M. A. (2003). The grandparents from a college student's perspective. *Psicologia em Estudo, 8* (special issue), 55–62.

Dias, C. M. S. B., Costa, J. M, & Rangel, V. A. (2005). Grandparents raising their grandchildren: circumstances and consequences. In T. Féres-Carneiro (Ed.). *Family and couple, effects of contemporaneity* (pp. 158–176). Rio de Janeiro: PUC.

Dias, C. M. S. B., Hora, F. F. A., & Aguiar, A. G. (2010). Young created by grandparents and one or both parents. *Psicologia, Teoria e Prática, 12*(2), 188–199.

Dias, C. M. S. B., Viana, M. C. L. L., & Aguiar, F. S. L. (2003). Self-perception of early grandparents. In T. Féres-Carneiro (Ed.), *Family and couple, arrangements and contemporary demands* (pp.119 – 140). Rio de Janeiro: PUC.

Fonseca, A. L. B., & Bastos, A. C. S. (2001) Maternity in cultural context: A study of adolescent mothers of two communities (one urban and one semi-rural) in Bahia. *Journal of Human Growth and Development, 11*(1), 80–89.

Gerondo, V. L. S. (2006). Elderly grandparents caregivers of hospitalized grandchildren. (Master's dissertation). Federal University of Paraná, Curitiba.

IBGE (Instituto Brasileiro de Geografia e Estatística) (2010). *Profile of elderly heads of households in Brazil.* Series Studies and Research – Demographic and Socioeconomic Information, no. 9. Rio de Janeiro: Brazilian Institute of Geography and Statistics.

IBGE (2012). *Woman in the market.* Brazilian Institute of Geography and Statistics. Retrieved from www.ibge.gov.br/home/estatistica/indicadores/trabalhoerendimento/pme_nova/Mulher_Mercado_Trabalho_Perg_Resp_2012.pdf

Koike, M. L. (2013). The abduction of children by the Argentine military dictatorship and the performance of the grandmothers of the Plaza de Mayo for the right to truth (legal and biological) and memory. *Journal of Gender and Law, 1,* 1–24.

Li, X., & Lamb, M. (2015). Fathering in Chinese culture: Traditions and transitions. In J. L. Roopnarine (Ed.), *Fathers across cultures: The importance, roles, and diverse practices of dads* (pp. 273–306). Santa Barbara, CA: Praeger.

Maggi, R., S. (2014). Indigenous health in Brazil. *Revista Brasileira Saúde Materna Infantil, Recife, 14*(1), 13–16.

Mainetti, A. C., & Wanderbrooke, A. C. N. S. (2013). Grandmothers who take care of grandchildren. *Pensando Famílias, 17*(1), 87–98.

Mariano F. L. O. R., & Fiamenghi Jr., G. A. (2011). Elderly grandmother caregivers of hospitalized grandchildren. *Aletheia, 34,* 138–150.

Munduruká, D. (2006). *Picking lice, telling stories.* Sao Paulo: Brinque-Book.

Oliveira, P. S. (1999). *Shared lives: Culture and co-education of generations in everyday life.* Language and Culture Collection. Sao Paulo: Hucitec, Fapesp.

Oliveira, G. A. S. (2015). *Perception of the links and relationships between adult grandchildren and their grandparents.* (Master's thesis). Catholic University of Pernambuco, Recife.

Oliveira, A. R. V, Gomes, L., Tavares, A. B., & Cárdenas, C. J. (2009). Relationship between grandparents and their grandchildren in the period of infancy. *Revista Kairós Gerontologia, 12*(2), 149–158.

Palmeira, F. S. (2012). Afrofeminin voices in Colombian literature. *Proceedings of SILIAFRO, 1,* 249–257.

Pedrosa, A. S. (2006). Elderly men grandfathers: meanings of grandchildren for everyday life. (Master's thesis). University of São Paulo, São Paulo.

Peixoto, C.E. (2004). *Family and aging.* Rio de Janeiro: FGV.

PNAD. (2013). *National Survey by Household Sample Survey.* Retrieved from www.ibge.gov.br/home/estatistica/populacao/trabalhoerendimento/pnad2013/

Portal Brasil (2015). *Divorce taxes increase more than 160% in the country.* Retrieved from www.brasil.gov.br/cidadania-e-justica/2015/11/em-10-anos-taxa-de-divorcios-cresce-mais-de-160-no-pais

Prato, A., Hernandez, A. L., Techera, L., & Rivas, R. (2012). Grandparents and grandchildren: A necessary relationship? *Biomedicine, 7*(2), 22–36.

Rabinovich, P. E., & Azevedo, T. (2012). Participation of grandparents in the daily care of young grandchildren. In M. G. C. Castro, A. M. C. Carvalho, & L V. C. Moreira (Eds.), *Family care dynamics* (pp. 205–238). Salvador: EDUFBA.

Ramos, A. C. (2006). Child culture and aging: What children say about old age? A study of boys and girls from the outskirts of Porto Alegre. (Dissertation). Federal University of Rio Grande do Sul, Porto Alegre.

Ramos, A. C. (2011). My grandparents and I: Intergenerational relationship between grandparents and grandchildren from the perspective of children. (Doctoral thesis). Federal University of Rio Grande do Sul, Porto Alegre.

Ramos, A. C. (2014). About grandparents, grandchildren and cities: Intertwining intergenerational relations and urban experiences in childhood. *Revista de Educação, 35*(128), 629–696.

Rocha, S. (2013). Affective and virtual ties between grandparents and grandchildren. *Proceedings of the Second International Congress on Interdisciplinary Social and Humanities – II Coninter*. Federal University of Minas Gerais.

Santos, T. M, Silva, S. S. C., & Pontes, F. A. R. (2011). The participation of grandparents in grandchildren are in a riverside community. *Psicologia, Teoria e Prática, 13*(1), 182–197.

Schuler, M. F. G. (2015). "Orphans of Mobility": Mother's migration impact on the lives of their children. (Doctoral thesis). Catholic University of Pernambuco, Recife.

Silva, C. J. (2012). In the networks of family solidarity: a study of grandparents raising or caring grandchildren. (Master's thesis). Federal University of Sergipe, Aracaju.

Silva, D. V., & Salomão, N. M. R. (2003) Motherhood in the perspective of adolescent mothers and maternal grandmother. *Estudos de Psicologia (Natal), 8*(1), 135–145.

Silva, J. T. S., Coelho, R. S., Oliveira, E., Borges, F. C., & Oliveira, K. (2010). Parents abroad and grandchildren under full responsibility of grandparents: An analysis of this reality. *Revista Encontro de Psicologia, 13*(8), 59–70.

Weisbrut, M. A., & Giraudo, N. (2012). Concepts and perceptions of grandmothers about their grandchildren's care: Qualitative study and publication of the Italian Hospital of Buenos Aires. *Archivos Argentinos of Pediatria, 110*(2), 126–131.

PART III
Europe and Russia

5

GRANDPARENTHOOD IN GERMANY

Intimacy at a Distance or Emeritus Parents?

Katharina Mahne, Daniela Klaus, and Heribert Engstler

PROVERBS

1. "Not until you become a grandparent can you begin to understand your children." (*Erst bei den Enkeln ist man dann so weit, dass man die Kinder ungefähr verstehen kann*)

    Erich Kästner, famous German writer, author of several books
    for children (1899–1974)

2. "For children, grandparents are like holidays from the parents." (*Großeltern sind für Kinder Urlaub von den Eltern*)

    (see p. 104 for interpretations)

CASE STORY: HELGA, A TYPICAL GERMAN GRANDMOTHER

Helga, widowed and almost 80 years old, lives in a middle-sized town. She has three children, four grandchildren, and one great-grandchild. Growing up toward the end of World War II, she left school early and started an apprenticeship to become a tailor. She stopped working after getting married to her husband Karl at the age of 21. One year later she gave birth to her first child, Petra. Her second daughter, Susanne, was born in 1959 and son Michael in 1962 when Helga was 27 years old. While a housewife Helga was occasionally paid for doing sewing jobs at home. When her youngest child reached high-school age she started a part-time job as a sales clerk in a department store nearby. At the age of 46, Helga stopped working in order to care for her mother until she died three years later.

Around that time (1981) her oldest daughter Petra, who had married Wolfgang, gave birth to Stefan, Helga and Karl's first grandchild. Two years later, Stefan's sister Katrin was born. Living nearby, Helga was in close contact with both grand-children. She regularly cared for the two kids, which was very helpful when her daughter returned to her part-time job and no places were available in the local kin-dergarten. At that time, Grandpa Karl still had a full-time job and saw his grand-children mainly at the weekends or on vacation. Helga's second daughter Susanne, a successful manager in the insurance business, remained childless. In 1990, Helga's son Michael had his daughter Jennifer, the third grandchild. As Michael lived more than two hours away, contact frequency between Helga and Jennifer was moderate but became even rarer when Michael divorced and moved to a more distant place. In 1998, Michael married his second wife, Heike, who already was mother of Martin. So Helga gained a 10-year-old step-grandchild and Michael and Heike became parents of Niklas.

Three years later, Helga's husband Karl died. Nevertheless, Helga has a comfort-able income from her widow's pension, some old-age pension and private savings. Contributions to the governmental health and long-time care insurance are low, as is the rent for her flat, so the relationships with her children and grandchildren are freed from financial demands. Helga is able to transfer some money to the younger family members just as she has done for the last 40 years.

Today, Helga has most frequent contact with her oldest grandchild, Stefan. He is already 34 years old, lives nearby, and helps her with the weekly shopping, as her driver sometimes, gives technical support, or just has a small talk. A special pleasure for Helga is to see Stefan's daughter, her only great-grandchild, at play. Sometimes the whole family takes a day trip and has dinner in a restaurant – Helga pays the bill. Whenever her granddaughter Katrin (32), who lives far away, comes to meet her parents, she drops in on her grandma Helga, too. This happens about once a month, but in between, Katrin and Helga call each other. In contrast, Martin (27), her step-grandson, very seldom shows up. At the age of 16 he moved in with his biological father, and today he lives far away with his girlfriend. It will be Helga's 80th birthday soon and there will be a big party. Maybe all the family members will come together again to congratulate Helga.

In an ageing Western world, grandparenthood is an emergent theme for both individuals and society. In Germany, most parents experience grandparenthood at some time (Engstler & Menning, 2005; Mahne & Huxhold, 2017). The grand-parent role has become a common family role for older adults and is infused with high subjective importance (Herlyn & Lehmann, 1998; Mahne & Motel-Klingebiel, 2012). The aim of this chapter is to provide a multifaceted analysis of contemporary grandparenthood in Germany. First of all, background information is given on demographic, cultural, and welfare state-related developments and conditions that characterize grandparenthood in Germany.

Demographic, Cultural, and Welfare State Background

Demography

It is only since the second half of the 20th century that the experience of grand-parenthood has become common in Western countries; "in earlier times multi-generational families with members of several lineage generations in one family, were simply a myth" (Lauterbach & Klein, 2004, p. 653). In Germany, only one-third of children born between 1941 and 1946 had all four grandparents alive at time of their birth and 13% had no grandparents at all (Lauterbach & Klein, 2004). Due to low life expectancy and high marital age, most individuals did not live to witness the birth of their first grandchild (Lauterbach, 2002).

As for the development of the generalized age structure in Germany, in 1974 there were about one million (1,053,281) individuals aged 10 years or older and less than half a million (430,771) individuals aged 85 years or more. Forty years later the age structure has rebalanced dramatically: there are 720,022 individuals aged 10 years or less and more than two million (2,147,596) individuals aged 85 years or more (Federal Statistical Office of Germany, 2016a; our calculations).

Today, the average life expectancy is 78 years for men and 83 years for women (Federal Statistical Office of Germany, 2015a). About half of the people in Germany aged 50 years and older live in three-generation families (Grünheid & Scharein, 2011), and at the age of 70 about 80% of parents have grandchildren (Engstler & Menning, 2005). The parallel existence of several family generations was promoted by the increase in life expectancy during the 20th century. Whereas an increase in life expectancy mainly affects the likelihood of grandchildren experiencing their grandparents (and not necessarily vice versa – see Uhlenberg & Cheuk, 2010), it has also prolonged the lifetime overlap between the genera-tions. Today in Germany, grandparents and grandchildren enjoy up to 30 years together (Grünheid & Scharein, 2011); this is illustrated in our case story: at nearly 80 years of age, grandmother Helga has not only watched her grandchildren grow up but has also lived to see the birth of a great-grandchild. However, the num-ber of households with three or more generations living under the same roof has decreased dramatically within the last 20 years: in 1995 there were 351,000 house-holds of three or more generations; in 2015 the number was 209,000, which is a decrease of more than 40% (Federal Statistical Office of Germany, 2016b).

Apart from changes in life expectancy, the transition to and the duration of grandparenthood depends on fertility. Today across Europe, postponement of the entry into parenthood and fertility rates below replacement level are observed (Frejka & Sobotka, 2008). Germany is among the countries in the European Union with the lowest fertility rates and the highest mean age for women at the birth of their first child (European Commission, 2013). In 2013, the period total fertility rate in Germany was as low as 1.42 (lower than every population group

FIGURE 5.1 A great-grandson (age 6) meets his great-grandmother (age 95) at her birthday party in a restaurant. Due to increased longevity in Germany, great-grandparenthood has become more and more common.

Source: Courtesy of DZA Photo Collection – Peter Zeman.

in Table 1.1 with the exceptions of Japan and Korea) and mean maternal age at birth of first child reached 29.2 years (Human Fertility Database, 2016). Since the transition to parenthood has previously and continues to take place much earlier in Eastern Germany, East German grandparents experience an earlier onset and a longer period of grandparenthood than grandparents in the Western part of the country (Leopold & Skopek, 2015). The mean age at transition to grandparenthood is 49 years in the Eastern and 54 years in the Western part of Germany (Mahne & Klaus, 2017). Germany also has one of the highest rates of childlessness worldwide. Around 22% of women born between 1968 and 1972 are estimated to remain childless (Federal Statistical Office of Germany, 2013), compared with about 20% in the UK, 18.8% in the US, and only 8.5% in Mexico.

Low fertility combined with longevity has resulted in a family structure labelled as "beanpole families" (Bengtson, Rosenthal, & Burton, 1990). In such families, living family members come from many generations, but there are few representatives of each generation. Due to this structural change, vertical (i.e., intergenerational) relationships within the family gain influence, whereas horizontal ties become weaker (e.g., those with siblings). However, the increase of childlessness in subsequent cohorts will result in significant proportions of older adults who will never have grandchildren (Uhlenberg & Cheuk, 2010). Due to the low total numbers of births grandchildren will be "in short supply" (Uhlenberg & Cheuk, 2010, p. 449). The rise in age at the birth of the first child increases the intergenerational gap and thus counteracts the effect that prolonged life expectancy has on grandparenthood. According to estimates, in the long run, the joint lifetime between generations, which has extended in the last decades, will decrease again (Grünheid & Scharein, 2011).

Early marriage was common in the 1950s but is less obligatory today. The mean age of marriage was 26 for men and 23 for women in 1970, but in 2009 it was 33 for men and 30 for women (Federal Statistical Office of Germany, 2011). Also, a growing number of extra-marital births can be observed. In 2013, 35% of all newborns had a mother who was not married to their father (Federal Statistical Office of Germany, 2016c). Lifetime marriage and partnerships have lost significance, as indicated by growing rates of divorce and separation, even among those who have (grand)children. Currently, the cumulated divorce rate of the 1990 marriage cohort after 25 years is about 39.3%; the total divorce rate in 2015 amounts up to 34.7, which means that by current durational dissolution rates around every third marriage would get divorced within 25 years (Federal Statistical Office of Germany, 2016d). In 2014, about 41% of all divorcees were parents of minor children (Federal Statistical Office of Germany, 2015b). However, re-partnering and re-marriage is widespread. Therefore, due to such profound changes in partnering and childbirth within the last decades, other forms of private living arrangements have been added to the still dominant nuclear family: cohabitation with or without children, living-apart together, single parent families, blended families, homosexual parents, etc. As a consequence, step-grandparenthood has gained in importance. In line with this trend, Helga in our case story has a step-grandson.

Cultural Contexts

Besides the impact of Germany's changing demographic structure, the meaning of grandparenthood and the arrangement of grandparent–grandchild relationships are embedded in longstanding, culturally rooted kinship systems. They provide normative orientation, customs, opportunities, and incentives with respect to family life. Historically, Germany belongs to the "Western European Marriage Pattern" (Hajnal, 1965), according to which marriage was only allowed if financial means enabled an independent, neo-local household formation; this pattern by definition also applies to the UK. The newlywed couple and their children form the primary unit of solidarity. As a result, and contrary to widely held belief, three-generation households (which are common in descent family systems) have not been the norm even in pre-industrialized times. During industrialization, this family formation pattern easily changed into the modern nuclear family with strong spousal and parent–child relationships (Klein & Nauck, 2005). Nevertheless, the isolated nuclear family with its weak connections to wider kinship and family generations outside the household – a response to needs of the industrialized economy (Parsons, 1943) – misses the reality of today's families in Germany. Many studies suggest close relationships even between adult children and their old parents on average – among other things, characterized by frequent contact and mutual exchange of support. Concepts like the "multi-location multiple-generation" (Nave-Herz, 2002, p. 234) better describe the network of intergenerational relationships. Familism and acceptance of filial responsibility in Germany are moderate by European standards (e.g., Kalmijn & Saraceno, 2008; Reher, 1998).

Compared to non-European countries, Germany seems to be culturally homogenous but heterogeneity exists for at least two reasons. First, there are regional differences as a result of Germany's recent history (Klein & Nauck, 2005). Specifically, before the foundation of the German Empire (in German, *Deutsches Reich*) in 1871, there were many autonomous states. Even today, the federal structure of Germany allows its member states a great amount of autonomy. A major demarcation line runs between the Lutheran Protestant North and the Roman Catholic South. Furthermore, the separation into two German nations after the breakdown of the Nazi regime – the Federal Democratic Republic in the West and the socialist German Democratic Republic in the East – entailed divergent family types due to country-specific social and family policies and ideologies. As a result of strong political involvement in individuals' life and great dissatisfaction with the limited opportunities outside the family, people in the authoritarian German Democratic Republic retired into their families. Even after the re-unification in 1990, family orientation remained stronger in East Germany compared to West Germany which, among other things, involves closer kinship relations (e.g., Szydlik, 1996). Thus, Germany has a long history of regional disparities.

Second, there is a growing ethnic heterogeneity because of immigration to Germany since World War II. Today, among the population aged 50 and older in Germany, around 12% are immigrants or born to immigrants, and this proportion is rising. Immigrants originate from a great variety of countries all over the world. Still, there were two major waves of immigration which formed the basis for today's elderly migrant population in Germany. First, starting in the early 1950s, ethnic German repatriates came to Germany from East Europe, mainly Poland and Romania. After the flow of post-war immigration ebbed away a couple of years later, a second peak was reached between the late 1980s and the mid-1990s. At that time, late repatriates (in German, *Spätaussiedler*) mainly from the former Soviet Union arrived in Germany as a result of the collapse of the socialist Eastern bloc. Altogether, German repatriates form the largest group of immigrants in Germany with around 4.5 million people who have immigrated since 1950 up to today (Vogel, 2012). Predominantly they came as families and aimed to settle in

Germany. They became German citizens on arrival and thus were granted access to public benefits. At present, they have been living in Germany for around 25 years on average. Second, between 1955 and 1973 Germany concluded several agreements on the recruitment of workers with Turkey and other Mediterranean countries. According to the political idea of a job rotation chain, the labor migrants (in German, *Gastarbeiter*) were expected to return home after a couple of years. But more than one-third of the approximately 10 million immigrants who entered Germany in that period, predominantly as labor workers but also in the context of family reunification, stayed in Germany (Schimany & Baykara-Krumme, 2012). By now they have been living in Germany for 45 years on average. Compared to the group of repatriates they are, however, less integrated. They are less educated and qualified, have fewer financial resources, own less property, and are of poorer health, not only compared to non-migrants but also compared to the group of repatriates (Klaus & Baykara-Krumme, 2017). The diverse cultural backgrounds and the variable socioeconomic resources of the different groups of immigrants has – in addition to their distinct immigration regulations – implications for their integration in general and for their family life, intergenerational relationships, and for the meaning of grandparenthood in particular. Originating in the US (see the discussion in Chapter 3 of subcultural variations), contextual theories in the tradition of the "three-generation-assimilation cycle" emphasize the second generation of migrants when studying the process of integration. Second-generation migrants are those who are born to migrants in the country of immigration. Due to Germany's short history of immigration, at present their share among the older population is very small but it is expected to grow in the near future. Second-generation migrants are, however, most telling when it comes to an examination of processes of assimilation among migrants in terms of the meaning and behavioral patterns of grandparenthood.

Welfare State

Generally, the existence of different family cultures has coincided with the degree of expansion of the welfare state. In the non-Western world, social security is poorly developed. In Europe, regional patterns in welfare state regulations exist, according to which southern European countries leave much responsibility to the family to take responsibility for the risks of life (Esping-Andersen, 1990; Ferrera, 1996). In contrast, Scandinavian countries strongly encourage the independence of partners or familial generations by providing a broad coverage with public childcare and universal and generous payments in the event of illness or need for care, and in old age. The conservative welfare regime in Germany, which is largely insurance-based, ranges in between these types and provides restricted access to benefits at moderate levels. In general, older family members in Germany are financially independent of their offspring. Basically they live from their public pension and public health and care insurance. Poverty rates among retirees have been decreasing since the 1950s, and currently around 12% of people aged 65 are poor, defined as having an income below 60% of the average median income in Germany (Motel-Klingebiel & Vogel, 2013).

However, due to persistent cutbacks that have taken effect within the last few years, public pensions are about to decline, resulting in a re-increase of poverty among the elderly (Motel-Klingebiel & Vogel, 2013), which will eventually change means and needs of family generations. *De jure*, mutual financial support is obligatory only between parents and grown-up children. For instance, according to their financial opportunities, children are requested to provide monetary resources to parents who need to move to a care home which they cannot afford by themselves.

In contrast, norms, expectations, or welfare state regulations relevant to the grandparent–grandchild relationship are nearly absent. However, grandparents do fulfil family tasks. As today's grandparents are relatively young, healthy, and well-off, much of grandparenting takes the form of continued parenting such as care for young grandchildren (Herlofson & Hagestad, 2012). This is partly in response to the growing share of mothers working at least part time after one or two years of parental leave. Occupational orientation and career aspirations of women have substantially increased due to educational expansion and higher qualifications since the 1960s. In 2012, 32% of all mothers with children under age 3 were gainfully employed. When the youngest child is between 3 and 5 years old, 62% of women are already employed (Federal Statistical Office of Germany, 2014). The majority (70–73%) of working mothers with young children work part time (Federal Statistical Office of Germany, 2014). As a consequence, a fundamental increase of subsidized childcare facilities has occurred. Between 2008 and 2015 the proportion of children under age 3 visiting a daycare centre (or being looked after by a state-subsidized child-minder) rose from 18% to 33%, and almost all 3–5-year-old children (95%) receive this kind of care (Federal Ministry for Family Affairs Senior Citizens Women and Youth, 2015; Federal Statistical Office of Germany, 2016e). However, there are still tremendous regional disparities. In Western Germany, 28.2% of children aged under 3 visit a daycare centre whereas the rate is 51.9% in Eastern Germany (Federal Statistical Office of Germany, 2016e). Still, public provision of childcare facilities does not cover parents' demand, which requires private arrangements like involvement of grandparents. As for the discussion whether a strong welfare state "crowds out" or "crowds in" intergenerational family help, it is rather a "mixed responsibility" for childcare, i.e., a combination of family and formal help, that operates in Germany. Institutional childcare provides reliable everyday service, while grandparents' childcare is more flexible and spontaneous. There is an ebb and flow of grandparents' involvement in childcare over time, following the different paces of relevant societal trends such as women's (mothers' and grandmothers') employment rates or the amount of institutional childcare being provided. For more information on childcare, see also the literature review section below.

Taken together, demographic changes, the pluralization of private lifestyles and family forms, the weakening of traditional gender roles, and generous but changing social welfare all affect the reality of grandparenthood. This means that there is a great variety in grandparents and grandparenting styles across cohorts, ethnic backgrounds, regions, and social strata in Germany that makes it hard to describe a "typical" situation.

Theoretical/Conceptual Approaches

Over the past decades, sociological and gerontological studies on families and family relationships in later life have accumulated. However, theory development on the multigenerational family of later life has not kept up with the mounting empirical knowledge. Grandparenthood research is still inadequately theorized and the field lacks a general research agenda (Szinovacz, 1998a, 1998b; Timonen & Arber, 2012). Propositions rooted in the sociology of family and sociology of ageing may guide the study of grandparenthood in Western industrialized societies including Germany.

Family Sociology Perspectives on Grandparenthood

Parsons' (1943) and Durkheim's (1921) classic theses of the crisis of the family and their descriptions of the isolated modern nuclear family serve as a reference point in contemporary diagnoses and future prognoses for the family. Although not targeted at a description of grandparenthood, they gave rise to ideas about the respective role of grandparents and the relationships between grandparents and grandchildren. Parsons' (1943) modern nuclear family is composed of a married couple with minor children who are economically independent of the couple's parent generation. Family solidarity is assumed to be high within the nuclear family, but low within the context of the extended family system. As offspring become independent through marriage and professional life, the relationship between older parents and adult children weakens. Time and motivation to care for older family members become sparse and the older parents grow lonely. As for the role of grandparents, this means that relationships with grandchildren remain rather remote, distant, and weak. This view, however, does not apply to contemporary family relationships in Germany. Phrases such as "intimacy at a distance" (Rosenmayr & Köckeis, 1963, p. 418) or "internal closeness through external distance" (Tartler, 1961, p. 79) provide a more appropriate picture of the actual relationships between kin. Even if older parents and adult children do not share a household, family members usually live nearby.

Sociology of Ageing Perspectives on Grandparenthood

There are two approaches affiliated to the discourse on ageing which are mainly referred to in empirical research on grandparenthood: (1) role theory, and (2) the model of intergenerational solidarity.

As to role theory, research on the relevance of the grandparent role for ageing individuals is often framed by discussion about role occupancy and well-being in later life or debate about levels of activity and adjustment to old age (Adelmann, 1994). The role strain hypothesis (e.g., Goode, 1960; Merton, 1957) predicts that occupying many roles has negative consequences for psychological well-being. Grandparents might suffer from incompatible demands between their roles or overload by cumulative role obligations (e.g., being employed and taking care of grandchildren). The role enhancement hypothesis (e.g., Marks, 1977; Sieber, 1974), in contrast, predicts that multiple roles may promote well-being.

In a similar vein, there is a debate about the relationship between the level of activity and adaptation to old age. Disengagement theory (e.g., Cumming & Henry, 1961) predicts an abandoning of roles and reduced interaction by older individuals which is functional and welcome. Activity theory (e.g., Hochschild, 1975), on the other hand, predicts that continued activity is central to well-being and optimal adjustment. In this sense, grandchildren may offer developmental tasks that help grandparents not only to stay active, but also to cope with the process of ageing. Likewise, Baltes and Baltes (1990) state that older people have competencies, remain active agents of their lives, and provide resources. According to Rosow (1976), later life provides only tenuous roles which are vague and have only a few or no normative elements. As tenuous roles do not offer the same social benefits as institutional roles, it could be that, contradictory to activity theory and the role enhancement hypothesis, multiple roles in later life have no effect on well-being.

Meanwhile, according to the model of intergenerational solidarity, intergenerational relations can be described by means of six components, all of them characterized as specific forms of solidarity between family members (Bengtson & Roberts, 1991): (1) *affectual solidarity*: feelings toward and relations with other family members; (2) *associational solidarity*: type and frequency of interaction between generations; (3) *consensual solidarity*: the degree of agreement on opinions, values, and orientations; (4) *functional solidarity*: donation, reception, and exchange of help and support; (5) *normative solidarity*: commitment to familistic values and obligations; and (6) *structural solidarity*: opportunity structures for intergenerational relations such as number, gender, and geographical proximity of family members.

One major criticism of this model addresses its focus on successful family relationships and its incapacity to describe relationships that are not based on geographical and emotional closeness or mutual support. The term "solidarity" itself has been questioned (e.g., by Lowenstein, 2007), as follows: do problematic intergenerational relations imply the absence of solidarity? Negative, conflictual, and weakening ("non-affirming") aspects of intergenerational relations were hence later subsumed under the term "intergenerational conflict" (Clarke, Preston, Raksin, & Bengston, 1999). However, these aspects remain conceptually as well as empirically disconnected from the model of intergenerational solidarity. In addition, partly as a reaction to shortcomings of the solidarity model, the concept of "intergenerational ambivalence" (Lüscher & Pillemer, 1998) was developed.

The model of intergenerational solidarity was originally developed to under-stand relationships between older parents and adult children, but is supposed to be equally suited for the study of relationships between non-adjacent fam-ily generations. However, it is an open question as to whether or not the rela-tionships between grandparents and grandchildren can be characterized by the same dimensions of solidarity and conflict. For example, mutual instrumental support ("functional solidarity"), a major concern of parent–child relations in later life, is much less existent in grandparent–grandchild relations (Mahne & Motel-Klingebiel, 2010). Most importantly, relationships between grandparents and their grandchildren cannot be adequately described, analysed, or understood without conceptualizing the role of the middle generation. The concept of the "multi-local, multigenerational family" (Bertram, 2002) encourages research on non-adjacent family generations and a three-generation perspective. One aspect of a three-generation perspective that has been the main focus of discussion in the literature so far is the idea of "bridges" (Hagestad, 2006). Children in the middle generation have a bridging function, in that they act as gatekeepers or facilitators for the relationships between grandparents and grandchildren.

None of the preceding theories have been especially developed to conceptualize grandparenthood or to describe grandparents' situation in Germany. However, they reflect relevant aspects of grandparenthood that exist in Germany just like as in other Western countries or regions. Theoretical advancement in consideration of grandpar-enthood in Germany (and other Western countries) will need to address the question as to whether grandparent–grandchild relationships are characterized by the same dimensions as parent–child relationships or if other conceptualizations are needed. It remains unclear, so far, whether and in which aspects the grandparent role actually differs from the parent role. Grandparents continue to provide family functions, they appear as "emeritus parents" (Gutmann, 1987, p. 234) as, for instance, the provision of grandparental childcare takes the form of support for their children.

Moreover, a distinction between the different conceptual levels for the study of grandparenthood is crucial (Szinovacz, 1998b). Societal, family, dyadic, and indi-vidual characteristics need to be discussed as relevant contextual factors medi-ating the grandparent experience. As can be seen in the next section (review of research), the grandparent experience in Germany varies according to gender, age, cohort, partnership status, family structure, lifestyle, educational attainment, region, etc. However, theoretical notions to provide a framework for analyses on these different (conceptual) levels are lacking by and large.

Sociological research on grandparenthood is thematically narrow and focuses on the enactment of the grandparent role, such as contact frequency between grandparents and grandchildren, or grandparental childcare. Moreover, it is typi-cally conducted under the paradigm of "intergenerational solidarity" (Bengtson & Roberts, 1991; see above). This fosters an overly positive view of grandparenthood. Linkages and interrelations between the different dimensions of grandparenting (i.e., interdependencies between role importance, role enactment, and role out-comes) are needed to gain a holistic understanding of the grandparent role.

Review of Research on Grandparenthood in Germany

Research on grandparenthood in Germany is relatively sparse compared to the US and compared to research on parent–child relations in Germany. During the 1980s a series of unpublished master's theses was carried out (see Sticker, 1987, 1991, for a summary) that were based on small, non-representative samples using semi-structured explorative interviews. At least a decade later, a multi-themed study on grandparenthood was conducted (Herlyn & Lehmann, 1998). Although representative nationwide it sampled grandmothers only. Since then, research on grandparenthood in Germany has focused almost exclusively on grandparental childcare (e.g., Hank & Buber, 2009). The lack of research on grandparenthood is partly due to a lack of large-scale data sources. Since 2008, the German Ageing Survey (DEAS – Klaus et al., 2017) has provided information on several aspects of grandparenthood, such as age at transition to grandparenthood, subjective importance of the grandparent role, contact frequency, emotional closeness, conflict with grandchildren, and involvement in childcare. Being representative of the community dwelling population aged 40–85 in Germany, the DEAS provides a unique data source for analyses on grandparenthood. Information in DEAS is collected for Germans and non-German citizens residing in Germany. However, the participants are interviewed exclusively in German.

The grandparental role comprises several dimensions that need to be addressed in order to fully understand grandparenthood. Szinovacz (1998b) identifies this multidimensionality as a challenge for research on grandparenthood and postulates more attention being given to possible linkages between these different dimensions. The following literature review is therefore structured along different aspects of grandparenthood: role meaning, role enactment, and role outcomes.

Role Meaning

Generally speaking, little is known in Western countries about attitudinal and symbolic aspects of the grandparent role. However, the grandparent role is one of the few novel roles that can be adopted in later life and therefore provides potential for adult socialization processes. In fact, becoming a grandparent has a taken-for-granted nature for most parents in Germany and is expected to happen as a part of the way things are (representative for grandmothers in Germany: Herlyn & Lehmann, 1998). The majority of family members perceive grandchildren as important for grandparents (Sticker, 2008). Grandchildren provide grandparents with a feeling of being needed, of staying young, and of living on in the grandchildren's generation. Grandparents, in contrast to parents, can have "the joy without the burden" (Sticker, 2008, p. 35) when they interact with grandchildren. Although the enactment of grandparenthood was found to be quite varied, its importance was rated very high among German grandmothers during the 1990s (Herlyn & Lehmann, 1998). Most recent findings show that the subjective importance of the grandparent role is high and stable over a period of six years (based on DEAS: Mahne & Klaus, 2017). For the majority of grandparents, their role as a grandmother or grandfather is important. While only a small minority describes the grandparental role as completely unimportant, more than half of all grandparents (about 56%) describe grandparenthood as very important and about one-third (36%) say it is important to them. Even for about two-thirds of parents (60%) that do not yet have grandchildren, becoming a grandparent in the future is very important (Mahne & Klaus, 2017). This indicates that in Germany, the grandparent role is central to grandparents' and parents' lives.

Moreover, the grandparent role is of high importance regardless of grandparents' social class; neither the level of education, nor household income, nor occupational prestige is associated with the importance of the grandparent role for grandparents (Mahne & Motel-Klingebiel, 2012). This is a contrast, for example, with the significance of socioeconomic status for grandparenting in Brazil (see Chapter 4) and in the US, where higher social classes generally attach more meaning to social roles outside of the family (e.g., employee) and therefore do not rate grandparenthood as central (James, Witte, & Galbraith, 2006; Silverstein & Marenco, 2001). As found elsewhere, gender differences exist; grandfathers in Germany perceive their role as less important than grandmothers (based on DEAS: Mahne & Motel-Klingebiel, 2012). Grandparenthood is of equal importance to grandparents in West and East Germany. Employed grandparents and those who are retired or not working rate grandparenthood as equally important. Time restrictions due to employment are not obviously related to variation in grandparent role importance but grandparents with health problems are associated with lower levels of grandparent role importance (Mahne & Motel-Klingebiel, 2012). Altogether, social class indicators and socio-demographics of the grandparents explain very little variance in the importance of grandparenthood (see also: Herlyn & Lehmann, 1998), but characteristics of the relationships with grandchildren do (Herlyn & Lehmann, 1998; based on DEAS: Mahne & Motel-Klingebiel, 2012). That is, the more grandchildren a grandparent has, the more importance he or she attaches to the grandparent role. More involved grandparents evaluate their role as more important, whereas low contact frequency is associated with moderate importance. The stronger the emotional ties between the generations, the higher the perceived importance of the grandparent role.

For grandmothers in Germany it was found that they attach meaning to their grandparent role in accordance with their general lifestyle, which has changed somewhat across cohorts (Herlyn & Lehmann, 1998). For family-orientated women that lived a life mainly as a homemaker, being a grandmother is a very central and unquestioned part of later life. This may apply to Helga, the grandmother in our case story. Today, older grandmothers like her emphasize the transmission of tradition and family values. In contrast, work-orientated women do not see grandparenthood as central to their identity. They prefer independent and individual relationships with grandchildren and do not want to be labelled a "granny". These grandmothers are younger. In between, dual-orientation grandmothers value both family and worker roles, and they understand their grandparenting behaviour as some kind of voluntary engagement that provides a new twist to later life.

Role Enactment

A central concern of empirical sociological research on grandparenthood is the enactment of the grandparent role, and its correlates (e.g., Timonen & Arber, 2012). Studies generally witness a diversity of grandparenting styles, sometimes illustrated by typologies (e.g., Neugarten & Weinstein, 1964). The function that grandparents have for grandchildren and "grandparenting styles" is said to vary with the age of the grandchild (Sticker, 1991); the fun-seeking style dominates among grandparents with toddlers as well as with grandchildren up to 12 years. Grandparents as a reservoir of family wisdom are common among elementary school children and grandchildren up to 12 years. Among grandparents with young adult grandchildren, a more formal and distant style is also present.

As to contact frequency, recent findings for Germany suggest that about one-third (29%) of all grandparents have at least weekly contact with their adult grandchildren. Another third (about 29%) have contact at least once a month and the remaining 42% report contact less frequently than monthly (based on DEAS: Mahne & Klaus, 2017). Contact frequency between grandparents and grandchildren decreases with the age of both grandparents and grandchildren (based on DEAS: Mahne & Huxhold, 2012; Sticker, 1991). For grandchildren in their adolescence and adulthood, contact rates do not vary according to gender, neither their own nor their grandparent's (based on DEAS: Mahne & Huxhold, 2012).

Just as described for the US (see Chapter 3), German grandparents interact less often with grandchildren who live further away (Sticker, 1991), and contact frequency is considerably lower for grandparents who are divorced or separated (based on DEAS: Mahne & Huxhold, 2012). In addition, grandparents actively taking part in the labour force have less contact than grandparents who do not work. Competing roles and time restrictions associated with employment affect grandparent–grandchild contact. Grandparents interact more often with grandchildren who are biological children, as also illustrated in our case story: Grandmother Helga meets her step-grandson very seldom. This is, however, mediated by emotional closeness, as close emotional bonds may buffer against less contact with step-grandchildren. Being an only child does not affect the frequency of contact (Mahne & Huxhold, 2012). In light of the growing numbers of step-families and the shrinking numbers of siblings in Germany, this is good news. As contact frequency is higher among grandparents who derive greater meaning from grandparenthood (Mahne & Huxhold, 2012), possible linkages between the different dimensions of grandparent–grandchild relations are indicated as suggested by Szinovacz (1998b), and thus the need to examine the dynamic interplay of grandparents' values and behaviour over time is emphasized.

Although necessary, few studies so far have simultaneously considered the specific impact of grandparents, adult children, and grandchildren on the relationships between grandparents and grandchildren. Such analyses indicate 35% of the variation in grandparent–grandchild contact is attributable to the family level i.e., characteristics of the grandparent (based on DEAS: Mahne & Huxhold, 2012). The larger part of the variation (65%), however, is explained by the different individual relationships with grandchildren that a grandparent experiences (i.e., at the individual level) (Mahne & Huxhold, 2012). In line with the literature on the bridging or gate-keeping influence of the middle generation, the less close bonds that exist between parents and sons influence grandparents' relationships with their grandchildren; grandparents interact less often with the offspring of their son (Mahne & Huxhold, 2012). As seen in our case story, Grandmother Helga has the strongest relationship with her daughter's son Stefan. Not only is the gender of the middle generation associated with grandparent–grandchild contact, but it is also related to the contact rate between the grandparent and the middle generation (Mahne & Huxhold, 2012). According to one-third of grandparents, the middle generation is an important agent for the grandparent–grandchild relationship and grandparents may act as a "safe haven in times of crisis" (Sticker, 2008, p. 36), for example, when parents break up. This, however, may only apply to daughters because a son's experience of marital or union dissolution results in lower contact rates between his parents and children (based on DEAS: Mahne & Huxhold, 2012). Having a harmonious relationship with their own children is important to grandmothers and implies a norm of "non-interference" especially concerning issues of child-rearing (Herlyn & Lehmann, 1998).

Despite an adequate supply of social welfare benefits and services, intergenerational relationships are characterized by frequent exchange of mutual support. This also includes the grandparent–grandchild relationship although to a lesser extent. Within Europe, monetary transfers provided to grandchildren are highest in Germany (Igel, 2012). According to recent findings from the DEAS, it is most prevalent among the elderly: More than one-fourth (28%) of grandparents aged 70–85 provide regular financial support, money, or major gift items to their grandchildren. In the opposite direction, however, only around 3% of them receive help with housework from their grandchildren (Klaus & Mahne, 2017). This suggests a support pattern that favours the young generation.

In the US there is a discussion about grandparents as "child savers" (e.g., Goodman & Silverstein, 2006; Herlofson & Hagestad, 2012). These are grandparents who take over custodial care for grandchildren, a phenomenon virtually non-existent in Germany. However, the European discussion of the family function of grandparents ranges between their role as "mother savers" and their role of "family savers" (Herlofson & Hagestad, 2012). In Southern Europe, a lower percentage of grandparents is engaged in childcare, but if childcare is provided, it is often full time (e.g., Igel & Szydlik, 2011). In this way, grandparents, or more explicitly grandmothers, compensate for the lack of public childcare. They act as "mother savers" as they enable their daughters to engage in employment. In contrast, in the Nordic welfare states, a higher percentage of grandparents is engaged in childcare, but intensity is low (Igel & Szydlik, 2011). They act as family savers or as a "reserve army" (e.g., Hagestad, 1985) and back up family life in times of need. Germany ranges in between the preceding examples. Besides public childcare institutions and childcare by parents (mainly the mothers) they are the most important providers of childcare, especially for children under the age of 3. While the proportion of grandparents providing some form of childcare dropped from about one-third to one-quarter between 1996 and 2008 (based on DEAS: Mahne & Motel-Klingebiel, 2010), currently, German grandparents are more involved again: about 30% look after their grandchildren (based on DEAS: Mahne & Klaus, 2017). Whereas the earlier drop in grandchild care might be a consequence of improved public childcare, the recent rise may indicate that mothers' shares of employment or working hours are rising faster than the supply of public childcare. Grandmothers are found to be more involved in grandchild care than grandfathers, and it is also the grandmothers who combine paid work and childcare (Mahne & Klaus, 2017). Probably very characteristic for Germany is the emergence of services to "rent a granny". Such services act as an agent between parents of small children and older persons that would like to take over responsibilities similar to a grandparent. It could be that the actual grandparents are dead or the family lives far away so that (grand)parents make use of such services.

Role Outcomes

Studies on subjective outcomes of grandparenthood such as subjective well-being are uncommon in Germany. They often deal with co-parenting or custodial grandparents (Erbert & Alemán, 2008; Smith, Palmieri, & Hancock, 2008), a social phenomenon that is important in the US, but non-existent in Germany where teenage pregnancies are very rare. In Germany, satisfaction with the grandparental role is high, especially among grandparents with younger grandchildren (Sticker, 1987). Role satisfaction seems to be associated with grandparents' general attitudes toward social interaction and grandchildren, with the middle generation's behaviour, and with individual images of ageing (Sticker, 1991). Grandparents' subjective well-being is related to relationship quality with grandchildren, independently from relationship quality with children. The higher the relationship quality, the higher the grandparents' life satisfaction and positive affect, and the lower the negative affect and loneliness (based on DEAS: Mahne & Huxhold, 2015). But not all grandparents profit from good relationship quality with grandchildren in the same way; only highly educated grandparents enjoy lower negative affect and less loneliness due to a high relationship quality with grandchildren (Mahne & Huxhold, 2015). This finding may indicate that education buffers negative experiences around grandparenthood in the sense that higher educated grandparents have more resources to cope with stressful aspects of the grandparent–grandchild relationship. For example, grandparents from higher social classes are able to spend money on holidays, leisure activities, or on private tutoring for school children. In the case that problems occur they may be more flexible dealing with them. Generally speaking, in families from higher social classes the generations are more independent from each other. In lower social classes, family members are more dependent on each other, for example financially, a situation that may cause problems.

Grandfathers in Germany

While research explicitly on grandfathers exists for example in the UK (e.g., Mann, Tarrant, & Leeson, 2016), research on grandparents in Germany has not yet explicitly addressed the specific situation of grandfathers. The first studies on grandparenthood in Germany were based on grandmothers only, and nowadays most studies deal with both grandmothers and grandfathers. The fact that research on grandparenthood was focused on grandmothers illustrates the social reality that family issues in Germany are still gendered. For a long time, it was seen as women's duty only to care for younger and older family members, and they are still considered the kinkeepers. In fact, grandfathers rate their role as a grandfather as less important than grandmothers, they feel less emotionally close with children and grandchildren, they report lower contact frequency with young grandchildren, and they provide childcare for young grandchildren less often (see preceding literature review).

FIGURE 5.2 A grandfather (62) reads a book to his grandchildren (ages 4 and 6) while they spend the weekend at the grandparents' home. While taking care of grandchildren is common in Germany, it is still gendered with grandmothers more involved. This grandfather can therefore be called a "new grandfather".

Source: Courtesy of DZA Photo Collection – Peter Zeman.

However, grandfathers in Germany recently have received more and more media attention, and "the new grandfather" is a catchphrase that is often used to portray contemporary grandfathers. They are now described as caring family members who support their children by taking care of the grandchildren. In earlier times, grandfathers were more likely to be labelled as rigid family patriarchs or grumpy old men. By spending leisure time with grandchildren they may now enact a role they had been missing as fathers. However, keeping in mind the latest research findings, the "new grandfather" seems to be more of a media phenomenon than a reality. Magazines have a tendency to make a good story, irrespective of its empirical foundation. The same phenomenon exists for grandmothers: for example, the "grandmother revolution" (see www.grossmuetter.ch) exists as a Swiss initiative that addresses the problem that some grandmothers no longer want to follow the traditional grandmother role. Although there surely are real grandfathers and grandmothers that do not want to act out traditional roles, gender roles and differences are very persistent in Germany and over the last decade not that much has changed concerning the enactment or quality of grandparent–grandchild relationships.

(Sub)Cultural Variations of Grandparenthood in Germany

As explicated earlier in this chapter, one characteristic of German society is its relatively large and growing proportion of migrant people and their descendants. Individuals who were socialized in another cultural environment contribute to the variety of grandparent experiences in Germany today. For example, the large group of labour migrants from Turkey originates from a region where the patrilineal descent kinship regime is predominant, which is fundamentally different from the traditional European pattern (Nauck & Klaus, 2005). It is characterized by a clear status differentiation according to age and gender, with the male patriarch as ultimate authority of the family, and intergenerational relationships are superior to spousal relationships. Obligations and expectations of mutual solidarity are strong along the lineage. Although less pronounced, the descent kinship regime also prevails in Eastern Europe, where numerous immigrants to Germany stem from (i.e., former Soviet Union, former Yugoslavia, and Romania; Hajnal, 1965), resulting in a greater strength of intergenerational obligations than in Western Europe (Daatland, Herlofson, & Lima, 2011). Labour migrants from Mediterranean countries like Greece, Italy, and Portugal come from a European region where family ties and intergenerational obligations are persistently much stronger than in north and central Europe (including Germany), but weaker than in West Asian countries like Turkey with their "strict allegiances and corporatism generated within enlarged family lineages and clans" (Reher, 1998, p. 215). Altogether, this may imply that the majority of immigrants to Germany may attach much greater importance to grandparenthood and grandparent–grandchild relationships than non-migrant families in Germany.

It is not only the cultural and socioeconomic background prevailing in the country of origin, but also the conditions of migration and characteristics of the country of immigration that affect family-related norms, expectations, and patterns. With respect to family ties and migration two opposing hypotheses are discussed, and pose different mechanisms (Baykara-Krumme, 2008b). On the one hand, solidarity between the generations may be higher in migrant than non-migrant families because of the familistic background of the majority of migrants and an increase of familial cohesion in order to cope with the challenge of migration (solidarity hypothesis). From another point of view, the potential for disagreements may be higher in migrant families as a result of unequal acculturation of the generations. Children and grandchildren of immigrants who were born in Germany may be less willing to respond to the traditional expectations of elderly family members, provoking intergenerational conflict and even detachment (conflict hypothesis).

While there are some studies on the family relations of migrants in Germany, empirical research on grandparent–grandchild relationships in particular is virtually absent. However, there is somewhat more evidence for the solidarity hypothesis. Studies indicate higher rates of co-residence in later life among migrant families, more frequent contact, and patterns of mutual intergenerational support similar to non-migrants with slightly higher rates of upward financial support (e.g., Baykara-Krumme, 2008a; Steinbach, 2013; Vogel & Sommer, 2013).

Most migrant research is dedicated to the large group of labour migrants from Turkey. In Turkish migrant families, a more intense intergenerational transmission of core cultural values such as relatedness is found compared to non-migrant families in Turkey (Nauck, 2001). The norm of filial obligation is not only high in the first generation of Turkish migrants but also in the second generation (Carnein & Baykara-Krumme, 2013). Compared to German natives, kin relationships including relationships to grandparents are very important for adolescents of Turkish origin (Nauck & Kohlmann, 1999) and not only grandmothers but also grandfathers of Turkish origin are involved to a greater extent in grandchild care than are German grandparents (Hubert, Althammer, & Korucu-Rieger, 2009, p. 55). Greater importance attached to grandparenthood among migrants is also suggested by the authors' calculations, based on DEAS 2008 and 2014 data. Controlling for group-specific demographics, the share of grandparenthood among those who are aged 40 to 85 is higher for labour migrants (60%) and ethnic German repatriates (62%) than for non-migrant Germans of the same age (50%), and migrants value the role of grandparent more than their non-migrant German counterparts. However, the rates of childcare provided by grandparents are nearly equal for labour migrants (28%), ethnic German repatriates (26%), and non-migrant Germans (25%).

Recent findings emphasize the importance of differentiating between distinct groups of migrants since patterns of intergenerational relationships are found to be very heterogeneous. Whereas migrants from the European Union resemble non-migrants, labour migrants and migrants from non-European and non-Western countries are most differentiated from non-migrants (Based on DEAS: Klaus & Baykara-Krumme, 2017). The findings also give rise to speculation that patterns of grandparenthood and grandparent–grandchild relationships may converge across the groups because relationships in the second generation of migrants are similar to those among non-migrants of the same age (Based on DEAS: Klaus & Baykara-Krumme, 2017). Cultural norms and customs may adapt to the prevailing social structure in Germany in the long run.

Social Policy Issues

As mentioned earlier in our discussion of the welfare state, welfare state regulations addressing the grandparent–grandchild relationship are nearly absent in Germany. Likewise, social policy in Germany does not directly address issues relating to grandparents. Sometimes social policy regulations implicitly or explicitly affect grandparents. Recent policy reforms aiming to make it easier for gainfully employed family members to combine work and care for children or frail kin added some entitlements to grandparents and grandchildren. But working grandparents do not have the same right to take grandparental leave or reduce work hours and get some state-financed earnings substitution as parents have when caring for the children. Only if grandparents have custody for a grandchild – which is extremely rare in Germany – are they entitled to the social provisions usually given to parents.

Another policy concerns keeping contact with grandchildren when conflictual relationships exist between grandparents and the parents of a grandchild or in the case of divorce in the middle generation; laws pertaining to this issue are shown in this book to differ country-to-country. Grandparents in Germany have the right to maintain contact with their grandchildren as long as this seems to be in the best interests of the child. Grandparents may ask the youth welfare office for help or even go to court. But few grandparents take these opportunities, and departments and courts are reluctant to enforce grandparental contact with a grandchild against the will of parents. As a growing number of divorcing couples accept joint custody and minor children keep contact with both parents, increasingly as members of multilocal families (Schier, 2015), there might be a decreasing risk of hindered grandparental contact following parental divorce.

Speculation About the Future of Grandparenthood in Germany

In Germany, being a grandparent is a common experience in the second half of life. However, future cohorts of parents are probably less likely to experience grandparenthood due to the rising incidence of childlessness in Germany. In light of the very highly subjective importance of the grandparent role, even among parents who do not yet have grandchildren, wishes and plans for later family life and its reality may diverge for a growing share of older people in Germany.

On the other hand, grandparenthood in Germany today is characterized by increasingly overlapping life spans between grandparents and grandchildren. This means that in the future it will be a common situation for many grandparents that they interact with adult grandchildren. It may well be that future grandchildren take over responsibilities like household chores or care for their grandparents to a greater degree, just like children typically do for their ageing parents today. Likewise, in the future more and more grandparents may take over parental responsibilities, especially concerning financial issues such as paying for the university education of their grandchildren. In addition, great-grandparenthood will be even more common in future cohorts. It could be that relationships with great-grandchildren become more like relationships with grandchildren, while those with grandchildren become more similar to those with children.

No one today may foresee how the current major wave of immigration of refugees will alter the German society in general and family life in particular. Parents who come to Germany from all over the world will become grandparents in the future, merging the traditions of their countries of origin and their experiences in Germany into something new. However, for many young refugees coming to Germany, lineage is broken, either because they have left their parents and grandparents in their home countries and have to manage their family relationships over an immense distance or because their family has died in war or terror. We certainly may anticipate that the experience of grandparenthood in Germany will become more culturally diverse.

Summary

In Germany, to be a grandparent is a common experience in the second half of life and most grandparents live to see their grandchildren as adults. Most grandparents and grandchildren are in frequent contact and grandparents describe their relationships as close. Intergenerational obligation is low and only few normative expectations exist concerning grandparents and grandchildren. Grandparents actively take part in childcare and more and more grandparents support their older grandchildren financially. It is also important to consider the middle generation because relationship quality between older parents and adult children is important for the grandparent–grandchild connection. Further, disruptive life events such as divorce in the middle generation affects the multigenerational family system. Lineage is important in this respect. Although gender roles are weakening in Germany, at least in more recent cohorts, it is the female family members that serve as the kin-keepers, which has consequences in the event of divorce or family breakup. Grandparenthood in Germany is varied, not only between families from different cohort, social, and cultural backgrounds, but also within families. The variety of different grandparenting experiences in Germany will probably increase into the future.

Appendix

Meaning of Proverbs

> "Not until you become a grandparent can you begin to understand your children."

This proverb may relate to the fact that relations between family generations in Germany are always relations between societal generations as well, with different socialization backgrounds. A second interpretation is that parents can more easily understand their children as soon as they see them in their role as a parent, because they have had the same experience.

> "For children, grandparents are like holidays from the parents."

This proverb relates to the fact that in Germany norms and obligations concerning the grandparent-grandchild relationship are looser than those for parent-child relations ("having the joy without the burden").

Additional Resources

www.grosseltern.de/
　The website contains a wealth of information, advice and hints to grandparents, and provides a platform to communicate on grandparent-related topics (in German only).

www.grosselterninitiative.de/
　An initiative by grandparents advocating the right to stay in contact with their grandchildren after a divorce in the middle generation, or after other family conflicts (in German only).

www.demografie-portal.de/
　A platform created by Germany's federal government for discussing policies on demography. The Portal of Demography provides facts about the ageing population and informs about local projects on demography. The Berlin based project where elderly step in as extra-grandparents on the request of single parents is one example (in German only).

Discussion Questions

1. Cleavages between the Lutheran Protestant North and the Roman Catholic South, and the divide between a Federal Democratic Republic in the West and a socialist German Democratic Republic in the East, have contributed to the heterogeneity of today's Germany. Do these cleavages affect grandparenthood in Germany today? If so, how?

2. Welfare state regulations relevant to grandparent–grandchild relationship are nearly absent in Germany. At the same time, a nationwide organization of grandparents advocates the right to stay in contact with their grandchildren after a divorce in the middle generation. Should the grandparent–grandchild relationship be regulated more than it is today? If so, in which areas?

3. Grandfathers in Germany perceive their role as less important than grandmothers, and they provide childcare for young grandchildren less often. In what ways could more involved grandfathers contribute to changes in the division of labour in the intergenerational family? How can grandfathers be motivated to take on more family responsibility?

References

Adelmann, P. K. (1994). Multiple roles and psychological well-being in a national sample of older adults. *Journals of Gerontology, 49*(6), 277–285. doi:10.1093/geronj/49.6.S277

Baltes, P. B., & Baltes, M. M. (Eds.). (1990). *Successful aging: Perspectives from the behavioral sciences.* New York: Cambridge University Press.

Baykara-Krumme, H. (2008a). Reliable bonds? A comparative perspective of intergenerational support patterns among migrant families in Germany. In C. Saraceno (Ed.), *Families, ageing and social policy: Intergenerational solidarity in European welfare states,* (pp. 285–311). Cheltenham, UK: Edward Elgar.

Baykara-Krumme, H. (2008b). *Migrant families in Germany: Intergenerational solidarity in later life.* Berlin: Weißensee Verlag.

Bengtson, V. L., & Roberts, E. L. (1991). Intergenerational solidarity in aging families: An example of formal theory construction. *Journal of Marriage and Family, 53*(4), 856–870. doi:10.2307/352993

Bengtson, V. L., Rosenthal, C. J., & Burton, L. M. (1990). Families and aging: Diversity and heterogeneity. In R. Binstock & L. George (Eds.), *Handbook of aging and the social sciences* (3rd ed., pp. 263–287). New York: Academic Press.

Bertram, H. (2002). The multi-local, multi-generational family: From neo-local and husband-centered to multi-local and multigenerational family. *Berliner Journal für Soziologie, 12*(4), 517–529.

Carnein, M., & Baykara-Krumme, H. (2013). Attitudes towards family solidarity in later life: A comparative analysis between Turks and Germans. *Zeitschrift für Familienforschung, 25*(1), 29–52.

Clarke, E. J., Preston, M., Raksin, J., & Bengston, V. L. (1999). Types of conflicts and tensions between older parents and adult children. *The Gerontologist, 39*(3), 261–270. doi:10.1093/geront/39.3.261

Cumming, E., & Henry, W. E. (1961). *Growing old: The process of disengagement.* New York: Basic Books.

Daatland, S. O., Herlofson, K., & Lima, I. A. (2011). Balancing generations: On the strength and character of family norms in the West and East of Europe. *Ageing and Society, 31*(7), 1159–1179.

Durkheim, E. (1921). La famille conjugale: Conclusion du cours sur la famille. *Revue philosophique, 90*, 1–14.

Engstler, H., & Menning, S. (2005). The transition to grandparenthood: Cohort-specific trends in prevalence, age, and duration of grandparenthood in Germany. *Mitteilungen der Deutschen Gesellschaft für Demographie, 4*(8), 7.

Erbert, L. A., & Alemán, M. W. (2008). Taking the grand out of grandparent: Dialectical tensions in grandparent perceptions of surrogate parenting. *Journal of Social and Personal Relationships, 25*(4), 671–695. doi:10.1177/0265407508093785

Esping-Andersen, G. (1990). *The three worlds of welfare capitalism.* Princeton, NJ: Princeton University Press.

European Commission. (2013). *EU Employment and Social Situation Quarterly Review March 2013* – Special Supplement on Demographic Trends. Luxembourg: Publications Office of the EU.

Federal Ministry for Family Affairs Senior Citizens Women and Youth. (2015). *Family report 2014: Benefits, effects, trends.* Berlin: BMFSFJ.

Federal Statistical Office of Germany (2011). Couples marry later. *Zahl der Woche.* Retrieved from www.destatis.de/DE/PresseService/Presse/Pressemitteilungen/zdw/2011/PD11_030_p002.html

Federal Statistical Office of Germany (2013). *Trends in births and family situation in Germany.* Wiesbaden, Germany: Statistisches Bundesamt.

Federal Statistical Office of Germany (2014). *On the way to gender equality?* Wiesbaden, Germany: Statistisches Bundesamt.

Federal Statistical Office of Germany (2015a). *Life expectancy for boys almost 78 years, for girls about 83 years.* Press release no. 143. Retrieved from www.destatis.de/DE/PresseService/Presse/Pressemitteilungen/2015/04/PD15_143_12621.html

Federal Statistical Office of Germany (2015b). *Statistic of court decisions concerning dissolutions of marriages 2014.* Wiesbaden, Germany: Statistisches Bundesamt.

Federal Statistical Office of Germany (2016a). Population in Germany by age group (1974–2014), own calculations based on GENESIS online database.

Federal Statistical Office of Germany (2016b). *There are 209,000 households with three or more generations.* Press release no. 263. Wiesbaden: Statistisches Bundesamt. Retrieved from www.destatis.de/DE/PresseService/Presse/Pressemitteilungen/2016/07/PD16_263_122.html

Federal Statistical Office of Germany (2016c). *Natural demographic development 2013.* Wiesbaden: Statistisches Bundesamt.

Federal Statistical Office of Germany (2016d, July 15). *Decreasing number of divorces in 2015 by 1.7 percent.* Press release no. 249. Retrieved from www.destatis.de/DE/PresseService/Presse/Pressemitteilungen/2016/07/PD16_249_12631.html

Federal Statistical Office of Germany (2016e). *Daycare – regional results 2015.* Wiesbaden: Statistisches Bundesamt.

Ferrera, M. (1996). The "Southern model" of welfare in social Europe. *Journal of European Social Policy, 6*(1), 17.

Frejka, T., & Sobotka, T. (2008). Fertility in Europe: Diverse, delayed and below replacement. *Demographic Research, 19*(3), 15–46.

Goode, W. (1960). A theory of role strain. *American Sociological Review, 25,* 483–496.

Goodman, C. C., & Silverstein, M. (2006). Grandmothers raising grandchildren: Ethnic and racial differences in well-being among custodial and coparenting families. *Journal of Family Issues, 27*(11), 1605–1626. doi:10.1177/0192513X06291435

Grünheid, E., & Scharein, M. G. (2011). On developments in the mean joint lifetime of three- and four-generation families in Western and Eastern Germany: A model calculation. *Comparative Population Studies, 36*(1). doi:10.4232/10.CPoS-2011-01en

Gutmann, D. (1987). *Reclaimed powers: Towards a new psychology of men and women in late life.* New York: Basic Books.

Hagestad, G. O. (1985). Continuity and connectedness. In V. L. Bengtson & J. F. Robertson (Eds.), *Grandparenthood* (pp. 31–48). Beverly Hills: Sage.

Hagestad, G. O. (2006). Transfers between grandparents and grandchildren: The importance of taking a three-generation perspective. *Zeitschrift für Familienforschung, 18*(3), 315–332.

Hajnal, J. (1965). European marriage patterns in perspective. In J. Hajnal, D. V. Glass & D. E. C. Eversley (Eds.), *Population in history* (pp. 101–143). London: Edward Arnold.

Hank, K., & Buber, I. (2009). Grandparents caring for their grandchildren: Findings from the 2004 Survey of Health, Ageing, and Retirement in Europe. *Journal of Family Issues, 30*(1), 53–73.

Herlofson, K., & Hagestad, G. O. (2012). Transformations in the role of grandparents across welfare states. In S. Arber & V. Timonen (Eds.), *Contemporary grandparenting: Changing family relationships in global contexts* (pp. 27–50). Bristol, UK: Policy Press.

Herlyn, I., & Lehmann, B. (1998). Grandmotherhood in a multigenerational context: An empirical study from the perspective of grandmothers. *Zeitschrift für Familienforschung, 10*(1), 27–45.

Hochschild, A. (1975). Disengagement theory: A critique and proposal. *American Sociological Review, 40*, 553–569.

Hubert, S., Althammer, J., & Korucu-Rieger, C. (2009). *Socio-demographic characteristics and psycho-physical condition of older Turkish migrants in Germany.* Schriftenreihe des Bundesinstituts für Bevölkerungsforschung, 39. Retrieved from www.bib-demografie. de/EN/Publications/BZB/archive.html?nn=3197368

Human Fertility Database. (2016). Max Planck Institute for Demographic Research (Germany) and Vienna Institute of Demography (Austria). Retrieved from www.humanfertility.org

Igel, C. (2012). *Grandparents in Europe: Intergenerational solidarity in the welfare state.* Wiesbaden: Springer.

Igel, C., & Szydlik, M. (2011). Grandchild care and welfare state arrangements in Europe. *European Journal of Social Policy, 21*(3), 210–224.

James, W. B., Witte, J. E., & Galbraith, M. W. (2006). Havighurst's social roles revisited. *Journal of Adult Development, 13*(1), 52–60.

Kalmijn, M., & Saraceno, C. (2008). A comparative perspective on intergenerational support. Responsiveness to parental needs in individualistic and familialistic countries. *European Societies, 10*(3), 479–508.

Klaus, D., & Baykara-Krumme, H. (2017). The living situation of persons with and without migrational background in the second half of life. In K. Mahne, J. K. Wolff, J. Simonson, & C. Tesch-Römer (Eds.), *Altern im Wandel: Zwei Jahrzehnte Deutscher Alterssurvey* (pp. 359–379). Wiesbaden: Springer.

Klaus, D., Engstler, H., Mahne, K., Wolff, J. K., Simonson, J., Wurm, S., & Tesch-Romer, C. (2017). Cohort profile: The German Ageing Survey (DEAS). *International Journal of Epidemiology.* doi:10.1093/ije/dyw326

Klaus, D., & Mahne, K. (2017). Time for money? The exchange of support between the generations. In K. Mahne, J. K. Wolff, J. Simonson, & C. Tesch-Römer (Eds.), *Altern im Wandel: Zwei Jahrzehnte Deutscher Alterssurvey* (pp. 247–256). Wiesbaden: Springer.

Klein, T., & Nauck, B. (2005). Families in Germany. In B. Adams & J. Trost (Eds.), *Handbook of world families* (pp. 283–312). Thousand Oaks: Sage.

Lauterbach, W. (2002). Grandparenthood and multigenerational families: Social reality or demographic myth? *Zeitschrift für Gerontologie und Geriatrie, 35*, 540–555. doi:10.1007/s00391-002-0128-z

Lauterbach, W., & Klein, T. (2004). The change of generational relations based on demographic development: The case of Germany. *Journal of Comparative Family Studies, 35*(4), 651–663.

Leopold, T., & Skopek, J. (2015). The delay of grandparenthood: A cohort comparison in East and West Germany. *Journal of Marriage and Family, 77*(2), 441–460. doi:10.1111/jomf.12169

Lowenstein, A. (2007). Solidarity conflict and ambivalence: Testing two conceptual frameworks and their impact on quality of life for older family members. *Journals of Gerontology Series B: Psychological Sciences and Social Sciences, 62*(2), 100–S107. doi:10.1093/geronb/62.2.S100

Lüscher, K., & Pillemer, K. (1998). Intergenerational ambivalence: A new approach to the study of parent–child relations in later life. *Journal of Marriage and the Family, 60*(2), 413–425.

Mahne, K., & Huxhold, O. (2012). Social contact between grandparents and older grandchildren: A three generation perspective. In S. Arber & V. Timonen (Eds.), *Contemporary grandparenting: Changing family relationships in global contexts* (pp. 225–246). Bristol, UK: Policy Press.

Mahne, K., & Huxhold, O. (2015). Grandparenthood and subjective well-being: Moderating effects of educational level. *Journal of Gerontology: Social Sciences.* doi:10.1093/geronb/gbn147

Mahne, K., & Huxhold, O. (2017). Intimacy at a distance: Do the relationships between older parents and their adult children remain positive despite growing spatial distance? In K. Mahne, J. K. Wolff, J. Simonson, & C. Tesch-Römer (Eds.), *Altern im Wandel: Zwei Jahrzehnte Deutscher Alterssurvey.* Wiesbaden: Springer.

Mahne, K., & Klaus, D. (2017). In between joy and duty: The meaning and enactment of relationships between grandparents and grandchildren. In K. Mahne, J. K. Wolff, J. Simonson, & C. Tesch-Römer (Eds.), *Altern im Wandel: Zwei Jahrzehnte Deutscher Alterssurvey* (pp. 231–245). Wiesbaden: Springer.

Mahne, K., & Motel-Klingebiel, A. (2010). Intergenerational relationships. In A. Motel-Klingebiel, S. Wurm, & C. Tesch-Römer (Eds.), *Altern im Wandel: Befunde des Deutschen Alterssurveys* (pp. 188–214). Stuttgart: Kohlhammer.

Mahne, K., & Motel-Klingebiel, A. (2012). The importance of the grandparent role: A class specific phenomenon? Evidence from Germany. *Advances in Life Course Research, 17*(3), 145–155. doi:10.1016/j.alcr.2012.06.001

Mann, R., Tarrant, A., & Leeson, G. W. (2016). Grandfatherhood: Shifting masculinities in later life. *Sociology, 50*(3), 594–610. doi:10.1177/0038038515572586

Marks, S. (1977). Multiple roles and role strain: Some notes on human energy, time, and commitment. *American Sociological Review, 42*, 921–936.

Merton, R. K. (1957). *Social theory and social structure.* New York: Free Press.

Motel-Klingebiel, A., & Vogel, C. (2013). Poverty in old age and the later phase of life. In C. Vogel & A. Motel-Klingebiel (Eds.), *Altern im sozialen Wandel: die Rückkehr der Altersarmut?* (pp. 463–480). Wiesbaden: Springer.

Nauck, B. (2001). Intercultural contact and intergenerational transmission in immigrant families. *Journal of Cross-Cultural Psychology, 32*(2), 159–173.

Nauck, B., & Klaus, D. (2005). Families in Turkey. In B. N. Adams & J. Trost (Eds.), *Handbook of world families* (pp. 364–388). Thousand Oaks: Sage.

Nauck, B., & Kohlmann, A. (1999). Kinship as social capital: Network relationships in Turkish Migrant families. In R. Richter & S. Supper (Eds.), *New qualities in the life-course: Intercultural aspects* (pp. 199–218). Würzburg: Ergon.

Nave-Herz, R. (2002). Family changes and intergenerational relationships in Germany. In R. Nave-Herz (Ed.), *Family change and intergenerational relations in different cultures* (pp. 215–248). Würzburg: Ergon.

Neugarten, B. L., & Weinstein, K. K. (1964). The changing American grandparent. *Journal of Marriage and the Family, 26*(2), 199–204.

Parsons, T. (1943). The kinship system of the contemporary United States. *American Anthropologist, 45*(1), 22–38.

Reher, D. S. (1998). Family ties in Western Europe: Persistent contrasts. *Population and Development Review, 24*(2), 203–234.

Rosenmayr, L., & Köckeis, E. (1963). Propositions for a sociological theory of ageing and the family. *International Social Science Journal, 15*, 410–426.

Rosow, I. (1976). Status and role change through the life span. In R. H. Binstock & E. Shanas (Eds.), *Handbook of aging and the social sciences*. New York: Van Nostrand Reinhold.

Schier, M. (2015). Post-separation families: Spatial mobilities and the need to manage multi-local everyday life. In C. M. Aybek, J. Huinink, & R. Muttarak (Eds.), *Spatial mobility, migration, and living arrangements* (pp. 205–224). Cham, Switzerland: Springer.

Schimany, P., & Baykara-Krumme, H. (2012). On the history and demographic relevance of older migrants in Germany. In H. Baykara-Krumme, A. Motel-Klingebiel, & P. Schimany (Eds.), *Viele Welten des Alterns: ältere Migranten im alternden Deutschland* (pp. 43–73). Wiesbaden: Springer.

Sieber, S. (1974). Toward a theory of role accumulation. *American Sociological Review, 39*, 567–578.

Silverstein, M., & Marenco, A. (2001). How Americans enact the grandparent role across the family life course. *Journal of Family Issues, 22*(4), 493–522. doi:10.1177/019251301022004006

Smith, G. C., Palmieri, P. A., & Hancock, G. R. (2008). Custodial grandmothers' psychological distress, dysfunctional parenting, and grandchildren's adjustment. *International Journal of Ageing & Human Development, 67*(4), 327–357. doi:10.2190/AG.67.4.c

Steinbach, A. (2013). Family structure and parent–child contact: A comparison of native and migrant families. *Journal of Marriage and Family, 75*(5), 1114–1129.

Sticker, E. J. (1987). Relationships between grandparents and grandchildren: Recent findings of explorative studies in Germany. *Zeitschrift für Gerontologie, 20*(5), 269–274.

Sticker, E. J. (1991). The importance of grandparenthood during the life cycle in Germany. In P. K. Smith (Ed.), *The psychology of grandparenthood: An international perspective* (pp. 32–49). London: Routledge.

Sticker, E. J. (2008). The role of grandparents: On the relations of generations. *Demografischer Wandel. Themenheft der Zeitschrift "Die Politische Meinung", 469*, 33–37.

Szinovacz, M. E. (1998a). Grandparent research: Past, present, and future. In M. E. Szinovacz (Ed.), *Handbook on grandparenthood.* (pp. 1–20). Westport, CT: Greenwood Press.

Szinovacz, M. E. (1998b). Research on grandparenting: Needed refinements in concepts, theories, and methods. In M. E. Szinovacz (Ed.), *Handbook on grandparenthood* (pp. 257–288). Westport, CT: Greenwood Press.

Szydlik, M. (1996). Parent–child relations in East and West Germany shortly after the fall of the Wall. *International Journal of Sociology and Social Policy, 16*(12), 63–88.

Tartler, R. (1961). *Age in modern society*. Stuttgart: Enke.

Timonen, V., & Arber, S. (2012). A new look at grandparenting. In S. Arber & V. Timonen (Eds.), *Contemporary grandparenting: Changing family relationships in global contexts* (pp. 1–24). Bristol, UK: Policy Press.

Uhlenberg, P., & Cheuk, M. (2010). The significance of grandparents to grandchildren: An international perspective. In D. Dannefer & C. Phillipson (Eds.), *The SAGE handbook of social gerontology* (pp. 447–458). London: Sage.

Vogel, C. (2012). Intergenerational relations of ethnic German repatriates: State of research and exemplary findings on attitudes towards familial support. In H. Baykara-Krumme, A. Motel-Klingebiel, & P. Schimany (Eds.), *Viele Welten des Alterns* (pp. 289–313). Wiesbaden: Springer VS.

Vogel, C., & Sommer, E. (2013). Financial transfers between adult children and parents in migrant families from the former Soviet Union. *Journal of Comparative Family Studies*, *44*(6), 783–796. doi:10.2307/23644596

6

CHANGING ROLES OF GRANDPARENTS IN THE UK

Emergence of the "New" Grandfather

Ann Buchanan

PROVERBS

1. "Blood is thicker than water."
2. "Grandparents should feel free to advise, but should never interfere."

(see p. 129 for interpretations)

CASE STORIES

Two case stories illustrate aspects of British grandparenting. The first is a case story of a prosperous upper-class family where the grandparents' emphasis is on supporting their children and grandchildren, while at the same time keeping "a stiff upper lip" (i.e., to maintain their dignity and the reputation of their family in the face of multiple life challenges); the second illustrates both how grandfathers are taking on a new role and how the UK has become a multi-cultural country with the arrival of some remarkable immigrants.

1. AN ENGLISH/SCOTTISH GRANDMOTHER

My grandmother was one of nine children. She came from a prosperous middle-class family with homes in London and the home counties. In both places, she would have had a household of servants, and it was important whatever challenges life threw at you, a "stiff upper lip" was maintained. You should not show your feelings. At 19 she met and married in London a Scotsman some 20 years older. He took her "home" to Scotland to live in a large 10th-century priory which had previously been a monastery. There was no road or telephone – the only access was by boat and this frequently was unable to sail because of the weather. She had six children in quick succession. Her husband was head of the family and ruled the family with firm expectations. He died prematurely, leaving my grandmother as a 40-year-old widow, alone in a desolate part of the Highlands. Every Sunday she went to the Kirk, where the minister lectured on sin and the Devil. Three of her brothers were killed in World War I, three of her sons were wounded or captured in World War II, and a daughter died in childbirth. My grandmother brought this child up until her father remarried.

During World War II, while my father was away fighting, my grandmother gathered up her daughters and daughters-in-law and their children to live together in Scotland. "Never a man was allowed to cross the threshold." At the end of the war all the women were returned to their husbands.

I had a particularly close relationship with my grandmother. I remember her telling me "Never feel sorry for yourself…it is in your hands to make things the best they can be." Though not particularly religious, she had a strong sense of her duty and held the view that families should support each other. Her example of a "stiff upper lip", which came from her background and her own upbringing, was very influential on her children and grandchildren.

2. A REMARKABLE INDIAN GRANDFATHER WHOSE DAUGHTER IMMIGRATED TO THE UK

The daughter was born in 1946, the sixth of seven children in a small town in southern India. When she was 3 years old, her own mother passed away leaving her father as a single parent. The father combined his job as a civil servant with charity work for a home for poor students from remote villages.

Bringing up seven children as a single father was no mean feat, and there was no formal welfare system to fall back on and family help was limited. The father's view of education was holistic and included exposure to literature and arts, compassion, and sharing with others, in addition to academic training.

Besides advocacy of independence for India, the father had two particularly strong values which were based on the fundamental principle of equality. The first was that caste discrimination was an abomination. When two of his daughters told him that they wished to marry men of a different caste whom they had chosen themselves, he supported them fully in spite of great opposition. This approach flew in the face not only of the caste diktat, but also in the face of the practice of arranged marriage.

The father was also committed to equality for women and this was a value he lived up to without fail. He strongly believed that girls deserved as much education, encouragement, and opportunity as boys. He ensured that all his children became graduates, including his three daughters. It would have been easy to have given them away with some monetary dowry, but he refused. His daughters' dowry was their education and the values he had instilled in them. The youngest daughter immigrated to the UK and became one of the very few Indian women consultants in Scotland.

The father's values had a huge impact not merely on the lives of his own children but also on those of his grandchildren. He helped his grandchildren with their school and college work and encouraged them to take part in debates, sports, and games. Most of his grandchildren were not only graduates but also postgraduates, and entered professional life either in India or the UK. When one granddaughter read Law at Cambridge, he was delighted because Nehru had studied at Cambridge and went on to practise law. This grandfather was no doubt exceptional, but he illustrates, rather ahead of his time, both the new roles grandfathers of all ethnic groups are taking on and how the face of Britain has changed with our new arrivals.

Outline of Chapter

This chapter traces how the culture of grandparents in the UK, although based on a strong liberal Christian tradition, has changed in response to changes in society. In particular, the industrial revolution, the coming of the welfare state, the arrival of mass immigration and demographic factors have all influenced the roles of grandparents in the UK today. More recently, as men survive longer and stay healthier, there has been the emergence of the "new"'grandfather: he is no longer the stern patriarch of yesteryear, but a more nurturing and involved fig-ure. Throughout our history, there has been a class divide between those with resources and those without. In modern Britain, with increasing education and prosperity, many of these class divisions have become less obvious (Heath, Savage, & Senior, 2013). Yet three traditions remain. First, "non-interference" is a strong norm. This norm, however, is weaker in poorer families, and states that grandpar-ents should not interfere with how their children raise their grandchildren, and that parents should be independent and self-reliant. Perhaps this is a hold-over from the "stiff upper lip" tradition described in the first case story. Second, at the same time, grandparents are expected to "be there" for their grandchildren as "protectors", "confidants", "supporters", "benefactors", and "connectors". This is illustrated in both case stories. The third tradition is that the parents are the gatekeepers. Whether grandparents are able to be involved in their grandchildren's lives depends on the extent to which the parents allow this.

UK family policy, although not as generous as in Nordic countries, is well established, but with the recent recession and the change to a Conservative gov-ernment, state services have been cut back. Grandparents in many cases are filling the gap by providing massive amounts of free childcare. However, despite evidence of the important support they give and how their involvement is associated with greater child well-being, currently, under the law, grandparents have no rights of contact with their grandchildren if parents do not so wish. It is estimated that over a million grandparents are affected by this.

The UK today is made up of people from many cultures. Although throughout history immigrants have arrived on our shores from all over the world, the numbers coming in the last century, indeed in the last 50 years, have never been exceeded. These new Britons have all influenced the grandparent role. Grandparenthood is a social construction, i.e., it evolves according to the needs and demands of changing circumstances (Berger & Luckmann, 1966). But grandparenthood in the UK is also influenced by the culture and traditions of previous epochs. Newcomers bring with them their own cultural expectations but in the process of assimilation absorb some of the traditions and values of their chosen country.

Cultural, Historical, Economic, and Demographic Background

Early History of the UK

At base, the UK evolved from a Christian heritage. From a Christian perspective, a key function of grandparenthood involved the passing on of heritage and faith (Conroy & Fahey, 1985). Although parents were crucial to this process, grandmothers and grandfathers were also transmitters of a Christian perspective of life – its origins, memory, and values. The grandparents, if still living, were there to support the parents in bringing up the child with Christian values. The extent to which grandparents were involved in this process, however, depended on whether they had been blessed with a long life.

In medieval times military virtues were linked with those of Christianity, as epitomized by the Arthurian legend in England. In addition to military prowess and valour, and loyalty to God and the knight's feudal lord, they called for courtesy towards enemies and generosity towards the sick and oppressed, widows, and other disadvantaged people (Herlihy, 1985; Gayre, 2007). Women were respected and protected but were considered to be essentially frail creatures. Two sets of stories, written by Boccaccio and Chaucer in the 14th century, offer insight into young people's views of older people at that time and how the Black Plague shifted attitudes toward the elderly in the 14th century (Sandidge, 2007). Boccaccio's *Decameron* and Chaucer's *Canterbury Tales* offer significantly different descriptions of old people. Boccaccio upheld the view that the elderly were a source of wisdom and stability in society. However, in the 1348–1349 Black Death epidemics, those who died were mostly the older, wise figures who traditionally offered sage advice and helped to maintain the moral order. Moreover, older family members were no longer there for their children. Young people might be freed from patriarchal tyranny, but they also regretted the loss of mentors.

In Chaucer's works, however, the elderly received little respect. By the 1380s and 1390s it was the young people who succumbed to the plague. By ravishing first the elderly and then the young, the plague radically changed attitudes to old people. Chaucer displays young people regarding old men as foolish objects of ridicule, especially when they pursued young women, disregarding the ancient wisdom of old people's proper behaviour. The Black Plague altered class and economic structures but other social values, such as attitudes toward the elderly, may also have been transformed (Sandidge, 2007). When young men were plentiful, the scarce elders were respected. When young men were scarce, elders were less valued.

The Impact of the Industrial Revolution

The transformation to an industrial economy from an agricultural one took place from the mid-18th to early 19th century in certain areas in Europe and in Great Britain. Before the industrial revolution in England, "the household was not only the industrial centre but also the social centre, for its members derived social satisfaction from working together and from rustic amusements enjoyed at home or on the village green" (Gray, 1992, p. 244). The grandfather, if living, would be at the centre of the family. Industrialization brought considerable changes to family structure, leading to the weakening of intergenerational bonds. In pre-industrial societies there was an *extended family* structure, spanning many generations, with members probably remaining in the same location for generations. In industrialized societies the *nuclear family* predominated, consisting of only parents and their growing children. Families and children reaching adulthood became more mobile and tended to relocate to where the jobs were. Extended family bonds become more tenuous (Parsons & Bales, 1956). With the growth of industrial society, property and jobs moved away from family control and the elderly were often left behind. Industrialization also disrupted the traditional relationship between generations. The elderly were seen as burdens who needed to be supported. In conditions of severe poverty, any semblance of maintaining "family life" was challenging, with multiple families and individuals crowded into tiny dwellings to save on rent (Smith, 2011). There was no room for the elderly. In poorer families, many wives started working outside the home as the industrial revolution gathered momentum. This meant that caring for the home and children was no longer the exclusive duty of women; neither was earning a living and pursuing a public life the exclusive domain of men (Smith, 2011).

The dramatic shift brought about by the industrial revolution perhaps was responsible for the view that each generation should look after itself. Whereas in earlier times grandparents may not have survived until old age, in Victorian times there was a large rise in survival rates (Chase, 2009). For the Victorians, old age became a conspicuous public topic and problem, but at the same time it was also an intensely private preoccupation. Older people were both powerful and powerless. Those with resources retained a hold over their family; those with none were at the mercy of state institutions. Portrayals in Victorian literature, reflecting perceptions of the time, included a number of elderly villains. For example, in the novels of Charles Dickens there are characterizations of exploitative old men: Mr. Bumble (*Oliver Twist*), Mr. Dolls (*Our Mutual Friend*), and Arthur Gride (*Nicholas Nickleby*) (Chase, 2009). These portrayals illustrate changing perceptions of grandfathers, i.e., they were no longer revered but instead were mean old men who blocked the progress of younger members of society.

Coming of the Welfare State

There is considerable discussion in the academic literature on the impact of welfare provision on intergenerational bonds. On the one hand it was felt that as the state took over many of the responsibilities of the family, this would lessen the role of grandparents. But on the other hand, research has shown a rather different picture. In 1942, William Beveridge was given the task of outlining the kind of Britain that people wanted after the war. He identified the five giants that lead to poverty and social misery: poverty, disease, ignorance, squalor, and idleness. To defeat these giants, he proposed setting up a welfare state with social security, a national health service, free education, council housing, and full employment. The new Labour Prime Minister, Clement Attlee, announced that he would introduce the welfare state outlined in the 1942 Beveridge Report. This included the establishment of a national health service in 1948, with free medical treatment for all. A national system of benefits was also introduced to provide social security, so that the population would be protected from the "cradle to the grave". People at work still had to make weekly contributions, as did employers, but the benefits provided were now much greater (Abel-Smith, 1992). The Labour Party proceeded to implement many social policies, which became known as the welfare state. These included the Family Allowances Act 1945 (financial help for children), the National Insurance (Industrial Injuries) Act 1946 (benefits for those injured at work), the National Insurance Act 1946 (unemployment benefits), the National Health Service Act 1946 (free health care for all), the Pensions (Increase) Act 1947 (weekly allowances for the elderly), and the Landlord and Tenant (Rent Control) Act 1949 (more security in rented accommodation).

Although there was some rolling back of the welfare state in the UK, particularly under Margaret Thatcher in the 1970s and more recently under David Cameron, the National Health Service, which is free to all at point of need, is still considered the jewel in our welfare state. What impact has the welfare state had on cultural practices in family life? In many ways, the coming of the welfare state absolved the younger generation of primary responsibility for caring for their elders. The welfare state provided pensions and free health care to enable the elderly to remain independent. Similarly, the coming of the welfare state absolved the older generation of caring for their grandchildren. Families receive an allowance for each child from the state; education from age 5 (now from age 4) is free; and in more recent years some childcare for pre-schoolers has become free.

The literature, however, presents a more complex picture. The question is: does the existence of the welfare state "crowd out" intergenerational exchange or actually "crowd (the family back) in" (Igel & Szydlik, 2011)? When it comes to grandparents offering childcare, European studies demonstrate that family and state complement each other. Studies across Europe show that as the percentage of state-provided childcare provision in a country increases, parents are less likely to receive intensive childcare help from grandparents, but receive support in other ways, such as financially. In countries with low levels of state childcare, grandparents offer more intensive childcare with grandchildren. But the picture is further complicated by demographic changes in the numbers of children in a family and numbers of women working in each European country.

Arrival of New Britons in the 20th and 21st Centuries

A key influence on the culture of grandparenthood in England and Wales has been the high rate of immigration in the 20th and 21st centuries. These new Britons have brought with them their own traditions and cultures relating to older people and their involvement with children. In the UK, cultural diversity is most pronounced in the cities. According to the 2011 census, London had a population of over 8 million. Of this number, 44.9% were white British and 37% were born outside the UK, including 24.5% born outside of Europe (Office for National Statistics, 2011), and more than 300 different languages were spoken.

These various ethnic groups are now at different stages of growth and ageing, and some groups, such as black Caribbean, already include substantial proportions of elders. London also has several ethnic minorities within the white population, such as Irish, Cypriots, and East Europeans; again, some of these include large numbers of older people. While some groups are relatively concentrated, others are more widely scattered, forming very small minorities in a number of boroughs. These migrants have brought with them different traditions towards caring for their elders and different expectations of grandparents.

London elders from South Asian ethnic groups tend to live in larger families (see homeland comparisons in Chapter 8) and have more multi-generational households than white or black Caribbean elders. More black Caribbean and African older men live alone than do men from other minority ethnic groups. Minority ethnic groups have lower incomes, although there are some Indian elders among those in the highest income groups. Bangladeshi and black Caribbean elders are less likely to be owner-occupiers, and more likely to be living in social housing than white or Indian groups. Levels of overcrowding are especially high for older people from south Asian ethnic groups. In addition, mortality rates for different ethnic groups differ, and this affects whether older people will play a grandparental role. Generally, in London people of all ethnic groups live longer but mortality rates for the most recent migrant groups are significantly higher than the London average (Lowdell, Evandrou, Bardsley, Morgan, & Soljak, 2000).

A number of factors influence the roles grandparents play: cultural traditions towards care of the elderly may be imported from the homeland; for example, with the Chinese population there is the strong Confucian tradition of filial piety and obligation to care for the elderly (see Chapter 9). A key factor is whether elderly people live in multi-generational households or live alone. Other sources of variation are one's location of residence, health, income, and ownership of property.

If there has been some general agreement in the 21st century about the role of grandparents in Great Britain, it centres on the third stage hypothesized by Gratton and Haber (1996) in the USA. Their suggestion was that across history, first the grandparents are seen as "patriarchs/matriarchs"; then, as we saw in the plague and the industrial revolution, they became "burdens"; but then they finally become "companions" to their grandchildren. More importantly in the UK, they have found an invaluable role, filling gaps in our welfare state.

Demographic Factors in the UK that are Changing the Roles of Grandparents

As in other developed economies, a rapid increase in the numbers of surviving elders is apparent. In the UK, it is projected that by 2044 those aged 65 and over will represent 25% of the total population (the comparable figure was 18% in 2014 and 15% in 1984). These elders are also healthier than they have been in the past. Meanwhile, the percentage of the UK population aged 15 and under is projected to decrease from 21% to 17% between 1984 and 2044 (Office for National Statistics, 2014).

FIGURE 6.1 Baking has always been a grandmother's activity in the UK. There has been renewed interest in this type of grandmother–granddaughter interaction, following the popularity of the "Bake Off" television programme. Here a UK granny celebrates a baking success with her granddaughters.

Source: Courtesy of Richard Liston.

In addition, as reported elsewhere, the numbers of children who are raised in divorced families has also increased. One-third of all children aged 16 and under were not living with both of their birth parents in 2010 (ONS, 2012). A quarter of all children (fourth highest in Europe) were living with a lone single parent (never married or divorced). In addition, the number of mothers working has increased dramatically (ONS, 2013). As of 2010, more than two-thirds of all mothers worked in various paid sectors. Research from RIAS (insurance specialists) reveals that two-thirds (67%) of UK grandparents provide childcare for their grandchildren. This 9.2 million strong "Grandparent Army", up from 6.1 million in 2009, saves parents £15.7 (US$20.2) billion each year in childcare costs, equivalent to almost £1,700 (US$2,190) per family (RIAS, 2015).

The *21st century grandparent army report* of 2015 also shows that one-fifth (19%) of grandparents have seen their childcare roles increase in the last 12 months – a major reason being their children's increasing workloads and pressure to keep their job or get a pay rise. The vast majority (96%) of grandparent childminders receive no payment whatsoever from their children to cover the cost of looking after their little ones. They also expend over £400 each year for little ones' activities whilst they are in their care, a colossal combined £3.8 billion (RIAS, 2015). Although grandparents have been involved in childcare in the past, never before have so many been involved so intensively in caring for the next generation.

Theoretical Approaches

Within the historical, economic, and demographic contexts described above, the study of grandparents in the UK has involved many disciplines. For example, evolutionary biology research from the UK and elsewhere and anthropological studies have been important in helping us understand why grandparents care. The fields of developmental psychology and family psychology have led the way in showing the associations between the involvement of grandparents and child development. Whereas sociology has monitored the impact of changes in society, social-legal scholars have illustrated how these changes have impacted families, particularly in divorce cases.

The Evolutionary Biology Approach

The evolutionary biology approach was well illustrated by our first case story. The grandmother brought her children and grandchildren together to protect them in challenging times. The role of the grandmother within evolutionary biology has led to research on the grandmother hypothesis. The grandmother hypothesis proposes that grandmothers might have been the most knowledgeable, efficient, and motivated helpers for reproducing mothers throughout human history, and helped them to have more children and grandchildren. The grandmother hypothesis is currently used to explain why human female longevity extends beyond meno-pause. Coall, Hilbrand, Sear, and Hertwig (2016) noted, however, that evolution-ary studies on grandfathers do not show any protective function. Indeed, the few studies that there are suggest that grandfathers may have a negative influence on grandchild survival. The second case story, however, suggests that such a negative tendency may be changing.

Coall et al. (2016) summarized findings from evolutionary biology and anthro-pology on why grandparents care. They highlighted the broadest level of explana-tion, that humans are cooperative breeders. According to the cooperative breeding hypothesis, a mother does not raise her children by herself but is helped by other members of her social group. In both traditional societies and contemporary industrialized societies, one class of kin helper was often available and inclined to help: post-reproductive adults, i.e., grandparents.

Developmental Psychology Approaches

It is known that grandmothers and grandfathers, regardless of kinship status, are rated as important attachment figures by older adolescents (Creasey & Koblewski, 1991). In general, granddaughters reported better relationships than grandsons with their grandparents, and grandchildren reported better relations with grandmoth-ers than with grandfathers. But not only are grandparents important attachment figures, there is also evidence from the UK that their involvement with grandchil-dren may have a positive impact on their grandchildren's well-being (Buchanan & Flouri, 2008). These scholars report that grandparents' involvement may mitigate the impact if parents divorce and buffers the children in times of adversity.

Caregiving is not all undirectional. Some grandchildren are actually involved in caring for grandparents. A qualitative study in the US reported that adult grandchil-dren (21–29 years old) assisted grandmothers and grandfathers with instrumental activities of daily living (Fruhauf, Jarrott, & Allen, 2006). Reasons for providing care included grandparents' chronic illness or gradual ageing, and a crisis or event that left grandparents needing assistance. The grandchildren assisted their grandparents because the grandparents had looked after them when they were young children. It may be this intergenerational reciprocity which fosters well-being in grandchildren. Across history, although UK grandparents have mostly been valued family members, current demographic factors are changing their traditional role into a more active involvement with their grandchildren. This active involvement appears to benefit the grandchildren and may also be of benefit to the elders (Glaser et al., 2014).

Sociological Approaches

Ross, Hill, Sweeting, and Cunningham-Burley (2006), in a UK study, noted that grandparents have roles as "protectors", "confidants", "supporters", "benefactors", and "connectors". Although personal contact might decline in the adolescent years, emotional closeness between grandparents and grandchildren remains, if it were there already. There is also evidence that the family context may influence the type of grandparent/grandchild relationships. In the Ross et al. (2006) study, the grand-parents and grandchildren interviewed came from different settings in Scotland and the researchers found marked differences in the family dynamics of affluent families compared to those living in disadvantage. Generally speaking, grandchildren in dis-advantaged families had more contact with grandparents. But as we have discussed earlier, across the UK, families from different ethnic communities show wide diver-sity in their attitudes to, and practice with, intergenerational relations.

Clarke and Roberts (2004), in a representative study of 850 UK grandparents, found that when asked what they thought a grandparent should and should not do, 88% replied that "they should not interfere" in raising children. Other studies conducted on Anglo-American families have always found that the edict of "non-interference" is important (e.g., Bates, 2009, p. 338). But the dilemma is that non-interference may come into conflict with the need to protect the next generation when the grandparents feel they may be at risk. Harper and Ruicheva (2010), also from the UK, demonstrated that the non-interference rule may be less true for grandparents of lone-parent families, where grandparents can become "replace-ment partners" and "replacement parents".

The other key norm of contemporary grandparenting in the UK is the con-cept of "being there", also highlighted by the Clarke and Roberts study (2004). This means to be available if asked for support in caring and/or financial need. But both concepts are passive; that is, at heart the parents of the grandchildren were expected to be self-determining and independent.

The main challenge to the more active grandparent role is that parents, as the middle generation, are the gatekeepers of contact with grandchildren. This has been noted in a number of reports (e.g., Buchanan & Flouri, 2008; Clarke & Roberts, 2004; Buchanan & Rotkirch, 2016), and poses a particular dilemma when parents divorce. Social-legal scholars in the UK have been very active in this area. Under UK law, grandparents, as will be discussed later, have no legal rights for contact with their grandchildren if parents do not agree to this contact. A UK-based qualitative study explored the role of grandparents in divorced families and concluded that there was not sufficient evidence that grandparents should have a special role recog-nized by the law (Ferguson, Douglas, Lowe, Murch, & Robinson, 2004). However, Dunn and Deater-Deckard (2001), based on data from the Avon longitudinal study, showed that many grandparents, although they may not be recognized by UK law, are already heavily involved after family separation and divorce and are often key confidants for children (Dunn, Davies, O'Connor, & Sturgess, 2001).

Changing Traditions in Parenting

Changing traditions of parenting pose a key challenge for grandparents when they take on an intensive role in childcare. Conflict can arise over how best to care for a child. Fashions in parenting have changed over the grandparents' lives (Campbell, 2013). They themselves may have been brought up under the rubrics of Truby King: strict routines and "do not spoil the child". When rearing their own children, the more liberal regimes of Dr. Spock and Dr. Winnicott may have been in vogue. Both Drs. Spock and Winnicott believed that parents should trust their intuition. "It is when a mother trusts her judgement that she is at her best," Dr. Winnicott said. Parenting did not have to be perfect, but just had to be "good enough". Grandparents' children, however, now have different models to follow. Gina Ford (maternity nurse and media personality in UK) has brought back the return of "routine", and a television documentary with Jo Frost raised new issues about managing children's boundaries. In contrast, other experts such as Penelope Leach, who focuses on "child centred parenting", are still advocated by Dr. Tanya Byron (psychologist and media personality in UK). When grandparents have a more active role in childcare, these changes in parenting doctrine are challenging to say the least. In one family, different children may espouse different parenting methods, and woe betide the grandparent who undermines the parental regime!

What Do Parents and Grandchildren Think UK Grandparents Should Do/Be?

The following quotes illustrate how demography and other factors have influenced the role of grandparents. The quotes from grandchildren come from the UK National Grandparents Survey I undertook in 2006 (Buchanan & Flouri, 2008). The children came from many different ethnic and religious backgrounds, and broadly matched the current diversity in England and Wales. The views of the parents come from *Grandfathers: Global Perspectives* (Buchanan & Rotkirch, 2016). It is not possible to identify the ethnic/religious backgrounds of respondents, but the web-based parenting site *NetMums*, from which these quotes were extracted, has a nationwide membership of mothers from all ethnic and religious backgrounds.

In the study on grandparents, a key factor in grandparents' involvement was whether this involvement was welcomed by parents. One young man noted that he saw less of his paternal grandparents but was in touch with his maternal grandparents despite a difficult relationship between them and his father:

> You see, my Mum gets on with her parents really well, but my Father argues with his parents quite a lot. My Dad, he didn't like my Grandma and Granddad (Mum's parents) but Mum makes sure I see them.

Contact was also influenced by whether a child's parents had divorced:

> Well my Mum and Dad broke up when we were quite young...I seem to get along better with my Mum's Mum and Dad than my Dad's Mum and Dad as I grew up seeing them a lot more.

As noted earlier, some 25% of UK families are headed by a single parent. One young man of a single parent noted that he was very close to his mother's parents because he had lived with his grandparents and largely been looked after by them when he was young. Effectively they had become his surrogate parents.

A strong theme in the statements of young people was their grandparents' support and interest in their education and future careers. Many teenagers would drop in to grandparents after school while their parents worked and be given a meal and help with their homework. Some grandparents also attended parenting meetings at their school.

> My Grandma and Granddad are interested in how I'm doing at school and if...I had homework I didn't understand, they always helped me.
> Yes, when I got my SATs [standard achievement tests] results I got 3 x 5s so I was really happy so I rang them that night to tell them.
> My Grandma and Granddad are very interested about what I do when I'm older.

Grandparents were also reportedly important for access to contacts and net-works that would help them find employment when they left school. Young people also appreciated all the presents and money provided by grandparents. A key finding was that young people felt that grandparents were important "because they are family". Grandparents were seen as a safety net. If parents died or "mucked up", they would rather go to live with their grandparents than go into state care.

The other side of the coin is the parents' views. As reported by the parents, the principal barrier to grandparent involvement with grandchildren was diffi-cult intergenerational relationships. It was Tolstoy who said, "All happy families are alike; each unhappy family is unhappy in its own way" (Tolstoy, 2014, p. 1). This was vividly illustrated by the parents' remarks. Often, problems arose when the grandparents did not approve of their son/daughter's choice of partner. In one case this involved a cross-cultural marriage where the grandparents refused to get involved with their mixed-race grandchild but happily helped with their other white grandchildren. Grandparents' own divorce, particularly for grandfathers, often cut them out of ongoing relationships with the next generation.

> But ever since the breakdown of my stepfather and mother's marriage a few years ago, my stepfather's family have grown very distant – so much so that I'm feeling very pushed out. And I guess I just don't really know where I fit in anymore.

But parents also made decisions as to how safe their children were being cared for by grandparents, especially as the grandparents became older and frailer. Parents worried when grandparents smoked in the house and when they gave their child-ren junk food and unnecessary treats. Grandparents, on the other hand, accus-tomed to a more relaxed parenting style, sometimes felt that their children, as parents, worried too much about safety issues. Despite these concerns, there was real appreciation for all the work grandparents did in caring for their children and this appeared to cross all ethnic and religious groups. It was apparent that grandmothers and grandfathers, often on their own, were heavily involved in childcare. Parents were particularly grateful for childcare that enabled them to work.

> *My daughter is 3 yrs and my son is 8 months and from the age of 3 months they have stayed overnight at their nanna and granddad at least once a week due to mine and my husband's shifts. Now my daughter stays over every Friday night regardless of if we are working or not. She has a fantastic relationship with her grandparents.*

Grandparents were also seen to have other family roles. Principal among these was to care about the family history and to keep the grandchildren in touch with their ancestry.

Grandfathers

Although there has been a flowering of academic research into grandparents (which in most studies means grandmothers), there has been almost nothing on grandfathers. The following citations are from Buchanan and Rotkirch (2016). Just as grandparenting is a social construct, as we saw earlier in this chapter, grandfathering is even more of a construct. In Britain, traditionally a Christian democracy, the fall-back position is the family patriarch. In the past, how able a man was to fulfil this role was dependent on whether he had survived long enough to be a grandparent, and whether he had ownership of resources. Those elders who owned property and money were able to dictate how family life was organized. History shows that in times of social stress, such as during the plague and during industrialization in the 19th century, the elderly were seen more as a family burden than as family members who should be respected.

In recent years, it is interesting how the grandfather has reinvented himself to become a more caring and nurturing resource to his grandchildren (Buchanan & Rotkirch, 2016). Many of these men may have missed out on their own children when they worked (Lewis, 2013). They now appear to enjoy caring for their grandchildren. This movement to the "new" grandfather is not only a phenomenon in the UK but is also seen across Europe, where about 42% of grandfathers have recently undertaken or regularly undertake care of their grandchildren; only marginally less than grandmothers (Glaser et al., 2014).

However, this involvement is more likely if the man has a wife who is a grandmother, and where the grandparents have not separated or divorced. Divorced elders are often cut out from intergenerational contact (Buchanan & Rotkirch, 2016). As long as the care of grandchildren is not "intensive" (more than 30 hours a week), this is associated with the grandfather's own greater well-being. Similarly, his involvement, independent of grandmothers, is associated with greater well-being in the

FIGURE 6.2 Gardening is a national obsession in the UK. In this photo, a UK grandpa teaches the next generation how to rake leaves.

Source: Courtesy of Richard Liston.

grandchildren. Grandfathers' involvement appears to be different from that of grandmothers. Whereas grandmothers are more involved in nurturing, feeding, and cooking for grandchildren (similar to the activities described in several other chapters in this book), grandfathers get more involved in activities such as playing games and going to football matches. Grandfathers are also more involved in career guidance, future planning, and help with networks. Grandfather involvement is associated with greater child well-being, and this influence has been evidenced not only in the UK but also in Israel and South Africa (Buchanan & Rotkirch, 2016).

Generally speaking, parents welcome grandfather involvement, but parents have to make judgements about how competent the grandfather is at caring for their children. In addition, they may be aware of darker issues where a few grandfathers have been involved in abusive incidents (Buchanan & Rotkirch, 2016). The construction of the "new" grandfather has changed his traditional role in the UK. Fifty years ago most grandfathers would have found it quite unthinkable that they would be as involved in the care of their grandchildren as they are today.

Social Policies

As an advanced liberal democracy, the UK has well-developed maternity/paternity/child sickness leave arrangements and benefits to help parents to care for their children. Although the benefits may seem generous by US standards, they are not as generous as in Nordic countries such as Sweden, Norway, and Finland. Parental policies and child benefits are highly conditional on family or individual income. Childcare public services are currently severely limited, and are in the process of being cut back. Private market provision is to some extent filling the gap, but at a high cost to families.

Only recently, after much campaigning by the charity Grandparents Plus (see p. 129, now merged with the Grandparents' Association), some of the arrangements and benefits have been made available to grandparents who care for grandchildren. Research by Glaser et al. (2014) on grandparenting in Europe gives a useful and detailed comparative account of family polices across Europe, with a special section on the UK.

In England and Wales, grandparents can receive child benefits as long as they are the main carers of the grandchildren and the parents agree. The recently introduced National Insurance credits (available to grandparents who give up work to care for grandchildren under age 12) count towards later pension, and are a step forward in recognizing the valuable contribution of grandparents as providers of childcare. Under family law in England and Wales, grandparents with primary care of grandchildren can obtain parental responsibility for grandchildren if a court grants them a Residence Order or Special Guardianship Order. In such cases, a grandparent is allowed to make decisions about a grandchild but parents must also retain a say. Local authorities are required to help children "in need", (where a child's health or well-being is at risk) through a range of services, but many children in family and friends' care are not recognized by the local authority as children in need and so do not qualify for support. If formally fostered with grandparents, foster allowances are payable from the Local Authority until the child is 16 years old or 20 years old, where the grandchild is in non-advanced education or in approved training. Grandparents can also become legal guardians in the event of the death of one or both parents. They would then be entitled to a Guardian's Allowance which can be paid until the child's 16th birthday. The ongoing debate, highlighted by the internet mothers' discussion forum (www.netmums.com/coffeehouse), is whether grandparents should be paid for the vast amount of informal childcare they provide or whether low-paid parents can use the childcare vouchers provided by employees to pay grandparents (Buchanan & Rotkirch, 2016).

In public law, when decisions are made about children's futures and parents are unable to care for them, there is a much recognition by the courts in the UK that "the best interests of the child" are often better met by family and friends' care. The work of Grandparents Plus (www.grandparentsplus.org.uk) demonstrates the work many grandparents do as full-time kinship carers. These grandparents of course constitute a considerable resource. Not only is their care generally better for children than placements with strangers, but these kinship carers also save the Exchequer large sums of money. A major concern is that because carers are "family" they may not receive the help needed to enable them to cope with the challenging behaviour of some very damaged young people (Hunt & Waterhouse, 2013).

The Dilemma of Grandparent Rights

In private law, following parental divorce (in contrast with the German laws described in Chapter 5) UK grandparents have no rights to see or make contact with their grandchildren if parents do not consent to this contact. As a result, many grandchildren miss out on the support of grandmothers and grandfathers. Under English, Welsh, and Scottish law, despite the evidence of the possible value of ongoing contact with grandparents, there is strong legal resistance to allowing grandparents any rights, even visitation rights. The Grandparents' Association in England and Wales claims that over one million grandparents are denied contact with their grandchildren (www.grandparentsplus.org.uk). Paternal grandparents in particular may find themselves excluded from their former role in the child's life once the child's father no longer resides with the child.

In a study for the English Department of Constitutional Affairs on residence and contact orders (Smart, May, & Wade, 2003, p. 29) it was noted:

> In contact cases the courts seemed unlikely to go against a parent's wish by ordering contact with a grandparent. The grandparent's best chance of success seemed to lie in being able to persuade the residential parent of the importance of ongoing contact.

Courts are naturally reluctant in cases of high conflict to further add to the marital dispute by involving grandparents. In many Asian countries (e.g., China, Singapore), it would be unthinkable that grandparents would not have visitation rights to see their grandchildren (Buchanan & Rotkirch, 2016). Under Confucian teachings, family obligation means that members must *care* for each other: young for old and old for young. But it is hard to care if there is no contact. Many Asian families who have come to Britain still maintain these traditions.

In the US, after a massive effort on the part of grandparents (Jackson, 1994), visitation rights are now commonplace. In Germany and Italy, grandparents have visitation rights provided these are compatible with the child's welfare (Ferguson et al., 2004). In England and Wales, and under separate legislation in Scotland, grandparents have to apply for "leave of the court" to make an application for contact with grandchildren. For grandparents of limited means, this can be quite expensive. Both in England/Wales and Scotland there has been considerable debate about whether this hurdle should be removed. In a survey by Wasoff and Morrison (2005) in Scotland, 92% felt that paternal grandparents, perhaps reflecting the strong clan tradition, should have the same rights for contact as the father after separation. But under both legislatures, following reviews (Norgrove, 2011; Scottish Law Commission, 2005), it was decided that removal of the need to apply for leave would lead to vexatious applications and increased conflict for the children. As a token of recognition of the role grandparents play, the Grandchildren's Charter in Scotland aimed to foster greater cooperation between parents and grandparents; and in England and Wales, Parenting Plans that separated parents during mediation were encouraged to consider the child's links with grandparents and wider family.

It may be difficult to judge how grandparents should be treated by the courts in individual applications to see their grandchildren. According to Kaganas (2007), the Scottish organization Grandparents Apart Self Help (www.grandparentsapart. co.uk) goes further than most other campaigning bodies in the UK. It suggests that there should be a change in the law to give "presumption of contact" with the grandparents. The organization suggests that this will encourage those involved to attend conciliation/crisis counselling to assist in finding a compromise. They feel this has to be mandatory to avoid the parents cutting out the wider family from their child's life (Kaganas 2007). This presumption can of course easily be overruled where a grandparent may pose a risk for a child. Nothing in family law is straightforward but a presumption of contact may be the best way to ensure that British children do not miss out on the benefits they could acquire from their grandparents.

Summary

> Shouldn't we recognize that each person is a sort of unconscious anthology of all epochs of man; and that he may at times be moving simultaneously among different epochs?
>
> (Joaquín, 1988)

Grandparents in Britain today are indeed an unconscious anthology of all past epochs in the UK. At base, their roles and behaviour have evolved from our liberal Christian democracy and the values that go with this. Over time, however, as grandparents have lived longer, they have had to adjust to the realities of a changing society. Notably, these include the move away from extended family life in rural settings to the nuclear household largely living in towns; the coming of the welfare state after World War II, which both loosened and strengthened family bonds; the arrival of mass immigration, bringing with it new traditions and attitudes in the treatment of the older family members; and more recently the recession, which has cut back state-provided family services. In the context of all this change, grandparents have had to adapt to the new demography: fewer young people, and more elderly, divorced, single parents, and working mothers. In doing so, many UK grandparents have found a new role for themselves, as essential child carers, and family supporters. In particular, there has been the emergence of the "new" grandfather, who in many families is a more nurturing and involved figure than ever before.

Theoretical approaches from the UK and elsewhere suggest that many disciplines have contributed to our knowledge about grandparents. At base, evolutionary biology has tried to explain why grandparents care. Research evidence shows that grandmother care is mostly associated with higher survival rates in grandchildren but to date this does not hold for studies of grandfathers' care. But as our second case story illustrates, the "new" grandfather is a relatively new phenomenon. Psychological research shows that grandparent care is associated with greater child well-being; sociological and demographic research illustrates how changes in society are impacting on the grandparental role; and social-legal researchers are searching for a solution to the damage done to children from high conflict divorce.

Although family policy is moving in line with the new trends, family law, especially where it gives grandparents no rights to maintain contact with their grandchildren if parents do not wish this, is out of step with the new roles. There is evidence that grandparental involvement is associated with both their own greater well-being, as long as their childcare is not intensive, and that of their grandchildren. Although vexatious family conflict is always a worry and not good for children, and in a few cases there may be darker issues, such as abuse, which should limit access of grandparents, for most grandchildren their grandparents are a positive asset and grandchildren would miss out without this contact. As grandparents live longer and maintain their health, it is hard to imagine a UK where the importance of their role will diminish. With more women working, family breakdown, and austerity politics the importance of the role of the "new" grandfather is likely to increase. This will be good for children.

Appendix

Meanings of Proverbs

"Blood is thicker than water."

Most parents, if unable to care for children themselves, would rather their children be cared for by "family", and most grandchildren, if they cannot be looked after by their mother and father, would rather be looked after by their grandparents.

"Grandparents should feel free to advise, but should never interfere."

Grandparental non-interference is a strong mantra. Indeed, as we have seen in this chapter, parents are the gatekeepers. If parents do not wish grandparents to have contact with their grandchildren, they have the right to block this.

Additional Resources

Grandparents Plus (now amalgamated with the Grandparents' Association) (www. grandparentsplus.org.uk)

Grandparents Plus is the national charity which champions the vital role of grandparents and the wider family in children's lives – especially when they take on the carer role in difficult family circumstances and when they have lost contact with children. Helplines for kinship carers and also grandparents who have lost contact (with free legal help).

Office for National Statistics (www.ons.gov.uk)
For all statistics on the family in the UK. Many articles are written in accessible language.

American Grandparents Association (www.grandparents.com)
The American Grandparents Association (AGA), established by Grandparents. com, is a non-political group dedicated to enhancement of the lives of grandparents and their families. With nearly two million members, the AGA recognizes that grandparenting today is like at no other time in history. The AGA offers a host of services, discounts, and resources that help UK grandparents, although the website is from the US.

Discussion Questions

1. Why do UK grandparents now have a greater role in caring for their grandchildren than in the past? Illustrate you answer with examples.
2. Discuss this comment: "the Welfare State in the UK has undermined intergenerational relations."
3. With reference to the UK, what do parents and grandchildren want from their grandparents?

References

Abel-Smith, B (1992). The Beveridge report: Its origins and outcomes. *International Social Security Review, 45* (1–2), 5–16.

Bates, J. S. (2009). Generative grandfathering: A conceptual framework for nurturing grandchildren. *Marriage & Family Review, 45,* 331–352.

Berger, P. L., & Luckmann, T. (1966). *The social construction of reality: A treatise in the sociology of knowledge.* London: Penguin Books.

Buchanan, A., & Flouri, E. (2008). Involved grand parenting and child well-being: Non-technical summary (research summary). ESRC End of Award Report, RES-000-22-2283. Swindon: ESRC.

Buchanan, A., & Rotkirch, A. (2016). *Grandfathers: Global perspectives.* London, UK: Palgrave Macmillan.

Campbell, A. (2013). Six childcare gurus who have changed parenting. *BBC.* Retrieved from www.bbc.co.uk/news/magazine-22397457

Chase, K. (2009). *The Victorians and old age.* Oxford: Oxford University Press.

Clarke, L., & Roberts, C. (2004). The meaning of grandparenthood and its contribution to the quality of life of older people. In A. Walker and C. Hagan Hennessy (eds), *Growing older: Quality of life in old age* (pp. 188–208). Milton Keynes: Open University Press.

Coall, D., Hilbrand, S., Sear, R., & Hertwig, R. (2016). A new niche? The theory of grand-father involvement. In A. Buchanan & A. Rotkirch (Eds.), *Grandfathers: Global perspectives* (pp. 21–38). London, UK: Palgrave Macmillan.

Conroy, D., & Fahey, C. (1985). Christian perspective on the role of Grandparents. In V. Bengtson & J. Robertson (Eds.), *Grandparenthood* (pp. 195–207). Beverly Hills: Sage.

Creasey, G. L., & Koblewski, P. J. (1991). Adolescent grandchildren's relationships with mater-nal and paternal grandmothers and grandfathers. *Journal of Adolescence, 14*(4), 373–387.

Dunn, J., & Deater-Deckard, K. D. (2001). *Children's views of their changing families.* York, UK: Joseph Rowntree Foundation.

Dunn, J., Davies, L., O'Connor, T., & Sturgess, W. (2001). Family lives and friendships: The perspectives of children in step-, single-parent, and non-step families. *Journal of Family Psychology, 15*(2), 272–287.

Ferguson, N., with Douglas, G., Lowe, N., Murch, M., & Robinson, M. (2004). *Grandparenting in divorced families.* Bristol, UK: Policy Press.

Fruhauf, C. A., Jarrott, S. E., & Allen, K. R. (2006). Grandchildren's perceptions of caring for grandparents. *Journal of Family Issues, 27*(7), 887–911.

Gayre, R. (2007). Chivalry. *Grolier Multimedia Encyclopedia.* Grolier Online.

Glaser, K., Price, D., di Gessa, G., Ribe, E., Stuchbury, R., & Tinker, A. (2013). *Grandparenting in Europe: Family policy and grandparents' role in providing childcare.* London, UK: Grandparents Plus.

Gratton, B., & Haber, C. (1996). Health and health care of African American elders: Three phases in the history of American grandparents: Authority, burden, companion. *Generations, 20,* 7–12.

Gray, R. (1992). *The factory question and industrial England.* Cambridge, UK: Cambridge University Press.

Harper, S., & Ruicheva, I. (2010). Grandmothers as replacement parents and partners: The role of grandmotherhood in single parent families. *Journal of Intergenerational Relationships, 8*(3), 219–33. doi:10.1080/15350770.2010.498779

Heath, A., Savage, M., & Senior, N. (2013). Social class. The role of class in shaping social attitudes. *British social attitudes.* Retrieved from www.bsa.natcen.ac.uk/media/38459/bsa30_social_class_final.pdf

Herlihy, D. (1985). *Medieval households.* Cambridge, MA: Harvard University Press.

Hunt, J., & Waterhouse, S. (2013). *It's just not fair! Support, need and legal status in fam-ily and friends care.* Family Rights Group/Oxford University Centre for Family Law and Policy. Retrieved from www.frg.org.uk/its-just-not-fair-support-need-and-legal-status-in-family-and-friends-care

Igel, C., & Szydlik, M. (2011). Grandchild care and welfare state arrangements in Europe. *Journal of European Social Policy, 21,* 210–224. doi:10.1177/0958928711401766.

Jackson, A. (1994). The coming age of grandparent visitation rights. *American University Law Review, 43,* 563–601.

Joaquín, N. (1988). *Culture and history.* Manila: Anvil.

Kaganas, F. (2007). Grandparents' rights and grandparents' campaigns. *Child and Family Law Quarterly, 19*(1), 17–42.

Lewis, C. (2013). Fatherhoood and fathering research in the UK: Cultural change and diversity. In D. Shwalb, B. Shwalb, & M. Lamb (Eds.), *Fathers in cultural context* (pp. 332–357). New York: Routledge.

Lowdell, C., Evandrou, C., Bardsley, M., Morgan, D., & Soljak, M. (2000). Health of eth-nic minority elders in London: Respecting diversity. Health of Londoners Project Directorate of Public Health East.

Norgrove, D. (2011). *Family justice review.* Retrieved from www.gov.uk/government/uploads/system/uploads/attachment_data/file/217343/family-justice-review-final-report.pdf

Office for National Statistics. (2011). *A summary of countries of birth in London.* Census update. London: Office for National Statistics.

Office for National Statistics. (2012). *Children of divorced couples.* Retrieved from www.ons.gov.uk/ons/dcp171778_351693.pdf

Office for National Statistics (2013). *Women in the labour market.* Retrieved from www.ons.gov.uk/ons/rel/lmac/women-in-the-labour-market/2013/rpt---women-in-the-labour-market.html

Office for National Statistics (2014). *Overview of the UK population.* Retrieved from www.ons.gov.uk/ons/rel/pop-estimate/population-estimates-for-uk--england-and-wales--scotland-and-northern-ireland/mid-2014/sty---overview-of-the-uk-population.html

Parsons, T., & Bales, R. F. (1956). *Family socialization and interaction process* Abingdon, UK: Psychology Press.

RIAS (2015) *Twenty-first century grandparent army report.* Retrieved from www.rias.co.uk/about-us/news-and-press-releases/we-salute-you-britains-grandparents-save-mums-and-dads-15.7bn-annually-in-childcare-costs/

Ross, N., Hill, M., Sweeting, H., & Cunningham-Burley, S. (2005). Grandparents and teen grandchildren: Exploring intergenerational relationships. Report for ESRC, Centre for Research on Families and Relationships.

Sandidge, M. (2007). *Old age in the Middle Ages and the Renaissance: Interdisciplinary approaches to a neglected topic.* Berlin: Walter de Gruyter.

Scottish Law Commission. (2005, June). Newsletter, Issue 1. Edinburgh: Scottish Law Commission.

Smart C., May,V., & Wade,A. (2003). *Residence and contact disputes.* Vol. 1. London: Department of Constitutional Affairs.

Smith, N. (2011). The impact of the industrial revolution on families in New England and America. *Myriad.* Retrieved from www.articlemyriad.com/impacts-industrial-revolution-families-new-england/

Tolstoy, L. (2014). *Anna Karenina.* Translated by R. Bartlett. Oxford: Oxford University Press.

Wasoff, F., & Morrison, A. (2005). *Family formation and dissolution in Europe: Scotland in a European context:* Legal Studies Research Findings No.56/2005, Edinburgh: Scottish Executive. Retrieved from www.scotland.gov.uk/Publications/2005/07/28102739/27419

7

GRANDMOTHERS IN RUSSIA'S MATRIFOCAL FAMILIES

Shoring Up Family Life

Jennifer Utrata

PROVERBS

1. "Even your grandma wouldn't know whether it will rain or snow." Бáбушка (гадáла, да) нáдвое сказáла (– то ли дóждик, то ли снег, то ли бýдет, то ли нет) (*Babushka [gadala, da] nadvoye skazala [– to li dozhdik, to li sneg, to li budet, to li net]*)
2. "The person whose grandma tells fortunes is happy." Хорошо тому жить, кому бабушка ворожит (*Khorosho tomu zhit', komu babushka vorozhit*)

(see pp. 152–153 for interpretations)

CASE STORY: SVETLANA'S ENDURING COMMITMENT TO WORK AND FAMILY

A special education teacher, former Communist Party member, and divorced mother of two children with one granddaughter, Svetlana wants to help her 32-year-old divorced daughter just as her own parents helped her years ago when she left her husband. To manage two young children under 5, along with work and Party responsibilities, would have been much harder without her parents' help. Her mother's steadfast support, in particular, allowed her to attend a special education training course a few hours away in Moscow for a full year, knowing that her children were in good hands. However, she explained that today it is even harder for single, working mothers. Now there is more competition for jobs which were once guaranteed, less state support, fewer after-school activities for kids, and more grandparents working for pay after retirement.

Svetlana hopes to contribute to the outlay of expenses traditionally expected at the start of a new school year, which includes the new backpack her granddaughter Olga covets. But it is challenging to do so with the prices for meat at the local market increasing every month while her own salary has stagnated. Svetlana loves Olga, and doesn't really mind cooking for her 29-year-old unmarried son Pavel, currently back home with her, as well as her daughter and Olga who live nearby. Yet making ends meet is not easy. Her pension is stable but insufficient, and time is another challenge. Svetlana enjoys spending time with Olga on the many evenings when her daughter works (Svetlana cares for Olga for several hours most weekday evenings and many weekends) but at the same time she often feels tired after commuting and working at an intense job all day. She wishes she had more time for herself in retirement, to go to the theatre as she used to or perhaps see her boyfriend Victor more often. But even if her pension were sufficient, Svetlana would still work after her retirement. "My work is important! Our government does not seem to consider it important based on what it pays, and it is not prestigious work, but these children need my expertise!"

As she balances paid work after retirement with significant caregiving and household work on behalf of her granddaughter and adult children, Svetlana is fairly typical of Russian grandmothers in the transition to market capitalism. Grandmothers are often more involved with care for grandchildren than grandfathers in Russia, due to cultural traditions and men's rates of mortality and alcoholism since the early 1990s. Svetlana loves her children, but she sometimes wishes she were appreciated a bit more for her efforts, whether in words or through some occasional financial support. Moreover, she is frustrated by how little money she earns at a job that is so important for society. She once compared a ride at a local, privately owned carnival in town to the amount she earns for one day's work with special needs children. "My labor appears to be worth 30 minutes in the bouncy house!" Svetlana exclaimed incredulously.

Svetlana's life trajectory provides important clues for our understanding of contemporary Russian grandparenthood. Grandfathers are frequently absent due to divorce, heavy drinking, or premature mortality, whereas bonds between mothers and adult daughters form networks of caregiving support exchanged over time. Like many grandmothers, Svetlana loves her job and enjoys her granddaughter; yet she feels caught in the middle between paid and unpaid work, and sometimes feels underappreciated at home. She is not alone in trying to "do it all" all over again as a grandmother, as she cares intensively for a grandchild and also works for pay, but doing so during a period of economic and social transition is a challenge on many levels. She is uncertain about her own future given all of the changes she has gone through, and hopes her daughter will reciprocate for her efforts over time.

Despite their importance to families, there is much less research on Russian grandparents relative to parents, especially mothers. And just as motherhood features more prominently than fatherhood in studies of Russian parents, (Utrata, Ispa, & Ispa-Landa, 2013), grandmotherhood garners more attention than grandfatherhood. To bring together strands of the varied research on Russian grandparents, this chapter begins with the cultural and historical backgrounds that have shaped grandparenthood in the Soviet period (1917–1991) and the post-Soviet period (1991–present). I then elaborate on a theoretical framework to analyze Russian grandparenting, review the existing literature, and discuss the marginalization of grandfathers, subcultural variations, and social policies that affect grandparents. I conclude with some comparisons between Russia and other regions of the world, and include speculation and suggestions about the future of Russian grandparenting.

Cultural, Historical, and Demographic Backgrounds

To understand contemporary Russian grandparenting requires us to grapple with a variety of cultural, historical, and demographic factors related to families. The Russian grandmother (or *babushka*), in particular, has long held symbolic and practical significance in family life, while little attention has been paid to the role and importance of the grandfather in Russian families. This discrepancy requires an analysis of gender relations and families under state socialism, when Russia was part of the Soviet Union. Just as there has been much less research on fatherhood than on motherhood in Russia (Utrata et al., 2013), there is a long historical and cultural legacy of grandmothers as major linchpins of support in families (Utrata, 2011, 2015). Although this trend of much less attention being paid to grandfathers is reported in almost all chapters of this book, Russian grandfathers have been uniquely marginalized or absent from family life.

The Soviet Period (1917–1991)

During most of the Soviet period, Russians lived under state socialism and all citizens considered work as the central part of their lives. Toward the end of this period the Soviet Union had the highest rate of female labor force participation in any industrialized country (Ashwin & Lytkina, 2004). Women as worker-mothers were entitled to benefits to help them balance paid and unpaid work responsibilities, such as state-subsidized childcare and other guarantees. However, their burden was still heavy, given the frequent shortages of consumer goods and that they had few of the time- and labor-saving conveniences available in other parts of the world. In contrast to the multiple responsibilities expected of women, men were encouraged by the Soviet state to focus their efforts nearly exclusively on paid work, including management and leadership of state enterprises. Compared to women, men maintained higher social status and their roles were much more narrowly defined (Ashwin, 2000).

Even though gender ideals in the early part of the Soviet period had the revolutionary potential to ensure equality for women and men, in practice male dominance was left unchallenged as a norm in the Soviet Union. Rather than challenging the gender division of labor at home, the Soviet state periodically tried to shift the basis for masculine identity from patriarchal power at home to the realm of paid work. However, patriarchal ideology proved resistant to change (Kukhterin, 2000). Ultimately, the Soviet gender order offered a façade of liberation (Utrata, 2015) – the state mandated women's participation in the labor force but also allowed gender traditionalism to flourish at home. Given that there was no women's movement to challenge the domestic division of labor or feminine responsibility for most domesticity in addition to women's paid labor, scholars agree that this "emancipation was always thinner than it seemed" (Pascall & Manning, 2000, p. 262). While the Soviets encouraged men to be powerful leaders at work, they also saw men "as the weak link in the family…particularly in relation to drink" (Kukhterin, 2000, p. 83). The state relied on women's unpaid labor at home on top of their paid labor and preserved the gender wage gap, paying only lip service to gender equality. As long as men contributed to the household economy and aspired to be primary breadwinners, men saw their role at home mostly as helping out with traditional masculine tasks.

Most women therefore served as secondary breadwinners. If troubles at home proved to be too much, then women were encouraged to turn to the Soviet state as their ultimate father and patriarch. Although two-parent families were considered the ideal family structure throughout the Soviet period, divorce rates were still very high; the Soviet Union had the second-highest divorce rate after the US in the mid-1970s (Moskoff, 1983). Nowadays the Russian divorce rate is even higher than the 36% divorce rate in the US (Stanton, 2015).

The matrifocality of Soviet families and the frailty of heterosexual relations relative to intergenerational kin bonds (Ashwin & Lytkina, 2004; Rotkirch, 2000) are key aspects of Russian family life that are relevant to grandparenting. In matrifocal families, "the mother–child unit is more central culturally than the father–child unit or the mother–father conjugal relationship" (Utrata, 2015, p. 6). In the Soviet period, mothers had a much more elaborated role than fathers in Russian families (Ashwin & Lytkina, 2004; Fogiel-Bijaoui, 2013; Utrata, 2008), and the dynamics of matrifocality extend to grandmothers and still continue in today's families.

Given that this gender status quo had long shaped parenthood in Soviet Russia, it is not surprising that it has likewise shaped grandparenthood. Focusing on how grandparents contribute to grandchildren, scholars note the ubiquitous finding that the grandmother "has held a prominent and venerated position in Russian history, and her importance in the family continues up to the present" (Uhlenberg & Cheuk, 2010, p. 452). Of course, it is also critical to note that Russian families have undergone various forms of upheaval in the 20th century, including World War I, the 1917 Bolshevik Revolution, Stalin's political purges, World War II, and the economic struggles citizens faced after the 1991 collapse of the Soviet Union. With so many women working full time and so many men absent due to military service or travel for work, death, or divorce, both men and women were frequently absent from families (Ashwin & Lytkina, 2004; Kelly, 2007; Utrata, 2015). Therefore, grandparents had a major role in assisting their adult children with childcare, and especially their adult daughters, because women were traditionally expected to deal with family issues.

Many Soviet children were closer to their grandparents than their own parents, which in some ways reduced the Soviet regime's influence over children's socialization yet also preserved traditional roles in families (Kukhterin, 2000). Whether children visited grandparents for summer vacations or spent weekdays with them while parents worked, children were exposed to the more traditional values of the older generation. Extended family living arrangements remained the norm in the 1950s and 1960s, partly due to a shortage of separate housing for families (Semenova & Thompson, 2004). Although not all co-resident grandparents helped with childcare, Kelly (2007) concluded that throughout the Soviet period most probably did. By the 1960s the Soviet press began to suggest that active pensioners might be well suited to care for grandchildren, "emphasizing that state child-care facilities would only be able to cope if parents and grandparents helped – say, by acting as assistant to overworked supervisors" and suggesting that "if parents were absent or unsatisfactory, grandparents could offer compensation" (Kelly, 2007, pp. 415, 422). Grandparents were often expected to indulge grandchildren, e.g., entertaining them with traditional folk tales (*skazki*) and family stories.

Soviet family and work policies fluctuated over time, but generally the postwar period (1944–1967) was critical in establishing grandparents' roles in Russian families. The Soviet Union lost approximately 27 million soldiers and civilians during the war, i.e., about half of all World War II casualties. Given that so many men lost their lives in the war, there were many more mothers and grandmothers available to provide care. These events forced many mothers to depend on their children's grandmothers to provide childcare, buy gifts, allow them to finish their education and find better jobs, do housework, shop, cook, and much more.

Soviet grandmothers, in particular, were encouraged by the state and society to step in to compensate for both the state's inadequacies and for the frequent absence of both fathers and grandfathers. Households composed of several generations were common, with early marriage typical and often encouraged by the state. Even when fathers were present in the Soviet period, research suggests that everyday life was supported by extended mothering to provide stability in times of change (Gurko, 2003; Rotkirch, 2000; Teplova, 2007). Women developed intricate networks to carry out predominantly female care work. Unlike the ideology of intensive mothering which predominates in US white middle-class households, an ideology that views childrearing as "child centred, expert-guided, emotionally absorbing, labour intensive and financially expensive,"

(Hays, 1996, p. 8), Russian-style extended mothering is authoritarian, family-guided, socially integrated, and based on informal networks (Rotkirch, 2000). Grandmothers, adult daughters, and grandchildren form the core of these support networks, and effectively, even if not purposively, marginalize men as fathers and grandfathers.

The assistance *babushka* provided to Soviet society was critical. "Female and kin solidarity thus compensated for the often underdeveloped social infrastructure and lack of household goods, as well as for the mistrust experienced toward public institutions" (Rotkirch, Tkach, & Zdravomyslova, 2012, p. 134). In a longitudinal survey of young adults in Moscow born in the 1960s, one-third of the adults lived with a grandparent and three-quarters had contact with a grandparent at least weekly. Moreover, Semenova & Thompson (2004, p. 129) note that "It is very striking how much more often there seems to have been a confiding intimate relationship between the child and its grandmother than with the parents." In addition, Boss and Gurko (1994) found that Soviet women sometimes expressed a great sense of dissatisfaction when their husbands' parents did not help them sufficiently with childrearing.

The Post-Soviet Period (1991–present)

Since the breakup of the Soviet Union in 1991, Russian society has been undergoing many dramatic changes. But the marginalized status of men in family life, both as fathers and as grandfathers, extended into the post-Soviet period. At the same time the transition to capitalism has incrementally influenced the institution of grandparenthood. Yet the matrifocality of Russian family life, whereby mothers, grandmothers, and children continue to form the course of family life, continues to endure. Though grandmothers were vital to family life after World War II due to demographic and social changes, in post-Soviet Russia they have also provided stability during economic, political, and cultural crises and changes. Grandparents serve as a source of stability in many families, providing income, childcare, and emotional support to adult children and their families, yet many grandparents also want to work for pay after retirement, enjoy increased leisure, and engage in other activities besides minding children. While many welcome these new pursuits, when grandparents devote their time elsewhere it makes the hard work of care for the next generation more difficult and precarious for families accustomed to depending on the grandmothers' support.

Moreover, cultural, economic, and demographic changes in the transition from state socialism to market capitalism have compounded the problems faced by Russian grandparents. For instance, while drinking has long been primarily a masculine ritual, in recent years Russian men drink more and die earlier than ever before. In fact, Russia has the world's largest gender gap in both drinking and life expectancy (Gavrilova & Gavrilov, 2009). Drinking, especially vodka, is a widespread cultural custom, and survey data affirm that about one-third of Russian men binge drink at least once per month. During the post-Soviet period, men's drinking has become even more normalized and entrenched, and the practice of binge drinking is associated with the crisis in male mortality that intensified in the 1990s. Today the gender gap in life expectancy is still high at 12 years, with men's life expectancy at 64.7 years and women's at 76.6 in Russia (Table 1.1). Overall, Russia is a country with low gender equality, high female participation in labor markets, and very low fertility. Although most women aspire to have two children, they end up with just one. The average number of children is now 1.6, lower than in Soviet times, and most women have their first child at a relatively young age, typically in their early 20s (Temkina, 2010). The combination of low fertility, heavy male drinking, and a large gender mortality gap has severe implications for family life. Besides small family size in recent years and a continued pattern from Soviet times for women to have their first child relatively early, there are simply more grandmothers (even young grandmothers) than grandfathers alive and available to help families. These demographic and cultural trends are powerful forces which reinforce Russia's matrifocal families and the centrality of grandmothers rather than grandfathers in family life.

FIGURE 7.1 A 56 year old grandmother from Kaluga shares a tender moment with her 10-year-old grandson. She can no longer work full time for health reasons, but she enjoys the time she spends with her grandson after he gets home from school each day, when she prepares some of his favorite snacks and talks to him about what he learned in school.

Source: Courtesy of Jennifer Utrata.

Scholars have noted that the premature mortality crisis is concentrated among men at the bottom of the labor market, who are more likely to be poor and marginalized and form about 15–20% of the overall population (Gavrilova & Gavrilov, 2009). Russians with university degrees or residence in Moscow have mortality rates closer to those in Western countries (Shkolnikov, Field, & Andreev, 2001). Because most alcohol-related deaths occur between the ages of 45 and 55, Gavrilova and Gavrilov (2009) argue that the elderly can be considered a group less likely to abuse alcohol. Hence, as occurred in the Soviet period, grandparents may serve as a source of family stability. While in most countries there is a feminization of population aging (Gavrilova & Gavrilov, 2009), Russian women's longevity relative to men compounds this feminization. Even though the meaning and practices of being a grandmother are in flux in Russia, most studies suggest that grandmothers continue to serve as major sources of stability and continuity in family life (Kosterina 2012; Utrata, 2011, 2015).

The significance of grandmothers in Russian society, and the marginalization of men as fathers and grandfathers are noteworthy, but it is not necessarily as unique as it might first appear. For example, in many kinship networks the relationship with one's mother is often considered most salient (Nauck, 2009). Nauck's comparative study focused on tight-knit relationships with mothers in Russian, Chinese, and German societies, and reported that 64% of Russian women maintained close relationships with mothers, compared to 53% and 27% for Chinese and German women, respectively. Although recent studies note that grandmothers provide more childcare than grandfathers do in many parts of the world, the findings do not clearly explain the reasons for the differential levels of their involvement (Leopold & Skopek, 2014). The grandmothers' support and caregiver role is thus taken for granted in many societies (Ashwin & Lytkina, 2004; Utrata, 2015).

Theoretical/Conceptual Approaches

Research on the contours of Russian family life, including grandparenting, is minimal, and with few exceptions it focuses on the consensus that grandparents make large contributions to family life with close ties between the generations. Much of this research focuses on Russian grandparenting without building on or extending broader theories of grandparenting in family life. Nevertheless, research on grandparents in other contexts calls attention to the idea that children and the elderly are age groups in conflict over scarce welfare supports. Alternatively, critics of age group conflict theories argue instead that individuals or groups should not be seen as "separate from their households, wider networks of family relations, support and social obligations" (Kanji, 2009, p. 372). Instead of an emphasis on conflicts between age groups, this second group of theorists foregrounds intergenerational interdependence; it emphasizes that kinship structures, familial bonds, and normative expectations condition people's actions. Some argue that increased lifespans actually create opportunities for more intergenerational cooperation over time (Bengtson, 2001).

Some arguments in this chapter are informed by these two theoretical perspectives: intergenerational conflict versus solidarity. The relationship between Russian grandparents and adult children and grandchildren certainly involves both conflict and cooperation. Generally, I seek to move beyond these two paradigms. I draw upon social constructionist theories of gender as key to understanding the cultural beliefs and practices of grandparents in Russia. Scholarship has framed parenting as a highly gendered practice in most societies, and I view grandparenting as similarly gendered. To theorize about the experience of grandparenthood, we should recognize the importance of grandchildren's and grandparents' gender, age, social class, race/ethnicity, and sexuality. As they care for their grandchildren, grandparents engage in gendered activities; moreover, through their care work grandparents are "doing gendered age" (Utrata, 2011). This does not mean that many grandmothers do not feel genuine love and joy when they spend time with grandchildren. However, there is so much more to the story. Grandmothers in particular are expected to feel love and affection for their grandchildren, and to embody feminine self-sacrifice as they assist their adult children with domestic work and caring for grandchildren. Gendered expectations change over the lifespan, but many studies treat age as merely a number; instead, I view age as a socially constructed power relation on a par with other axes of power and inequality, since gender, class, race, and sexuality also shape behavior (Krekula, 2007; Utrata, 2011, 2015).

Gender, like age, is produced and performed by individuals. It is an ongoing process with both men and women "doing gender," held accountable to these performances by institutions and in interactions with others (West & Zimmerman, 1987). Of course, social expectations for doing gender, and gendered age, change over time. In the Russian context, especially during the transition to market capitalism over the past few decades, fluidity in gender and age performances has intensified. Past cultural expectations still shape what grandparents do and how they feel about it, but newer market pressures and institutions also influence grandparents' feelings and behavior in relation to their grandchildren and adult children.

In the case of grandparents, men and women are held accountable to gender expectations but also to their socially perceived age. In this way, grandparents are expected to behave according to their gendered age (Utrata, 2011). Russian women perceived as of a certain age are especially encouraged and even pressured by society to dedicate themselves to their grandchildren and to assist their adult children, in spite of their motivation to continue with paid work, travel, and personal relationships, or take some leisure after a lifetime of significant care work.

Although gender relations from the Soviet era remain mostly intact, there are new challenges as Russia transitions from state socialism to market capitalism. According to Tartakovskaya (2000, p. 128), "gender relations are in flux and old certainties have dissolved." There are now weaker supports for families than there were previously, and Russian families are in the throes of a significant "quiet revolution" (Utrata, 2015). Although some suggest that there may be a "crisis of grandmother's role in the family" (Zdravomyslova, 2010, p. 204), others find that grandmothers in particular perform a great deal of unpaid, and often unreciprocated, care work for their adult children and grandchildren (Utrata, 2011, 2015). Russia is an interesting case of significant grandmother support for adult children in times of cultural change, because these women are bound to gendered work to ensure the family's survival, in an environment with a heightened possibility for tension and conflict between the generations.

Research on Russian Grandparents

Russian grandparents have not been as well studied as have grandparents in some Western countries (e.g., the US, Chapter 3, and Germany, Chapter 5). In part this is due to the fact that during the Soviet period (1917–1991), sociology "was thoroughly controlled by the party-state" (Voronkov & Zdravomyslova, 1996, p. 40), as was psychology, and research centered mainly on the state's interests and public opinion surveys, with scant attention paid to family life. There is still inadequate space for an inadequate autonomy for a social science independent of the market and the state (Zdravomyslova, 2008). Research in both the Soviet and post-Soviet periods has emphasized the importance of close intergenerational ties and matrifocal, female-dominated networks of caregiving in Russian families. Most cultural traditions centered around the *babushka*, the word for "grandmother" in Russian. *Babushka* is used as a polite form of address for any woman in Russia "of grandmotherly age," whether or not she is actually a grandmother.

Much of the cultural fixation on grandmothers rather than grandfathers can be linked to longstanding traditions and recent demographic changes in Russia, described earlier in this chapter. Svetlana, the Russian grandmother in the case story, is not unusual for having been divorced herself in the Soviet period, but besides divorce other grandmothers may have lost partners to premature death or the sometimes fatal effects of drinking. Because early childbearing is still normal in Russia (Zakharov, 2008), Russian men and women become grandparents at a relatively early age, typically after 40. Russia also has an early retirement age relative to most other countries, age 55 for women and 60 for men. Once women, in particular, reach this age, they are expected to have more time to assist adult children and their families. This is so even though many women, like men, still want and need to work for pay (Ashwin, Tartakovskaya, Ilyina, & Lytkina, 2013). There has been much discussion recently about a change in the age at which Russians are eligible to receive a pension, but currently the early ages remain in place. Given that the average life expectancy of men barely exceeds the official retirement age of 60, any change to the age of retirement faces strong popular opposition (Gavrilova & Gavrilov, 2009).

Grandparents cope with a range of uncertainties due to huge cultural, social, and economic changes as a result of the transition to market capitalism after 1991. Many of these experiences are shaped by gender and class. For instance, a relatively high number of older Russian women live alone, but a recent study found that older Russian men were the least likely group to live alone in the former Soviet Union and Eastern Europe (Gavrilova & Gavrilov, 2009). Still, in Russia today about 20% of families live in three-generational households (Nauck, 2009). In addition, even though the healthcare system in Russia officially provides free services, in practice "many pensioners report difficulties in obtaining qualified medical care" (Gavrilova & Gavrilov, 2009, p. 128); the same may be said about its childcare system. Kravchenko (2012, pp. 195–196) describes Russia more generally as "a society with a rather high degree of corruption at all levels." Given these sources of anxiety, many grandparents feel uncertain about who will care for them as they age, or what the quality of that care will be. As a result, many feel as if they have no choice but to do whatever they can to help their adult children, in hopes that their caregiving work will be reciprocated as they age (Utrata, 2011).

Pensions have been crucial to the survival of many Russian households (see Chapter 12 for a similar discussion of pensioners in Southern Africa). Specifically, Kanji's (2009) research highlights that many households with children in Russia rely on the pension income of the grandparents. Kanji (2009, p. 383) notes "pensioners add to the material security of children but at their own cost," which emphasizes that pensioners in Russia are generally economically active, much more so than in many other countries, with at least 40% of their income derived from sources other than pensions. Women more than men suffered from non-payment of their pensions in the late 1990s, and while this has stabilized somewhat women are still more vulnerable to pension non-payments (Kanji, 2009). Overall, transfers of economic resources in Russia during the transition to market capitalism have flowed from the older to the younger generations (Gavrilova & Gavrilov, 2009).

Much of what we know about grandparents until recently relied on anecdotal evidence and stereotypes about older Russian women. In the Soviet period, one dominant narrative suggested that although some Soviet women chose to work after retirement, most freely chose the *babushka* role. For instance, Sternheimer (1985, p. 328) argued that "The *babushka*, in effect, takes full responsibility for her daughter's home, freeing up both daughter and husband to participate unhampered in the work force…voluntary assumption of the *babushka* role is, in part, a reflection of the love that frequently transcends the generations." Considering how these depictions tend to sideline intergenerational conflicts and power relations, newer research data questions some aspects of these former assumptions (Utrata, 2011).

While research on contemporary grandmothers is still nascent, we know that conflicts are a part of most intergenerational relationships. In spite of conflicts, most Russians expect their mothers to support them to some degree (Utrata, 2015). When women lack a mother to provide this kind of support, they often look for a mother-substitute in the form of a neighbor or hired nanny. Some Russian scholars argue that one way to mark oneself as middle class in Russia today is to hire a domestic worker or nanny, instead of relying on the grandmother or another unpaid relative (Patico, 2016). The role of "working grandmothers"

FIGURE 7.2 This grandmother was able to leave her full-time job early to accompany her 6-year-old granddaughter to her first dance recital. Her own daughter was busy with work until a few minutes before the recital started. She is one of many grandmothers who works full time but also finds ways to provide extensive support to their grandchildren and adult children.

Source: Courtesy of Jennifer Utrata.

has gradually become more legitimized and expected, as a replacement for the later Soviet model of a "grandmother bringing up her grandchild" (Patico, 2016, p. 27). Ultimately, social inequalities among mothers are reinforced in this situation, whereby some middle-class mothers have upward career mobility through new forms of class inequality.

While the grandmother's place in society is in transition, traditional expectations often still hold sway. In Kosterina's (2012) article about rural women, she noted that "after the birth of a child, mothers often appeared in the participants' interview narratives as accessible, free nannies who enabled young parents to go to work or to socialize, and often the women had found a job as a result of assistance from their mother, for example, by tapping into her mother's networks and communications" (p. 1885). Power dynamics among the women shifted over time, "but, in some cases, where daughters began to offer material support to parents or, to help them with more physically demanding domestic chores, mothers began to feel dependent on their daughter and lost a form of control as a result" (Kosterina, 2012, p. 1886). I observed similar patterns in my own research, i.e., compared to the guarantees by state socialism of basic needs, contemporary Russian life is characterized by distrust of the state and anxiety about the future.

While the phenomenon of grandmothers who care for grandchildren endures in contemporary Russia, newer research shows that the institution of *babushka* support is much less stable than it was in the Soviet period (Utrata, 2015; Zdravomyslova, 2010). In the transition to market capitalism in Russia, grandparents have many more lifestyle options after retirement. Many grandmothers, for instance, prefer to continue working for pay while receiving pension income, or simply to have more time for personal relationships and leisure (Utrata, 2011, 2015). Although working-class grandmothers may feel somewhat less entitled to leisure, values of self-fulfillment are ascendant in Russia. Many women who are not yet of grandmotherly age benefit from a kind of "youth privilege" (Utrata, 2011, p. 618). That is, newer values of feminine self-care and leisure are expected to apply mostly to younger women. Younger women also face pressures to do it all at home and work, as they attempt to seamlessly juggle paid work and unpaid childcare. Still, it is the generation of older women, especially grandmothers, who are expected to serve as a reserve army of feminine self-sacrifice, with caregiving mapped onto older women, and much less so on younger people or older men. In spite of strong pressure on older women to serve as caregiver grandmothers, it is possible that the transition to a market economy will eventually lead to a greater number of grandmothers who set limits on the support they provide adult children and grandchildren. This could, in time, lead to weaker *babushka* support.

Increasingly, some grandmothers put some limits on the care work they provide; the following are all excerpts from Utrata (2015). For example, a 62-year-old grandmother named Luba emphasized the importance of boundaries: "When my granddaughter was born, I clearly said to myself, yes, I'm a *babushka*. But not constantly...I also have my own plans!" Another grandmother said she admired grandmothers who took care of themselves while they also helped their adult children in a way that would not undermine their own life plans. Alyona noted,

> Natalya Ivanovna took in her grandson at her own expense and now the parents are complaining...And then there's Aleftina Mikhailovna – oh, how I admire that woman! She helps out only when she considers it necessary. She takes care of herself as a woman should – she reads, dresses well, devotes time to herself. But when she has free time...she says, 'I'll go buy some groceries for them.' That is, when it's not to the detriment of her own life.

Even though many grandmothers yearn for more appreciation for their efforts and contributions, I found in my research that grandmothers talk about enforcement of limits more often than they actually enforce such limits. After all, given the political and economic transition in Russia after the collapse of state socialism in 1991, many worry about their future and feel dependent on their children. Ruslana, a 65-year-old grandmother who helps her 40-year-old daughter significantly with daily cooking and babysitting while also working for pay, explained: "What choice do I have? I worked my whole life for nothing;

I have not even a penny to show for it. And what if I get sick? I cannot expect anything from the state. I can only count on my daughter." Besides this feeling of dependence, some grandmothers feel that things are actually harder for working-age adults today, especially in the job discrimination most women face. Women can lessen the effects of this discrimination by telling employers they have a *babushka* who can provide backup care support for children. One single mother I interviewed, a librarian named Yuliya, reflected on whether she would face discrimination if she had to suddenly look for work:

> No, I wouldn't. If I didn't have her [*babushka's*] support, then yes, I'd face discrimination … Therefore, I'm a little bit protected. And I can let myself work more in general. This is a big advantage. I have an entire detachment at home – my grandma, great-grandma, and my sister!

Not only does access to a grandmother's support allow her to feel protected, but she feels she can improve her career and breadwinning prospects further through evening freelance work in addition to her lower-paid day job. Svetlana, in our case story, tried to set some limits on the support she provided her adult children, but she felt she should try to do what her own mother had done for her while raising her children as a divorced woman in the Soviet era. Under market capitalism today, she observed, there are even more stresses and anxieties for young people, with fewer guarantees or supports.

The negotiations for mutual support between adult daughters and grandmothers are complex and are shaped by broad institutions such as labor markets and marriage markets. While many grandmothers work for pay beyond retirement age, they are also frequently pressured to take sick leave to help adult daughters with childcare in emergencies, since they face less societal pressure to be successful in their jobs than their adult children do. Many assume that the early career-building years should be prioritized for younger women. Marriage markets, too, place a premium on relative youth, with grandmothers often expected to provide childcare for adult daughters, who feel more entitled to have a social life. Some grandmothers try to carve out time for themselves besides working and helping adult children with housework and childcare, but it is often an uphill battle. In Russia, where masculine values of independence, autonomy, and success in the marketplace are increasingly prized in the transition to a market economy, values of feminine self-sacrifice and selfless caregiving are often assumed to apply most to older women, especially *babushki*. However, rather than forming distinct groups of grandmothers, older women tend to vacillate between newer discourses of femininity emphasizing self-fulfillment and autonomy and older discourses foisting unpaid work on grandmothers. In this way, the institution of grandmother support in Russia is in a time of flux.

At a dinner gathering during my fieldwork, one woman reflected on grandmothers' contributions to families during a toast:

In this country, as long as you have your mother, you're fine. A mother is the closest person a woman can have. She is one of your own, not a stranger as a husband can be, and only one of your own will not abandon you in a time of need!

While many are less reflective than this particular woman, mothers without a *babushka*'s support feel much more insecurity and worry about their child's future. A lack of support from the grandmother in the family, whether due to death, illness, or living far away, is experienced as a tragedy by many Russians, especially mothers (Utrata, 2015). Kravchenko (2012, p. 198), too, noted that "The importance of extended networks becomes much more evident in the narratives of families who do not have them." The presence of a *babushka* provides emotional and social supports that, while difficult to quantify, are as significant as material supports – if not more so.

Grandfathers

Compared to grandmothers, grandfathers' contributions to family chores including childcare are modest in matrifocal Russian families (Tiaynen-Qadir, 2016; Utrata, 2015). As indicated earlier, matrifocality structures family life and represents "predominantly female, cross-generational social, emotional and economic relations" (Rotkirch, 2000, p. 160). Fatherhood in Russia has long been marginalized relative to motherhood (Utrata, Ispa, & Ispa-Landa, 2013), and in many ways a parallel argument can be made about grandfatherhood relative to grandmotherhood. Grandfathers' involvement in childcare and family routines has long been minimal. Whereas grandmothers have long specialized in provision of childcare and maintenance of extended families, grandfathers' involvement is less pronounced, especially given a construction of masculinity that de-emphasizes care and encourages men to instead realize themselves in the public sphere. Masculine ideals of men as breadwinners are not only still dominant culturally, but they are even stronger and more pronounced today than they were previously. Today people expect even more of breadwinning men. Given that detached fatherhood and involved motherhood have been cultural norms in Russia (Ispa, Ispa-Landa, & Utrata, 2013), it may take some time before the contributions beyond breadwinning for grandfathers will take shape.

While more research on grandfathers is needed in Russia, to some extent grandfathers may have been overlooked in research because grandmothers are so much more numerous. As noted earlier, Russia currently has one of the largest gender gaps in life expectancy in the world. In rural areas, this is combined with the out-migrations of young people, which exacerbates the situation. In rural villages every third person is an elderly woman. According to Kosterina's (2012) study, rural women most frequently cited their own mothers as the source of emotional closeness and trust as a confidant.

Although it is usually women who become professional grandparents after retirement (Rotkirch, 2000), some research shows that grandfathers can also find alternatives to employment in grandparenthood, as long as they are of pension age. Ashwin and Lytkina (2004, pp. 200–201) argue that retirement provides "a socially legitimate form of economic inactivity" such that "being an active grandfather does not represent a major deviation from locally accepted norms of masculinity." In a more recent study by Ashwin et al. (2013) on unpaid task assistance in Russia, grandfathers were reported to take care of children. However, "in all cases, this work was shared with their spouses, who, the men's comments revealed, played the leading role" (Ashwin et al., 2013, p. 404). Grandfathers can and do participate in childcare, but this participation is not perceived as obligatory (Ashwin et al., 2013) in the way that it still is for grandmothers.

Nevertheless, limited research data suggest that grandfathers may play an important role in support of childcare work led by grandmothers and women. In particular, Russian men play a significant role in the care of elderly parents; they either assist their wives in this work or bear primary responsibility for it when wives or daughters are unable to (Rotkirch, 2000). Although some research has begun to highlight the voices of Russian fathers (Kay, 2006; Utrata, 2008; Utrata et al., 2013), more research is needed to highlight grandfathers' contributions to families, even within the context of the matrifocal family structure.

Subcultural Variations among Grandparents

In a country as vast and diverse as Russia, patterns of grandparenting vary by ethnicity, class, timing of the transition to grandparenthood, and rural–urban location. Although most research focuses on grandparents in large and mid-sized cities, some research focuses on rural–urban variations in grandparenting. The problems discussed previously in terms of men's drinking and premature mortality, the gender gap in life expectancy, and the availability of caregivers, are intensified in the Russian countryside. Russia has experienced a variety of crises in its transition to capitalism. With lower standards of living relative to the rest of Russia and weakened traditional rural values (Kosterina, 2012), the country-side has experienced a deeper level of social and economic crisis than the rest of Russia. The gap in living standards between rural and urban areas is wider than the gap between various regions (White, 2005). With the out-migration of young people from rural to urban areas and intensified economic and social crisis, the absence of men, including grandfathers, and the more widespread presence of grandmothers is likely amplified in rural Russia. Matrifocal patterns of intergenerational relationships, with grandmothers playing the lead roles in family life, are also intensified in rural settings. There also tends to be more gender traditionalism in rural families, which discourages men and grandfathers from domestic and childcare work in families (Kosterina, 2012; White, 2005). In urban households, Russian men have long participated in domestic work by repairing broken household items and perhaps taking out the trash (Ashwin & Lytkina, 2004), but in rural households more work (e.g., domestic food production, animal husbandry) has been expected of men at home. Furthermore, grandparents and parents in lower-income families are more dependent on each other than is the case in the middle class.

Social Policies that Affect Grandparents

There is a lack of data about how Russian family policy shapes the lives of ordinary citizens, including grandparents (Kravchenko, 2012). This reflects the limited importance of the autonomous social science field related to families, and the priorities of the party-state in the Soviet period (Voronkov & Zdravomyslova, 1996). In addition, it has largely been assumed by tradition that grandparents, especially grandmothers, would provide supplementary childcare and related support for adult children after their retirement.

Any analysis of social policy in contemporary Russia must consider the "flagship of contemporary Russian family policy" (Borozdina, Rotkirch, Temkina, & Zdravomyslova, 2016, p. 72) – Russia's maternity capital program. The maternity (family) capital program (*materinskii - semeinnyi - capital*) continues to marginalize fathers in families while it reinforces women's primary responsibility for the home and family. Valued at approximately US$10,000 and indexed to inflation, "capitals" are paid out to women who give birth to a second or third child, after the child turns 3 years old (Rivkin-Fish, 2010; Utrata, Ispa, & Ispa-Landa, 2013). Although recent research suggests that this program has influenced the timing of the second child but not so much the overall number of children families have (Borozdina et al., 2016), the existence of such policies highlights the gender traditionalism of the state, a legacy of the Soviet period, where women are assumed to be the default parents and caregivers. Grandparents are not a direct part of the maternity capital program, although grandparents contribute significant income, housework, and childcare on behalf of their grandchildren. To have a grandparent, especially a grandmother, nearby to assist with childcare helps working parents immensely, but this assistance is seldom considered from a policy perspective. Given that women are more likely to share childcare or housework with extended female kin than they are with male partners, the disregard for grandparents in policy practices and research is problematic as it provides a very limited perspective on family life (Kravchenko, 2012; Utrata, 2015).

Some social policies in the post-Soviet era do confirm and provide some support for grandparents' important role in the family. For instance, Article 256 of the 2001 Russian Labor Code gave some recognition to grandmothers' provision of childcare since a father, grandmother, grandfather, or other relative may request full or partial childrearing leave (see Rotkirch, Temkina, & Zdravomyslova, 2007). However, we know little about the actual effects of these changes to the Labor Code. Because "formal legal norms do not necessarily translate into actual administrative practice in the Russian context" (Kravchenko, 2012), much more research on policy issues remains to be done.

There have also been many efforts since 1991 to change the pension system in Russia, as well as the retirement ages of 55 for women and 60 for men. In 2001, Russia selected a World Bank model of pension reform which favors individual pension accounts. However, there have been many delays in its implementation, and "difficulties in reaching agreement between state, employers and employees postponed the introduction of such pension systems" (Gavrilova & Gavrilov, 2009, p. 126). The reformulation of the pension system will have implications for grandparents who provide direct care and financial support for their grandchildren.

Speculation

The institution of grandparenthood is now in a period of flux. However, the Soviet legacy of marginalizing men as fathers and grandfathers in families, in addition to cultural expectations for grandmothers to provide childcare and related assistance to grandchildren looms large in the contemporary period. Whereas Soviet grandparents were expected to retire after they reached pension age, and to help their adult children with summer garden plots, household work, and childcare, in the post-Soviet transition to market capitalism grandparents face both more uncertainty and more opportunities than in past generations. Grandparents are now uncertain about the state's promises to them for retirement. Russian citizens, including grandparents who have lived through various regime changes, generally have extremely high levels of distrust in government and related institutions (Borozdina et al., 2016; Shlapentokh, 2006). In addition, many grandparents are dissatisfied with their small pensions, and worried about their adult children's ability to provide for themselves and their families. Given their distrust in government and uncertain future, many grandparents choose to continue to work for pay after retirement.

There is a critical need for additional research on grandfathers. Today's grandfathers may step up their involvement with grandchildren because fathers are increasingly expected to help out with the care of children and other household chores (Utrata et al., 2013). However, this change will take time because they have not been expected to do so as grandmothers have. Grandfathers may choose to spend time with grandchildren, but they do not see this as an obligation (Ashwin et al., 2013) in the way that many grandmothers do. Furthermore, recent research suggests that women's "gifts of labor involve greater time and effort than men's but women report nonreciprocation" (Ashwin et al., 2013, p. 396). That is, much of the work that grandmothers perform is taken for granted and rendered invisible, while norms of gender and age inhibit reciprocity and recognition of their gifts. Even though individual fulfillment is increasingly seen as legitimate, grandmothers continue to be pressured to provide care, especially many grandmothers who feel uncertain about the state or a partner caring for them as they age.

Overall, as part of the quiet revolution in which families and gender relations are changing in Russia, the roles of grandparents, especially grandmothers, are evolving rapidly. While stereotypes, cultural pressures, and economic anxieties tend to support grandmothers' continued assistance in care for the next generation and in assistance to their own children, new opportunities in labor markets and cultural ideas about leisure and self-care in retirement also now shape grandmotherhood, albeit differently depending on age and class.

The historical and cultural legacy of a state and society that marginalized men as fathers and as grandfathers in family life, and the continued emphasis on the matrifocal organization of family life in Russia, make it difficult to argue that the place of grandparents will change much over the next couple of decades. But because the conversation about involved fatherhood has begun in Russia (Utrata et al., 2013), I am hopeful that there will be an increase in attention to all that grandfathers can and do provide for grandchildren in families. This anticipation is somewhat complicated because of the fact that Russia has the largest gender gap in life expectancy in the world, which reduces the number of grandfathers available to grandchildren. Masculine drinking rituals also make it difficult for grandfathers to readily embrace new kinds of care work in families. Even if men's health and longevity were to increase in the near future, it will take time for grandfathering to develop as a social practice, given the cultural and demographic dominance of grandmothers in Russian family life. The norm of matrifocal families has intensified since the population losses of World War II, and will likely persist for some time. Although matrifocality with different childcare dynamics is observed in other parts of the world (Roopnarine, 2013), it will be interesting to see how patterns of matrifocal family organization and grandmothering change in Russia. The emerging ideology of "successful aging" and its close ties to neoliberalism now encourage older women to remain active for their own sake (Rubinstein & de Medeiros, 2015).

Although this chapter focused on Russian society, Russia is an extreme case of more general regional trends. Countries in the former Soviet Union and Eastern Europe have some commonalities in terms of social policies and family laws, which have included women's earlier entry into the paid workforce relative to the West. Yet the diversity of paths various countries have taken since the collapse of state socialism makes it difficult if not impossible to generalize about grandparents in the region as a whole. As I indicated earlier, Russia is in many ways an outlier in terms of its divorce rates, gender gap in life expectancy, heavy male drinking, and rapidly expanding population of female pensioners. Rates of social and income inequality are higher in Russia than elsewhere in the region, in addition to a dramatic lack of adequate childcare facilities since the collapse of state socialism. However, there are some other major trends to consider. The Soviet era encouraged women's involvement as grandmothers in families, but at the same time the state "socialized the costs of motherhood" and "reduced women's dependence on their families" (Pascall & Manning

2000, p. 256). Nowadays, according to Pascall and Manning (2000, p. 256), "Across the region – though to different degrees – these costs are now being put onto families," which further increases women's dependence on their families. Intense involvement by grandmothers may be found elsewhere in the region, but it seems to be more pronounced in Russia.

While some Russians speculate that the *babushka* is dying out as a cultural institution, this kind of statement seems premature. Evidence suggests that Russian grandmothers have long served as steadfast sources of support for grandchildren and adult children, and they will likely continue to do so for years to come. While it is troubling that grandmothers' unpaid work on behalf of Russian families is seldom reciprocated and is taken for granted by the state and society, grandmothers' contributions to families are invaluable and necessary in times of transition. Yet their contributions must not remain invisible. The growing number of Russian single mothers and quasi-single mothers also suggests that matrifocal family networks, with strong links between grandmothers, adult children, and grandchildren, are here to stay into the foreseeable future.

Summary

Grandparents are key figures in Russian society and provide multiple forms of assistance to the younger generation. This assistance has become crucial in today's society, in the transition from state socialism to market capitalism. Grandmothers have special symbolic and practical significance in Russian society. Meanwhile, men as grandfathers are often on the margins of family life. Facing lower average lifespans and low cultural expectations for involvement with grandchildren, grandfathers frequently simply assist the grandmothers with childcare efforts. Yet given Russian men's drinking habits and premature deaths, even the low level of assistance from grandfathers is significant. Nonetheless, it is *babushki* who are considered ideal mother-substitutes. Grandmothers have long cared for grandchildren and have provided a great deal of invisible household labor in Russian families. While grandparents will continue to serve as a source of stability during a period of rapid change in Russia, many grandmothers are also likely to continue to provide childcare and work after retirement, and to have an increased appreciation for self-fulfillment, leisure, and autonomy.

Appendix

Meaning of Proverbs

"Even your grandma wouldn't know whether it will rain or snow."

This proverb is used for situations when an outcome or a result is uncertain or unpredictable; it means "no one can know for certain."

"The person whose grandma tells fortunes is happy."

This proverb signifies that a person can do well when they have someone to support them, or when circumstances are favorable for them.

Additional Resources

http://pensionerka.spb.ru/kompyuternye_uroki/kompyuternye_uroki.shtml
The unpaid care work of grandparents, and especially grandmothers, tends to be taken for granted. There are, however, several organizations and programs focused on fostering the social inclusion of older people, especially with a focus on digital literacy. This website provides an example of such a program (in Russian only). Contributions to Russian society is still very novel given that the unpaid carework grandparents, and especially grandmothers, provide tends to be taken for granted. There are, however, several organizations and programs focused on fostering the social inclusion of older people, especially with a focus on digital literacy. This website is an example of such a program.

www.gks.ru/
This Russian government statistics information site features a range of useful information about the health, longevity, and livelihood of older people (in Russian only).
www.seniorschool.ru/
Shkola Tretego Vosrasta [Third Age School]. Educational centers, or so-called "third age school," have begun to emerge in larger cities like St. Petersburg. The Third Age School in St. Petersburg seeks to improve the social position of older people in society by providing them with activities (in Russian only).

Discussion Questions

1.   Grandmothers in Russia's matrifocal families do more care work for the next generation than grandfathers. Explain why this gender gap is so marked in Russia. Is grandparenting gendered in similar ways in your own community?
2.   This chapter indicates that the institution of *babushka* support has been in flux since Russia began its transition to capitalism. While some grandmothers conform to traditional expectations, others set limits on the support they provide to grandchildren. Based on this chapter, what do you think will happen in the future among grandparents in Russia? Is grandparenthood in the West be in a similar state of flux? Why or why not?
3.   How have war, alcoholism, and premature mortality shaped patterns of Russian parenthood? Do you think that grandfathers may begin to play a bigger role in caring for the future, or will Russia continue its mostly matrifocal family patterns?

References

Ashwin, S. (Ed.). (2000). *Gender, state and society in Soviet and post-Soviet Russia*. London: Routledge.

Ashwin, S., & Lytkina, T. (2004). Men in crisis in Russia: The role of domestic marginalization. *Gender & Society, 18*(2), 189–206.

Ashwin, S., Tartakovskaya, I., Ilyina, M., & Lytkina, T. (2013). Gendering reciprocity: Solving a puzzle of nonreciprocation. *Gender & Society, 27*(3), 396–421.

Bengtson, V. L. (2001). Beyond the nuclear family: The increasing importance of multigenerational bonds. *Journal of Marriage and Family, 63*(1), 1–16.

Borozdina, E., Rotkirch, A., Temkina, A., & Zdravomyslova, E. (2016). Using maternity capital: Citizen distrust of Russian family policy. *European Journal of Women's Studies, 23*, 60–75.

Boss, P. G., & Gurko, T. A. (1994). The relationships of men and women in marriage. In J. W. Maddock, M. J. Hogan, A. I. Antonov, & M. S. Matskovsky (Eds.), *Families before and after perestroika: Russian and US perspectives*, (pp. 36–75). New York: Guilford.

Fogiel-Bijaoui, S. (2013). Babushka in the Holy Land: Being a Russian-Israeli grandmother in Israel today. *Journal of Comparative Family Studies, 44*(6), 725–739.

Gavrilova, N. S., & Gavrilov, L. A. (2009). Rapidly aging populations: Russia/Eastern Europe. In P. Uhlenberg (Ed.), *International handbook of population aging* (pp. 113–131). New York: Springer.

Gurko, T. A. (2003). *Roditel'stvo: Sotsiologicheskie aspekty [Parenthood: Sociological aspects]*. Moscow: Tsentr obshchechelovecheskikh tsennostei.

Hays, S. (1996). *The cultural contradictions of motherhood*. New Haven: Yale.

Kanji, S. (2009). Age group conflict or cooperation? Children and pensioners in Russia in crisis. *International Journal of Sociology and Social Policy, 29* (7,8), 372–387.

Kay, R. (2006). *Men in contemporary Russia: The fallen heroes of post-Soviet change?* Burlington, VT: Ashgate.

Kelly, C. (2007). *Children's world: Growing up in Russia, 1890–1991*. New Haven, CT: Yale.

Kosterina, I. (2012). Young married women in the Russian countryside: Women's networks, communication and power. *Europe-Asia Studies, 64*(10), 1870–1892.

Kravchenko, Z. (2012). Everyday continuity and change: Family and family policy in Russia. In H. Carlbäck, Y. Gradskova, & Z. Kravchenko (Eds.), *And they lived happily ever after: Norms and everyday practices of family and parenthood in Russia and Eastern Europe* (pp. 185–206). Budapest: Central European University Press.

Krekula, C. (2007). The intersection of age and gender: Reworking gender theory and social gerontology. *Current Sociology, 55*, 155–171.

Kukhterin, S. (2000). Fathers and patriarchs in Communist and post-Communist Russia. In S. Ashwin (Ed.), *Gender, state and society in Soviet and post-Soviet Russia* (pp. 71–89). London: Routledge.

Leopold, T., & Skopek, J. (2014). Gender and the division of labor in older couples: How European grandparents share market work and childcare. *Social Forces, 93*(1), 63–91.

Moskoff, W. (1983). Divorce in the USSR. *Journal of Marriage and the Family, 45*, 419–425.

Nauck, B. (2009). Patterns of exchange in kinship systems in Germany, Russia, and the People's Republic of China. *Journal of Comparative Family Studies, 40*(2), 255–278.

Pascall, G., & Manning, N. (2000). Gender and social policy: Comparing welfare states in Central and Eastern Europe and the former Soviet Union. *Journal of European Social Policy, 10*(3), 240–266.

Patico, J. (2016). Culturedness, responsibility and self-help: Middle-class contexts in post-Socialist Russia. In L. L. Marsh & H. Li (Eds.), *The middle class in emerging societies: Consumers, lifestyles and markets* (pp. 19–32). New York: Routledge.

Rivkin-Fish, M. (2010). Pronatalism, gender politics, and the renewal of family support in Russia: Towards a feminist anthropology of "maternity capital." *Slavic Review, 69,* 701–724.

Roopnarine, J. L. (2013). Fathers in Caribbean cultural communities. In D. S. Shwalb, B. J. Shwalb, & M. E. Lamb (Eds.), *Fathers in cultural context* (pp. 203–227). New York: Routledge.

Rotkirch, A. (2000). *Man question: Loves and lives in late 20th century Russia.* Helsinki: University of Helsinki.

Rotkirch, A., Temkina., & Zdravomyslova, E. (2007). Who helps the degraded housewife? Comments on Vladimir Putin's demographic speech. *European Journal of Women's Studies, 14,* 349–357.

Rotkirch, A., Tkach, O., & Zdravomyslova, E. (2012). Making and managing class: Employment of paid domestic workers in Russia. In S. Salmenniemi (Ed.), *Rethinking class in Russia* (pp. 129–148). London: Ashgate.

Rubinstein, R. L., & de Medeiros, K. (2015). "Successful aging," gerontological theory and neoliberalism: A qualitative critique. *The Gerontologist, 55,* 34–42.

Semenova, V., & Thompson, P. (2004). Family models and transgenerational influences: Grandparents, parents and children in Moscow and Leningrad from the Soviet to the market era. In D. Bertaux, P. Thompson, & A. Rotkirch (Eds.), *On living through Soviet Russia* (pp. 120–145). London: Routledge.

Shkolnikov, V. M., Field, M. G., & Andreev, E. M. (2001). Russia: Socioeconomic dimensions of the gender gap in mortality. In T. Evans, M. Whitehead, F. Diderichsen, A. Bhuiya, & M. Wirth (Eds.), *Challenging inequalities in health: From ethics to action* (pp. 139–155). New York: Oxford University Press.

Shlapentokh, V. (2006). Trust in public institutions in Russia: The lowest in the world. *Communist and Post-Communist Studies, 39*(2), 153–174.

Stanton, G. (2015). *What is the actual US divorce rate and risk?* Retrieved from www.thepublicdiscourse.com/2015/12/15983

Sternheimer, S. (1985). The vanishing *babushka*: A roleless role for older Soviet women? *Current Perspectives on Aging and the Life Cycle, 1,* 315–333.

Tartakovskaya, I. (2000). The changing representation of gender roles in the Soviet and post-Soviet press. In S. Ashwin (Ed.), *Gender, state and society in Soviet and post-Soviet Russia* (pp. 118–136). London: Routledge.

Temkina, A. (2010). Childbearing and work–family balance among contemporary Russian women. *Finnish Yearbook of Population Research, 45,* 83–101.

Teplova, T. (2007). Welfare state transformation, childcare, and women's work in Russia. *Social Politics, 14,* 284–322.

Tiaynen-Qadir, T. (2016). Transnational grandmothers making their multi-sited homes between Finland and Russia. In K. Walsh & Lena Näre (Eds.), *Transnational migration and home in older age* (pp. 25–37). New York: Routledge.

Uhlenberg, P., & Cheuk, M. (2010). The significance of grandparents to grandchildren: An international perspective. In D. Dannefer & C. Phillipson (Eds.), *The SAGE handbook of social gerontology* (pp. 447–458). Los Angeles, CA: Sage.

Utrata, J. (2008). Keeping the bar low: Why Russia's nonresident fathers accept narrow fatherhood ideals. *Journal of Marriage and Family, 70,* 1297–1310.

Utrata, J. (2011). Youth privilege: Doing age and gender in Russia's single-mother families. *Gender & Society, 25,* 616–641.

Utrata, J. (2013). The backbone of Russia: *Babushkas* in modern Russia. *Russian Life, 56*(5), 279–302.

Utrata, J. (2015). *Women without men: Single mothers and family change in the New Russia.* Ithaca, NY: Cornell.

Utrata, J., Ispa, J., & Ispa-Landa, S. (2013). Men on the margins of family life: Fathers in Russia. In D. W. Shwalb, B. Shwalb, & M. E. Lamb (Eds)., *Fathers in cultural context* (pp. 279–302). New York: Routledge.

Voronkov, V., & Zdravomyslova, E. (1996). Emerging political sociology in Russia and Russian transformation. *Current Sociology, 44*(3), 40–52.

West, C., & Zimmerman, D. H. (1987). Doing gender. *Gender & Society, 1*(2), 125–151.

White, A. (2005). Gender roles in contemporary Russia: Attitudes and expectations among women students. *Europe-Asia Studies, 57*(3), 429–455.

Zakharov, S. (2008). Russian Federation: From the first to the second demographic transition. *Demographic Research, 24,* 907–972.

Zdravomyslova, E. (2008). "Make way for professional sociology": Public sociology in the Russian context. *Current Sociology, 56*(3), 405–414.

Zdravomyslova, E. (2010). Working mothers and nannies: Commercialization of childcare and modifications in the gender contract (a sociological essay). *Anthropology of East Europe Review, 28,* 200–225.

PART IV
Asia

8

GRANDPARENTS IN BANGLADESH, INDIA, AND PAKISTAN

A Way Forward with Traditions and Changes in South Asia

Nandita Babu, Ziarat Hossain, Jessica E. Morales, and Shivani Vij

PROVERBS

1. "It is time for the grandfather to arrange my marriage." (*Dada kaeno amare bia koraina* – Bengali)
2. "A child is like capital; and a grandchild is like interest on that capital." (*Asal se sood pyara hota hai* – Indian)

(see p. 182 for interpretations)

CASE STORY

Abdul Hai, 56, is a Bangladeshi husband, father, and grandfather ("dada"). In search of a job and shelter, he and his family moved from rural Kishoregonj to Dhaka City in 2000. His current household consists of his wife, two daughters, two sons (one is married), a daughter-in-law, and two granddaughters. He completed three years of schooling and is currently employed as a day laborer. His wife works as a domestic maid and his son is employed as a garment factory worker. They all live in two 12x12 foot rooms in a Dhaka slum. Abdul is worried about his future, especially the future of his children and grandchildren. He hates having to live in a slum, but does not see any way out of this precarious lifestyle. He questions the prevalence of social injustice and even God's indifference toward social and income disparities in Bangladesh, and feels that he is no longer a strong family patriarch given his current socioeconomic condition. He is constantly stressed because income from his insecure, informal sector jobs fluctuates almost every month. His married son works long hours each day and has very little time to spend with his two young children. Similarly, Abdul has little time to spend with his grand-children. But he invests in his youngest daughter's and grandchildren's education so that they might achieve a better life in the future, and he prays to God for the future welfare of his family.

General Background

Like Abdul, many South Asian grandparents today still reside within an extended family structure and function as the head of the household. Grandparents in Asian countries such as Bangladesh, India, and Pakistan (known also as the Indian sub-continent, a geographic region of South Asia) are best understood within the age-old tradition of multigenerational family practices and sociocultural milieu of interconnected self and family identity. As such, the indigenous psychology of people on the Indian sub-continent underscores and recognizes the various roles grandparents play in the family system. Specifically, grandparents act as a binding force to maintain intergenerational bonds, family lineage, and the socialization and care of young children. After the arrival of a baby in the family, childbirth events often overshadow the transition from parenthood to grandparenthood, when grandmothers (in India and Bangladesh, the maternal grandmother is called *nani* and paternal grandmother is called *dadi*) and grandfathers (*nana* or *dada*) emerge to begin their much anticipated journey as actively engaged socialization agents and as links between the parents and the newborn child.

Very little attention has been paid by scholars to the roles of the elderly in the densely populated Indian sub-continent. Typically, the geo-political boundary of the Indian sub-continent includes Bangladesh, Bhutan, India, Nepal, Pakistan, and Sri Lanka. The sub-continent forms the greater part of the South Asian region that also includes Afghanistan and the Maldives. This chapter focuses on several contextual and cultural aspects of grandparenting in the Indian sub-continent. We address five topics: (1) demographic, socioeconomic, and cultural backgrounds of grandparents; (2) conceptual and cultural underpinnings of grandparenthood; (3) roles grandparents play in the family; (4) specific roles of grandfathers; and (5) subcultural variations and public policies relevant to grandparenthood. We conclude with speculative and personal comments about grandparents, along with some comparisons of grandparents across societies and thoughts about the future of grandparenthood in the region. Most of the information in this chapter is from Bangladesh, India, and Pakistan. In geographic terms (see regional map – Figure 8.1), we use the terms South Asia and the Indian sub-continent interchangeably because 95% of South Asians dwell in Bangladesh, India, or Pakistan.

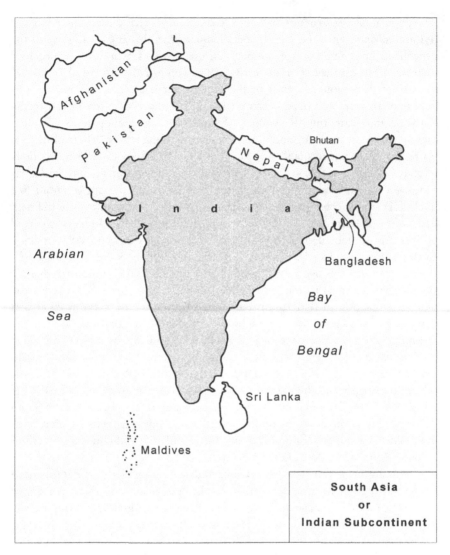

FIGURE 8.1 Map of South Asia

Source: Courtesy of Paul Larson.

Demographic and Sociocultural Contexts of Grandparenting

The current population of South Asia is 1.69 billion, and it is expected to rise to 2.32 billion by 2050 (World Bank, 2014), as the largest region within Asia. India is the most populous country in this region (76% of South Asians) followed by Pakistan (11%) and Bangladesh (9%) (Asian Development Bank [ADB], 2011). The remaining 4% live in Afghanistan, Nepal, Sri Lanka, Bhutan, and the Maldives.

The population age structure in South Asian countries has undergone rapid and dynamic change since the 1950s. Sociodemographic changes are leading to the growth of the community of South Asian grandparents, whose life expectancy increased from less than 40 in the early 1950s to 65 in 2010 (De Silva, 2003).

A brief discussion of trends in the elderly population on the Indian sub-continent is warranted here, because the word "elderly" is often linked to the status of grandparenting. Regardless of biological age, grandparents are often viewed as the last surviving and oldest generation of the family. Whereas the proportion of older persons (ages 60+) declined from 1950 to 1980 in Bangladesh, Pakistan, Nepal, and the Maldives, it increased in India, Bhutan, and Sri Lanka. However, the current proportions of the elderly within the age pyramid (see Table 1.1) are expected to converge across all South Asian countries in the next generation (De Silva, 2003). The elderly population (60+) in India is expected to increase substantially to over 11% by 2025 and to 20% by 2050, making India the most aged society in South Asia (Singh, Singh, & Arokiasamy, 2016). By mid-century, this age group is projected to include 323 million Indians, a number almost equal to the current total population of the US. Likewise, the elderly population in Bangladesh burgeoned from 4.8% to 5.2% in 2000, and is projected to increase to over 9% by 2025 and 17% by 2050. In Pakistan, the 60+ population is expected to surpass 9% by 2025 and 18% by 2050 (Mujahid & Siddhisena, 2009). Currently there are approximately 195 million South Asians over 55 years of age who live in India, Bangladesh, or Pakistan, and an over-whelming majority of the elderly in South Asia are grandparents (Winefield & Air, 2010). These demographic changes have the potential to reinforce the South Asian traditional practices of multigenerational living arrangements that inte-grate older persons and/or grandparents into family life and childcare functions (Edlund & Rahman, 2005; United Nations, 2011).

There are no national-level benchmark data to suggest the general pattern of the starting age for grandparenting on the Indian sub-continent. Anecdotal data and data for one's age at first marriage suggest that grandparenting usually begins when South Asians are in their 40s. The average age at first marriage for women in these societies is 18–22 years. Marriages are usually arranged or assisted, and men in the immediate family and in extended networks (e.g., uncles, grandparents) typically play a dominant role in facilitation of these early mar-riages, especially in rural families. Newlyweds are put under tremendous social pressure to meet the expectations of their parents to have a child as soon as they get married. Consequently, most parents welcome their first grandchild within a year or two of their children's marriage. The cultural necessity of grandchildren re-invigorates grandparents' caregiving and social roles in the family. Although this cycle continues across most families in South Asia, there has been a trend since the 1990s toward higher age at first marriage, delay of the childbearing stage, and lower fertility rates among educated and professional men and women in both rural and urban families. This scenario may eventually push the start of grandparenting for urban professionals into their 50s. To better comprehend grandparents in the Indian sub-continent, relevant sociocultural tapestries of grandparenting are described below.

Involvement and Well-being

In view of the increased life expectancy in the post-industrial era, the World Health Organization currently promotes *active aging* (a popular notion in gerontology) among elders worldwide. Active aging enhances one's physical, social, economic, cultural, and spiritual potential for involvement in society (Arifin, 2006). In addition, as a result of better health conditions, today's grandparents are more likely to be healthy, involved in the family system (e.g., as caregivers for grandchildren), economically independent, and to provide care for their own parents, compared with grandparents just a half-century ago. Indeed, it is a common scenario for active grandparents to be involved as caregivers in South Asian communities. However, the notion of active aging is not universal across all South Asian families, due to varied lifestyles and socioeconomic conditions. For example, there is evidence that as grandparents get older in Pakistan, they become more prone to disorders of immobility and geriatric syndromes associated with a sedentary lifestyle (Sabzwari & Azhar, 2011). Perhaps due to inactive lifestyles, the majority of the elderly population (aged 60+) may become dependent on other family members to meet their needs (Navaneetham & Dharmalingam, 2012). Research on Indian and Pakistani families discloses several risk factors that conspire against quality of life and active aging in the elderly population: high prevalence of disease, large-scale poverty, informal labor, limited work opportunities, and absence of adequate social assistance (Alam & Karim, 2006). As was evident in our case story about Abdul, abject poverty, lack of resources, illness, and social biases (such as lower class status) are among the many critical conditions that deprive grandparents of a better quality of life in South Asia (United Nations Economic and Social Commission on Asia and the Pacific [UNESCAP], 2005).

It is also important to note that interdependent lifestyles and communal living arrangements have a profound positive impact on the well-being of the elderly population in South Asia. Respect for the elderly and an inclusionary sense of family and social life encourage much-needed emotional support to grandparents. These types of family dynamics and filial dependence of the elderly are similar to the East Asian concept of *filial piety* (see Chapter 9, p. 203) and practice of *familismo* in Central America (see Chapter 2, p. 23). South Asian grandparents find meaning in life as they invest in childcare, participate in decision-making and socialization, and inculcate cultural values in their grandchildren. Feelings and experiences of responsibility and authority within the context of multigenerational family life thus keep South Asian grandparents active and healthy. These family norms, beliefs, and values are very similar to what we also observe in East Asian families.

Family Support and Care

South Asian grandparents are addressed and treated with respect, and elderly grandparents rely on their family members to satisfy their needs. Unlike the practice in many Western societies, family care of the elderly is rooted in a deep moral obligation that requires most South Asian grandparents to reside within an age-graded multigenerational family setting (Roopnarine & Gol-Guven, 2015; UNESCAP, 2005). Their close contacts and residential patterns also strengthen family ties and mutual commitment. There is a deep conviction that the care for the elderly, including parents and grandparents, is in fact a sacred responsibility of adult children. In particular, South Asian Muslims believe that they will not go to heaven if they ignore the needs of their parents and mistreat them. The Asian psychology of embedded identity, age-old traditional norms about family relations, and collective moral responsibility for family welfare all contribute to a definite obligation to support and care for the older generation.

On the other hand, a United Nations report (2011) highlights other factors such as urbanization, industrialization, migration, new attitudes toward marriage and the family, a growing sense of individualism, and demographic changes, all of which are beginning to cause a change in the family support and care system for South Asian elders. Whereas increased life expectancy means that many grandparents now need to provide care to their own parents (in many instances the great-grandparents of the family), a reduction in fertility rates implies that there are fewer children who will assume the roles of caregivers. Reduction of family income due to widespread poverty, development of a market economy, increased unemployment, and the necessity of finding employment opportunities far from home, all affect the family support and care system for grandparents (Alam & Karim, 2006). For example, increasing numbers of young family members leave home to seek jobs in larger cities, away from the grandparents. In addition, women comprise a growing portion of the paid workforce, which restricts their time to provide care for grandparents. It is apparent, in sum, that the traditional family support and care system for elderly grandparents faces a shift due to new and profound demographic, economic, and social changes (Singh et al., 2016).

Poverty and Economic Disparities

Approximately 600 million poor people live in South Asia (ADB, 2011). An overwhelming proportion of these people survive with an income of less than US$2 per day. It is estimated that about 18 million elderly people (60+) in India lived below the poverty line during 2004–2005 (Srivastava & Mohanty, 2012). Such an expansive landscape of poverty may explain why most countries in this region are unable to achieve even the minimal standards of the Millennium Development Goals (Navaneetham & Dharmalingam, 2012). This has dire implications for the care and welfare of elderly grandparents in South Asian families.

In South Asia, grandparents constantly deal with socioeconomic disparities and lack of employment opportunities, especially in rural areas (United Nations, 2014). Poverty among grandparents is a relevant concern because as people age their income decreases while expenses rise, due to health costs and consumption of other goods and services (Mahal, Berma, & NandaKumar, 2000). This scenario is not much different than what we observe even in affluent Western societies such as the US. Loss of income later in life leads to economic struggles for grandparents, mainly for those involved in agriculture and those engaged in marginal and informal sector employment as domestic laborers and part-time or seasonal workers (De Silva, 2003). This is reminiscent of the poverty dilemma facing grandparents in Brazil (Chapter 4) and Southern Africa (Chapter 12), who also bear a heavy responsibility for the care of their grandchildren. Agriculture is the primary source of income for hundreds of millions of grandparents in South Asia (India 49%, Bangladesh 47%, Pakistan 44%, Bhutan 56%, and Nepal 75%; Central Intelligence Agency, 2015). In addition, loss of agricultural jobs due to landlessness results in the migration of millions of people, who become employed in the informal economic sectors (e.g., shoe-shiners, housecleaners/cooks, bus conductors) in South Asian cities. Marginal sector occupations are characterized by extremely low incomes, insufficient or no pension income, and few opportunities for savings and insurance, all of which perpetuates a cycle of poverty, especially among elderly South Asians.

Living Arrangements and Living Conditions

As indicated earlier, grandparents in South Asia usually live in multigenerational and extended households (UNESCAP, 2005), and co-residence with a child or grandchild is the modal living arrangement among the elderly in the region (Arifin, 2006). Average household sizes are 4.6, 4.3, and 6.8 people in Bangladesh, India, and Pakistan, respectively (National Institute of Population Research and Training, 2013; National Institute of Population Studies, 2013). The Census of India (2011) shows that about 65% of households range typically from 4 to 8 members. It is common practice for grandparents to share a room with one or two young grandchildren within the family. Across the three societies, the mean household size is slightly larger in rural than in urban areas. Beyond the fact that grandparents live with more family members in rural areas, they are also exposed to less healthy living conditions with poor sanitation, congested living space, and poor or old homes unfit for habitation (Alam & Karim, 2006). Similar to Abdul's case story from Bangladesh, the majority of Indian grandparents reside with their adult children and grandchildren. Statistics also suggest that only about 16% of Indian grandparents live alone. Some of the reported motivations for living alone are to avoid family conflict, to be economically active, and to remain in their lifelong homes and avoid relocation; in other cases, their children had moved away (Jadhav, Sathyanarayana, Kumar, & James, 2013). Nevertheless, co-residence among grandparents, adult children, and/or grandchildren results from filial commitment as well as the necessity of social and economic reciprocity among family members (Szinovacz, 1998). South Asian value systems encourage grandparents to play both central and ceremonial (both actual and symbolic) roles in family socialization. Although meager or non-existent retirement pensions exacerbate dependence of elderly parents on their adult children, South Asian cultural beliefs lead to a dependency syndrome in that adult children are morally responsible for taking care of their elderly parents. In fact, most adult children take pride and invest in multigenerational and extended households as children are socialized to house the aged parents and care for them.

Marriage and Divorce

Marriage is a sacred commitment in South Asian families, and increased life expectancy has enabled many grandparents to enjoy the company of their partners longer now than did couples in past generations. Research on rural families in Bangladesh underscores that marital status is associated with higher quality of life among grandparents. Couples express that to share difficult and enjoyable moments in a marital union has a positive impact on their lives (Khan, Mondal, Hoque, Islam, & Shahiduzzaman, 2014). However, widowhood causes major emotional strains, especially for grandmothers, who usually outlive grandfathers. Specifically, elderly grandmothers have to cope not only with illness, dependency, and sometimes loss of authority, but also with single parenthood (De Silva, 2003) and feelings of loneliness and isolation that cannot be remedied by other family members (Rabindranathan, 2004).

Marriage dissolution and divorce among South Asian grandparents was a rare occurrence in the past, when a deep sense of responsibility toward the well-being of their children and grandchildren inspired couples to maintain married and selfless lives. However, this scenario has changed in recent years. Divorce among grandmothers in the age range 45–49 years has increased in Bangladesh, India, and Sri Lanka (De Silva, 2003); divorce statistics tend to be made less available for Pakistan. In 2011, the divorce rate among young South Asian grandparents (< 50 years old) was about 2% (Quah, 2015); even though this rate is high compared to the virtually non-existent divorce rate of the past, it is low compared to that in the US, UK, Germany, Russia, and elsewhere (see Chapters 3, 5, 6, and 7). Conservative belief structures regarding marriage and social stigmas and stereotypes regarding divorce still remain strong throughout South Asia. For women, divorce is associated with discrimination and shame that often undermine their social status and family support (De Silva, 2003). Such negative consequences of divorce may explain why South Asian grandparents tend to persuade their married daughters to stay in difficult or unsatisfactory relationships (Idrus & Bennet, 2003).

Religious beliefs and traditional practices clearly influence marriage and divorce in South Asian families. For example, Hindu couples with *Sanatan* ideologies see marriage as an eternal engagement, and therefore divorce is not conceivable (De Silva, 2003). Respect and the profound value of marriage are even manifested through fasts and prayers for the husband's health and well-being. Although Islamic practices allow divorce, Islamic Sharia law as tainted by male patriarchy gives legal authorities and men enough power to make divorce a difficult procedure for women (Quah, 2015). In contrast, the Maldives, a South Asian Island nation with a Muslim majority, is noted for its progressive attitudes toward marriage and divorce. Maldivians easily accept divorce because they envisage that it will happen at some point in life (Fulu, 2014). Unlike grandmothers in India or Bangladesh, Maldivian grandmothers do not tolerate spousal violence toward their granddaughters, and they support divorce when necessary.

Immigration

Sociohistorical and economic events such as British colonization, contemporary globalization, and international education and job prospects have encouraged thousands of South Asians to migrate every year to foreign destinations (e.g., US, UK, Australia, Canada, United Arab Emirates, etc.). For example, millions of young South Asians have migrated to oil-producing Arabian Gulf countries to work. In addition, about 182,000 Indian students study abroad each year; about 75% of them go to the US; on average about 11,000 Pakistani and 5,500 Bangladeshi students also study in American universities each year. The departure of young adults from the family noticeably impacts grandparents' lives in South Asian families, and the significant brain drain of adult children from South Asian countries leaves grandparents more vulnerable as they get older (Sabzwari & Azhar, 2011). Furthermore, close communication and interaction with grandchildren and adult-aged children are limited for grandparents who decide to stay behind in their home countries (Kennedy & Szinovacz, 1999). For those grandparents who migrate permanently with their offspring, adaptation to a new lifestyle is often difficult (Sabzwari & Azhar, 2011). Grandparents who occasionally visit their adult children in foreign countries are able to take care of and socialize their grandchildren. This arrangement is likely to encourage grandchildren to nourish their ethnic roots and speak and retain their native non-English languages. Not all grandparents, however, opt to be part of this immigration. For example, a married woman from Bangladesh who lives in the US with her husband and child pointed out to us that "My parents live in Bangladesh...My mother and father are both teachers, but my father is retired. My mother cannot come to visit us because she still works, and my father needs to take care of my grandfather because he is sick and my father is his only son" (Salma Yeasmin, personal communication, March 20, 2015). Recent data suggest that more Southeast Asian than South Asian grandparents follow the trails of their immigrant children, primarily to be with their grandchildren and to care for them (Phua & Kaufman, 2008).

Theoretical Approaches to Grandparenting

The philosophical bases of South Asian grandparenthood are grounded in cultural norms such as collectivistic lifestyles, reciprocity, age and gender-graded socialization, the value of children, and family welfare. Cultural identity formation and socialization foster reciprocal exchanges and interactions among members of multiple generations. Grandparents are intrinsically motivated to share their experiences and knowledge about childrearing, and to actively take part in childcare. Although several theoretical approaches have been employed to conceptualize grandparenting (Szinovacz, 1998), three concepts are most relevant here to explain South Asian grandparenting. *Social exchange theory* proposes that grandparenting involves both short-term and long-term exchanges. Grandparents take care of their children with the expectation that their children and/or grandchildren will take care of them later on (Silverstein, 2005). Their collectivistic value system thus promotes intergenerational exchanges across the family life cycle. Grandparents take care of grandchildren, and in turn grandchildren take care of them when they are older and weaker (Tang, 2009). Such reciprocity ensures connections, harmony, and peace between generations. Research in other Asian societies (like China) has shown that when grandparents choose not to participate in childcare for young grandchildren, their relationships with their children deteriorate gradually (Cong & Silverstein, 2012).

Unlike social exchange theory, the *altruism model* posits that grandparental care of grandchildren is based on culturally defined benevolence that does not imply any expectation of future exchanges. Here grandparents take care of grandchildren as a moral responsibility and do not expect anything in return. The South Asian disposition of altruism clearly underscores the fact that care by grandparents is a social norm and cultural expectation for grandparents. This mentality resembles the philosophy of humanistic or positive psychology as it highlights the symbolic role of grandparents who provide unconditional love, care, and a safe environment for grandchildren (Westheimer & Kaplan, 1998).

The *life span developmental perspective* also helps us understand grandparents' selfless role in the socialization of the young child. From this viewpoint grandparenthood is thought to occur at Erikson's 7th state as an expression of generativity (Kornhaber, 1996). This stage is associated with adults' commitment to make a difference in society as teachers and nurturers, which enables one to find meaning and purpose in life. As Woodbridge (2010) suggested, grandparenthood "provides the individuals with the opportunity to share their knowledge gained from years of experience with the new generation, therefore ensuring that some part of them remains once they are gone" (pp. 20–21). Grandchildren become a vessel in which the "wisdom, experiences and personal examples" of grandparents are stored, and grandchildren eventually transmit this information to successive generations (Kornhaber, 1996, p. 58). Such continuity in growth, self-worth, sacrifice, and connectedness describes well the pure motives of grandparents in South Asian societies.

FIGURE 8.2 A grandson (age 12) occasionally visits his grandmother (age 70) in a village in Bangladesh. The grandson was born to his immigrant parents in the US. This photo depicts the contemporary global immigration, lifestyle, and maintenance of intergenerational relationships through global travel, experienced by many South Asian families that live abroad.

Source: Courtesy of Ziarat Hossain.

Roles of Grandparents

In line with grandparental roles in other societies (e.g., see chapters on East Asia, Mexico and Central America, Brazil, and sub-Saharan/Southern Africa,), grandparents in India, Bangladesh, and Pakistan play an essential role in household activities and childcare in three-generation households (Coall & Hertwig, 2010; Szinovacz, 1998). They first have a symbolic role as authorities just by "being there," which imparts a special meaning to the family as a link between generations (Bengtson, 1985). Many also assume the role of family historian (Kennedy & Szinovacz, 1999) and lead the next generations by provision of their financial legacy and heritage, emotional support, and wisdom (Boldt, 2010). Sharing conversations and advice with their adult children and grandchildren is highly valuable for them and for their family members, which is probably why modern grandparents derive so much satisfaction from their roles as mentors and nurturers across Asian households (Mehta & Thang, 2012).

Grandparents play a crucial role as promoters of family togetherness. This role ensures harmony and well-being among its members, which is highly valued in South Asian families. They foster bonds and a good relationship among adult children within the family. Research suggests that Asian Indian grandparents living in the US enhance family togetherness and stability by contributing their time, attention, and care to family members, especially to the young generation (Mature Market Institute [MMI], 2010; Mehta & Thang, 2012). Although togetherness is at the heart of family socialization in South Asia, some obstacles to family interactions and relations remain, such as social separation, especially among grandmothers. Rapid urbanization with migration from rural to urban areas makes family unity difficult, which has led to the isolation of many grandmothers (UNESCAP, 2005). In particular, interactions between grandmothers and daughters-in-law in urban Indian families may be characterized by different levels of conflict. Co-residence and authority, interdependence, and management of daily family chores have increased the likelihood of conflicts (Fernandez, 1997). Family structural positions (e.g., daughter-in-law arrival into a grandparent-headed family), childcare, women's education and employment, issues of autonomy, division of household activities, and grandmothers' health problems exacerbate disagreements between the grandmother (especially as a mother-in-law) and her daughter-in-law (Rabindranathan, 2004; Vera-Sanso, 1999). The grandmother and the daughter-in-law have their own perspectives about roles and interactions in the family. According to Rabindranathan (2004), one Indian grandmother made this comment:

> My entire day is spent on running after the grandchildren. I can't even plan my holidays and indulge in the activities that give me satisfaction. To top it all, my daughter-in-law always finds fault with whatever I do even though I make all sincere efforts to provide care for the child. (p. 65)

Meanwhile, her daughter-in-law complained that:

> Though my mother-in-law has only a slight arthritic problem, she pretends to be totally handicapped to avoid doing the household chores. As a result I have to do all the work and if I go away even for a short period to my mother's house I am called back because the family's routine goes haywire. (pp. 73–74)

Examination of the South Asian psychology of family dynamics reveals an interesting array of conflict and relational patterns. However, some of the struggles and tensions that typically exist between the mother-in-law and the daughter-in-law are often mediated by other grandparents, especially the father-in-law (grandfather). Grandparents champion the primacy of their active engagement in authoritative and ceremonial family roles that resonate with the South Asian call for family harmony and peaceful co-existence among family members. In particular, "distant" Indian fathers create a harmonious family environment when they become grandfathers, and are more interactive and affectionate toward their grandchildren than they were as fathers (Chaudhary, 2013). Chaudhary's findings suggest that whereas an Indian father feels reserved and awkward in expressing emotional bonds with his children, later in life as a grandfather he can become a playful socialization agent for his grandchildren.

The previous two quotes from Rabindranathan (2004) also indicate that South Asian grandparents, especially grandmothers, invest heavily in childcare. In most cases, they conduct infant care through massage, feeding, bathing, holding, singing, and playing. These women sometimes travel long distances to assist the family in times of need (Winefield & Air, 2010), and over time grandfathers also provide childcare in the family. Overall, two-thirds of Indian grandparents take care of one or two grandchildren in their family. It is noteworthy to mention that several demographic (e.g., grandchild's and grandfather's age, sex of grandchild, ethnicity), individual (e.g., health of grandfather, personality traits), and familial variables (e.g., lineage, quality of parent–grandparent relationship) have also been shown to influence intergenerational interactions in European-American families (Bates & Taylor, 2013). Many of these variables like sex of grandchild, ethnicity or caste also impact the nature of grandparent–grandchildren interactions in South Asia. Although provision of childcare is a demanding role that can potentially change grandparents' lifestyles and daily routines as they assume greater responsibility in South Asian families (Rabindranathan, 2004), the childcare role often strengthens grandparent–grandchild relations.

One of the most valuable roles of South Asian grandparents is as a facilitator of the development of cultural identity among family members, especially for the younger generation (Kennedy & Szinovacz, 1999). They constantly communicate within the family, and inculcate language, religious beliefs, social norms, traditions, and other cultural values in their grown children and grandchildren. South Asian grandparents promote core family and social values such as respect for the elderly, loyalty to parents, duty to family, obedience, self-control, humility, collectivism, and inhibition of public displays of romantic affection (Boldt, 2010). In particular, Indian grandparents seek to transmit aspects of heritage/ancestry, cultural beliefs, holiday traditions, and social customs to their grandchildren. Likewise, they strive to pass down personal values such as honesty, good behavior, good health, and the idea that material possessions are not the top priority of life (MMI, 2010). This socialization fosters the development of cultural identities as Indians, Bangladeshis, and Pakistanis. Overall, involvement in childcare and at social gatherings such as wedding ceremonies provides the opportunity for context for grandparents to pass on their cultural identity, spend time together, and build cherished family memories (Winefield & Air, 2010).

Assisted marriages, traditionally known as arranged marriages, remain very common across South Asian societies. Although the father is the iconic authority who gives the daughter away in marriage (known as *kanyadaan* in India and Bangladesh), it is the grandparents who assume a direct and consequential role in the arrangement of marriages for their grown grandchildren. The Bengali proverb presented at the beginning of this chapter reflects this important role. Specifically, grandparents invite other adults in the family to identify and vet potential life partners for their grandchildren, and it is common wisdom that grandchildren–grandparent socialization is based on the ideals of trust and carefree interaction. A grandfather or grandmother is often recognized as a guardian or counselor of the grandchildren, and many grandchildren believe that their grandparents understand their needs, psychology, and personalities. Grandparents' opinions, experiences, insights, and social contacts often sway and determine the final selection of a marriage partner. There is even a proverb in Bangladesh that "If you would like to marry someone, then get her grandparents on your side." Through advice, persuasion, and humor, grandparents communicate about morality, intimacy, sexuality, and interpersonal relations with their grandchildren. Because pre-marital dating and practice-relationships are uncommon in South Asia, the grandparents' role as teachers helps emerging adults learn about partner relations and social skills. Grandparents often initiate activities, provide encouragement, and bring gifts to facilitate communication and interactions among the newlyweds who need this crucial support at the onset of their marriage.

Many grandparents also provide financial support to other family members. Adult children and grandchildren benefit from the grandparents' generosity and financial sacrifice, especially during economic hard times (MMI, 2010). For example, Pakistani grandparents commonly use their savings to support the family budget (De Silva, 2003), and about 31% of Indian grandparents were reported to directly provide financial support or monetary gifts toward their grandchildren's education (MMI, 2010). The degree of grandparents' contribution to the family economy varies according to their age, level of education, ability to work after retirement age, and their savings at age 50. Aside from these variables, the most important motivation behind grandparental financial contributions is to encourage autonomy and independence (De Silva, 2003). Finally, grandparents also seek to promote the cultural transmission within their extended family, interdependent relations, and benevolence.

Grandfathers

Patriarchal social structures and family systems have historically supported privileges and higher status for men across societies. As men, grandfathers have been the prime recipients of economic opportunities, honored social status, and positions of authority within their families. For instance, whereas the "Laws of Manu" in Hinduism accorded men an upper hand in society, women were expected to demonstrate self-sacrifice and absolute loyalty and devotion to the family (Roopnarine & Gol-Guven, 2015). This belief continues to elevate the grandfather's patriarchal authority in Indian and other South Asian (e.g., Nepal) communities. Even though grandfathers are expected to hand over their authority to the succeeding generation, they typically retain a position as a central authority figure, especially in South Asian families (Mines & Lamb, 2010). In line with South Asian beliefs and philosophies, grandfathers are treated with respect and dignity, and many of them still maintain their household position within the widely practiced multigenerational family system. Findings from limited research typically pay little attention to the roles of grandfathers in the family (Scraton & Holland, 2006). Much like the role of fathers in many cultural groups (Hossain, 2013; Roopnarine, 2015; Shwalb, Shwalb, & Lamb, 2013), traditional South Asian grandfathering has mostly been associated with the role of family head as a symbol of authority, ancestry, and wisdom, but without direct participation in household chores. The grandfather is regarded as the focal point in the delineation of family lineage and its standing in society. However, many contemporary South Asian grandfathers in the current generation have become more closely involved in various aspects of socioemotional development in grandchildren than in the past. They display more positive attitudes toward their grandchildren's lives and activities, express warmth and affection, and build strong interpersonal relationships with grandchildren (Roberto, Allen, & Blieszner, 2001). Therefore, grandfathers and fathers are shown by limited data to be potentially valuable resources for their grandchildren.

Broadly speaking, the measurement of grandfathers' role in the family system typically involves information about frequency of contact, participation in activities, and commitment (Bates & Taylor, 2013). The levels of grandfathers' involvement with grandchildren appear to have been impacted by various external factors. Just as immigration of adult children can limit the grandfather's access to grandchildren as a childcare provider, variations in geographic proximity impact the frequency of contacts between grandfathers and grandchildren. Grandfathers' responsibilities and activities also vary by urban and rural communities within South Asia. While urban grandfathers more often work in professional, political, private, and public settings, the lifestyle of grandfathers in rural areas is more sedentary and tranquil. Lamb (2000) described the everyday routines of retiree grandfathers in a rural Indian village as follows:

> They spent more of their days at others' houses chatting, playing cards, and drinking tea; resting on the cool platforms of temples; and loitering at shops or on roadsides, simply watching people come and go…seniority is seen as presenting opportunities for leaving the village to visit married daughters or undertake pilgrimages to faraway holy places. (p. 125)

Our own anecdotal data suggest that grandfathers often include their young grandchildren in such outings. When grandchildren enjoy such time with their grandfathers, their parents receive a much-needed respite to rest or complete household chores.

Subcultural Variations among South Asian Grandparents

Grandparents in Bangladesh, India, Pakistan, and other South Asian countries are awash in rich cultural diversity. This reminds us that family research in South Asia is often complicated by a "mindboggling" diversity (Chaudhary, 2013, p. 70) in language, religion, geography, and socioeconomic status (Hossain, 2013). Although grandparents across these nations share common ideals (e.g., devotion to religious values, respect for elders), they have other features like language and personal experiences that also distinguish them. Multilingualism and diverse ecological backgrounds define the way grandparents behave, their worldviews, and their living conditions. For example, a grandparent who is economically dependent on his grown children and a speaker of an indigenous language typically resides in a rural extended family system. His grandparenting experiences are expected to be different from a multilingual grandparent who is well educated, economically independent, and resides in a major city. Because of the high rate of urbanization and multiethnic composition of the Indian population, there are more Indian grandparents who fall in this latter group compared to Bangladeshi and Pakistani grandparents. Variations in social and cultural components such as values, beliefs, health practices, kinship organization, country of origin, urban/rural residence, and the lifestyle of a specific community also influence the meanings of being a grandfather and grandmother in South Asia (Ikels, 1998).

In particular, three social variations are very important in South Asian daily life: caste, class, and religion (Mines & Lamb, 2010). The caste system is often associated with, but not limited to, Hinduism. Although caste is illegal in contemporary South Asian societies, it still exists unofficially. Caste makes a group unique, and its definition has changed over time and from place to place. Whereas caste groups in urban India have become linked to the political landscape, low-caste grandparents in rural India are more concerned with economic adversity (Lamb, 2000; Mines & Lamb, 2010). The class system has remained a formidable context for grandparenting across contemporary South Asian societies. Our opening Bangladesh case story of Abdul exemplified how low-income grandparents are often preoccupied with the role as provider for the entire family including grandchildren. This vignette revealed the sense of uncertainty, the harsh lifestyles, and the human struggles of millions of families residing in slum neighborhoods in South Asia. The psychological, health, and social implications of living in economic hardship have an enormous negative impact on grandparents, parents, and their children. Economic hardship and lack of access to basic resources often undermine grandparents' and parents' roles as providers and caregivers in the family. Regardless of geopolitical and cultural differences, socioeconomic marginalization heightens family hardships and challenges, and this undermines the role of grandparents and child development in the family. There is an undeniable positive link between caste and economic well-being of the family. Due to lack of economic and social capital, poor and low-caste grandparents are typically very limited as they seek to perform the full array of grandparenting roles in the family.

South Asian grandparents observe diverse religious practices such as Hinduism, Islam, Sikhism, Jainism, Buddhism, Christianity, and Judaism. By and large, they adhere strongly to religious and spiritual lifestyles. Whereas 80% of Indians and 81% of Nepalese practice Hinduism, the majority of Bangladeshis and Pakistanis practice Islam (89% and 96%, respectively). Other religious groups are scattered throughout the Indian sub-continent. Grandchildren are encouraged to accompany their grandparents when they practice spirituality, meditation, and prayer, and when they visit places of worship and religious festivities. It is almost certain that a Muslim grandfather will ask his male grandchildren to go to the mosque with him for the Friday *Ju'mma* congregation and prayer. Likewise, a Hindu grandparent performs a role in the socialization of a grandchild with the religious messages of *dharma* (Hindu codes of conduct and duty) and *karma* (actions and thoughts that determine future fate and incarnation). Diet, remarriage, and lifestyle are also often linked to religious norms. For example, upper-caste Hindu grandfathers who are widowers often follow a special diet that excludes hot food (meat, fish, onions, and garlic), to avoid fleshly passions (Lamb, 2000). Although Maldivian Muslims widely tolerate divorce and remarriage, these practices are limited among upper and lower-caste Hindus, especially after widowhood. In fact, the lower-caste Hindu widow is not expected to remarry if she has a child. This situation may lead to a solitary lifestyle after she becomes a grandmother (Mines & Lamb, 2010).

There are additional subcultural variations in social support and family relations between grandparents and their adult children. Somewhat inconsistent with the traditional cultural precepts we have illustrated in this chapter, one recent study showed regional variations in emotional closeness among contemporary South Asian grandparents. For example, grandparents from the Indian state of Punjab (i.e., Indian Punjabi) and Sylhet district of Bangladesh (i.e., Bangladeshi Sylheti) have been largely characterized by a *lack* of mutual help and interdependence (Burholt & Dobbs, 2010). The nature of their relationships was independent, whereby grandparents did not provide or receive help. However, in this same study, grandparents from the Indian state of Gujrat reported interdependent and affectionate relations. Furthermore, sons were more likely to help their elder parents than daughters. Although this finding was striking in that adult daughters were thought to be the traditional care providers for grandparents, sons were expected to extend economic support toward their elder parents. Such mixed findings are probably also an indication of social changes due to the urbanization of the South Asian region.

Personal belief structures also account for subcultural variation in South Asian grandparenthood. For example, ethnographic research has depicted grandparents'

FIGURE 8.3 A middle class grandfather in his mid-50s is playing with his 1-year-old grandchild in New Delhi, India. This picture was taken on the terrace of the house when the grandfather was engaged in playful activities on a sunny winter day.

Source: Courtesy of Nandita Babu.

belief in *maya* in villages in the state of West Bengal in India (Lamb, 2000). *Maya* is a sense of affection or attachment to people, places, and objects, and is an essential attribute in a grandparent's life. The more *maya* grandparents are to someone, the more painful is the separation from the grandparents. The intensity of *maya* increases with age and often grandparents demonstrate greater *maya* to their grandchildren than to their own sons or daughters (Chaudhary, 2013; Lamb, 2000). Such emotional connections of *maya* enhance relationships in families that are especially deeply rooted in rural areas. This social norm of hierarchy allows grandparents to bestow blessings and guidance to the young, and in return to receive support and respect from them. Many grandparents also rise above the power of *maya* and relinquish their authority to their married sons. At this point, the grandparents' place shifts from the center to the periphery of the family, where they can enjoy retirement and concentrate on the welfare of their grandchildren.

The years of grandparenthood are associated with a period of physical decline, but it appears that rural and urban grandparents understand this physiological process somewhat differently. Both grandfathers and grandmothers in rural families define this period as a process of "cooling" and "drying" (Lamb, 2000). They perceive that cooling and drying are not only a physical manifestation of aging, but also involve several changes in their lifestyle, especially among upper-caste Hindu grandparents. They tend to practice celibacy, sleep in separate rooms, eat a vegetarian diet, and eat first before anyone else in the family. In particular, the process of aging makes them feel that it would be embarrassing or improper to engage in sexual relations. They tend to wear less colorful dresses because they believe that white clothing (a "cool" color) is symbolic of widowhood, celibacy, and sexual purity. Grandparents are further aware that the aging process diminishes their power and authority in the family. However, the process also empowers them with the acquisition of new privileges such as freedom, attention from the young, satisfaction of demands, and the right to complain. They are able to spend their days in religious and spiritual activities, address serious family issues when required, and share wisdom about vital topics such as *maya*, *dharma* and *karma*, rebirth, purity, contamination, and life struggles. Likewise, Bangladeshi grandparents in the UK teach their grandchildren about crops, vegetables, and rural settings including plants and animals (Ruby, Kenner, Jessel, Gregory, & Arju, 2007). Through such intergenerational communications grandparents teach young grandchildren about science and the environment. These grandparents may have less authority within the family but remain well connected with the family and community through their high social status. On the other hand, research findings from urban centers in Pakistan suggest that aging is not necessarily synonymous with a better quality of life (Ahmed, Chaudhry, & Farooq, 2014). Aging in this latter study was associated with illness and disease, isolation and ignorance, stress and depression, less social participation, increase of dependency, and the decline of mental and physical health. Such findings reveal that aging among urban grandparents can also be related to new concerns and misfortunes.

Shared values help us to gain a consistent view of grandparenthood in the South Asian region. There seems to be a symbiotic relationship between grandparents and grandchildren in these societies, by which positive human relations derive from grandparents' active engagement in care and socialization of their grandchildren. Grandchildren, in turn, help their grandparents to redefine their purpose in life and old age. The entire interaction process resonates with the principles of lifespan and psycho-social theories that underscore the dynamics of human development and relationships across societies. The social exchange and altruism models are also appropriate here, given the values of grandparents' devotion to deep human fidelity and connections that have been prevalent in South Asian cultures for centuries. Indeed, the beliefs and practices of giving and reciprocity are a foundation of South Asian psychology and ensure that grandparents are revered, respected, and duly acknowledged in every family and social accomplishment. However, social evolution and change are inevitable, and South Asian cultures are no exception to the rapid urbanization which has implications for the status and roles of grandparents. Empirical research is needed to understand the similarities and differences between grandparents in urban and rural ecologies and across socioeconomic classes in this region.

Social Policy Issues

As noted previously, traditional values emphasize the importance of and respect for grandparents in South Asian families. These values are supported by families and communities, and fundamental policies are needed to protect the welfare of grandparents. However, factors such as past colonization, urbanization, and globalized economic systems have eroded traditional collectivistic values of social norms with regard to South Asian families. These trends encourage individualistic attitudes toward life and create greater economic disparities among people. Furthermore, increases in life expectancy have added millions of people to the elderly age group. Changes in social patterns require us to explore social policies that preserve cultural values and still ensure the well-being of grandparents in South Asian families (Mujahid & Siddhisena, 2009). Although we cannot report on any national policies that specifically target grandparents, many eligible grandparents (65 years and older) benefit from programs designed for the elderly.

For example, development plans in 1997–2002 were the first notable national policies that addressed social security programs for the elderly in Bangladesh. The mission of this program was to help the most vulnerable elderly who live in extremely difficult high-risk situations (e.g., disability, widowhood, old age, abandonment, homelessness, violence). Under the Old Age Allowance Program enacted in 1998, each helpless, elderly person living in extreme poverty became eligible for a monthly cash allowance. By 2012, about 2.75 million elders (65+ for men and 62+ for women) benefited from this national program, while other organizations (e.g., Bangladesh Girl Guides Association, Bangladesh Education Board, Retired Employee's Welfare Association, Bangladesh Society of Gerontology, and other NGOs) also initiated activities such as outdoor and indoor medical care, maintenance of old age homes, and recreation facilities for old people. Grandparents benefit from these programs, which strategically support the family system through assistance and counseling, and promote family responsibility for the elderly while increasing the current old age allowance (Mujahid & Siddhisena, 2009).

Article 41 of the 1950 Indian Constitution guaranteed elders' rights and promoted public assistance in vulnerable settings (e.g., unemployment, old age, sickness, and disability). In 1995, India created the National Social Assistance Program, which included the National Old Age Pensions Scheme and the National Policy on Older Persons. In addition, Indian policies recognized aging as a national concern and attempted to ensure protection and well-being for this population in terms of financial capacity, food security (*Annapurna*), health care, shelter, mental health, living arrangements, and other basic needs (Singh et al., 2016; Ugargol, Hutter, James, & Bailey, 2016). These national policies have the potential to buffer some of the negative effects of urbanization as they embolden Indians to sustain the values of respect for elders and an age-integrated society. For example, the Maintenance and Welfare of Parents and Senior Citizens Act of 2007 articulated family responsibilities and obligations for elderly family members. This act provided an impetus for relatives and children to care for the elderly, in line with social mores of benevolence and self-sacrifice for the vulnerable in society.

In 2004, Pakistan adopted a National Policy for Elders that provided many grandparents with free membership to all public libraries, expedition of pension cases without delay, reduced rates for basic services (discounts for electricity, gas, water, telephone), exemption from payment of taxes on recreational activities, preferential service counters at major hospitals, airport check points, and railway stations, and special identification on their national identity card to receive preferential treatment and discounts. In a way, the introduction of these benefits recognized the elders' contributions to society and showed respect for them. Approval of the Pakistan Senior Citizen Welfare Act in 2007 expanded these privileges for the elderly throughout the country. Likewise, Sri Lanka and Nepal have begun to develop social programs, e.g., the *Samurdhi* and *Asmi*, to benefit elders including many grandparents (Chalise, 2006; Mujahid & Siddhisena, 2009).

Although social policies specifically targeted at grandparents are not well developed in South Asia, we can conclude that several laws are now being developed to protect the elderly and ensure their well-being. Recent policies constitute a first step toward a systematic treatment of issues relevant to grandparents in the changing societies of South Asia. They are of course essential, because many contemporary South Asians are drifting away from traditional values and norms of collective welfare and identity.

Speculation and Conclusions

Future demands for elderly health services will increase substantially, as a result of increased urbanization and further demographic changes throughout South Asia. Yet countries in this region are not well prepared for these challenges (United Nations, 2014). For instance, recent findings suggest that a significant proportion of Bangladeshi grandparents suffer from various diseases and sicknesses (Khan et al., 2014). Accessibility to health care services represents another challenge for grandparents, especially in rural areas where it often requires a long journey to visit a health clinic (Khan et al., 2014). Private health care is available in urban centers but is very expensive, and most elderly grandparents still work in the informal sector economy with no retirement or health care benefits. Work flexibility is crucial for grandparents because they need income to achieve good standards of living, but simultaneously need time to enjoy with their grandchildren and other family members. There is also an urgent need to develop social policies that ensure a decent quality of life, because many older people work hard until a later age. Impoverished grandparents also may lack proper housing and many of them have to resort to informal shelter in temples and monasteries (Mujahid & Siddhisena, 2009). It is encouraging that since 2000 the Ministry of Social Justice and Empowerment in India has undertaken projects to build low-cost housing for the poor, especially for qualified elderly grandparents.

In addition to health care and housing, family and community factors are highly salient for grandparents. It is important to strengthen traditional family bonds and social relations because these are signature cultural features of South Asian families. Many grandparents, especially grandmothers, feel insecure when they lose authority over the family due to widowhood or after the arrival of a daughter-in-law (Rabindranathan, 2004). In Pakistan, the grandparents' role in family decision-making, and reverence for grandparents, has weakened due to changes in the family structure (Sabzwari & Azhar, 2011). Evolution of the living environment of grandparents directly contradicts the South Asian belief that family and community are valuable sources of care, support, respect, and reciprocity. We predict that this situation will get worse as urbanization intensifies and the globalized economy forces millions of families to move away from sustainable, collectivistic lifestyles.

In these economic and demographic contexts, normative daily interactions between a grandparent and a grandchild often include a new question: "When was the last time you talked with your grandparents?" We anticipate that the inclusionary view of grandparents that once afforded them a grandiose position in the family and society will no longer remain as a guiding principle, as we try to anticipate the future status and role of grandparents in South Asia. Concepts such as agism and an exclusionary sense of self have already resulted from the urbanization and Westernization of this region. Many people tend to value grandparents less nowadays and stereotype them more and more as old, feeble, and burdensome.

As indicated earlier, social policies must address grandparenting within the emerging context of the spread of individualism worldwide. Such a change in orientation is likely to have economic, social, and psychological effects on grandparents. Meanwhile, technology and the pursuit of individual material gain leave the younger generation little time for relationships with their elders. Childcare and early education today are increasingly provided by institutional support systems that undercut the traditional importance of grandparents as teachers within the family, and television programs and video games also compete against grandparents as socialization agents who once provided children with heritage, stories, and histories. Consequently, grandparents may often feel increasingly isolated and unwanted. We wonder if such changes foreshadow the beginning of a new psychopathology that may break the strong human bonds which once characterized grandparent–grandchild relations and enhanced the social prestige of grandparents.

Historically, South Asians have been resilient as they conserved Asian values of collective welfare and constructive social hierarchy in human growth and relationships. How can they stave off the current forces that isolate grandparents who were once considered the mantle of a family? Is it time to reinstitute age-old traditional values that safeguarded the social status, family roles, and the quality of life of grandparents in South Asian families?

This chapter has shown the need to pay attention to changes in demographic structures, rural–urban and international migration patterns, and marriage and divorce, and also to the impact of modernization, unemployment, and poverty, in order to gain a contextual view of the roles and status of contemporary grandparents in South Asia. In particular, an increase in the wealth gap, and in the life expectancy and size of the elderly population, and the decline of multigenerational family units create a context in which institutional policies and programs for the elderly and for grandparents will be essential. At the same time, we believe that cultural norms that value grandparents must be sustained. Finally, future research should focus on health care, housing, poverty, and the family and community life of grandparents in this diverse and populous region.

Summary

While grandparenthood has increasingly captured the interest of Western scholars over the last few decades, little research attention has been paid to grandparents in South Asian families. This is unfortunate because South Asian grandparents have historically played a vital role, especially in multigenerational family units. Grandparents by tradition assumed significant roles in social leadership, provision of family authority and togetherness, financial stability, childcare, and cultural socialization of the young generation. Despite major religious, language, and ethnic diversity within South Asia, grandparents have generally been well respected and were an integral part of their families across South Asian nations.

Many grandparents in this region dedicate their entire later lives to the social-ization and raising of grandchildren (Rangila & Sharma, 2005). Children learn from them about their cultural and historical traditions and the roles they are expected to play in society. Although traditional families in South Asia are now in transition, primarily due to urbanization, most households still have co-resident grandparents. Even if grandparents do not live with their grandchildren, their emotional bonds are still maintained by frequent visits and by caring for them when there is a crisis. In most South Asian families, for example, the grandmother (*nani* or *dadi*) is the first to help a new mother. The grandmother, through her rich experiences with childrearing, helps the new mother to take care of her baby. Grandparents are also known as the best transmitters of culture for their grand-children (Thang, 2010). Based on their wisdom and lifelong experiences they can transmit cultural, religious, and moral values to young children through activities as simple as storytelling. This "giving back" resonates with Erikson's theoretical concept of generativity. In addition, the grandfather (*nana* or *dada*) maintains an expanded family role when he becomes more involved in certain duties such as childcare and support for grandchildren's academic achievement. Although grand-parents across South Asian nations share many common ideals and practices (e.g., devotion to religious values and provision of childcare), they also have unique features (e.g., personal beliefs, language, caste) that make them diverse. While there are no specific programs or policies in place to support grandparents, a number of national ones are emerging to benefit some grandparents in South Asia.

Appendix

Meaning of Proverbs

"It is time for the grandfather to arrange my marriage."

This Bangladeshi proverb embodies the expectation of an adult grandchild that the grandfather will arrange marriage for the grandchild. Through friendly and engaged socialization, the grandfather understands the personality and tastes of the grandchild, and thus the grandfather is entrusted with the decision and to take the measures to find a suitable mate for the grandchild.

"A child is like capital; and a grandchild is like interest on that capital."

This Indian proverb conveys a common message of mutual interests in the support and the probable functions of grandparents and grandchildren. Such reciprocity is based on age-old traditions of filial support and multigenerational family system.

Additional Resources

Child Rights Initiative for Shared Parenting (www.crisp-india.org)

This organization advocates for the rights of grandparents to access and take care of grandchildren.

Bangladesh Rural Advancement Committee (www.brac.net)

This Bangladesh-based international anti-poverty organization offers programs and support to benefit the literacy, health, and nutrition of impoverished elders including grandparents.

Agha Khan Foundation (www.akdn.org)

This non-profit international development agency supports many arts and crafts, literacy, and education programs that benefit many elders including grandparents in Pakistan.

Discussion Questions

1. What are the major socioeconomic and cultural parameters that help us understand the role and status of grandparents in South Asian families? Do grandparents seem to be equally involved in childcare in Bangladesh, India, and Pakistan?
2. In what ways do South Asian grandfathers still act as the family patriarch? What kind of role do they play to maintain harmonious family interactions?
3. Describe the nature of interactions between the daughter-in-law and grandmother (i.e., mother-in-law) in South Asian families? How are these interactions similar or different from your own cultural practices?

References

Ahmed, A., Chaudhry, A. G., & Farooq, H. (2014). Older persons and ageing phenomena: Exploratory study based on perceptions of elders about old age. *American Research Thoughts*, *1*(2), 1029–1035.

Alam, M., & Karim, M. (2006). Changing demographics, emerging risks of economic-demographic mismatch and vulnerabilities faced by older persons in South Asia: Situation review in India and Pakistan. *Asia Pacific Population Journal*, *21*(3), 63–92. Arifin, E. N. (2006). Growing old in Asia: Declining labour supply, living arrangements and active ageing. *Asia-Pacific Population Journal*, *21*(3), 17–30.

Asian Development Bank (ADB). (2011). *Key indicators of Asia and Pacific: Framework of inclusive growth indicators*. Research report no. 42. Mandaluyong City, Philippines: ADB.

Asian Development Bank (ADB). (2014). Key indicators of Asia and Pacific: Poverty in Asia, a deeper look. Research report no. 45. Mandaluyong City, Philippines: ADB.

Bates, J. S., & Taylor, A. C. (2013). Grandfather involvement: Contact frequency, participation in activities, and commitment. *Journal of Men's Studies*, *21*(3), 305–322. doi:10.3149/jms.2103.305

Bengtson, V., L. (1985). Diversity and symbolism in grandparental roles. In V. L. Bengtson & J. F. Robertson (Eds.), *Grandparenthood* (pp. 11–25). Beverly Hills, CA: Sage.

Boldt, S. M. (2010). iRelate: Relationship formation of South Asian in the West. In T. Kulanjiyil & T. V. Thomas (Eds.), *Caring for the South Asian soul: Counseling South Asian in the Western world* (pp. 83–95). Bangalore, India: Primalogue Publishing Media.

Burholt, V., & Dobbs, C. (2010). Caregiving and carereceiving relationships of older South Asians: Functional exchange and emotional closeness. *GeroPsych: Journal of Gerontopsychology and Geriatric Psychiatry, 23*(4), 215–225.

Census of India (2011). Analytical report on houses, household amenities and assets: Use of census houses, ownership, family size, couples and rooms. Report no. 23-022-2011. Madhya Pradesh, India: Government of India.

Central Intelligence Agency. (2015). *The world factbook.* Retrieved from www.cia.gov/library/publications/resources/the-world-factbook/

Chalise, H. N. (2006). Demographic situation of population ageing in Nepal. *Kathmandu University Medical Journal, 4*(3), 354–362.

Chaudhary, N. (2013). The father's role in the Indian family: A story that must be told. In D. Shwalb, B. Shwalb, & M. Lamb (Eds.), *Fathers in cultural context* (pp. 68–94). New York: Routledge.

Coall, D. A., & Hertwig, R. (2010). Grandparental investment: Past, present, and future. *Behavioral and Brain Sciences, 33*(1), 1–19. doi:10.1017/S0140525X09991105

Cong, Z., & Silverstein, M. (2012). A vignette study on elders' gendered filial expectations in rural China: Children's migration, child care responsibilities, and actual support provided. *Journal of Marriage and Family, 74*(3), 510–525.

De Silva, I. (2003). *Demographic and social trends affecting families in the south and central Asian region: Major trends affecting families: A background document.* New York: United Nation Publications.

Edlund, L., & Rahman, A. (2005). *Household structure and child outcomes: Nuclear vs. extended families: Evidence from Bangladesh.* (Unpublished manuscript). Retrieved from www.columbia.edu/~le93/nuclear.pdf. Columbia University, New York.

Fernandez, M. (1997). Domestic violence by extended family members in India: Interplay of gender and generation. *Journal of Interpersonal Violence, 12*, 433–452.

Fulu, E. (2014). *Domestic violence in Asia: Globalization, gender and Islam in the Maldives.* New York: Routledge.

Hossain, Z. (2013). Fathers in Muslim families in Bangladesh and Malaysia. In D. Shwalb, B. Shwalb, and M. Lamb (Eds.), *Fathers in cultural context* (pp. 95–121). New York: Routledge.

Idrus, N., & Bennet, L. R. (2003). Presumed consent: Marital violence in Bugis society. In L. Manderson & L. R. Bennet (Eds.), *Violence against women in Asian societies* (pp. 41–60). London, UK: Routledge Curzon.

Ikels, C. (1998). Grandparenthood in cross-cultural perspective. In M. Szinovacz (Ed.), *Handbook on grandparenthood* (pp. 46–58). Westport, CT: Greenwood Press.

Jadhav, A., Sathyanarayana, K. M., Kumar, S., & James, K. S. (2013). *Living arrangements of the elderly in India: Who lives alone and what are the patterns of familial support?* Busan, Korea: International Union for the Scientific Study of Population.

Kennedy, G. E., & Szinovacz, M. E. (1999). Handbook on grandparenthood [book review]. *Journal of Marriage and the Family, 61*(4), 1082–1083. doi:10.2307/354029

Khan, M. N., Mondal, M. I, Hoque, N., Islam, M. S., & Shahiduzzaman, M. (2014). A study on quality of life of elderly population in Bangladesh. *American Journal of Health Research, 2*(4), 152–157. doi:10.11648/j.ajhr.20140204.18

Kornhaber, A. (1996). *Contemporary grandparenting.* Thousand Oaks, CA: Sage.

Lamb, S. (2000). *White saris and sweet mangoes: Aging, gender, and body in North India.* Berkeley, CA: University of California Press.

Mahal, A., Berman, P., & NandaKumar, A. K. (2000). Health expenditures and the elderly: A survey of issues in forecasting, methods used, and relevance for developing countries. Research report no. 01.23. Cambridge, MA: Harvard University.

Mature Market Institute (MMI). (2010). Asian Indian grandparents imparting lessons, legacy, and love. New York: Metlife.

Mehta, K. K., & Thang, L. L. (2012). *Experiencing grandparenthood: An Asian perspective.* New York: Springer.

Mines, D. P., & Lamb, S. E. (2010). *Everyday life in South Asia* (2nd ed.). Bloomington, IN: Indiana University Press.

Mujahid, G., & Siddhisena, K. A. P. (2009). Demographic prognosis for South Asia: A future of rapid ageing. Research report No. 6. Bangkok, Thailand: UNFPA.

National Institute of Population Studies (NIPS). (2013). Pakistan demographic and health survey 2012–13. Islamabad, Pakistan: NIPS and ICF International.

National Institute of Population Research and Training (NIPORT). (2013). Bangladesh demographic and health survey 2011. Dhaka, Bangladesh: NIPORT, Mitra and Associates, and ICF International.

Navaneetham, K., & Dharmalingam, A. (2012). A review of age structural transition and demographic dividend in South Asia: Opportunities and challenges. *Journal of Population Ageing, 5*(4), 281–298. doi:10.1007/s12062-012-9071

Phua, V. C., & Kaufman, G. (2008). Grandparenting responsibility among elderly Asian Americans: The effects of householder status, ethnicity, and immigration. *Journal of Intergenerational Relationships, 6*(1), 41–59. doi:10.1300/J194v06n01_04

Quah, S. R. (Ed.). (2015). *Routledge handbook of families in Asia.* New York: Routledge.

Rabindranathan, S. (2004). Intergenerational co-residence: Conflict and resolution in familial contexts in India. *Asian Journal of Women's Studies, 10*(4), 58–78. doi:10.1080/12259276.2004.11665980

Rangila, D., & Sharma, D. (2005). The role of grandparents in the socialization of children with disability. *Childhood Disability Update, 4,* 26–29.

Roberto, K. A., Allen, K. R., & Blieszner, R. (2001). Grandfathers' perceptions and expectations of relationships with their adult grandchildren. *Journal of Family Issues, 22*(4), 407–426. doi:10.1177/019251301022004002

Roopnarine, J. L. (Ed.) (2015). *Fathers across cultures: The importance, roles, and diverse practices of dads.* Santa Barbara, CA: Praeger.

Roopnarine, J. L., & Gol-Guven, M. (2015). Indian fathers: Traditional with changes on the horizon. In J. L. Roopnarine (Ed.), *Fathers across cultures: The importance, roles, and diverse practices of dads* (pp. 251–272). Santa Barbara, CA: Praeger.

Ruby, M., Kenner, C., Jessel, J., Gregory, E., & Arju, T. (2007). Gardening with grandparents: An early engagement with the science curriculum. *Early Years, 27,* 131–144.

Sabzwari, S. R., & Azhar, G. (2011). Ageing in Pakistan: A new challenge. *Ageing International, 36*(4), 423–427. doi:10.1007/s12126-010-9082-z

Scraton, S., & Holland, S. (2006). Grandfatherhood and leisure. *Leisure Studies, 25*(2), 233–250. doi:10.1080/02614360500504693

Shwalb, D., Shwalb, B., & Lamb, M. (Eds.). *Fathers in cultural context.* New York: Routledge.

Silverstein, M. (2005). *Focus on intergenerational relations across time and place: Annual Review of Gerontology and Geriatrics.* Vol. 24. New York: Springer.

Singh, L., Singh, P., & Arokiasamy, P. (2016). Social network and mental health among older adults in rural Uttar Pradesh, India: A cross-cultural study. *Journal of Cross-Cultural Gerontology, 31,* 173–192. doi:10.1007/s10823-016-9286-0

Srivastava, A., & Mohanty, S. K. (2012). Poverty among elderly in India. *Social Indicators Research: an International and Interdisciplinary Journal for Quality-of-Life Measurement, 109*(3), 493–514. doi:10.1007/s11205-011-9913-7

186 Babu, Hossain, Morales, and Vij

Szinovacz, M. E. (Ed.). (1998). *Handbook on grandparenthood*. Westport, CT: Greenwood Press.

Tang, Y. (2009). A literature review of concept "filial piety." *Asian Social Science, 3*, 21–32.

Thang, L. L. (2010) Intergenerational relations: Asian perspectives. In D. Dannefer & C. Phillipson (Eds.), *The SAGE handbook of social gerontology* (pp. 202–214). Los Angeles, CA: Sage.

Ugargol, A., Hutter, I., James, K., & Bailey, A. (2016). Care needs and caregivers: Associations and effects of living arrangements on caregiving to older adults in India. *Ageing International, 41*, 193–213. doi:10.1007/s12126-016-9243-9

United Nations (2011). *Men in families and family policy in a changing world*. Department of Economic and Social Affairs, Division for Social Policy and Development. New York: United Nations. Retrieved from www.un.org/esa/socdev/family/docs/men-in-families.pdf

United Nations (2014). The world population situation in 2014: A concise report. Department of Economic and Social Affairs, Population Division. New York: United Nations.

United Nations Economic and Social Commission on Asia and the Pacific (UNESCAP). (2005). *Economic and social survey of Asia and the Pacific 2005: Dealing with shock*. Thailand: United Nations.

Vera-Sanso, P. (1999). Dominant daughters-in-law and submissive mothers-in-law? Cooperation and conflict in South India. *Journal of the Royal Anthropological Institute, 5*, 577–593.

Westheimer, R., & Kaplan, S. (1998). *Grandparenthood*. New York: Routledge.

Winefield, H., & Air, T. (2010). Grandparenting: Diversity in grandparent experiences and needs for healthcare and support. *International Journal of Evidence-Based Healthcare, 8*(4), 277–283. doi:10.1111/j.1744-1609.2010.00187.x

Woodbridge, S. (2010). Exploring the relationship between grandparents and their grandchild who has a disability. (Doctoral dissertation). Queensland University of Technology, Brisbane, Australia.

World Bank. (2014). *South Asia [Data & Statistics]*. Retrieved from http://data.worldbank.org/

9

GRANDPARENTS IN JAPAN, KOREA, AND CHINA

From Filial Piety to Grandparenthood

Jun Nakazawa, Jung-Hwan Hyun, Pei-Chun Ko, and David W. Shwalb

PROVERBS

Japan

1. "Grandparents' childrearing is three-penny cheap." 年寄りっ子は三文安い. (*Toshiyorikko wa sanmon yasui.*)
2. "Grandchildren's arrival and departure are both pleasing." 孫は来て良し帰って良し. (*Mago wa kite yoshi, kaette yoshi.*)

Korea

1. "A badly behaved child pulls the grandfather's beard." 행실이 나쁜 아이는 할아버지 수염을 잡아당긴다. (*Haengsil-i nappeun aineun hal-abeoji suyeom-eul jab-a dang-ginda.*)
2. "Even if they love their grandchild, they will eat rice which is soiled by the runny nose of their grandchild." 손자를 귀여워하면 코 묻은 밥을 먹는다 ~ 조부모는 손자를 귀여워해도 그 손자의 덕은 볼 수 없다. (*Sonjaleul gwiyeowohamyeon ko mud-eun bab-eul meogneunda.*)

China

1. "An oldster at home is a treasure to your own." 家有一老, 如有一宝 (*jiā yǒu yī lǎo, rú yǒu yī bǎo*)
2. "To mouth malt-sugars and dally with one's grandson...an old man enjoys life with no cares." 含饴弄孙 (*hán yí lòng Sūn*)

(see pp. 213–214 for interpretations)

OVERVIEW

Improvements in hygiene, nutrition, and medical conditions have extended life expectancy for many in East Asia, while increases in maternal employment and soaring divorce rates have necessitated an increase in grandparents' involvement in childrearing. There have also been precipitous declines in fertility and rising expectations for children's higher education throughout East Asia in recent decades, which have further increased the need for grandparental support, despite the decline in the numbers of three-generation families.

This chapter will discuss grandparents in three major East Asian nations. East Asia includes China (People's Republic of China: PRC), Taiwan (Republic of China), South Korea (Republic of Korea), North Korea (Democratic People's Republic of Korea), and Japan. The scope of this chapter will be limited, however, to information from Japan, South Korea ("Korea" hereafter), and China. These three countries are linked by geography, a shared Confucian tradition in their cultural and historical backgrounds, and important shared demographic trends. They differ in their respective political frameworks, economic systems, and in the current impact of Confucian traditions. We have excluded Taiwan, other worldwide locations of Chinese culture, and North Korea from these discussions due to space limitations, and also because of the particular lack of research evidence on grandparenting from North Korea (see Mehta & Thang, 2012 for other coverage of Asian populations).

The contemporary Japanese cultural context features long life expectancies, a large population of elderly people, relatively small numbers of children, and an economic recession that has festered since the 1990s. The Japanese Confucian tradition of the father/grandfather-centered family system (*ie*) faded notably after the end of World War II. Meanwhile, Korea is also now a society with a high percentage of old people and an even smaller number of children compared to Japan. In addition, we believe that Korea may be the most strongly oriented toward educational achievement among the three East Asian countries, and it has become an international economic force. In Korea, the traditional Confucian ideology of respect for older persons is still active, although as we shall see it is in decline. Chinese society has been characterized by dual-income families and until only recently by its One Child Policy. The communist PRC regime had criticized Confucian ideology as reactionary during the Cultural Revolution, but more recently Confucianism has been reappraised in China.

In this chapter, we describe the background of grandparenthood, psychological research about grandparenting, grandparents in cultural context, and social policy issues relevant to grandparents in each country. Finally, we seek to identify some commonalities and differences in grandparenting between Japanese, Koreans, and Chinese.

Japan

CASE STORY

Ichiro Yamato is 70 years old and his wife Hanako is 68. Five years have passed since Ichiro retired from his work as a businessman. Their son lives in a town 30 minutes away by car, with his wife and one school-age child. Since the son's wife stays home, Ichiro and Hanako do not provide direct childrearing support to this grandchild. Their daughter lives nearby with her husband and two preschool children. Since she works full-time, Ichiro and Hanako have taken care of their two grandchildren when needed, e.g., they escort them to a day nursery and provide some meals.

When each grandchild was born, Ichiro and Hanako presented traditional Japanese dolls to their families as a symbol of wishes for a good life. They also started an educational endowment insurance account for each grandchild, partly because gifts for educational finance from grandparents to grandchildren are not taxed. They attend their granddaughter's piano recitals and grandson's baseball matches to root for them. As grandparents they believe that childrearing is the responsibility of parents, so they try not to interfere with their adult children's parenting. But if they are asked to care for a grandchild, they are willing to do so. For now, they take the greatest delight when they have weekend dinners with their grandchildren.

Contextual Background of Grandparenting in Japan

Two key demographic issues in Japan are its aging population and a drastically low birthrate. Specifically, the average life expectancy in 2015 was 80.8 years for men and 87.1 years for women (Ministry of Health, Labor and Welfare, 2016a), the proportion of elderly (> 65 years old) in 2015 was 26.7%, and the proportion of children under the age of 14 in the population was only 12.7% (Ministry of Health, Labor and Welfare, 2016b). Meanwhile, maternal employment increased from 54.2% in 1995 to 68.1% in 2015 (Ministry of Health, Labor and Welfare, 2016c). National surveys (Ministry of Health, Labor and Welfare, 2016b) have also revealed an increase in single-parent families with children from 4.2% in 1986 to 7.3% in 2015. Meanwhile the percentage of three-generation families with children decreased from 27.0% in 1986 to 16.0% in 2015 (Ministry of Health, Labor and Welfare, 2016b). Day nurseries are so insufficient that the number of children on waiting lists exceeded 20,000 in 2016 (Ministry of Health, Labor and Welfare, 2016d). Looking at these trends together, we can say that grandparents have become a viable option for the care of grandchildren in the context of normative maternal employment and increases in single-parent families.

Japanese childrearing in the past was strongly influenced by Confucianism (Shwalb, Nakazawa, & Shwalb, 2005; Shwalb & Shwalb, 1996). One of the virtues within traditional Confucian ideology was 孝 (filial piety), i.e., that elders (especially the paternal grandfather) were revered, respected, and obeyed by younger people. Another Confucian directive engendered male work and female responsibility for housework and childrearing. Following these traditions, the eldest son of the grandfather was the heir of the family system (家 – *ie*) and the son's family lived as a three-generation family. The paternal grandfather controlled the family as leader while the paternal grandmother (mother-in-law of the mother) controlled the mother's housework and childrearing work. Thus, maternal childrearing received excessive control by the grandparents. Nowadays there is another popular type of three-generation Japanese family that lives with the maternal grandparents. In these families, the grandmother and mother have a parent/child relationship and communicate easily with each other. In both types of three-generation families, the modern grandfather is a democratic rather than as an autocratic family leader.

Theoretical Approaches in Japan

Although there have been numerous empirical studies of grandparents in Japan, the literature is generally atheoretical. One example of a theory-driven approach was the "grandmother hypothesis" in evolutionary psychology (Hawkes, O'Connell, Jones, Alvarez, & Charnov, 1998). It stated that while animals die when they lose reproductive ability, post-menopausal humans (i.e., grandmothers) instead help take care of their grandchildren as surrogate mothers, which contributes to the mother's fertility and as a result increases the number of offspring who share the same genes as the grandmother. To test this theory, Jamison, Cornell, Jamison, and Nakazato (2002) analyzed the population registers in one Japanese village from the Edo Era (1671–1871), and compared the mortality rate of children in families who lived with the paternal or maternal grandfather or grandmother. This mortality rate was lowest in the family that lived with the maternal grandmother, which Jamison et al. asserted fit with the grandmother hypothesis.

In addition, sociocultural theory (Vygotsky, 1978), would predict that grandparent–grandchild interactions facilitate information transmission from generation to generation, and as a result build high-level cultures. However, several studies in Japan have found that even grandchildren who live with grandparents do not incorporate the grandparents' religious consciousness (Nishiwaki, 2007) or the grandmother's traditional foods and taste preferences (Miura, 2009). These results suggest that even in three-generation families there is a big generation gap between grandparents and grandchildren in modern Japan. Further, the decrease in three-generation families in Japan has resulted in the loss of opportunities for daily grandparent–grandchild interactions, which makes it increasingly difficult to transmit traditional values between the generations.

Research on Grandparents in Japan

Meaning of the Existence of Grandchildren and Grandparents

Two studies have examined the meaning of grandchildren's existence to their grandparents, and they showed that grandchildren make the grandparent's life richer and give grandparents the opportunity to reflect on their own past and future lives. Tabata et al. (1996) developed a scale to assess the functions of grandchildren for grandparents (> 60 years old, $n = 107$). Their factor analysis revealed

FIGURE 9.1 Japanese grandparents (both age 65) visit their daughter's home for the first time since the birth of their first grandchild (17 days old). The young parents live near the grandparents and are both employed. When maternity leave ends, the grandparents will provide support dropping off and picking up the baby girl at a nursery school. The young father is an active participant in childrearing, and grandfathers will be expected to be more active in his generation.

Source: Courtesy of Jun Nakazawa.

five functions of grandchildren: time perspective ("grandchildren help me realize the importance of the rest of my life"; "grandchildren make me reflect on my past life"); instrumental information support ("grandchildren teach me about the latest fashions"); acceptance of existence ("grandchildren are the cornerstone of my life"); succession of generations ("grandchildren make me aware of what I gained from my own ancestors"); and daily emotional support ("grandchildren understand and care about me"). Elsewhere, Miyata, Okawa, and Tsuchida (2013) also explored the meaning of the existence of grandchildren to grandparents (*n* = 174) in a factor analysis of questionnaire data, and they derived five similar factors of meaning (sources of improvement in daily life, sources of life enrichment, encouragement of active behavior and motivation, support and care in illness, and promotion of mental satisfaction).

In addition, two research teams have examined the meaning of grandparents' existence for grandchildren, and have shown that grandparents provide a safe base for grandchildren, pass on their culture across generations, and impart life perspectives to grandchildren. For example, Tabata et al. (1996) also developed a scale to assess the functions of grandparents for their grandchildren (junior high, high school, and university students, $n = 551$). They found four factors: acceptance of existence ("the existence of grandparents is a relief to me"; "grandparents are a rock when I am in trouble"); daily emotional support ("grandparents understand me"); time perspective ("grandparents help me think about life and death"); and succession of generations ("I inherited some similarities from my grandparents"). In another study on the meaning of the existence of grandparents, Maehara, Kinjo, and Inatani (2000) examined the perceptions of high-school students in the Okinawa islands (the southern-most part of Japan). Their factor analysis identified three functions of grandparents: as transmitters of tradition/culture, a safe base, and teachers of the meaning of life and death. In this study, granddaughters gave the highest scores for perceptions of maternal grandmothers as transmitters of tradition/culture and a safe base. In contrast, grandsons gave higher ratings to their paternal grandfathers on all three factors. In traditional Okinawan culture, there still remains a remnant of the *ie* system whereby the grandfather took the role as family leader. In this way the paternal grandfather was a role model for grandsons (who will succeed them as family leaders) in terms of their interpersonal behavior in the community, enactment of traditional events, and strong masculine leadership.

Effects of Grandparents on the Development of Grandchildren

Other studies have examined the effects of grandparents on the development of grandchildren. Most grandchildren have four grandparents (paternal grandfather and grandmother, maternal grandfather and grandmother). However, almost no research has separated out the effects of each grandparent statistically. In addition, most researchers have not collected concurrent data from parents. It is thus difficult to exclude the direct and indirect effect of parents from the effects of grandparents on the development of grandchildren.

Aramaki (2012) examined the effects of academic background of grandparents on grandchildren, in an analysis of national survey data from the Japan Society of Family Sociology. He found, even after statistical control for parental academic background, that the academic background of grandparents directly influenced their grandchildren's academic background. The effects on grandchildren were the same for paternal and maternal grandparents. Aramaki also found that there were cumulative effects of the academic background of grandparents and parents. In addition, the effects of grandparents were strongest on their first grandchild.

Yoshida (2014) examined the relationship between childrearing support by grandparents ($n = 170$: grandfather $= 28$, grandmother $= 142$) and grandchildren's social skills, as evaluated by kindergarten teachers. Self-control skills of granddaughters whose grandparents provided frequent childrearing support (once or more weekly) were stronger than whose grandparents provided low frequent support (less than once per week). However, there were no such differences for grandsons.

Grandparents' Support for Parents

Onodera (2004) interviewed grandmothers who lived nearby their grandchildren ($n = 11$). Most of the grandmothers (10/11) agreed with this statement, "Since childrearing is the mother's job, a grandmother should not interfere with the mother's childrearing." But only one grandmother agreed with the statement, "Grandmothers should actively participate in childrearing." In such "non-interference" responses (see also Chapter 6 from UK), Japanese grandmothers expressed respect for their adult children's rearing, and that their grandparenting is an indirect support for parental childrearing.

Ando (2011) examined the determinant factors of grandparenting for the first grandchild by grandfathers ($n = 146$) and grandmothers ($n = 176$, all ages 60–77 years) by logistic regression analysis. He found two determinants: the residential location of the grandchild (grandchild lived nearby grandparent) and maternal employment (mother was employed full-time). Elsewhere, Matsuoka, Miyanaka, and Iwawaki (1996) examined the effects of grandparents for their 3-year-old grandchildren among 205 pairs of grandmothers and mothers. They found that the more grandmothers participated in rearing, the more satisfied mothers were with the grandmother's participation. Grandmothers' "socio-cultural support" (e.g., teaching manners, discipline, book reading, play, etc.) promoted mothers' feelings of "pleasantness of childrearing" and "competence in childrearing."

In a unique experimental study, Okitsu and Hama (1997) investigated the effects of grandmothers on mothers' disciplinary behavior. Their participants were mothers, grandmothers (14 paternal grandmothers and 8 maternal grandmothers), and children (4–7 years old) from three-generation families. Mothers watched their children's problem-solving behavior on a television screen, and whenever the child made an error during a task the mothers had to reduce the reward. The mothers decided the amount to be reduced on the advice of the grandmother via a computer; the children's performance and the grandmothers' advice was actually manipulated by the experimenter. It was notable that mothers living with paternal grandmothers modified their decisions in accord with the advice, while mothers living with maternal grandmothers did not. Although this small-sample study must be replicated, the finding that paternal grandmothers were more influential than maternal grandmothers suggests that grandmothers influence mothers' childrearing in paternal three-generation families (the traditional *ie* system).

Effects of Grandparenting on Grandparents Themselves

Miyanaka (2001) examined the mental health of grandmothers ($n = 528$) who participated in grandchild-rearing (3–5-year-olds). Most of these grandmothers (72%) stated that care of their grandchild was a motivator in life. Good mental health (low depression and high morale) of grandmothers was related by these data to "congruity of childrearing philosophy between grandmother and mother," "likes to take care of the grandchild," "frequent participation in direct grandchild-rearing," and "less physical fatigue." Elsewhere, Onodera's (2004) interview study showed that grandmothers who provided "mental support" to mothers (through advice and information about childcare) felt greater self-satisfaction than grandmothers who provided either "physical support" or "financial support." Nakahara (2011) found through multiple regression analyses that the grandparents ($n = 226$; male $= 125$, female $= 101$; ages 65–74) thought that grandparenthood was their central self-concept, had a positive identity as grandparent, and met more frequently with their grandchildren. This positive grandparental identity both directly and indirectly influenced their positive subjective wellbeing, via satisfaction in the grandparental role.

Japanese Grandfathers in Cultural Context

Under the traditional Confucian order of family life, the father was a worker and the mother took care of their children at home. Although this ideology receded throughout Japanese society after World War II, Japanese grandparenting research still focuses on grandmothers and there have been very few research publications about grandfathers. Onodera's (2005) work focused on the participation of grandfathers, as she interviewed ten grandmothers and their husbands (grandfathers). Most grandfathers told Onodera that "Care of grandchildren has been women's work since the old days." Compared with "physical support" and "mental support," more grandfathers described "financial support" as their responsibility. As to physical support, grandfathers reported activity only in teaching (riding bikes, writing, reading) and playing with grandchildren. Onodera's other (2004) interview study also found that "congruity of grandchild-rearing philosophy with the grandfather" and "the grandfather is a good partner in support of grandchild-rearing" were related to a higher level of grandmothers' "mental support" for mothers. That is, grandfathers may indirectly influence grandmothers' grandchild-rearing. Today's Japanese fathers have become concerned with childrearing because of increasing maternal employment and an egalitarian view of gender roles (Nakazawa, 2015; Nakazawa & Shwalb, 2013), and future Japanese grandfathers are thus likely to become more involved with grandchildren.

Social Policy Issues Related to Grandparents in Japan

Tax policy. The Japanese government began to initiate policies in support of grandchild-rearing. For example, tax policies from 2013 to 2019 have allowed tax-exempt gifts of up to ¥15,000,000 (US$130,000) toward educational expenses for grandchildren (National Tax Agency, 2013). The government also proposed a policy to promote an increase in three-generation families by offering tax benefits for the acquisition of three-generation houses (Ministry of Finance, 2016).

Pocket handbook for grandparents. The Japanese government now distributes a "maternal and child health handbook" to the mother of every newborn baby;

this pocket-sized notebook is used to record and track the child's health and development, and mothers bring this pocket handbook to regularly scheduled health examinations. Local governments recently began to distribute a "paternal handbook" for fathers, and Saitama City (2016; see Appendix, this chapter) now distributes a handbook for grandparents. The contents of this handbook focus on the merits of grandparenting for family members (grandchild, parents, and grandparents), common sense notions of childrearing, how to get along with the other generations, how to play with grandchildren, and about "public childrearing centers" and the childrearing support system.

Grandparenting leave. Some private Japanese companies are just beginning to introduce a support system for grandparenting. Toho Bank Company, for example, has begun a new system of grandparenting leave (Asahi Shimbun, 2015). In this system, workers who are grandparents can take paid leave of up to 120 days until their grandchildren graduate from elementary school.

Grandparenting magazine. A magazine titled *Mago no Chikara* ("Power of Grandchildren" – see Appendix, this chapter) has been published bimonthly from 2011 to 2016 as a source for grandparents who are interested in grandchild-rearing. The titles of some of the articles appearing in this magazine have included: "OK, we have grandchildren (after the earthquake and tsunami disaster in 2011)," "Let's live with grandchildren," "How to use money for the happiness of grandchildren," "Let's learn with grandchildren (after-school learning such as piano, art, yoga, golf)," "How to travel with grandchildren," and "How to take pictures of grandchildren."

Speculation and Conclusions for Japan

With negative population growth already a reality, Japan as an aging society faces a drastic decline in its population of children and is also an aging society. In addition, a shortage of workers already makes maternal employment a national necessity. These factors, we believe, will increasingly promote the grandparental role of grandchild-rearing. Social policies are just beginning to react to these social trends, and this social atmosphere has even led to the publication of a grandparenting magazine.

In a society with increased longevity and fewer children, Japanese grandparents want to have good relations with and enjoy their grandchildren for a long time. The modern role of Japanese grandparents is not as autocratic family leaders, and they do not control parents' childrearing. They are now indirect supporters of their adult children's childrearing. They provide advice and financial support in childrearing. Even if they provide direct support in grandchild-rearing, they tend to believe that parents have primary responsibility for childrearing, and their support is often partial and temporary. These changes in the grandparental role derive from a decline in the influence of the Confucian tradition (weakened *ie* system and gender roles), and respect for individuality (for their own lives, their adult children's parenting, and their grandchild's lives).

A widening income gap between rich and poor that followed a long recession, and an increase in the divorce rate (currently similar to the rate in Korea and slightly lower than that in China), may lead to a future in which Japanese grandparents will become more heavily involved or even act as surrogate parents. In such a case, we may confront many new problems such as value conflicts between grandparents and grandchildren, and difficulties with childrearing due to the health problems of aged grandparents.

Republic of Korea

TWO CASE STORIES

> *Mrs. Kim is a 75-year-old woman who has taken care of eight grandchildren over the past 15 years. She recently told us, "I have no regrets about the upbringing of my grandchildren…it's just a shame that my health has gotten worse. But if it helps my sons to succeed, it will have been worth it for me living this long. I don't regret my sacrifices for the grandchildren at all; it was hard but it gave my sons the freedom to succeed. I guess that all these years I have not really lived for myself, but I'm not that frustrated. Anyway, nobody can say I was a bad mother to my sons." Given that Koreans typically prioritize the family over the individual, this grandmother sacrificed herself for the sake of her family, an example of a deep-seated Korean value: placing the family unit above the individual (Kwon, Lee, & Kim, 2015).*
>
> *Mrs. Go is a 60-year-old who lives with her husband and helps care for the son of her daughter, who is employed. She told us, "When I take care of my grandson I feel disconnected from the world. I seldom go to gatherings with friends, and one friend has told me that I'm passing up the golden years of my life to take care of the boy. My friends say I don't enjoy life as I should, and that I don't seem happy even though I still have my health. Maybe this is true, and I am still young and healthy. My daughter has some financial flexibility, but I am willing to give up this time of my life to be a grandparent." This case story illustrates another grandmother who is ambivalent about her life, knowing that she is giving up her social life and healthy years for the sake of her daughter and grandson (An & Kim, 2015).*

Background of Korean Grandparenting

South Korean families have changed rapidly since the 1990s. For example, the fertility rate has declined (from 2.10 children in 1980 to 1.24 in 2015; Statistics Korea, 2015), and the population has aged (with the population 65 years of age and older rising from 7.0% in 2000 to 13.1% in 2015 and expected to reach 30.0% by 2040; Statistics Korea, 2014). Meanwhile, dual-income households have become normative (47.5% in 2015: *JoongAng Ilbo*, 2016). These data all closely parallel the population trends we have just presented from Japan.

Also as in Japan, the traditional family values of Korean society once included patriarchy, prioritization of family over individual family members, and a strict separation of gender roles. In addition, support of one's parents by married children has been considered a virtue based on Confucian filial piety, which once predominated throughout East Asia. However, the percentage of adults who agreed that children should be responsible to support elderly Korean parents dropped from 70.7% in 2000 to 36.0% in 2010 (Lee & Koh, 2011). The first reason for this decline was that "it has become more difficult to look after the financial problems of the elderly," but there has also been a change in the mentality of the elderly, who gave such reasons as "I don't want to be an economic burden to my children," and "not only my children but also society should bear some responsibility for me."

Childrearing assistance by Korean grandparents has come to take three forms: (1) three-generation households in which family members share the upbringing of grandchildren (in 2015, 6.1% of families, only 5.4% in the capital city of Seoul; Seoul Statistics, 2015); (2) older-generation families who live near the younger nuclear family, where the grandparents assist with childrearing in place of the parents; and (3) co-residence of grandparents and grandchildren in cases where parents are divorced or deceased, or have economic problems. The most common of these configurations is (2), and these families are referred to as the "new nuclear family' or "2.5-generation family" (Lee & Lee, 2012). We are not aware of the use of the "2.5-generation" idiom outside of Korea.

Research on Grandparents in Korea

Images, Roles, and Meanings of Grandparents

Traditionally, the functions of Korean grandparents in the past era of larger families were to pass down the history of one's family, transmit moral beliefs, and have responsibility for the emotional stability and discipline of grandchildren (Lee & Park, 2000). They bestowed especially on their grandsons, the rich experience and wisdom of their elder generation, the traditional goal of socialization was to instill in the children morality and courtesy. Recently, however, expectations have increased for alternative caregivers (i.e., the grandparental generation) to provide for auxiliary care in assistance of the mother, as different from the traditional emphasis on grandparental relations with grandsons (Shin, 2015).

Effects of Grandparents on Development of Grandchildren

When a Korean grandparent reads folk stories and fairytales to grandchildren, this interaction forms an intimacy between grandparents and grandchildren, and this is thought by experts to affect the social and emotional development of children

FIGURE 9.2 A Korean grandfather and two grandmothers tell folk stories to 5-year-old children at a social welfare center program near Seoul that connects independent-living elderly with children. The purpose of the program is to help grandparents feel the value of living, and for children to have intimate time with grandparents.

Source: Courtesy of Jung-Hwan Hyun.

(Jang & Kwon, 2010). Reading together brings about an emotional exchange with the grandchildren and fosters emotional growth. The literature (Yoo, Lee, & Choi, 2015) reports observational evidence that in kindergartens and nursery schools the elderly engage in a variety of activities with children, e.g., native music, writing Chinese characters, puppet shows, and telling fairytales, which seem to be effective to encourage children's emotionality and prosocial behavior, as illustrated by Figure 9.2. In all of these research examples the elderly provided a bridge to knowledge of past traditions and cultural customs.

Determinants of Grandparents' Support of Childrearing

The social and economic context of Korean families includes several social factors that relate to childrearing by grandparents. These include an increase of two-income households (*JoongAng Ilbo*, 2016), the lack of a secondary child support system, and long working hours. In fact, at 2,256 hours Koreans have the greatest number of annual work hours of any OECD nation (Park, 2013). Reluctance to take parental work leave is based on finances under the corporate system salary is reduced to 40% of base during leave (Yang & Shin, 2011) and a lack of nursery school facilities. There is also a traditional belief in Korea that children under the age of 3 should be raised at home by the mother. It is better for grandparents to provide grandchild-rearing in the home than for parents to seek the assistance of nursery schools (Cho, 2014). In Japan, the same belief is expressed as the "3-years myth," and this belief has weakened with the proliferation of maternal employment.

The first individual determinant of childrearing support by grandparents is one's relationship with the child. Specifically, this predictor includes a high degree of intimacy between the grandparent and their adult children, consistency of parenting values across generations, active interest in grandparenting, and frequency of contact with one's grandchildren (Kim & Doh, 2011), all of which parallel findings reported from Japan. As to role identity, grandchild-rearing provides a grandparent with an identity, and the higher the positive recognition of this role the more involved grandparents are in childcare (Chung, Choi, & Kang, 2015). Finally, grandparenting appears to change with the age of the children, with grandparents' involvement highest when the child is young and a shift from a caring role for younger children to a focus on education when the grandchildren are older (Yi, 2004).

Effects of Grandparenting on Parents and Grandparents Themselves

Grandparents have been found to have a positive effect on mothers' planning for childbirth. However, studies of motivation for grandparental involvement with future grandchildren are correlational, and it is not clear from such data whether grandparents have direct effects on mothers' behavior or attitudes (Kim & Kim, 2012; Joung & Choi, 2013).

The pleasure of learning to take on a new role through grandchild-rearing appears to have a positive effect on the lifestyles of the grandparents (Choi & Cha, 2013). According to another study, on a sample of 500 grandparents who provided care for their grandchildren, the largest percentage of respondents agreed with the statement that they "feel a purpose in life by helping my daughter" (66.0%). The next most common response was that "it is pleasurable to see the growth of my grandchild" (65.4%; Korean Women's Development Institute, 2015). In addition, family relationships were reported as enhanced when grandparents provided support, and grandparents felt that grandparenting activities gave them satisfaction, which helped them overcome the psychological alienation of old age (Paik, 2013). Apparently, grandparents who take care of their grandchildren have an overall higher life satisfaction than grandparents who do not have such involvement, and this involvement also has a positive effect on their own emotional stability and self-esteem (Cho, 2012).

On the other hand, and different from the findings reported in Japan, for some Korean grandparents there is a reported decrease in quality of life due to the burden of care for grandchildren (Shin, 2015). This is evidenced in their loss of health, social life, and time for recreation activities. A report by the South Korean National Language Institute in 2012 coined the term "grandchild sickness" (in Korean 손자병 – *Sonju Byeong*) in reference to physical exhaustion, loss of time, and financial stress (An & Kim, 2015). The mass media now uses an expression that represents childcare by grandparents as "twilight childcare" (in Korean *Hwanghon Yukga*), and has publicized many serious cases of depression among grandparents who provide childcare (*Kukmin Daily*, 2014).

One negative effect of taking care of grandchildren for grandparents is on their physical fitness (Cho, 2014). The average age of Korean grandparents who take care of grandchildren is 59.2 years, and at this age most grandparents have not yet experienced a major decline in physical strength (Cho, 2014). The psychological burden and stress of grandchild-rearing leads in some cases to depression and anxiety (Choi, 2014). In addition, grandparents who are involved in childcare may be cut off from their social connections (Chung, Park, & Ki, 2015). The 500 grandparents interviewed in a survey by the Korean Women's Development Institute (2015) were asked at one point: "In the future do you want to continue to take care of your grandchildren? Among the 73.8% of respondents who answered "No, if I do not have to" to this question, most gave as reasons for this response their physical limitations and the loss of friendships and social life. Elsewhere, a September 2012 survey in Seoul of adults in their 60s found that the activity they most looked forward to was "leisure life" and their least desirable activity was "taking care of grandchildren" (Cho, 2014). Thus, the complex impact of childrearing on grandparents contains both strongly positive and negative effects. These effects seem somewhat more negative than was the case in the Japanese data, but since no comparative studies have been undertaken between the two countries a direct cultural comparison is not possible.

Generational Conflict Between Grandparents and Parents

Research suggests that there is sometimes conflict between parents and grandparents about the upbringing and education of children (Cho, 2014), and the most common conflict is over methods of childrearing (39.7%). Grandparents may, for example, tend to provide more unconditional acceptance and have a generous attitude toward their grandchildren, and some parents may be concerned that this will spoil or otherwise harm the development of their children. The Korean proverb "The habits of the 3-year-old last until age 80" (세 살 버릇 여든까지 간다 – *Sesal beoleus yeodeunkkaji ganda*) is very similar to the Japanese proverb "The soul of the 3-year-old child lasts until age 100" (三つ子の魂百まで – *Mitsugono tamashī hyaku made*). That is, parents in both societies are sensitive to the impact of the habits learned and the personality formed by grandchildren early in life.

Sandwich Generation

Korean grandparents are aware that traditional family values have encouraged people to support their elderly parents as an expression of filial piety. As such they are increasingly asked to care for and provide economic support to their children, and thus constitute an elderly "sandwich generation." This differs from the usual notion of a sandwich generation in that the generation now being squeezed is the older generation rather than the middle generation. According to research, young parents nowadays have relatively little sense of filial piety toward their own parents, and today's younger generation of parents strongly believes that it is natural for them to receive economic assistance and childcare support from the elderly grandparents (Chang, 2011). As a result, grandparents nurture both their children and grandchildren even after they have nurtured their own parents, and these responsibilities can accumulate into a heavy physical, mental, and economic burden.

The Grandparent–Grandchild Home

Divorce, runaways from home, death, disease, poverty, drug addiction, and imprisonment are all reasons that some parents cannot raise their own children. Homes in which Korean grandparents live with grandchildren and raise them tripled from 58,058 in 2005 to 152,992 in 2015 (Yeom & Yeom, 2015), which is a very important social trend. In these grandparent–grandchild homes, the grandparents may tend to experience physical fitness problems and psychological stress more than grandparents who provide temporary support or supplemental assistance to their grandchildren. They may also have strong anxiety about their role performance and future as surrogate parents (Kim, 2009). In addition, the majority of grandparent–grandchild families live below the poverty line (Park, 2010), and there may be psychological problems between these grandparents and grandchildren. For example, some of these grandparents cannot express their feelings when they do not want to convey negative information to the grandchildren about their parents. At the same time grandchildren may hesitate to say that they want to see their parents, so as not to hurt the grandparents' feelings. As a result, grandparents and grandchildren in a rapidly growing number of households may maintain a delicate balance in their relationships (Kim & Yoon, 2015).

Social Policy Issues Related to Grandparents in Korea

Government measures to support the upbringing of Korean children by grandparents are more common at the local level than at the national level. In 2010, in its S and G districts, Seoul became the first Korean city to devise policies to support grandchild-rearing by grandparents. Specifically, grandparents under the age of 70 were offered 25 hours of childcare education as implemented by their local ward. The contents of the curriculum emphasize applied topics such as "knowledge of child development," "how to play with children," "baby massage," "solutions in emergency situations," and "knowledge about the Grandparental Health Management Act." Grandparents who take care of their grandchildren (up to 40 hours/month) can also receive an allowance of 6,000 *won* (about US$5.37) per hour. In the G district outside Seoul, since 2011, households where grandparents alone take care of grandchildren under the age of 8 are paid an allowance of 250,000 *won* (about US$224) per month. Given that the average monthly per capita income in Seoul is 3.14 million *won* (about US$2,810), this allowance is miniscule at only 8% of per capita monthly income. Importantly, on a national level, the Bureau of Gender Equality and Families began to consider a national expansion of the allowance payment policy to grandparents in 2015, but this policy has not yet been implemented (Kwon, Lee, & Kim, 2015).

In addition, grandparents can now benefit from grandparenting education programs at comprehensive support centers and health centers of various local governments. For example, the Korean Population Health and Welfare Association (2015) published a parenting guide book for grandparents, and operates grandparenting classes on a regional basis. There are also grandparent library programs at the local level. One such program is called "The grandma who reads books for you." Intimate relationships are formed between the generations in such public settings where grandmothers read fairytales to young children, and research has indicated that these programs have positive effects.

Speculation and Conclusions for Korea

Many young Korean parents now expect support from the grandparents, both financial and in assistance with their children. They tend to depend on their parents after marriage, due to structural problems faced by Korean society, along with the legacy of Korean traditions that prioritized the family over the individual and close relationships between households. These values remain relatively strong and we do not expect them to weaken immediately.

On the other hand, grandparents are becoming more aware that they have been asked to sacrifice their later years to the family, and they want to live their own lives. Therefore, Korean grandparents are pulled between traditional collectivism and contemporary individualism, and the future role and aspirations of Korean grandparents will have to coexist with traditional values that emphasize the family. According to a white paper issued by the Korean Women's Policy Research Institute in 2015, titled "2030 Korea: Scenarios and Policy Direction of the Family of the Future," the most ideal scenario for families is a "lenient and intimate family." Based on this recommendation, future Korean society may see a shift from its emphasis on family life to individual life. If this trend occurs we would predict a weaker sense of obligation and stronger intimacy between the generations, and that grandparents will change in accordance with changes in families and society overall.

China

CASE STORY

> *Mr. Cheng, 70, lives in Jinjingzhen City in Fujian Province. He and his wife take care of their son's 1-year-old daughter while his son works part time in Shenzhen, Guangdong Province (372 miles away). His son was divorced over financial issues, and to make more money after the divorce he went to work in Shenzhen, leaving his daughter behind in the care of her grandparents. The son remits 1,000 Chinese*

renminbi (US$149) to his parents every three months. In addition, Grandfather Cheng decided to spend his days scavenging the streets for sellable or recyclable items, in order to afford sufficient food and clothing for his granddaughter. Mr. Cheng said that he would rather wear ragged clothes and work overtime than let his granddaughter do without. This devotion to his granddaughter in a difficult financial situation is sometimes misunderstood by people who don't know Mr. Cheng. For example, people on the street once reported him to the local police for kidnapping, because Mr. Cheng in torn clothes was accompanied by a well-dressed little girl. Upon investigation, the police determined the truth about Mr. Cheng and decided to provide welfare services and social assistance. This story attracted great attention on social media in China, as a symbol of the ultimate love of grandparents, and an enormous amount was donated to the family by the public in hope of improving the Chengs' lives (Fuzhou News, 2015).

Contextual Background of Grandparents in China

As a cultural foundation that has shaped Chinese society (Yao, 2000), Confucianism provided several ethical principles for intergenerational relationships in public and private domains. For example, it suggested that the parent–child relationship is based on closeness, especially between the father and son (Park & Chesla, 2007). Among these Confucian guidelines and virtues, filial piety (孝 – xiao) was most often related to the role of grandparents in Chinese families. Filial piety includes two elements: respect and obligation (Sung, 1999), which indicate that children should show respect to their elderly parents and fulfill the obligations to support elderly parents in order to repay their indebtedness. Meanwhile, aged parents were expected to enjoy time with their children and grandchildren (Sung, 1999). Nevertheless, grandparents' roles and relationships with younger generations departed from the Confucianistic ideals pictured when China implemented its One Child Policy and experienced rapid economic development and internal labor migration from the early 1980s. The One Child Policy triggered renegotiations of responsibility for care and support between aged parents and adult children, as families strived to be certain that the only child would receive the best resources (Short, Zhai, Xu, & Yang, 2001). Inevitably, the arrangement of childcare responsibilities fell increasingly upon grandparents, especially when both husband and wife worked to maximize the economic resources of the household. Grandparents also became childcare providers because childcare facilities were inadequate in China. In addition, rapid economic development generated a demand for labor that resulted in mass labor migration from rural areas to urban areas. As young couples became migrant workers and left their older parents and young children in rural villages, grandparents became primary childcare providers in places where public care centers were insufficient (Chen, Liu, & Mair, 2011). As a result, traditional Confucian ideals morphed in the context of the practical considerations of modern China, characterized by reciprocal exchanges between grandparents and adult children (Chen, Liu, & Mair, 2011).

FIGURE 9.3 A Chinese grandmother (age 59) is pictured with her daughter and maternal grandchildren during a trip in Taipei, Taiwan. It is a common practice for Chinese grandmothers to look after their grandchildren, to support their working daughters.

Source: Courtesy of Pei-Chun Ko.

To sum up, in a comparison of Chinese, Japanese, and South Koreans on a spectrum of collectivistic and individualistic values, China as a society most clearly emphasizes collective advancement based on the family unit over individual goals. What is unique in the study of grandparents in China is that labor migration in China has indirectly forced rural grandparents to take responsibility for childcare because adult children's work in cities is a financial boon to the whole family. It is reasonable to assert that this migration issue in China is unique within East Asia, and nothing comparable has occurred on such a massive scale in Japanese or Korean society.

Theoretical Approaches to Chinese Grandparenting

The theoretical perspectives most appropriate to investigate determinants and outcomes of Chinese grandparents' involvement involve cultural norms and the "corporate model," and intergenerational solidarity, including intergenerational support. These perspectives enrich our understanding of research on Chinese grandparenthood by focusing on cultural norms, living arrangements, exchanges between grandparents and adult children, and support from extended families.

First, filial piety in Confucianism in general implies that the elderly should enjoy being with their adult children and grandchildren (Sung, 1999), and it provides a cultural foundation that emphasizes grandparents' role in rearing and educating grandchildren for the betterment of the family unit. Silverstein, Cong, and Li (2006) explained that the involvement of grandparents as caregivers to grandchildren was traditionally important in Chinese families when their adult children worked during the day and when daughters in-law were considered to be rearing children in an improper manner. In the context of the corporate model, this model explains why family members optimize resources and support the collective wellbeing of the family (Cong & Silverstein, 2012a). However, the corporate model emphasizes that investment in children's human and economic capital will contribute to the improvement of the wellbeing for the whole family, and not just be limited to the grandparent–adult child dyad.

The intergenerational solidarity framework can also be used to explain the prevalence of Chinese grandparents who provide childcare. Structural solidarity has been seen in the living arrangements between grandparents and grandchildren, which is relevant to understanding their intensity of care provision (Chen, Liu, & Mair 2011; Chen, Short, & Entwisle, 2000). The involvement of grandparents can further be viewed with the application of the functional solidarity approach. That is, in the face of women's labor participation and important contribution to family economics, especially in rural China, provision of childcare by grandparents is not only viewed as adaptive strategy but also maintains intergenerational relationships between three generations: grandparents, adult children, and grandchildren (Chen, Liu, & Mair, 2011; Silverstein, Cong, & Li, 2006). This functional solidarity concept may be further utilized to explain reciprocal exchanges described as "intergenerational time-for-money exchanges" (Cong & Silverstein, 2008). For example, under the restrictions of *hukou* (the household registration system), migrant workers cannot easily leave their rural homes. Hence, they leave their children in the ancestral village and send remittances home to support their children and their aged parents who provide grandchild-rearing care. For grandparents, the provision of childcare becomes a strategy to secure continuous support from their children, and the adult children's financial support remains the key resource in rural Chinese families (Croll, 2006).

Research on Grandparents in China

In a questionnaire survey, Xu and Chi (2011) investigated the life satisfaction of rural Chinese grandparents. They found that older adults who perceived their children as expressing filial piety viewed their families as harmonious, while those who received instrumental or financial support from their grandchildren had greater life satisfaction. Their respondents stated that co-residence with adult children helped bring about more life satisfaction in grandparents, because the multigenerational family in China was the combined product of cultural norms, state policies, and socioeconomic conditions. In terms of reciprocity, grandparents in their sample provided care to grandchildren and also received support from their children.

Health Outcomes of Grandparents Who Take Care of Grandchildren

Silverstein, Cong, and Li (2006) found in rural China that living with adult children and grandchildren was beneficial to grandparents in a psychological sense, and that the benefits extended to grandparents' health outcomes. Guo, Pickard, and Huang (2008) noted that grandparents who provided grandchild-rearing had better physical and mental health than those who did not provide childcare, based on their analysis of the 1994 Survey on Aging and Intergenerational Relations in Baoding City. However, the intensity of care provision was the key element in understanding the health benefits of childcare. Chen and Liu (2012) investigated the health implications for grandparents of taking care of children in China, and showed that grandparents who provided intensive care to grandchildren hastened their own decline in health, while grandparents who provided a moderate amount of care enjoyed better health. Their findings supported role enhancement theory (Moen, Robison, & Dempster-McClain, 1995) in that grandparents who provided a low or moderate level of childcare did not suffer from physical exhaustion. Their findings also supported role strain theory (Goode, 1960) in that grandparents who provided intensive childcare were physically exhausted and squeezed out of their resources. These negative health outcomes of intensive care provision suggest that the societal ideal of having grandchildren around points to a moderate level of involvement in childcare. The findings of exhaustion and other negative effects of grandchild-rearing remind us further of the ambivalent attitudes of Korean grandparents toward their role as caregivers (see pp. 199–200, this chapter).

Characteristics of Grandparents Who Provide Childcare

Chen, Short, and Entwisle (2000) investigated the impact of grandparental proximity on childcare in China, specifically how the availability of grandparental involvement in childcare affected mothers' time spent in childcare. Their data indicated that paternal and maternal grandparents who lived with their daughters reduced the amount of time mothers gave to childcare. Neighboring paternal grandparents also seemed relevant to mothers' childcare, in that paternal grandparents who lived nearby were associated with a decrease in mothers' childcare involvement. These results reflect the patrilineal nature of the family system in China in that the husband's parents were more involved in childcare in the family even if paternal parents did not live with their adult children. Moreover, their study found that proximity between parents differed between urban and rural areas. Urban grandparents stayed in the same household with children or live nearby, and were more likely to provide childcare than are rural grandparents, which is explained partly by a lack of public transportation which decreases access to childcare in rural areas. Their study not only revealed that the patrilineal system indirectly influences how distance matters to paternal and maternal grandparents in childcare provision, but it also implied that transportation in rural and urban areas may enhance grandparents' opportunities to provide childcare. Jiang et al. (2007) similarly noted high rates of assistance in childcare by grandparents in urban areas, for as many as 50–70% of younger children. Chen, Liu, and Mair (2011) documented the structural and functional solidarity of grandparental care for grandchildren based on the China Health and Nutrition Survey of nine Chinese provinces. They found that many grandparents lived with their grandchildren and that the time they spent taking care of their grandchildren was as much as the mothers'. Furthermore, if the mother was employed and her work was less flexible, grandparents would spend more time on childcare. The factors of living arrangements, proximity, and maternal employment were all similar to the findings for Japanese and Korean grandparents described earlier in this chapter.

In addition, based on the pilot wave of the China Health and Retirement Longitudinal Study, on the affluent and impoverished areas of Zheijang Province, Ko and Hank (2014) found that grandparental childcare was positively associated with the grandparents' financial support from adult children. Here, childcare provision was negatively associated with the grandparents' age and their having a partner.

Grandparents as Primary Caregivers

Grandparents who were primary caregivers have been investigated in some other studies. Goh (2006) conducted focus groups and in-depth interviews to understand how grandparents and parents provided care for children in single-child households in Xiamen, an urban city in southern China. She found that grandparents were the primary caregivers, whereas parents who were secondary caregivers were more involved in the evenings and weekends at work in urban areas. Her interviews also revealed that grandparents felt exhausted and unable to plan their own activities, and that parents likewise had mixed feelings about sharing the caregiver role. Another study by Goh (2009) showed that grandparents attributed their involvement to their sense of family obligations and indebtedness. That is, grandparents were embedded in a tightly knit network and bound by familial expectations from their adult children and from society. This study portrayed grandparents who took major responsibility for childcare as meeting collectivistic expectations. This was quite different from the Confucian ideal of later life that grandparents felt a low level of life satisfaction and wellbeing, when those grandparents felt exhausted from intensive childcare. This implication is reminiscent of Chen and Liu's (2012) findings, cited earlier.

Cong and Silverstein (2012b) conducted interviews on custodial grandparents, their children, and their grandchildren in the rural area of Anhui Province to understand the extent of financial remittances to custodial grandparents, closeness between adult children and grandparents, and the obligations of adult children in skipped-generation households. Their findings showed that grandparental care increased the adult children's responsibilities toward their parents and led them to prioritize the needs of the grandparents. However, they did not note an increase in emotional closeness between parents and grandparents in skipped-generation households. This study supported a corporate model of the skipped-generation households in which family members share their resources with those who are in need. That is, adult children's absence indirectly increased the obligations of grandparents to take care of their grandchildren. Such childcare provision reinforces the adult children's sense of obligation to support their aged parents, who are the main caregivers in skipped-generation households.

Grandparental Childcare and Support from Extended Family

Cong and Silverstein (2012a) investigated how support from adult children across the whole family was affected by the grandparents' involvement in childcare, based on a corporate model. In a corporate model, seeing one family member devote their time and resources to improve the wellbeing of the whole family reinforces support from other family members, who provide resources and help that family member. In rural China, grandchild-rearing is regarded as an important task because investment in grandchildren is expected to improve the family's long-term socioeconomic condition. Hence, when adult children see their grandparents take care of grandchildren, all adult children within an extended family provide their support and help to the grandparents. Cong and Silverstein (2012a) found that emotional support from all adult children was enhanced when grandparents provided childcare but not financial support for their other grandchildren. Their study provided partial support for the corporate model suggesting that childcare is a collective task in rural China.

In sum, research on Chinese grandparents includes findings about health outcomes of grandparental childcare, intergenerational solidarity (financial support and living arrangements), and grandparents' roles in skipped-generation households. There are similarities between Chinese grandparents' provision of childcare and that of their Japanese and Korean counterparts. Across societies, maternal employment and co-residence with grandchildren were associated with grandparental childcare provision. In addition, the health benefits of grandparental childcare were the same as those in Japanese and Korean studies: provision of a moderate amount of childcare was associated with better mental and physical health. However, we should also point out some China-specific findings in these studies. Specifically, the prevalence of reciprocal intergenerational support and the effects of a corporate model of support for grandparents' childcare provision seems to have been more relevant to Chinese grandparents than to their Japanese or Korean counterparts.

Chinese Grandfathers in Cultural Context

Similar to the research literature from Japan and Korea discussed above, it is not common in Chinese studies to find much coverage of grandfathers as addressed separately from grandmothers. Confucianism did not explicitly address the gender of grandparents, apart from its focus on the father–son relationship ("the father should be kind while the son should be filial"). Meanwhile, in research, the gender of grandparents was typically regarded as a control variable in the analyses of most studies. In one exceptional study, Chen, Liu, and Mair (2011) documented that grandfathers' time spent in the care of grandchildren (7 hours/week) was much less than that of grandmothers (21.1 hours/week). The same research team (Chen & Liu, 2012) also found that grandfathers who provided a large amount of care to grandchildren were more likely to have a rapid health decline. This suggested that grandfathers, who are not expected by Chinese society to be in the role of caregiver, tended not to provide grandchild-rearing care if grandmothers are present. Hence, a lack of normative support may make it stressful for grandfathers to provide care to their grandchildren.

We anticipate that research on the roles of grandfathers will increasingly be addressed as being as important as that on grandmothers in childcare in the future, as China introduces institutional support for maternal leave and promotes egalitarian attitudes in household chores. Indeed, as more Chinese fathers become involved in childcare and household chores, the patrilineal tradition that regarded men as breadwinners may transform into a more egalitarian approach, and at that point grandfathers' involvement in childcare would receive more scientific attention.

Speculation and Conclusions for China

Pension reform in China has provided minimum financial resources to the older population, especially for those in rural China. The New Rural China Pension was implemented in 2009 to provide institutional support for older adults in rural China (Lei & Lin, 2009; Shen & Williamson, 2010). This was the first time that the pension system covered the rural population, which had been largely excluded from the public social security system previously. Up until the present time, the possible effects of financial support on grandparents' childcare behavior have remained unknown. Since the amount of the pension is about 55 yuan per month (US$8.83 – Vilela, 2013), it may only have a limited psychological effect on grandparents' wellbeing in rural China. We also anticipate that the intensity of provision of childcare will not be much affected by pension reform, and that grandparents may even use their pensions to invest in their grandchildren's education, as long as the skipped-generation family remains prevalent.

One result of China's termination of its One Child Policy in 2015 may be a long-term increase in family size. We speculate that the demands of childcare may increase in light of this demographic change. Grandparents' provision of childcare will be crucial to young families if institutional support for childcare remains insufficient. Future research must investigate the impact of grandparental childcare in the era after the One Child Policy, as it may well affect grandparents' wellbeing and retirement plans.

As we have seen, recent research has also emphasized that Chinese grandparents in urban and rural areas have different resources available to them as they take care of grandchildren. In our opinion, filial piety remains stronger in rural China and grandparents' care for grandchildren has become a strategy to secure support, while in urban China grandparents are relatively independent because they have better institutional resources and greater financial security.

General Conclusions and Discussion

Across Japan, Korea, and China, grandchild-rearing appears to compensate for a lack of societal childcare resources. In this region, grandparents' love became concentrated on a small number of children, due to low fertility and, in China the One Child Policy, and this concentration has promoted grandparenting. Based on Confucian ideology, older people were for centuries respected and supported by their children and grandchildren. However, nowadays there are massive numbers of elderly people who are in good health, and they are now enlisted in support of their children and grandchildren. In one sense, this represents a reversal of the direction of support, with the trend being toward support of the young by the old. The impact of Confucianism has always varied among the three countries (Shwalb, Nakazawa, Yamamoto, & Hyun, 2010) and within each country, i.e., traditional roles remain stronger in rural areas than in urban areas (e.g., Okinawa in Japan, and the Chinese countryside).

We can detect gradual changes toward grandparental involvement in all three societies as a reflection of both economic needs and family-centered values. In Japan, nurturing by grandparents is most often considered to be supplemental to the childrearing role of young parents. We have also observed among Koreans how the grandparental role constrains or defines grandparents' own way of life. And especially in rural China, grandparents often become surrogate full-time caregivers in reaction to maternal employment and the migration of workers from rural toward urban locations. Grandchild-rearing is not only a cultural practice for Chinese grandparents, but it also requires family support from adult children. Compared to the situations in Japan and Korea, the economic necessity of grandchild-rearing stood out dramatically here in the case of China.

East Asian studies of grandparental involvement, to varying extents in the three societies, have documented the physical, psychological, and economic impact of grandparenting on grandchildren, children, and the grandparents themselves. The most obvious predictors of grandparental involvement appear to be maternal employment and the residential location of the grandchild (either co-residential or living nearby) across all three societies. In our view, active participation by grandparents in childrearing usually appears to have a positive impact psychologically and on identity, although stress reportedly also takes a toll on those Korean and Chinese grandparents who provide a heavy amount of childcare. However, it is difficult to assign causal effects here because most of the studies that examined the effects of grandparenting were correlational studies. Typically, research about the effects of grandparents on grandchildren has not accounted for the effects of parents' economic or health conditions. We therefore need better research designs to clarify the effects of grandparenting, and this recommendation is not unique to East Asian research.

Japanese and Korean data show that for grandparents to provide stable care to their children, it is preferable that the childrearing philosophies of parents and grandparents be compatible. In this era of drastic societal changes, it is difficult to maintain continuity in childrearing philosophy across generations, yet this stability is important for families. We can also observe how difficult it is to manage discrepant cultural values and traditions, within even a three-generation East Asian family. Bridging the generation gap between grandparents and grandchildren is therefore another important task for families.

In East Asia, as has been discussed throughout this chapter, childrearing has been regarded as a women's traditional responsibility, in accordance with Confucian ideology. Compared to the South Asian societies discussed in Chapter 8, "religion" was seldom mentioned in this chapter as a guiding foundation of grandparenthood in East Asia. Rather, economic conditions, societal preoccupations with children's educational attainment, and mass migrations within China were more notable in defining societal expectations for grandparents. In this context, grandmothers might take a direct childrearing role while grandfathers would provide indirect support or serve only as a playmate for grandchildren. However, many young fathers have become highly invested in direct childrearing throughout the three East Asian societies; when today's young fathers become grandfathers it will not surprise us to see their paternal concern transformed into grandparental concern. That is, we speculate that the future will hold generations of more active East Asian grandfathers.

Social policies to support grandparents have emerged in Japan at both national and local levels, and policies to encourage and support grandchildrearing are beginning to emerge in Korea. In China, we have already seen policy changes in terms of pension reforms and health care for the elderly. In Japan, income inequalities are widening as the percentage of single-parent families increases. We expect that the numbers of grandparents who become full-time surrogate parents will also increase, and that financial and health support for these grandparents will become larger issues for government policy-makers. We also believe that Confucian ideology now remains somewhat more influential in Korea than in Japan. As a result, Korean grandparents tend to care for their parents based on filial piety, and provide financial and physical support for their children along with grandchild-rearing. Social support will be needed, especially in Korea, to decrease the burden of grandchildren, within the context of the current Korean shift from family-centered to individual-centered values. The One Child Policy in China terminated in 2015, and the lack of nursery facilities to accommodate the future increase in the numbers of children will probably result in a bigger demand on the elderly to take care of their grandchildren.

In sum, family configurations and structures in Japan, Korea, and China have changed drastically over the past half-century, and we predict that negative population growth in Japan and Korea will influence grandparenthood, while the end of the One Child Policy in China will also impact on intergenerational relationships. As life expectancy continues to lengthen across East Asia, in all three societies the elderly expect post-retirement lifestyles that include more than grandparenting, despite differences in the societal contexts between these societies. Future research on grandparents in East Asia cannot avoid the impact of changes in these contextual variables, as the nature and activities of grandparenthood continues to change.

Summary

This chapter focused on contextual factors and research on grandparents in East Asia (Japan, South Korea, and the People's Republic of China). In all three societies, we discussed first the legacy of Confucian ideology on family relations and the roles of the elderly within the family and society. However, the impact of Confucian ethics has evolved differently in each of the societies, based on their different patterns of historical, cultural, demographic, and other contextual changes.

Japan was viewed here as a rapidly aging society with a precipitously low birth rate. Therefore, a growing percentage of the elderly population is involved with the upbringing of historically small numbers of children. We have observed that maternal employment has increased the demand for support from grandparents, and that while grandchild-rearing has an impact on children's cognitive and social development and on the mother, there has been less study of the impact of the grandparental role on grandparents themselves. Laws and social policies relevant to support of grandparental involvement have been most notable in the area of taxation policies. Korea also has an extremely low birth rate, and maternal employment in Korea has required increased involvement in grandchild-rearing. As in Japan, traditional Korean ideology had promoted the preference of raising children within the family rather than in institutional settings, and in the past preference for males had made it especially important for grandparents to help with the oldest grandson. This latter preference is no longer the case, and the ambivalence of Korean grandparents toward the sacrifices they must make to provide grandchild-rearing stood out within this chapter as a potential problem for Korean grandparents. This may be the reason that grandparenting classes are more common in Korea, compared with Japan and China. Labor migration and the One Child Policy are major contextual influences on grandparents in China, and both of these phenomena have put special pressure on rural grandparents to provide childcare. The collectivistic nature of Chinese families also stood out as an important influence on grandparents.

In all three countries, most studies of grandparents have focused on grandmothers. Little research has been done on grandfathers, and there has been a tendency to study grandparents on the individual or dyadic level in all three societies, rather than studying families from a systems perspective.

Appendix

Meanings of Proverbs

"Grandparents' childrearing is three-penny cheap."

This means that care by Japanese grandparents detracts from the autonomy of grandchildren and devalues them, and that grandparents are seen as overprotective in discipline.

"Grandchildren's arrival and departure are both pleasing."

This implies that for a grandparent interaction with the grandchild is pleasurable yet exhausting. Many modern Japanese grandparents want to maintain only a moderate level of contact with their grandchildren.

"The badly behaved child pulls the grandfather's beard."

This signifies that even in a society with filial piety, Korean children can be disrespectful toward the grandfather, and that discipline and polite behavior are important at a young age.

"Even if they love their grandchild, they will eat rice which is soiled by the runny nose of their grandchild."

This means that Korean grandparents do not always receive much benefit in return from grandchildren. But since the love of grandparents is selfless, they do not expect anything in return.

> "An oldster at home is a treasure to your own."

This Chinese proverb describes the family values that view the aged as precious resources in the household.

> "To mouth malt-sugars and dally with one's grandson…an old man enjoys life with no cares."

This proverb promotes an ideal old age of leisure enjoyment with grandchildren.

Additional Resources

Saitama City, (2016). *Pocket handbook for grandparents*, (www.city.saitama.jp/007/002/012/p044368_d/fil/sofubotechou.pdf (in Japanese only))

Mokurakusha, (2016). "Mago no Chikara"(*Power of Grandchildren* magazine), (www.magonochikara.com (in Japanese only))

www.grandparents.or.kr/

This website gives the curriculum and outline of a program for grandparenting classes, including essential information about grandchild-rearing and discussions about grandparents' experiences at the school (in Korean only).

www.swd.gov.hk/tc/index/site_pubsvc/page_family/sub_listofserv/id_projectcct/

Experimental childcare curriculum for grandparents in Hong Kong.

Discussion Questions

1. What aspects of Confucian ideology affect grandparenting in Japan, Korea, and China?
2. What are three factors that explain differences in grandparenting between Japan, Korea, and China?
3. What are the effects of population aging and fertility rate decline in each of the three East Asian societies?

References

Japan (and also Overview, and General Conclusions and Discussion sections)

Ando, K. (2011). Recognition of surrogate grandparenting and family changes: The influence of de-housewifing on grandparenthood. *Studies in Humanities and Cultures, Nagoya City University, 15*, 17–39.

Aramaki, S. (2012). Effects of grandparents' education on grandchildren's education: Interactions by paternal/maternal distinction, gender, and birth order. *Japanese Journal of Family Sociology, 24*, 84–94.

Asahi Shimbun. (2015, September 7). Grandparenting leave is OK. *Asahi Shimbun*, evening ed., p. 5.

Hawkes, K., O'Connell, J. F., Jones, N. G., Alvarez, H., & Charnov, E. L. (1998). Grandmothering menopause, and the evolution of human histories. *Proceedings of the National Academy of Science of the United States of America, 95*, 1336–1339.

Jamison, C. S., Cornell, L. L., Jamison, P. L., & Nakazato, H. (2002). Are all grandmothers equal? A review and a preliminary test of the "grandmother hypothesis" in Tokugawa Japan. *American Journal of Physical Anthropology, 119*, 67–76.

Maehara, T., Kinjo, I., &Inatani, F. (2000). Relationships of grandchildren with paternal and maternal grandparents. *Japanese Journal of Educational Psychology, 48*, 120–127.

Matsuoka, T., Miyanaka, F., & Iwawaki, Y. (1996). Effect of grandmother's rearing participation on mothers. *Japanese Journal of Maternal Health, 37*, 91–98.

Mehta, K. K., & Thang, L. L. (Eds.). (2012). *Experiencing grandparenthood*. New York: Springer.

Ministry of Finance. (2016). *Foundation of tax benefit to promote an increase in three-generation families.* Retrieved from www.mof.go.jp/tax_policy/tax_reform/outline/fy2016/request/cao/28y_cao_k_04.pdf

Ministry of Health, Labor and Welfare. (2016a). *Summary of abridged life table in 2015.* Retrieved from www.mhlw.go.jp/toukei/saikin/hw/life/life15/index.html

Ministry of Health, Labor and Welfare. (2016b). *Research on demographics in 2015.* Retrieved from www.mhlw.go.jp/toukei/saikin/hw/jinkou/suikei15/

Ministry of Health, Labor and Welfare. (2016c). *National livelihood survey.* Retrieved from www.mhlw.go.jp/toukei/saikin/hw/k-tyosa/k-tyosa15/dl/02.pdf

Ministry of Health, Labor and Welfare. (2016d). *The number of children on waiting lists for day nursery in 2015.* Retrieved from www.mhlw.go.jp/stf/houdou/0000078441.html

Miura, K. (2009). Comparison of grandmother's cooking with mother's cooking. *Memories of the Faculty of Human Development, University of Toyama, 3*, 47–54.

Miyanaka, F. (2001). Relationship between mental health of aged women and their involvement in child-rearing: Effectiveness on grandmothers. *Journal of Japanese Society of Psychosomatic Obstetrics and Gynecology, 6*, 173–180.

Miyata, M., Okawa, I., & Tsuchida, N. (2013). The meaning of grandchildren: Analysis of the psychological relationship between grandparents and grandchildren. *Journal of Care and Behavioral Sciences for the Elderly, 18*, 61–73.

Nakahara, J. (2011). The relationship between grandparent role and subjective well-being of young-olds. *Japanese Journal of Psychology, 82*, 158–166.

Nakazawa, J. (2015). Fathering in Japan. In J. L. Roopnarine (Ed.), *Fathers across cultures* (pp. 307–324). Santa Barbara, CA: Praeger.

Nakazawa, J., & Shwalb, D. W. (2013). Fathering in Japan: Entering an era of involvement with children. In D. W. Shwalb, B. J. Shwalb, & M. E. Lamb (Eds.), *Fathers in cultural context* (pp. 42–66). New York: Routledge.

National Tax Agency. (2013). *Tax free system on donation of educational finance from grandparent.* Retrieved from www.nta.go.jp/shiraberu/ippanjoho/pamph/sozoku-zoyo/201304/01.htm

Nishiwaki, R. (2007). Grandparents' and parents' influence on the religious development of their children. *Shirayuri Christiano Cultural Studies, 8*, 112–140.

Okitsu, M., & Hama, H. (1997). The effects of paternal and maternal grandmothers on mother's disciplinary behavior. *Japanese Journal of Psychology, 68*, 281–289.

Onodera, R. (2004). The discussion on the grandmother's support for grandchildcare. *Bulletin of Faculty of Education, Hokkaido University, 95*, 119–141.

Onodera, R. (2005). Fluctuation of grandmother's view of gender division of labor derived from rearing grandchildren. *Journal of 21st Century Research Organization for Human Care, 10*, 95–106.

Saitama City. (2016). *Pocket handbook for grandparents.* Retrieved from www.city.saitama.jp/007/002/012/p044368_d/fil/sofubotechou.pdf

Shwalb, D. W., & Shwalb, B. J. (Eds.). (1996). *Japanese childrearing: Two generations of scholarship.* New York: Guilford Press.

Shwalb, D. W., Nakazawa, J., & Shwalb, B. J. (Eds.). (2005). *Applied developmental psychology: Theory, practice, and research from Japan.* Charlotte, NC: Information Age Publishing.

Shwalb, D. W., Nakazawa, J., Yamamoto, T., & Hyun, J. H. (2010). Fathering in Japan, China, and Korea: Changing contexts, images, and roles. In M. E. Lamb (Ed.), *The role of the father in child development* (5th ed., pp. 341–387). New York: Wiley.

Tabata, O., Hoshino, K., Sato, A., Tsuboi, S., Hashimoto, T., & Endo, H. (1996). Development of scales of relationships between grandchildren in adolescence and grandparents. *Japanese Journal of Psychology, 67*, 375–381.

Vygotsky, L. S. (1978). Mind in society: Development of higher psychological processes. Edited by M. Cole, V. John-Steiner, S. Scribner, & E. Souberman. Cambridge, MA: Harvard University Press.

Yoshida, A. (2014). A study of the correlation between the development of social skills in grandchildren under the care of their grandparents and the mood state of these grandparents. *Studies in Comparative Culture, 113*, 263–272.

Korea

An, H. L., & Kim, S. M. (2015). A qualitative study of interpretations of grandmothers' childrearing experiences. *Journal of Korean Family Resource Management Association, 19*(1), 93–109.

Chang, K. S. (2011). Social reproduction in an era of "risk aversion": From familial fertility to women's fertility. *Family and Culture, 23*(2), 1–23.

Cho, K. P. (2014). Problems involved in the rearing of the children of working parents by grandparents and their suggested solutions. *Korea Journal of Child Care and Education, 84*, 283–299.

Cho, Y. J. (2012). A study on the satisfaction of grandchild rearing activities: Focused on the elders' generativist and family support. *Health and Social Welfare Review, 32*(2), 267–294.

Choi, I. H. (2014). The impact of grandparenting on life satisfaction among female older adults: Focusing on the effects of grandmothers' willingness to care and subjective perceptions of grandparenting. *Family and Culture, 26*(4), 118–138.

Choi, Y., & Cha, T. (2013). The effects of caregiving characteristics on the perceived life satisfaction of the grandparents who providing care for their grandchildren. *Journal of Korean Association of Social Welfare Policy, 40*(3), 183–206.

Chung, M. R., Choi, H. J., & Kang, S. K. (2015). An exploratory study of the variables affecting the child-rearing role of grandmothers. *Journal of Korea Open Association for Early Childhood Education, 20*(3), 119–141.

Chung, S. D., Park, A. L., & Ki, J. H. (2015). The longitudinal relationships between patterns of grandparenting role and life-satisfaction and family-relationship-satisfaction. *Journal of Survey Research, 16*(3), 45–73.

Jang, Y. H., & Kwon, H. J. (2010). An inquiry on response of elderly volunteer's story telling activities for young children. *Early Childhood Education & Care, 5*(2), 157–186.

JoongAng Ilbo. (2016, February 4). A social column. *JoongAng Ilbo.* Retrieved from http://koreajoongangdaily.joins.com/

Joung, E. H., & Choi, Y. S. (2013). The factors associated with the birth plan for second child and second birth for married women in Korea. *Health and Social Welfare Review, 33*(1), 5–34.

Kim, H. S. (2009). The fostering experience of custodial grandmother in low-income grandparent-grandchild family. *Journal of Gerontological Social Welfare, 43*, 61–92.

Kim, J. H., & Doh, H. S. (2011). Types of grandmothers with preschool-aged grandchildren and their correlates: Demographic characteristics, contacts between grandmothers and grandchildren, and closeness between grandmothers and mothers. *Journal of Child Studies, 32*(1), 13–29.

Kim, H. S., & Kim, J. Y. (2012). Effects of coresidence with parents on first childbirth. *Health and Social Welfare Review, 32*(3), 5–32.

Kim, M. Y., & Yoon, H. M. (2015). Grandparent-headed families in poverty: A qualitative approach focusing on family roles. *Journal of Korea Society of Child Welfare, 50,* 145–177.

Korean Population and Health Welfare Association. (2015). *Childrearing guidebook for grandparents.* Retrieved from www.ppfk.or.kr/Eng/

Korean Women's Development Institute. (2015). *2015 report.* Retrieved from http://eng.kwdi.re.kr/

Kukmin Daily. (2014, October 1). *Kukinews.* Retrieved from www.kukmindaily.co.kr/

Kwon, E. B., Lee, J. H., & Kim, S. M. (2015). Supporting child care and dynamics of family in transition. *Journal of Korean Family Resource Management Association, 19*(1), 111–138.

Lee, Y. J., & Koh, S. K. (2011). Resource transfers between mothers and adult children: Financial resources and caregiving. *Journal of Korean Home Management Association, 29*(6), 137–151.

Lee, Y. M., & Lee, J. E. (2012). A comparative study on the perception of the traditional child-rearing practices between the parents' generation and grandparents' generation. *Asia Studies Review, 29*, 267–299.

Lee, Y. S., & Park, H. Y. (2000). A study on the grandparent role expected by preschool grandchild. *Korean Journal of Early Childhood Education, 20*(3), 211–232.

Paik, J. A. (2013). Experiences of grandmothers raising their grandchildren: The familial response to the absence of care work in family. *Damron201, 16*(3), 67–93.

Park, C. S. (2010). A Study on the formation process of grandparents-grandchildren families, raising experiences, and life satisfaction of grandmothers. *Korean Journal of Family Welfare, 15*(2), 105–125.

Park, J. S. (2013). Gauging gender equality in terms of household labor division and gender-role perception. *Health and Welfare Policy Forum, 199,* 28–38.

Seoul Statistics. (2015). Family structure and change of supporting family. *e-Seoul Statistics 93.* Retrieved from http://stat.seoul.go.kr/jsp3/

Shin, Y. J. (2015). Grandparenthood revisited. *Andragogy Today: Interdisciplinary Journal of Adult & Continuing Education, 18*(4), 29–47.

Statistics Korea. (2014). *Statistics of the aged.* Retrieved from http://kostat.go.kr/portal/eng/index.action

Statistics Korea (2015). *Birth statistics.* Retrieved from http://kostat.go.kr/portal/eng/index.action

Yang, S. N., & Shin, C. S. (2011). Work–family conflicts: Challenges of working mothers with young children. *Journal of Korea Institute for Health and Social Affairs, 31*(3), 70–103.

Yeom, J. S., & Yeom, J. H. (2015). The meaning of family from the lives of grandmothers and their single parent grandchildren. *Early Childhood Education Research & Review, 19*(3), 319–342.

Yi, Y. S. (2004). A study on the grandparents' role in their relationship with grandchildren in adolescent. *Journal of Korean Association of Human Ecology, 13*(5), 673–681.

Yoo, K. J., Lee, K. M., & Choi, S. Y. (2015). Analysis of situation and awareness of teachers about developing grandparents' traditional storytelling program for enhancement of pro-social behaviors of children. *Journal of Children's Literature and Education, 16*(1), 115–136.

China

Chen, F., & Liu, G. (2012). The health implications of grandparents caring for grandchildren in China. *Journals of Gerontology Series B: Psychological Sciences and Social Sciences, 67B,* 99–112.

Chen, F., Liu, G., & Mair, C. A. (2011). Intergenerational ties in context: Grandparents caring for grandchildren in China. *Social Forces, 90*(2), 571–594.

Chen, F., Short, S. E., & Entwisle, B. (2000). The impact of grandparental proximity on maternal childcare in China. *Population Research and Policy Review, 19*(6), 571–590.

Cong, Z., & Silverstein, M. (2008). Intergenerational time-for-money exchanges in rural China: Does reciprocity reduce depressive symptoms of older grandparents? *Research in Human Development, 5*(1), 6–25.

Cong, Z., & Silverstein, M. (2012a). Caring for grandchildren and intergenerational support in rural China: A gendered extended family perspective. *Ageing and Society, 32*(3), 425–450.

Cong, Z., & Silverstein, M. (2012b). Custodial grandparents and intergenerational support in rural China. In K. K. Mehta & L. L. Thang (Eds.), *Experiencing grandparenthood* (pp. 109–127). New York: Springer.

Croll, E. J. (2006). The intergenerational contract in the changing Asian family. *Oxford Development Studies, 34*(4), 473–491.

Fuzou News. (2015). Elderly scavenger went out with a child in clean clothes: Unselfish Love? Kidnapping? *Fuzhou News.* Retrieved from www.qzwb.com/gb/content/2015-12/17/content_5249328.htm

Goh, E. C. (2006). Raising the precious single child in urban China: An intergenerational joint mission between parents and grandparents. *Journal of Intergenerational Relationships, 4*(3), 6–28.

Goh, E. C. (2009). Grandparents as childcare providers: An in-depth analysis of the case of Xiamen, China. *Journal of Aging Studies, 23*(1), 60–68.

Goode, W. J. (1960). A theory of role strain. *American Sociological Review, 25,* 483–496.

Guo, B., Pickard, J., & Huang, J. (2008). A cultural perspective on health outcomes of caregiving grandparents: Evidence from China. *Journal of Intergenerational Relationships, 5*(4), 25–40.

Jiang, J., Rosenqvist, U., Wang, H., Greiner, T., Lian, G., & Sarkadi, A. (2007). Influence of grandparents on eating behaviors of young children in Chinese three-generation families. *Appetite, 48*(3), 377–383.

Ko, P.-C., & Hank, K. (2014). Grandparents caring for grandchildren in China and Korea: Findings from CHARLS and KLoSA. *Journals of Gerontology Series B: Psychological Sciences and Social Sciences, 69*(4), 646–651.

Lei, X., & Lin, W. (2009). The new cooperative medical scheme in rural China: Does more coverage mean more service and better health? *Health Economics, 18*(S2), S25–S46.

Moen, P., Robison, J., & Dempster-McClain, D. (1995). Caregiving and women's well-being: A life course approach. *Journal of Health and Social Behavior, 36,* 259–273.

Park, M., & Chesla, C. (2007). Revisiting Confucianism as a conceptual framework for Asian family study. *Journal of Family Nursing, 13*(3), 293–311.

Shen, C., & Williamson, J. B. (2010). China's new rural pension scheme: Can it be improved? *International Journal of Sociology and Social Policy, 30* (5/6), 239–250.

Short, S. E., Zhai, F., Xu, S., & Yang, M. (2001). China's one-child policy and the care of children: An analysis of qualitative and quantitative data. *Social Forces, 79*(3), 913–943.

Silverstein, M., Cong, Z., & Li, S. (2006). Intergenerational transfers and living arrangements of older people in rural China: Consequences for psychological well-being. *Journals of Gerontology Series B: Psychological Sciences and Social Sciences, 61*(5), S256–S266.

Sung, K.-T. (1999). An exploration of actions of filial piety. *Journal of Aging Studies, 12,* 369–386.

Vilela, A. (2013). *Briefings on social protection in older age: Pension coverage in China and the expansion of the new rural social pension.* London, UK: HelpAge International. Retrieved from http://socialprotection.org/discover/publications/pension-coverage-china-and-expansion-new-rural-social-pension-scheme

Xu, L., & Chi, I. (2011). Life satisfaction among rural Chinese grandparents: The roles of intergenerational family relationship and support exchange with grandchildren. *International Journal of Social Welfare, 20*(S1), S148–S159.

Yao, X. (2000). *An Introduction to Confucianism.* Cambridge, UK: Cambridge University Press.

PART V
Africa and the Middle East

10

GRANDPARENTS IN THE MIDDLE EAST AND NORTH AFRICA

Changes in Identity and Trajectory

Mahmoud Emam, Yasser Abdelazim, and Mogeda El-Keshky

PROVERBS

1. "If you know his father and grandfather you can trust his son." (Morocco)
   (إذا كنت تعرف والده وجده فإنك تستطيع أن تثق بابنه)
2. "More precious than our children are the children of our children." (Egypt)
   (أعز من أبنائنا هم أبناء أبنائنا)

   (see p. 240 for interpretations of proverbs)

CASE STORY

[Ziad, a 14-year-old young man, talked with his father about their extended family and particularly his grandparents.]

A 60-minute conversation with my father revealed much about his experiences and memories of his father. He recalled the invaluable lessons he still keeps in his heart. These lessons became an integral part of his memories and have had an impact on his daily life while definitely shaping his future. Bedtime stories, a blend of facts and fantasies, inspired him and he reflected on my grandfather's struggles. My father recollects that my grandfather was a farmer who inculcated a love of the land in his son. A retired veteran, my grandfather believed in patriotism to build up the nation, and was keen to pass these values on to me as his grandson. I was 12 when he passed away. However, I still remember every single word he said when we conversed. He wanted to ensure that my father and I would carry the flag of the nation and complete the journey. One of the early lessons from my grandfather was that the best time to learn and study school lessons was early morning, precisely at Fajre time (dawn).

In a religious family and environment, Ziad grew up learning to be accountable for his deeds to Almighty Allah. His grandfather explained the significance of the Al Fajr prayer, that Allah blesses the one who performs this prayer before the sun rises. When Ziad lost his grandfather at age 12, he realized how strong a support his grandfather had been. After graduation from school, Ziad's grandfather had joined the army, and he was proud to speak at length about it. "My father learned from him that in those days literate volunteers were requested to join the army," said Ziad. His monthly salary was 13 pounds when he participated in the wars of 1967 and 1973, which were historical milestones for Egypt and the MENA region in general. Ziad's grandfather always keenly stressed the importance of teaching him the Arabic language. Having grown up close to his grandfather in the three-story house of their extended family, says Ziad, my father admits that he was not able to repeat my grandfather's level of courage to join the army. He also observed that my grandmother helped bring up her grandchildren, which showed him the valuable role a woman plays in support of the family, and that my grandmother demonstrated this same value in their family.

Introduction

Changes in the social roles of grandparents due to a global array of contextual factors have motivated researchers to better understand the meaning and identity of grandparenthood in dynamic social contexts (Assaad & Roudi-Fahimi,

FIGURE 10.1 A drawing of Ziad's grandfather by a skillful artist. The facial expressions reflect the serious life he led since he joined the army. Ziad's grandfather was an example of a MENA grandparent who cared for his children and was careful to inculcate his wisdom in his grandchildren.

Source: Courtesy of Yasser Abdelazim.

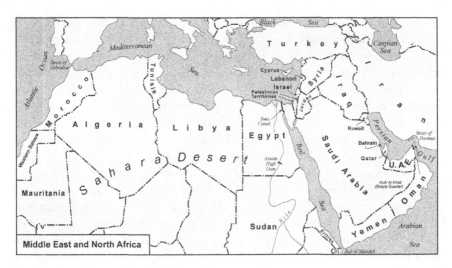

FIGURE 10.2 Map of the MENA region

Source: Courtesy of Paul Larson.

2007; Flemming, 1999). Understanding grandparenthood as a cultural phenomenon in the Middle East and North Africa region (hereafter, MENA) first requires a description of contexts and background. Sometimes referred to as the "Arab World," MENA consists of Egypt, Sudan, Somalia, Djibouti, Saudi Arabia, Bahrain, Iraq, Jordan, Kuwait, Lebanon, Oman, Qatar, Syria, the United Arab Emirates, West Bank and Gaza, Israel, Yemen, and Turkey (Middle East), in addition to Mauritania, Morocco, Algeria, Tunisia, and Libya (North Africa) – see Figure 10.2. Although Israel usually aligns itself with the Western world, it is located in the broader geographical definition of the MENA region. Therefore, the overall sociocultural description of the MENA region may not reflect Israeli values well.

Islam is the predominant religion and Arabic is the dominant language in the MENA region, but the area is also the home of substantial numbers of Jews and Christians (World Bank, 1999), and is known as the cradle of the world's three major monotheistic religions (i.e., Judaism, Christianity, and Islam) (Doumani, 2012). Most MENA countries share several common cultural practices which guide daily life, despite important variations in ethnicity, tradition, history, and spoken Arabic dialects. Although there are also social, political, and economic variations among MENA countries, most people in the region share a cultural heritage based on geographical location, language (Arabic), and religion (Islam). Each country has been impacted somewhat differently by modernization and certainly by the discovery of crude oil in some countries. Islam dictates all aspects of Muslims' lives, as in the expression: "Islam creates a legal framework for economic, social-cultural, and political interactions" (Elsaman & Arafa, 2012, p. 3), and this is probably a stronger influence than among people of other religions and beliefs in the region.

For example, Islamic law states that fathers should provide their children with all life resources to support their survival and growth (Ahmed, 2013; Qur'an 1:33). In cases where the child's father is dead or unable to care for the child, or if the child does not have any inherited resources, the paternal grandfather and other paternal relatives are responsible by Islamic law to provide for the child. Thus, grandparents have an inherent key role to play even though they are at a late stage of life. But what is the nature of the relationship between grandparents and grandchildren within Arabic culture as shared by MENA countries, and what factors are likely to influence grandparental roles?

Traditional religious roots, whether Islamic, Christian, or Jewish, place a significant emphasis on family ties in general, and particularly on grandparental ties with grandchildren (Sonnheim, 2004; Yousef, 2004). The empirical study of grandparenthood in MENA societies, however, is still in a preliminary stage (Katsenelson & Raviv, 2009; cited in Tourjeman, Doron, & Cohen, 2015). With the exception of a number of international reports by the United Nations and World Bank (described below), there is little statistical data available about several key issues regarding MENA grandparents. Indeed, we know very little from research, for example, about how grandparenthood has evolved over the past four decades, or what effects globalization and regional conditions have had on changes in grandparents in MENA societies.

In this chapter we discuss the characteristics and practices of MENA grandparents in terms of roles, duties, and responsibilities, and changes in trajectory and identity. Prior to a historical examination of grandparenthood in the MENA region, we will provide some background information about the region and its families. This should help the reader understand how the concept of grandparenthood is best delineated and described for the MENA region. In general, our aims are threefold: to (1) describe the cultural factors that shape(d) the roles of grandparents in the MENA region, (2) explore different perspectives including a historical review, and practices of the family and wider society in relation to grandparents, and (3) examine factors that have impacted on changes in the normative roles of grandparents. We also look at how these changes may have resulted from modernization and other economic and social factors.

Cultural, Historical, Social, Economic, and Demographic Background

In MENA countries, there is a general emphasis on extended family structure, where the husband, wife, and children live with other family members such as grandparents, uncles, aunts, nephews, cousins, and nieces. The typical practices of extended families imply that each of the elder members of the family provides support care to the younger members. The family system is generally patrilineal, a common kinship system in which an individual's family membership derives from and is traced through his or her father's lineage (Gregg, 2005).

Within Islamic belief, which has historically guided family system mechanisms, children of the elderly are expected to take full care of and responsibility for their aged parents. On the other hand, the elderly are expected to act as advisors to their children and grandchildren on family and cultural matters, since they have considerable life experience and knowledge of the history and culture of the society. Such long-standing beliefs, however, became vulnerable to change due to economic and social factors associated with globalization. In current modern societies it could be that some grandparents may play motherly roles with their grandchildren, acting either as advisors or sole caregivers. In spite of changes in patterns of grandparent–grandchild relations, we cannot claim that any emerging new pattern can be seen as entirely negative, and there is also some continuity in beliefs, for example that the grandparent should care for grandchildren even if they are old, poor, and barely able to take care of themselves.

In past generations it was rare to have all of one's grandparents alive (Hafez & Slyomovics, 2013), but nowadays it is common for several grandparents to act as caregivers. More recently there have been signs of strain on the family system due to industrialization, improved health services, urbanization, wars and conflicts, and Westernization (Yousef, 2004; Akkari, 2004). Despite the pressure these factors place on the family system in the MENA region, the family remains the primary system of support. This pattern appears to be just as strong among Arabs who have emigrated and have lived in the Western world (Akkari, 2004), and for Israelis (Sigad & Eisikovits, 2013). Different researchers claim that these contextual factors have both increased and decreased individual grandparents' involvement in their role. Change is particularly notable among grandmothers, who have begun to play a more active and positive role in the lives of their grandchildren either as advisors or caregivers. In the past the grandfather was the main catalyst for all practices within the family, while grandmothers used to play a supportive role under the authority of grandfathers. The education of women and the influence of feminism within the MENA region in the second half of the 20th century contributed to this change (Abudabbeh, 2005).

Between 1950 and 2000, the Middle East experienced explosive population growth, from 92 million to 349 million. With a huge surge in migration from the Western world and increasing numbers of Westerners working in the region, particularly in the Gulf countries whose economies are based on oil production, indigenous people were exposed to alternative ways of life which were seen by some as an improvement over traditional life. This promoted several changes in cultural practices and implicit changes in family systems. For example, as a majority of men began to practice monogamy, families had fewer children and girls in some societies began to have more educational opportunities. But despite changes in cultural beliefs and practices, individuals remained committed to the values of collectivism (emphasizing the needs of the group over the needs of the individual) over individualism, and individuals continued to value kinship relationships in accord with Islamic beliefs. This helped maintain the traditional concept of the extended family. Even when extended families divided into separate nuclear families in different locations inside or outside their country, the extended family concept remained strong and reasserted itself on social occasions or in the teaching of values to the young.

A careful examination of these contextual changes shows that modern transformations have had an impact on the quality of relationships between grandparents and grandchildren. Grandparents now have the opportunity to know their grandchildren as babies, teenagers, young adults, and middle-aged adults. This is partly because of increasing life expectancy as a result of better health services (Silverstein & Long, 1998). Hence, contemporary parent–child relationships could last 6–7 decades, and grandparent–grandchild bonds could continue for 3–4 decades. In the past, with shorter life expectancy, many children had no surviving grandparents and a relatively high proportion lost their parents before reaching adulthood (Uhlenberg, 1996). Harper (2005) reminds us that demographic shifts in many countries have increased the number of generations but have also decreased the absolute number of relatives. As elsewhere, intergenerational connections that include grandparent–grandchild relationships have become more socially prominent and personally significant in the MENA region (Even-Zohar & Sharlin, 2009; Harper, 2005). As a result, grandparents are becoming more and more prominent figures within the extended family.

According to Roudi-Fahimi and Kent (2007), the total population of the MENA region was about 430 million in 2007 and it is expected to exceed 700 million in 2050. In addition, the Population Reference Bureau Report (Roudi, 2001) showed that the percentage of the total population over the age of 65 in the MENA region was 4.7%. After the 1980s, the total regional fertility rate declined drastically, from 5 children to 2.2, due to improvements in maternal/infant health, increased levels of education of females, female participation in the labor force, and urbanization from the 1950s and especially since the 1970s (Rizk et al., 2015). Additionally, life expectancy at birth in the MENA region increased between 1940 and the present from 30 to 71 years for males and 33 to 76 for females. In 2023, this number is expected to reach 73 and 79 for males and females, respectively (United Nations Department of Economics, 2005). These figures differ widely among the diverse MENA nations.

Divorce is another phenomenon that has led to the increased importance of grandparents in caregiving, as has been observed in many chapters of this book. Almost 95% of the MENA region population is Muslim (Pew Research Center, 2009), and the Muslim population in the MENA region is the second largest worldwide, with 20% of the global Muslim population (the largest is in the Asia-Pacific region). Under Islamic law, although a Muslim woman can divorce her husband, a man can divorce his wife simply by saying, or nowadays even by texting, "I divorce you" three times. After a divorce, the man remains financially responsible for the expenses (known as *nafaqa* under Islamic Law) of the wife and children. If the court finds the mother to be incompetent, custody of a child, regardless of age, can be given to the father or the child's paternal grandmother. Judgment of the mother's incompetence is made solely by the Sharia (Islamic Law) judge who assesses whether the mother has the necessary resources (e.g., emotional stability and financial capability) to care for the child (Elsaman & Arafa, 2012; Bakar, 2011). Divorce within other religious groups in the MENA region, however, does not follow Islamic Law, as both Jews and Christians follow their religious practices or secular divorce laws.

Other social, economic, and political conflicts have contributed to the significant role of grandparents in caregiving. Specifically, it is argued that since 1990 21 destabilizing events have occurred in the Middle East. From Operation Desert Storm in 1990 to the Anbar Clashes in 2013, the area has witnessed major and minor political/military disruptions, in addition to the Arab Spring revolution of 2011. Most grandparents who lost their sons and daughters in war and conflicts now take responsibility for their grandchildren (Joseph, 2013). Wars and other conflicts have given rise to very high migration and refugee rates, which in turn has led to large numbers of broken families. A recent example was the unrest and war which followed the Arab Spring protests. Subsequent and current Syrian, Yemeni, and Libyan civil wars have led to the largest wave of Arab refugees in history, impacting emigration to countries including Germany (see Chapter 5), UK (Chapter 6), and to a much lesser extent the US (Chapter 3). The clashes in Syria, which have shocked the world, are an ongoing example of the political, social, and economic conflicts that have been dramatically changing grandparents' roles (Malik & Awadallah, 2013).

At the same time, many nuclear families have replaced extended families, and the numbers of people living only in their urban, nuclear family has increased. Over recent decades people have looked for better life opportunities, setting aside the traditional value of "flocking together" within an extended family. Other parents, especially fathers, have left their children behind to work in other countries, often leaving responsibility for their children to the grandparents and the mother. As a result, growing numbers of MENA grandparents now bear the burden of caring for their grandchildren (Hafez & Slyomovics, 2013).

Research Literature on Grandparenthood

Families are central to local culture in MENA societies, and the importance placed on family solidarity is exhibited by indicators such as high rates of intergenerational living, shared family meals and leisure time, children's contact with grandparents, and family observation of traditional cultural practices (Even-Zohar & Sharlin, 2009; Reitzes & Mutran, 2004; Hatton-Yeo & Ohsako, 2000). Important MENA values include collectivism, respect for parents and elders, cherishing of children, and strong expectations of family obligation (Doumani, 2012; Abudabbeh, 2005; Apt, 2002, 2001).

As we have noted, MENA countries share common cultural and religious practices (Elsaman & Arafa 2012). This is mostly because of the common religion embraced by most of the Arab population in the region, with only a small minority comprised by Christians, Jews, or other believers. The Muslim community is characterized as patrilocal, patriarchal, endogamous, and sometimes polygamous. Other religious groups in the MENA region may differ in their attitude toward polygamy but still share with the Muslim community common cultural characteristics that guide people's lives (Bakar, 2011). Christians in the MENA region, for example, follow the Orthodox church and do not allow polygamy. They, however, share the cultural characteristic of viewing the husband as the pivotal figure in the family. It can therefore be argued that the religiousness which characterizes people throughout the MENA region has given grandparents a pivotal status in the family. The Qur'an places great importance on respecting the elders, and treating grandparents with kindness and respect comes before all else, except for the practice of *Tawhid* (belief that God is the Almighty one). There is also an Islamic belief, exemplified by the family from Egypt in the case story of Ziad's grandfather, that much can be learned from having three generations living under the same roof, and that co-residence strengthens the bonds within the family. Extended family members also play a crucial role. In Islamic history one reads that families often lived near one another. This is not necessarily true today, because many families live farther away from each other due to the social and economic demands of modernization. Yet close family bonds are still a dominant theme in Islamic and other religious societies in the MENA region even now, and the extended family is seen as the primary source of assistance during times of conflict within the immediate family.

Several studies have been performed in the Jewish community in Israel on various aspects of grandparenthood, and these studies reveal several similarities to our contextual descriptions of Arab societies. Tourjeman, Doron, & Cohen (2015), for example, investigated how increased life expectancy placed grandparents at risk when they lost a grandchild. They examined qualitative data about the ways grandparents experienced the loss of a grandchild, and found that the loss of a grandchild was characterized by a complex tension between two related forces of distancing and becoming closer to the grandchild and his or her parent. Elsewhere, in the context of the Israeli–Palestinian conflict, Possick (2015) focused on the meaning of grandchildren's deaths to their grandparents. She concluded that the loss was interpreted within a personal context in some cases or collective context in some others. Furthermore, Werner, Buchbinder, Lowenstein, and Livni (2007) critically examined the congruence in grandparent–parent–grandchild triads, and showed that relationships between the three generations were either (1) congruent and strongly connected, (2) congruent but non-connected, or (3) non-congruent. Finally, Ben-Shlomo (2014) recently evaluated the contributions of socio-demographic characteristics, stress, and cognitive appraisals of grandparenthood to life satisfaction among new Israeli grandparents. His results showed that higher levels of life satisfaction were associated with younger age of onset of grandparenthood, higher levels of physical health and economic status, and lower grandparent distress.

While these Israeli studies, as is so often the case in research on grandparents, looked at distinct aspects of grandparenthood and are not comparable with each other or with data from Islamic research samples, they serve as examples to reveal a growing interest in the new social status of grandparents within the unique culture of Israel. In our view, these research examples also suggest that Israeli grandparents share many of the experiences that are also common in MENA Muslim communities.

Grandparents and Grandchildren: Emerging Roles

Grandparents play an important role in building connections between the past, present, and future, and in shaping family identity and history (Reitzes & Mutran, 2004). Changes in grandparents–grandchild relations in the Arab world, as stated earlier, may best be viewed in the contexts of industrialization, urbanization, wars and conflicts, and Westernization (Abudabbeh, 2005). Modernization is defined as a transformation from a traditional, rural, agrarian society to a secular, urban, industrial society (Apt, 2002, 2001), and as convergence toward a system of modern values. One of the main effects of modernization is the transformation of the extended family system in economically underdeveloped societies to the nuclear family system characteristic of industrial societies (Chapin, 2014; Mazzanti, 2002).

It has been argued that better healthcare facilities, which lead to increased life expectancy, have resulted in an increasingly impactful role of grandparents in the lives of their grandchildren (Silverstein & Giarrusso, 2010; Mazzanti, 2002). Increased life expectancy and the outbreak of several conflicts have given rise to one prominent issue that has become characteristic of grandparenthood in the MENA region: many grandparents are at risk of losing their grandchildren. A worldwide increase in the absolute and relative size of the elderly population, as a result of changes in life expectancy and fertility rates (Hooyman & Kiyak, 2008) has specifically been related to improved sanitation, medical care, immunizations, better nutrition, and decreasing birth rates. According to United Nations statistics, the elderly population is expected to grow by 50% in developed nations between 2009 and 2050; and for developing nations it was projected to jump to 80%, i.e., from 264 million to 416 million. This will ultimately lead to a world population of which 12% will be 65 years or older by the year 2030, compared to 7% today (United Nations Department of Economics, 2005). These statistics apply to the MENA region, which includes both developed and developing countries. Israel (see demographic data, Table 1.1) is the only developed country in the MENA region, according to most criteria approved for classification by the United Nations, and some oil-producing Gulf countries are referred to as "high-income developing countries." In addition, longer life expectancy has generally increased the duration of grandparenthood. Once an individual becomes a grandparent, she or he will have that status for a much longer time than in past generations. It is now typical in the MENA region for people to become grandparents in their 40s, and some people, particularly women, become grandparents in their 30s (Timberlake & Chipungu, 1992).

Parental divorce has also been identified by various researchers as one of the factors leading to the changing role of grandparents in children's life (Fuller-Thomson & Minkler, 2000). In the past, divorce cases favored the mother of the children in Western countries (Silverstein & Giarrusso, 2010), but within Muslim societies in the MENA region mothers might remain responsible for the child until the child is older, at which point she could return the child to the paternal family. When the mother took the child back to the paternal home, the grandmother typically then assumed the caregiver role (Abudabbeh, 2005).

A number of scholars have argued that grandparental caregiving can be very rewarding (Even-Zohar & Sharlin, 2009; Giarrusso, Silverstein, & Feng, 2000), and that both grandfather and grandmother can benefit mutually from this relationship. Grandparents can enjoy close relations with their grandchildren as confidants and companions (Hayslip & Kaminski, 2005). Gatt and Musatti (1999) noted that the grandparent caregiver role could also enhance a grandparents' sense of having a purpose in life and contribute to satisfaction from maintainance of the family's identity and well-being. Additionally, scholars have argued that grandparents who serve as confidants to grandchildren sometimes help them with decision-making (Harwood & Lin, 2000; Roberto, Allen, & Blieszner, 1999).

Even-Zohar and Sharlin (2009) conducted a study of Jewish Israelis in which they explored the roles, expectations, and obligations of adult grandchildren. Specifically, 216 pairs of adult grandchildren (average age: 24.9 years) and their grandparents (average age: 78.3 years) responded to their questionnaires. Their findings demonstrated that role perceptions of the adult grandchild were shaped and increased in value by intergenerational transmission and through internalization of the norms and behavior patterns of parents. As expected, perceptions of the grandchild's role were more positive among grandchildren who experienced their grandparents as caregivers in their childhood, than among grandchildren who did not have such experiences. These grandchildren clearly had a perception of filial obligation and responsibility toward grandparents, and in fact they expressed more positive opinions than did the grandparent about grandparents' caregiving. In spite of the religious differences between these Israelis and Muslims in other MENA countries, we regard their sense of obligation and responsibility as similar, and note that both groups face the related contextual influence of life in a conflict region.

Cultural Beliefs and Practices

According to educational psychologist Aldhafri (personal communication, September 13, 2016), the author of a book published in Arabic titled *Parenting Styles in Oman*, parenthood in the extended family is best investigated through

FIGURE 10.3 Middle-class paternal grandfather (age 75) and grandmother (age 75) spending time indoors in a hotel with their 10- and 6-year-old grandsons in Muscat, Oman. Grandparents in the MENA region generally ensure that grandchildren are cared for, but many grandchildren lose that care due to various social, political, and economic factors.

Source: Courtesy of Mahmoud Emam.

an examination of how children perceive parenting styles. Aldhafri believes that personality traits influence how parents and grandparents practice childrearing in both the nuclear family and the extended family. The Muslim family was described earlier as characterized by extended, patrilocal, patriarchal, endogamous, and sometimes polygamous relations, and the extended family structure was seen as characteristic of the MENA region, whereby grandparents are responsible for teaching tradition and cultural practices to their grandchildren (Doumani, 2012). Other kinship ties are also particularly powerful influences in the MENA region. In most MENA countries more than 40% of children lived in households with other adults besides their parents, including grandparents, uncles, aunts, and cousins. This differs from what children experience in places where extended household members have lesser roles in daily life (Apt, 2002).

According to the Qur'an (17:23–24) and the Bible (Exodus 20:8), God commanded children to honor their parents. In addition, the Sharia commanded that maternal and paternal grandparents should have the same rights as parents. From these perspectives, children should reciprocate as they provide grandparents with food, shelter, healthcare, and clothing, and overall grandparents should receive the respect and honor they deserve, even after they become aged or feeble (Elsaman & Arafa, 2012).

Grandfathers versus Grandmothers in Cultural Context

Based on our discussion thus far, the roles of grandfather and grandmother may be differentiated as follows (Roberto, Allen, & Blieszner, 2001). First, in the absence of a child's father the grandfather often assumes the role of substitute father and the grandmother assumes the role of mother-figure. Metaphorically, the MENA grandfather acts as the family's "chairman" while the grandmother assumes the role of "secretary of interior affairs." Compared to grandmothers, grandfathers in the MENA region have been neglected by researchers (Metcalfe, 2006). Researchers have also contended that grandfathers have always had conflicting motivations to be active in their grandchildren's lives while trying to meet the expectations associated with their other roles as men (Clarke & Roberts, 2004). From a cultural perspective, grandfathers in the MENA region who assume the responsibility of a father take on the following roles in their grandchildren's lives:

- They provide food, shelter, education, clothing, and security.
- They create a family legacy, providing mentorship, discipline, and direction to grandchildren.

The case story which began this chapter exemplified how many Arab grandchildren perceive their grandfathers' role in their lives. Their functions include transmission of family history to grandchildren, a history that is vivid and full of examples of ethics, achievements, adversity and hardship, and dreams of the future.

The overall social-cultural context of the MENA region is characterized by a space-based patriarchy, whereby men are associated with the public space and women with the private space. Additionally, as an elder who has been through a long life journey that included many hardships and successful experiences, the grandmother uses her wisdom and experience in providing support, mentorship, and direction to her grandchildren, and dealing with marital and social issues (Aubel, 2012). Researchers agree that grandmothers play an influential role in the socialization of grandchildren, and that they also educate grandchildren and supervise their progress in school (Akkari, 2004; World Bank, 1999; Heyneman, 1997). Recently, the many wars and conflicts that have occurred in the MENA region have increased the burdens of grandmothers, who take responsibility for the care of orphaned grandchildren.

Although Israel is much more closely aligned with Western values than are other MENA societies, a close inspection of its societal and family values indicates that its religious orientation makes it possible to say that its grandparental roles are somewhat similar to those depicted throughout this chapter. In this regard, Findler (2000) conducted a study on grandparents of children with disabilities in Israel. He examined the structural and functional dimensions of perceived social support, with an emphasis on the importance of grandparents as support providers, among mothers of 3–7-year-old children with cerebral palsy and other special educational needs. Findler reported that mothers ranked the grandparents highly in comparison with other support providers; maternal grandmothers were perceived to be the most important figures. They were viewed as providing significantly more emotional support than instrumental support, and received the highest score among support givers in terms of maternal satisfaction. Generally, MENA grandfathers' roles include provision of food and shelter for the family, i.e., responsibility for the economic needs of the family. Meanwhile, grandmothers were perceived as taking full responsibility to provide care and nurturance as the affective and emotional sources of support for the family (Hafez & Slyomovics, 2013; Doumani, 2012).

Subcultural Variations in Grandparents

In the MENA region, two common, competing views of grandparental roles are:

*   Mentors for parents and grandchildren, and transmitters of values and heritage, and socialization agents for grandchildren;
*   People whose company parents and grandchildren enjoy, but without direct responsibility for childrearing practices (Ramachandran, 2012).

According to a global perspective on grandparenthood and based on psychological studies, Ramchandran (2012) argued that race and ethnicity are powerful influences on how grandparents are viewed by grandchildren. Variations in grandparenthood are largely influenced by the meaning attached to being a grandparent, rather than by culture or tradition. Such meaning, however, is shaped by the level of one's education, modernization, and exposure to other cultures. Therefore, variations in grandparenthood may be analyzed in terms of cultural beliefs and practices, and in terms of demographics, modernization, migration patterns, and divorce.

The roles of MENA grandparents also appear to differ based on socioeconomic status, as we saw for Brazil in Chapter 4. In higher socioeconomic status families, grandparents are more committed to transmitting traditional values. Grandfathers in these families are often idealized by their grandchildren based on their life examples. Meanwhile, in the middle class the emphasis is more on maintenance of the social order and acquisition of knowledge and talents, and poorer and working-class families usually expect their children to find their life path through natural growth while providing information about what to expect at different phases of life. They may be unable to intervene, but their insights are believed to help the grandchildren to adapt and survive.

Demographic Sources of Variations

The growth of the elderly population varies worldwide due to a number of factors including health outcomes and migration patterns. Apt (2002, p. 288) argued that "Ageing and longevity have together occupied the world's platform of popular concerns in the past century." While aging has drawn considerable attention in developed societies for several decades, in MENA countries aging has been perceived as a potential future demographic change. We believe that MENA countries will inevitably face demographic changes, and therefore changes in the roles of grandparents and grandparental caregiving should be anticipated. Apt (2002, p. 291) also stated that "The world population is aging and this presents a major policy issue in the developing world." In the MENA region, aging is a crisis that is just emerging. At present, the more notable MENA crisis is in the family. In demographic terms, the population that is aged 65 and over in the MENA region stands at 50 million (Kronfol, Sibai, & Rizk, 2014). Nevertheless, Yount and Sibai (2009), and also Sibai, Rizk, and Kronfol (2014) posited that aging in the MENA region represents more of an opportunity than a demand on families, in that the elderly are potential resource for the family in terms of provision of support and care for the younger generation.

Also, the current demographics of the MENA region have triggered different governments to take actions to intervene in taking care of the elderly, to take the burden off the shoulders of the young whose attitudes may not be favorable toward the historical and culturally rooted tradition of caring for the elderly. For example, public and private centers have been established across MENA countries to provide multidisciplinary services to the elderly. These services include medical, social, emotional, and psychological support. Additionally, public and private residence centers for the elderly have been set up to help those whose children are unable to care for them or whose children can afford to pay for the care centers. This reflects a shift from traditional societal values which stood against change over time, and within this paradigm shift grandchildren are at risk of being deprived of support and socialization from grandparents, who are increasingly moving into public homes for the elderly.

The Variable Effects of Modernization

Studies have found that modernization is another source of variability that has contributed to the changing roles of grandparents in the family today. One of the effects of modernization has been the abandonment of traditional ways, including those that encouraged positive grandparent–grandchild relations. In traditional Arab culture there is an emphasis on extensive honor, affection, and respect for the elderly. This varies across countries in the region, even though grandparents are commonly expected to give care to and receive care from their children. In other words, they provide an intergenerational link whereby cultural values and norms are maintained and passed on, while enjoying care and provisions from their children. However, in recent times, there has been a gradual and extensive shift from this paradigm as grandparents are left alone to either care for themselves or be taken care of by the government. A number of changes that have triggered this shift may be traced to immigration by Westerners into the MENA region or emigration of MENA people to Western countries in search of better life and education.

Recent studies in MENA societies show that some males still marry more than one wife, which often creates complex multi-relational grandparenting experiences for grandchildren. Also, some families live separately from their extended families; this trend indicates a change from the past, although some rural areas are unaffected by it. It is not surprising today to find women who work far away from their homes, and some of these women have difficulty with their maternal role. As a result, grandmothers may step into the situation. In addition, most families who emigrate to other countries either to escape from conflicts and war, or in search of better life conditions, leave their grandparents behind. These grandparents are not able to stay involved in the lives of their grandchildren, and also need to receive care from their own children. This situation is more prevalent in urban areas than in rural areas. In addition, due to the increasing rates of poverty in some MENA countries, many older people nowadays are not valued. Rather, they are increasingly considered old, burdensome, and obsolete. The younger generation holds the belief that grandparents are not well acquainted with and or adapted to current changes in the world and, therefore, they are not in a position to be helpful. This indeed has harmed the relationship grandchildren should have with their grandparents.

Social Policy Issues

Recent research studies have examined the effects of the increasingly aged population, along with the subsequent increased role of grandparents in caregiving, and suggest that social policies relevant to grandparenting should be prioritized (Chapin, 2014). For example, a report by the UNESCO Intergenerational Programs (Hatton-Yeo & Ohsako, 2000) focused on a demographic shift and its impact on grandparenthood in several countries including Palestine, which was the only MENA locale included in their report. Hatton-Yeo and Ohsako (2000) made the following points: (1) life expectancy has increased and consequently so have the numbers of older people; (2) economic and welfare patterns have changed, with the consequent risk of older people being seen either as a burden or less valuable or respected than previously; (3) there have been changes in the family structure, often exacerbated by the need for mobility for individuals engaged in economic activity; (4) a life-long learning movement has emerged; (5) relations between the young and the old have changed, and are often characterized by a mutual lack of understanding; and (6) social policy must engage with the whole community in a way that is both positive and recognizes the reciprocal relationships among different groups. Based on these findings, the report recommended the following: (1) generations of families that have been separated by migration should be reunited; (2) transmission of history and culture of the older to the younger generation should be encouraged; (3) resources should be shared among generations by encouraging the elderly who can work to engage in gainful activities; (4) social support networks should be built to foster the rehabilitation of isolated older people; and (5) life-long learning should be fostered to bring out the potential for shared learning across generations. While this report only named Palestine from within the MENA region, we believe that these recommendations are relevant to grandparents throughout the entire region.

Speculation, Conclusions, and Recommendations

The role of grandparents in the MENA region has changed over history, and the identities of grandparents have changed as a result of a number of contextual factors including divorce, migration, modernization, and the demographic changes the MENA region has witnessed over the last three or four decades. These factors are interwoven, and therefore an estimation of the contribution of each factor requires further empirical investigation. We believe that grandparents have not received their due attention from researchers in the region. It may be argued that a change in cultural values regarding the roles and value of grandparents, and the shift from extended families to nuclear families has brought about a paradigm shift in care for the elderly as well as caregiving provided by grandparents to grandchildren. This could be attributed to acculturation and modernization effects, i.e., new life patterns which have resulted from exposure to internal and external conflicts. These effects also need to be studied empirically.

Today, the tradition of caring for one's elderly parents is downplayed in our region, and grandparents are increasingly left alone to care for themselves or to bear the burden of caring for their grandchildren alone. This, in turn, has interfered with the traditional role of MENA grandparents as transmitters of cultural heritage and values to their grandchildren. Younger MENA families are gradually losing their identity as they move into practices and cultures that conflict with their traditions and deeply rooted culture. This is reflected in a quote by Denis Guenoun (2014), author of *A Semite: A Memoire of Algeria*. Guenoun, an Algerian who inherited French citizenship, discussed the situation with his son:

> We were swept along. The future picked us up and carried us away. Your great-grandfather spoke Arabic, your grandfather spoke Arabic and French. I, your father, speak French and a little Arabic. You, French only. You've broken with that world, you're the child of another place and another time. (Guenoun, 2014, p. 21)

This chapter has shown that demography, divorce, modernization, and migration are all reshaping grandparenthood in the MENA region. Emigration from MENA countries to Western nations in search of attractive jobs and education has increased in this century, and grandparents have found it difficult to cope with Western culture when their families decide to stay together, or they have become isolated back in their homeland when left behind. Ongoing political conflicts in MENA regions have intensified these problems even further (Bommes, Fassman, & Sievers, 2014).

Demographic trends reveal that strategies and action plans must be crafted to educate the public, both young and old, about the outcomes of such ongoing social changes. This is important because we must alleviate the perception held by many in the younger generation that the elderly population is a burden. Instead, the MENA region is in urgent need of a change in perception, to view the elderly as an asset and resource for socialization and mentorship. Support for grandparents who assume the responsibility of a caregiver should be prioritized in MENA societies, and further steps should be taken to ensure that grandparents obtain employment opportunities that help them secure a monthly income to care for their grandchildren. In poorer MENA countries, healthcare amenities should also be made available and subsidized for grandparents, which could enable them to access resources for their grandchildren. As will be seen in Chapters 11 and 12, poverty may be an even more dire issue in sub-Saharan and Southern Africa than in much of Northern Africa, as it impacts the grandparents' urgent role as caregivers for grandchildren.

In cases of divorce where grandparents are given the custody of the child, it is important that they receive training and education on how to support grandchildren, who are often under emotional duress from the separation of the parents. Grandchildren should be counseled by psychologists who understand the circumstances they have been through before the children are simply given over completely to their grandparents. We may speculate that social factors such as divorce, political factors such as wars and conflicts, and economic factors like the pace of modernization and migration from and to the region could result in more changes in the trajectory and identity of grandparents in the MENA region. This would represent a new phase for grandparenthood associated with new roles, responsibilities, values, and identities.

Conflicts between Israel and Palestine have led to the framing of a law of return whereby Jews who were ousted during the initial days of conflict could return to Israel, a Jewish state (Bahour, 2013). For the elderly, or grandparents who have to relocate with their families, this could be a challenge because they must adapt to the changes and take care of their grandchildren in the context of new societal ideologies. Young people's life view has also changed, e.g., many MENA women and girls want an education and a job before they get married and raise children. As a result, many grandparents in the region may have to delay their experience of grandparenthood, unfortunately until they are less likely to be fit enough to take adequate care of their grandchildren. In addition, economic growth stagnation in the MENA region coupled with falling oil prices are a cause of distress for grandparents who have to live on their own finances or support their children and grandchildren financially (World Bank, 2015).

Concerning families separated by emigration, the recommendations of UNESCO's Intergenerational Programs were that families who have been separated should be reunited and that access to better means of family communication should be prioritized in the MENA region. Governments and communities in the MENA region should develop platforms to bridge the gap between the younger generation and the elderly generation, so that relations between grandchildren and grandparents may improve.

Summary

This chapter first described cultural factors that shaped the roles of grandparents in the MENA region. We argued that the system of the extended family and the strong influence of religion have traditionally shaped the roles of grandparents. In modern times, however, traditional interdependence between grandparents and grandchildren is being reshaped. We next explored different perspectives and practices of the family and wider society with regard to the historical role of grandparents. Grandparents have always been present to instill tradition, and to connect the grandchildren to their roots, especially in families where divorces have taken place. Finally, we examined factors that have had an impact on changes in the typical roles of grandparents: political disturbances, emigration to the Western world, changing societal values, modernization, and demographics. Some grandparents now seem to play a more distanced role towards their grandchildren, within today's technologically modernized society. We believe that grandparenthood will be shaped and further changed by globalization whereby local cultural influences will gradually weaken. This will inevitably lead to a disconnect between grandparents and grandchildren in the MENA region. We hope that this can be prevented, because it would have the unfortunate effect that the cultural legacy characteristic of the MENA region over the millennia would eventually be lost.

Appendix

Meaning of Proverbs

"If you know his father and grandfather you can trust his son." (Morocco)

This quotation is pertinent to this chapter because it indicates that grandparents represent the source from which the offspring is shaped. If the source is adequate the outcome and extracts are adequately shaped and vice versa.

"More precious than our children are the children of our children." (Egypt)

This proverb indicates that in traditional Egyptian culture and the MENA region as a whole, grandparents regard their grandchildren as more precious than their own children and this is the reason why they provide them with thorough care and support.

Additional Resources

The Executive Board of Health Ministers for Gulf Cooperating Countries: http://sgh.org.sa/en-us/technicalprograms/healthcare/elderlyhealthcare.aspx
This resource was developed after several initiatives were endorsed by the member countries of the Gulf to provide social and health services to the elderly, available in English and Arabic.

Cairo University Center for Elderly Services: https://cu.edu.eg/ar/page. php?pg=contentFront/SubSectionData.php&SubSectionId=289:
A public university center which provides multidisciplinary services to elderly people in Egypt (in Arabic only).

Elderly Options Agency in Israel: http://eoisrael.co.il
A private agency that provides multidisciplinary services to the elderly in Israel.

Discussion Questions

1. What factors identified by this chapter appear to have caused a change of identity among grandparents in the Middle East?
2. The MENA region has cultural aspects that are consistent across the region. How do these aspects of culture influence the roles of grandparents in the MENA region?
3. The MENA region has experienced many conflicts. How have these conflicts influenced the identities and roles of grandparents?

References

Abudabbeh, N. (2005). Arab families. In M. McGoldrick, J. Giordano, & N. Garcia-Preto (Eds.). *Ethnicity and family therapy* (pp. 333–346). New York: Guilford Press.

Ahmed, R. (2013). The father's role in Arab societies. In D. W. Shwalb, B. J. Shwalb, & M. E. Lamb (Eds.), *Fathers in cultural context* (pp. 122–147). New York: Routledge.

Akkari, A. (2004). Education in the Middle East and North Africa: The Current Situation and Future Challenges. *International Education Journal, 5*(2), 144–153.

Apt, N. (2001). Rapid urbanization and living arrangements of older persons in Africa: Ageing and living arrangements of older persons: Critical issues and policy responses. *Population Bulletin of the United Nations*, (42–43), 288–310. Retrieved from www.un.org/esa/population/publications/bulletin42_43/Frontcover_note_preface.pdf

Apt, N. A. (2002). Ageing and the changing role of the family and the community: An African perspective. *International Social Security Review, 55*, 39–47.

Assaad, R., & Roudi-Fahimi, F. (2007). *Youth in the Middle East and North Africa: Demographic opportunity or challenge?* Washington, DC: Population Reference Bureau.

Aubel, J. (2012). The role and influence of grandmothers on child nutrition: Culturally designated advisors and caregivers. *Maternal & Child Nutrition, 8*(1), 19–35.

Bahour, S. (2013), *Diaspora Jews must speak out against the Israeli Law of Return, Mondoweiss*. Retrieved from http://mondoweiss.net/2013/04/diaspora-against-return/#sthash.mokhKKrp.dpuf

Bakar, O. (2011). Family values, the family institution, and the challenges of the twenty-first century: An islamic perspective. *Islam and Civilisational Renewal*, 3(1), 12–36.

Ben Shlomo, S. (2014). What makes new grandparents satisfied with their lives? *Stress and Health, 30*(1), 23–33.

Bommes, M., Fassman, H., & Sievers, W. (Eds.). (2014). *Migration from the Middle East and North Africa to Europe*. Amsterdam: Amsterdam University Press.

Chapin, R. (2014). *Social policy for effective practice: A strengths approach*. New York: Routledge.

Clarke, L., & Roberts, C. (2004). The meaning of grandparenthood and its contribution to the quality of life of older people. In A. Walker and C. H. Hennessy (Eds.), *Growing older: Quality of life in old age* (pp. 188–208). London: Open University Press.

Doumani, B. (Ed.). (2012). *Family history in the Middle East: Household, property, and gender.* Albany: State University of New York Press.

Elsaman, R. S., & Arafa, M. A. (2012). Rights of the elderly in the Arab Middle East: Islamic theory versus Arabic practice. *The Marquette Elder's Adviser, 14*(1), 1–54.

Even-Zohar, A., & Sharlin, S. (2009). Grandchildhood: Adult grandchildren's perception of their role towards their grandparents from an intergenerational perspective. *Journal of Comparative Family Studies, 40*(2), 167–185.

Findler, L. (2000). The role of grandparents in the social support system of mothers of children with a physical disability. *Families in Society: Journal of Contemporary Social Services, 81*(4), 370–381.

Fleming, A. A. (1999). Older men in contemporary discourses on ageing: Absent bodies and invisible lives. *Nursing inquiry, 6*(1), 3–8.

Fuller-Thomson, E., & Minkler, M. (2000). The mental and physical health of grandmothers who are raising their grandchildren. *Journal of Mental Health and Aging, 6,* 311–323.

Gatt, F. L., & Musatti, T. (1999). Grandmothers' involvement in grandchildren's care: Attitudes, feelings, and emotions. *Family Relations, 48,* 35–42.

Giarrusso, R., Silverstein, M., & Feng, D. (2000). Psychological costs and benefits of raising grandchildren: Evidence from a national survey of grandparents. In C. B. Cox (Ed.), *To grandmother's house we go and stay: Perspectives on custodial grandparents* (pp. 71–90). New York: Springer.

Gregg, G. S. (2005). *The Middle East: A cultural psychology.* Oxford: Oxford University Press.

Guénoun, D. (2014). *A Semite: A memoir of Algeria.* New York: Columbia University Press.

Hafez, S., & Slyomovics, S. (Eds.). (2013). *Anthropology of the Middle East and North Africa: Into the new millennium.* Bloomington: Indiana University Press.

Harper, S. (2005). Grandparenthood. In M. L. Johnson (Ed.), *The Cambridge handbook of age and ageing* (pp. 422–428). Cambridge: Cambridge University Press.

Harwood, J., & Lin, M. C. (2000). Affiliation, pride, exchange, and distance in grandparents' accounts of relationships with their college-aged grandchildren. *Journal of Communication, 50*(3), 31–47.

Hatton-Yeo, A., & Ohsako, T. (2000). *Intergenerational Programmes: Public Policy and Research Implications – An International Perspective.* UNESCO Institute for Education, Beth Johnson Foundation. Retrieved from www.unesco.org/education/uie/pdf/intergen.pdf

Hayslip, B., & Kaminski, P. L. (2005). Grandparents raising their grandchildren: A review of the literature and suggestions for practice. *The Gerontologist, 45*(2), 262–269.

Heyneman, S. P. (1997). The quality of education in the Middle East and North Africa (MENA). *International Journal of Educational Development, 17*(4), 449–466.

Hooyman, N. R., & Kiyak, H. A. (2008). Aging in other countries and across cultures in the United States. *Social gerontology, A,* 44–68.

Joseph, S. (2013). Anthropology of the future: Arab youth and the state of the State. In S. Hafez & S. Slyomovics (Eds.), *Anthropology of the Middle East and North Africa: Into the new millennium* (pp. 105–125). Bloomington: Indiana University Press.

Kronfol, N. M., Sibai, A. M., & Rizk, A. (2014). *Ageing in the Arab region: Trends, implications and policy options.* New York: Economic and Social Commission of Western Asia.

Malik, A., & Awadallah, B. (2013). The economics of the Arab Spring. *World Development, 45,* 296–313.

Mazzanti, M. (2002). Cultural heritage as multi-dimensional, multi-value and multi-attribute economic good: Toward a new framework for economic analysis and valuation. *Journal of Socio-Economics, 31*(5), 529–558.

Metcalfe, B. D. (2006). Exploring cultural dimensions of gender and management in the Middle East. *Thunderbird International Business Review, 48*(1), 93–107.

Pew Research Center (2009). *Mapping the global Muslim population: A report on the size and distribution of the world's Muslim population.* Retrieved from www.pewforum.org/files/2009/10/Muslimpopulation.pdf

Possick, C. (2015). Grandparents' meaning construction of the loss of a grandchild in a terror attack in Israel. *Journal of Loss and Trauma, 20*(3), 214–228.

Ramachandran, V. S. (2012). *Encyclopedia of human behavior.* Vol. 3. San Diego: Academic Press.

Reitzes, D. C., & Mutran, E. J. (2004). Grandparent identity, intergenerational family identity, and well-being. *Journals of Gerontology Series B: Psychological Sciences and Social Sciences, 59*(4), S213–S219.

Rizk, A., Kronfol, N. M., Moffatt, S., Zaman, S., Fares, S., & Sibai, A. M. (2015). A survey of knowledge-to-action pathways of aging policies and programs in the Arab region: the role of institutional arrangements. *Implementation Science, 10*(1), 1.

Roberto, K. A., Allen, K. R., & Blieszner, R. (1999). Older women, their children, and grandchildren: A feminist perspective on family relations. *Journal of Women and Aging, 11,* 67–84.

Roberto, K. A., Allen, K. R., & Blieszner, R. (2001). Grandfathers' perceptions and expectations of relationships with their adult grandchildren. *Journal of Family Issues, 22,* 407–426.

Roudi, F. (2001). *Population trends and challenges in the Middle East and North Africa.* Washington, DC: Population Reference Bureau.

Roudi-Fahimi, F., & Kent, M. K. (2007). *Challenges and opportunity: The population of the Middle East and North Africa.* Washington, DC: Population Reference Bureau.

Sibai, A. M., Rizk, A. & Kronfol, K. M., (2014). *Ageing in the Arab region: Trends, implications and policy options.* Beirut, Lebanon: United Nations Population Fund. Retrieved from www.csa.org.lb/cms/assets/csa%20publications/unfpa%20escwa%20regional%20ageing%20overview_full_reduced.pdf

Sigad, L. I., & Eisikovits, R. A. (2013). Grandparenting across borders: American grandparents and their Israeli grandchildren in a transnational reality. *Journal of aging studies, 27*(4), 308–316.

Silverstein, M., & Giarrusso, R. (2010). Aging and family life: A decade review. *Journal of Marriage and Family, 72*(5), 1039–1058.

Silverstein, M., & Long, J. D. (1998). Trajectories of grandparents' perceived solidarity with adult grandchildren: A growth curve analysis over 23 years. *Journal of Marriage and the Family, 60*(4), 912–923.

Sonnheim, M. (2004). *Welcome to the club: The art of Jewish grandparenting.* Jerusalem, Israel: Devora Publishing Company.

Thompson, E. H. (Ed.). (1994). *Older men's lives.* Vol. 6. Thousand Oaks: Sage Publications.

Timberlake, E. M., & Chipungu, S. S. (1992). Grandmotherhood: Contemporary meaning among African American middle-class grandmothers. *Social Work, 37*(3), 216–222.

Tourjeman, K., Doron, I., & Cohen, M. (2015). Losing a grandchild: The mourning experience of grandparents in Israel. *Death studies, 39*(8), 1–9.

Uhlenberg, P. (1996). Mortality decline in the twentieth century and supply of kin over the life course. *The Gerontologist, 36*(5), 681–685.

United Nations Department of Economics. (2005). *World population prospects: Sex and age distribution of the world population.* Vol. 2. New York: United Nations Publications.

Werner, P., Buchbinder, E., Lowenstein, A., & Livni, T. (2007). Grandmothers', mothers' and granddaughters' perceptions of grandparenthood: A qualitative analysis of congruence across generations. *Journal of Intergenerational Relationships, 5*(3), 7–26.

World Bank. (1999). *Education in the Middle East and North Africa: A strategy towards learning for development,* Washington, DC: World Bank.

World Bank. (2015, October). *The economic outlook for the Middle East and North Africa.* Retrieved from www.worldbank.org/en/region/mena/brief/economic-outlook-middle-east-and-north-africa-october-2015

Yount, K. M., & Sibai, A. M. (2009). Demography of aging in Arab countries. In K. M. Yount & A. M. Sibai (Eds.) *International handbook of population aging* (pp. 277–315). Dordrecht, Netherlands: Springer.

Yousef, T. M. (2004). Development, growth and policy reform in the Middle East and North Africa since 1950. *Journal of Economic Perspectives, 18*(3), 91–115.

11

CARER GRANDPARENTS OF SUB-SAHARAN AFRICA

"Foster to be Fostered"

Magen Mhaka-Mutepfa, Elias Mpofu, Ami Moore, and Stan Ingman

PROVERBS

1. "Foster them and they will also foster you" (*Chichengete chigokuchengetawo*, Shona language, Zimbabwe/Mozambique; *Amapango ya mailo*, Bemba language, Zambia)
2. "One is elderly only to one's significant others (partners)" (*Chembere mwenewayo*, Shona language)

(see p. 264 for interpretations)

CASE STORY

Consider the case of a 62-year-old grandmother from rural Zimbabwe, who is a carer for four of her grandchildren because their parents died from HIV/AIDS. She is also a person living with HIV/AIDS. She highlighted her carer responsibilities and resources as follows:

> *I take care of my elderly mother, four grandchildren, and my two daughters who are in high school. I also look after my late brother's three children who have dropped out of school from lack of school fees. The government used to pay for them but has since stopped due to inadequate finances and the increasing number of orphans. My surviving daughter is not gainfully employed because of her poor health. She also lives here with her two children, thereby increasing my burden. I did not do much farming last year because I was nursing my husband, who eventually succumbed to an ailment. I had no respite and our meagre financial resources were all used up. Given the resource shortages, I struggle to care for my grandchildren and the rest of my family. I would have liked a less taxing carer burden, having raised six of my own children.*

My extended family cannot assist with care of my grandchildren as they have needs of their own. However, I persevere through prayer, and from knowing that it is my responsibility to care for my grandchildren. I wish I had the resource support for the care I provide, so that my grandchildren can have a future.

This case story highlights several caregiver issues of frequent concern to grandparents in sub-Saharan Africa: role overload with overstretched personal and social resources, significance of cultural expectations, spirituality as a primary resource for care provisioning, and personal resilience and optimism regarding the future of their charges. Sub-Saharan Africa is the area of the continent of Africa that lies south of the Sahara Desert, and thus includes 49 of the 54 countries of Africa, excluding only Egypt plus the five countries of Northern Africa referred to in Chapter 10 as part of MENA (Middle East and North Africa). What we call sub-Saharan Africa includes the sub-region of "Southern Africa", which is the focus of Chapter 12. Figure 11.1 is a map of Africa; note that we have labelled in bold those countries which are specifically mentioned in this chapter, and have drawn an artificial sub-regional boundary to demarcate sub-Saharan Africa, MENA, and Southern Africa.

This vast geographic region includes families and groups (e.g., Hausa, Yoruba, Hutu, Massai, Aka Pygmies) with diverse economic, cultural, and religious-spiritual beliefs and practices. The focus is on grandparents in cities and towns rather than on hunter-gatherer populations of this region (Lamb & Hewlett, 2005). Several of the countries (e.g., South Africa, Lesotho, Botswana, Swaziland, Ethiopia, Mauritius, and Namibia) include support for the elderly in their national social development policies, but pay scant attention to implementation plans. Thus, state support for grandparent carers across sub-Saharan Africa remains meagre, and this constitutes a serious problem in terms of health and material deprivation for both grandparents and their charges. This chapter does not emphasize the hunter-gatherer communities of Eastern and Central Africa; readers are referred to the references for discussion of the family dynamics of such communities.

Personal and social resilience are critical for those in caregiver roles, in the contexts of food insecurity, under-developed or poorly implemented social welfare policies, and failing personal health from disease and the ageing process (Nyasani, Sterberg, & Smith, 2009). Grandparenting of minor children is a typical role in the family- and clan-based cultures of sub-Saharan Africa.

By tradition in sub-Saharan Africa, older people lived in extended, multi-generational family structures where they provided care to the grandchildren. This still occurs to a great extent, although the effects of modernization, migration, civil wars, and population depletion from communicable diseases have changed the traditional extended family structures so that members can provide comparatively less care for each other. As an example, the HIV/AIDS pandemic and civil wars in some parts of Africa have resulted in a high prevalence of skipped-generation family patterns (Hosegood, 2009; Reijer, 2013) or households in which grandparents

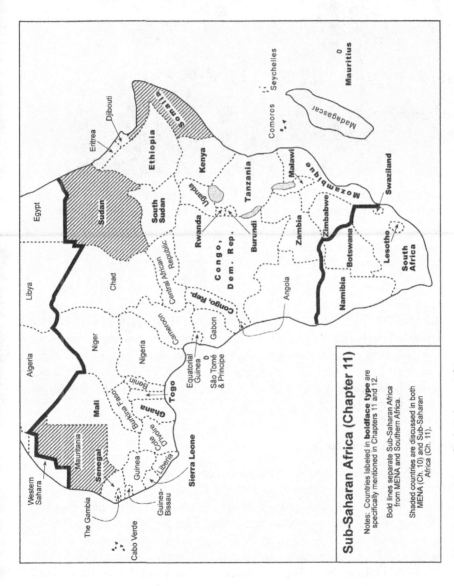

FIGURE 11.1 Map of sub-Saharan Africa

Source: Courtesy of Paul Larson.

FIGURE 11.2 A 90-year-old grandmother with her grandchildren in Togo. This grandmother is happy to show off all the grandchildren that she cares for and loves dearly.

Source: Courtesy of Ami R. Moore.

are primary care providers to their grandchildren (Hosegood, 2009; Schatz & Seeley, 2015). There is evidence to suggest that sub-Saharan grandparents who are caregivers of orphaned children are willing and compassionate about caregiving (Mhaka–Mutepfa, Mpofu, & Cumming, 2014). However, it is also the case that the grandparent carers are disproportionately maternal, female, older, single, and burdened by a lack of resources (Matshalaga, 2004; Nyasani, Sterberg, & Smith, 2009; Schatz & Seeley, 2015).

Theoretical Approach

This chapter applies structural lag theory concepts (Baker, Silverstein, & Putney, 2008) to understanding carer grandparenting in the sub-Saharan region. Structural lag is a tenet of the age and society paradigm (Baker et al. 2008) and posits that society is evolving in these modern times. While people are living longer, especially in the developed world, new developments are occurring on different fronts (internal conflicts, pressures and necessity to migrate, rapid spread of HIV/ AIDS, etc.) that have severe negative effects on many people's lives in the developing world including the sub-Saharan African region. However, social norms, roles, expectations, and social structure are not changing fast enough to keep up with developmental changes. This creates a mismatch between what people are expected to do and what society offers them in provision of expected goods and/ or services. In the sub-Saharan African context, the effects of the structural lag

FIGURE 11.3 A 90-year-old grandfather and 86-year-old grandmother at their family home in rural Zimbabwe. Their visiting grandchildren live and go to school in a city. Grandparents are much loved by the grandchildren for their unconditional availability and their deep emotional bonds with their grandchildren.

Source: Courtesy of Maidei Machina.

with skipped generations are yet to be well understood. However, it is clear that grandparents here carry significant family responsibilities beyond what they would normally carry, and these grandparents may be in need themselves due to the ageing process and deprivations common in the developing world.

This chapter emphasizes carer grandparenting, and personal and contextual resourcing in carer roles, in the rapidly changing sub-Saharan region. As indicated, use of structural lag theory helps us understand how grandparents in caregiver roles contend with mounting challenges as different social structures (e.g., unavailability of alternative and reliable childcare options, inadequate or no social assistance programmes, etc.) lag behind changes in familial life from modernization and voluntary and involuntary migration events. First, this chapter considers the context of caregiving in sub-Saharan Africa, including variations in care provisioning statuses, and caregiving and social protection affordances. Second, we provide an overview of research on health and wellbeing, coping strategies and support, caregiver burdens, and caregiver living arrangements. Third, we discuss personal and social resourcing for grandparent carers. The chapter concludes with an examination of the future of grandparenting in the sub-Saharan context, including implications for social policy in supporting grandparents in their carer roles.

Historical, Social, Economic, and Demographic Contexts of Grandparenting

Cultural Parameters

From time immemorial, grandparents have lived with their children and grandchildren in three-generational households. The children would sit with their grandparents after a meal to hear about their family's history, ancestral beliefs, and local fables. This fostered children's socialization and training and reinforced bonds between physically dispersed kinsmen. The caregiving of grandparents for their grandchildren is shaped by cultural perspectives, as discussed below. As previously noted, grandparents in traditionalist Africa provide care to both their adult children whenever needed, and to grandchildren as part of their extended family. This includes provision of care to grandchildren whose parents have either migrated or are deceased. They do so with very limited resources, which creates considerable stress on grandparents.

Despite these realities, care provision for minors and vulnerable others is grounded in the African worldview of *ubuntu* (Nguni/Sotho language, spoken in Southern African countries) or "beingness" (Goduka, 2000; Ramose, 1999). The *ubuntu* worldview is a pan-African social construct and applies to all of sub-Saharan Africa. It is about recognition and appreciation of the humanity in others and engagement in actions to express one's own sense of being. From an *ubuntu* cultural perspective, people are viewed as social and interdependent beings. For instance, caregiving is seen as a form of *ubuntu* and a way of showing humanity.

This is explained by the fact that caregiving occurs with a high sense of social interest and justice, as in actions to promote communal wellbeing. Grandparents in their care shape the personal and cultural identities of their grandchildren (Howard et al., 2006; Nyambedha, Wandibba, & Aagaard-Hansen, 2003, Oppong, 2006).

Impact of HIV/AIDS

Historically, African grandparents and other relatives have raised grandchildren, although the need is greater now due to AIDS mortality among the younger childbearing generation (Henderson & Cook, 2005). As in our opening case story, grandparents in sub-Saharan Africa face significant challenges from the triple jeopardies of having lost their own children to AIDS-related death, having lost their sources of economic support, and having to raise grandchildren with significant challenges (Reijer, 2013). Orphans from HIV may be stigmatized (Mudavanhu, Segalo, & Fourie, 2008) and caring for the infected could carry courtesy stigma by association for primary caregivers from neighbours, and other community members (Ogunmefun, Gilbert, & Schatz, 2011). In comparison, the incidence of HIV/AIDS is relatively lower in the grandparents' own generation.

The World Health Organization (WHO, 2013) estimated the number of AIDS-related orphans at 15 million, 80% of whom are in sub-Sharan Africa, the epicentre of the HIV/AIDS pandemic. Grandparents are the primary providers of care to this burgeoning HIV/AIDS orphan population, as 40–60% of orphans are in grandparent-headed households in sub-Saharan Africa (Reijer, 2013; UNICEF, 2012). Grandparent-headed households are always the most disadvantaged because they take in grandchildren whose parents have died or emigrated. Emigration has slowed delivery of social and public health services, which has affected the gains articulated in the Millennium Developmental Goals (MDG) for this region.

Sub-Saharan Africa has a very youthful population with 600 million (62%) of the population below the age of 24 and a low average life expectancy estimated at 56 years (WHO, 2013). This region thus comprises the youngest and the shortest-living population under consideration in this book (see Table 1.1 for stark contrasts within and outside Africa), although the region may see more of a trend towards ageing in the next generation (see also Chapter 12, for a discussion of Southern African projections for ageing). An estimated 40% of adults (ages 40–85) in sub-Saharan Africa take care of their grandchildren (UNICEF, 2012; Reijer, 2013). This statistic is likely an underestimate given the fact that nearly every family in sub-Saharan Africa has to care for grandchildren. Additionally, the impact of HIV/AIDS has been most devastating to the continent because a high proportion of young adults have fallen victim to this scourge. Households in countries with high HIV/AIDS prevalence are increasingly headed by the elderly leading to increased vulnerability to poverty (Aboderin & Beard, 2014; Nabalamba & Chikoko, 2011). However, with a lower life expectancy of 56 years, sub-Saharan's youthful population is at risk of mortality from HIV/AIDS, exacerbating child carer needs and with a diminishing adult population from the AIDS pandemic. The next section considers significant contextual influences on grandparenting in the sub-Saharan context.

Contextual Influences on Grandparents Who Assume Carer Roles

Grandparent caregivers' decisions to assume the surrogate parenting role in sub-Saharan Africa is influenced by the following important factors: historical and cultural traditions and customs, social and economic disparities, lack of availability of other caregivers (e.g., due to death, divorce, or immigration), spirituality, political systems, imposition of the decision by the dependent person, anti-institutional feelings, the caregiver's personal characteristics, gender, feelings of duty and obligation, and a lack of social institutions to care for children (Matshalaga, 2004; Mhaka-Mutepfa et al., 2014). Becoming a grandparent caregiver is not an easy task because one has to know how to cope with this new responsibility that often affects the health and wellbeing of the caregiver. In their new duties as caregivers, factors such as emotional and instrumental support, mental skill, and ability to cope with the daily demands of parenting are important in the enablement of grandparent carers (Oburu & Palmerus, 2005).

Population Migrations From Civil Wars and Labour Opportunities

As previously noted, internecine civil wars, particularly in the western, central, and northeastern regions of sub-Saharan Africa, have escalated the need for grandparenting of orphaned or abandoned children. For example, sub-Saharan Africa has 4.4 million refugees, mostly hosted in Ethiopia, Kenya, Uganda, and Tanzania. The countries from which most of the refugees originated were Burundi (221,000), Democratic Republic of the Congo (541,500), and Somalia (714,000) (UNHCR, 2015). Indeed, these incessant civil wars account for another source of need for grandparent carers. In South Sudan, Somalia, and Democratic Republic of the Congo, all torn by civil strife, grandparents may be the only care providers, which results in the elderly taking care of orphaned and displaced children. Access by humanitarian relief organizations, particularly for international staff, remains restricted in some areas, which hampers the UNHCR's ability to fulfill its mission.

Civil wars are also a major impediment to the eradication of endemic diseases (most notably HIV and malaria), which also impact the would-be child carers and their grandchildren. Health control and prevention campaigns cannot be conducted within countries with civil strife. Armed conflicts also divert government expenditures away from provision of economic services (e.g., social protection grants) towards military expenditures, so that support for family child carers is overlooked while the wars continue. Civil wars result in an increase of grandparent-headed households, making them poorer, which further impedes the economic development of many countries.

Grandparent carer demands in sub-Saharan Africa are also a result of labour migration among the younger generation of Africans who seek livelihood opportunities away from their historical habitats, including regional and international destinations (Kimuna & Makiwane, 2007). For instance, it is estimated that at least three million Zimbabweans (over 20% of the population) have left the country since the 1990s, at a monumental social-economic cost for a declining economy.

Historical Cultural Traditions and Customs

Cultural traditions and expectations also influence the grandparenting role in sub-Saharan Africa. Among these are ancestral beliefs (e.g., rituals), teaching specific skills (e.g., grinding nuts into peanut butter), and transmission of family values (e.g., family history, customs, and norms). Despite the fact that most young people in sub-Saharan Africa seek to maintain a Western lifestyle, some still follow specific principles of traditional African cultural views. This means that the elderly are still viewed with high respect and prestige as fountains of tried and true wisdom and as custodians of tradition. The elderly are still sought out for advice, especially on family matters.

Ancestral reverence for ancestors is central to the worldview of many cultural groups in sub-Saharan Africa, in that departed ancestors are perceived to be involved in the lives of the living, including the lives of their grandchildren (Bogoba, 2010; Shaibu, 2013; Yancura & Greenwood, 2013). Grandparents seek to transmit to their grandchildren the cultural traditions important to their personal and cultural identities (Nyambedha et al., 2003; Howard et al., 2006). For example, children learn to respect all the elderly in their communities just as they would revere their own grandparents. Nevertheless, economic and social disparities also influence the ways in which grandparents enact their carer roles.

Economic and Social Disparities

Twenty-six of the world's 32 lowest-income countries (81%) are in sub-Saharan Africa (World Bank, 2016). This economic context makes for a challenging carer setting for grandparents, in consideration of the lack of resources provided by social welfare programmes in these countries. Most research from sub-Saharan Africa and other parts of the world reports that grandparents who foster orphans tend to live in poverty (Kidman & Thurman, 2014; Mudavanhu et al., 2008; Nabalamba & Chikoko, 2011; Nyirenda et al., 2013; Shaibu, 2013; Skovdal, Campbell, Madanhire, Nyamukapa, & Gregson, 2011), even when they remain in the labour force. This is particularly true of those in small-scale agriculture, who often lack food security. Older people constitute a substantial share of these small-scale farmers, as a result of labour force losses through rural–urban migration and also diminished interest in farming among younger adults. For instance, in Kenya the average age of farmers is estimated at 60 years, which may be true of other African countries.

The effect of immobility due to the ageing process, combined with inadequate resources to buy agricultural implements (Nyambedha et al., 2003; Kidman & Thurman, 2014), is that over one-third of sub-Saharan grandparent caregivers live in poverty. Nevertheless, there is evidence that, despite extreme poverty, grandparents in sub-Saharan Africa (e.g., Zimbabwe, Kenya, Uganda, Botswana, South Africa) are committed to raising their grandchildren (Howard et al., 2006; Mhaka-Mutepfa et al., 2014; Mudavanhu et al., 2008), and show remarkable resilience as caregivers (Ferreira, 2004; Ice, Heh, Yogo, & Juma, 2011; Kamya & Poindexter, 2009; Kasedde, Doyle, Seeley, & Ross, 2014; Mhaka-Mutepfa et al., 2014; Sabella, 2012; Shaibu, 2013). Grandparent caregivers with positive perceptions and resilience are more willing to reach out to others for support and develop or implement a specific plan of action, indicative of active coping.

Pathways to Grandparenting

Pathways to grandparent caregiver roles in sub-Saharan Africa vary along a continuum of voluntarism, from those who opted to provide care, to those who drifted into it believing they had no choice or there were no alternative caregivers, and to those for whom it was natural (Lewis & Meredith, 1988). For example, kinship fostering in southern Ghana, in which grandchildren are "claimed" or "begged" by kin, serves to provide labour or companionship for the elderly. In Togo, Lallemand (1994) viewed the circulation of children as part of a system of gift exchange, and in Sierra Leone Bledsoe et al. (1989) found that grandparents typically care for young children who are later fostered by urban-based relatives when they attend school. Kinship fostering of children is valued for its social rather than material benefits. For instance, care fostering of grandchildren meets the kinship obligations of social alliance building within families through education and apprenticeship (Alber, Martin, & Notermans, 2013). For example, in the urban slums of Nairobi, Kenya, in addition to caring for their grandchildren, more than 30% of older women and 20% of older men (age 60 years or older) care for one or more children who are not their biological relatives. A cultural emphasis on social harmony in African cultures encourages people to share personal assets or extend help to the larger family. This may facilitate harmony and wellbeing in the family, but sharing of personal problems or making requests of the larger family may also disrupt harmony (Cheng, Linda, & Kwok, 2013), because material requests may be seen as burdensome, which also affects the wellbeing of the elderly. We believe that the former trend is more prevalent in African societies than elsewhere.

"Foster Them to Be Fostered by Them"

Sub-Saharan cultural communities in their diversity hold to the care provisioning proverb, "Foster them and they will also foster you" (*Chichengete chigokuchengetawo*, Shona, Zimbabwe/Mozambique language; *Amapango ya mailo*, Bemba language, Zambia), which in part explains the reciprocity between grandparents and grandchildren. We chose this proverb as the sub-title of this chapter because cultural groups in sub-Saharan Africa hold in high regard the principle of reciprocity (give-and-take), filial obligation, and a sense of responsibility to provide care to older family members. Thus most grandparents are willing to participate in caregiver roles, and hope to be provided for in the future (Kasedde et al., 2014; Ssengonzi, 2009). Family care is a fundamental value in sub-Saharan African communities. For that reason, the rate of institutionalization for African elders and children is very low in sub-Saharan Africa, based on the belief that foster home placement implies abandonment of kith and kin; this would infuriate spiritual powers and lead to punitive measures (Matshalaga, 2004). As a result, grandparents are caregivers at their homes even as they may be cared for, too.

Variations in Care Provisioning

Care provision takes place in both multi-generational households (when grandparents live with own children and grandchildren) and skipped-generation households (grandparents living with grandchildren only; Mhaka-Mutepfa et al., 2014). For example, a multi-generational household in Uganda typically comprises seven people, including elders and extended family members. The impetus for these intergenerational caregiver systems in sub-Saharan Africa is explained by the fact that care for grandchildren is shared among families within the overall extended family, which strengthens kinship ties through intergenerational flow of resources (Ssengonzi, 2009).

As previously noted, women provide most of the direct carer provisioning in the sub-Saharan context. This is explained in part by the fact that they are socialized to render nurturing care from an early age, to prepare them for increasing carer provisioning as they mature into adulthood (Bogoba, 2010; Mackinnon, 2009). Early socialization to carer roles pre-equips these grandparents to network for resources with others in the community (Killian, 2004). For instance, under-resourced grandmothers in Uganda remain resilient despite their lack of valued resources to efficiently care for their grandchildren, because of a high level of community engagement (Kamya & Poindexter, 2009). However, community engagement may be influenced by the cultural context of the region. For example, grandmothers in previous studies reported that their spouses did not provide physical support, and hence they were exhausted.

Grandfathers and Grandmothers in Cultural Context

Gender education for men and youth tends to increase interest in caregiving. As previously stated, caregiving is mostly provided by women in many developing countries. This is reinforced by patriarchal power dynamics which consign women to servitude (Bogoba, 2010). However, men and boys will increasingly be in carer service roles as gender mainstreaming of education is expected to erode patriarchal beliefs and practices in this region. For example, the Southern African Gender Protocol on Gender and Development (2011) provides gender equity education for men, which will likely result in more men in direct carer roles in their communities than has been the case previously.

Role of grandfathers in patriarchal societies. The extent of older people's caregiving is increasingly recognized in the context of HIV/AIDS. For instance, in Kenya grandfathers foster orphaned grandchildren and other vulnerable children alongside grandmothers. Their co-carer provisioning with grandmothers suggests fluidity of gender-appropriate work (Skovdal et al., 2011) in the context of subsistence economies of rural Africa. In such contexts, grandfathers and grandmothers are interchangeable as care providers although there may be differences in the care-related tasks involved. For instance, grandfathers may be perceived as providing more of the community access leadership such as networking between families, while grandmothers may attend to family support needs that tend to be mostly of a nurturing nature (Mpofu, Ruhode, Mhaka-Mutepfa, January, & Mapfumo, 2014). However, with the absence or non-availability of grandmothers, grandfathers can also fulfil a nurturing carer role.

Maternal and paternal grandparenting. Family grandparenting of children by the maternal side of the family is also more prevalent than paternal family grandparenting. Most women trust their own parents to take good care of their offspring. In addition, single female adult children often live with their parents, who would automatically take over childcare in time of crisis. One exception to this tendency is in Kenya, where the kinship care structure is patrilineal and not matrilineal. This means that it is customary for orphans in Kenya to be looked after by paternal grandparents (Nyambedha et al., 2003), unlike other African countries where most orphans are cared for by maternal grandparents. Paternal family grandparenting might also be hampered by the perception that fathers for some single orphans were alive but offered no assistance (Mhaka-Mutepfa et al., 2014; Shaibu, 2013). Although many African countries have child custody and protection laws, they often lack enforcement, leaving the children vulnerable to lack of proper care even though the parents are living or even gainfully employed.

Research on Grandparent Caregivers in Sub-Saharan Africa

Table 11.1 outlines the findings of several outstanding research projects on grandparents in sub-Saharan Africa. It is first notable that while grandparents raising grandchildren is a theme discussed throughout this book (e.g., Chapter 3 – US, Chapter 8 – South Asia, and Chapter 12 – Southern Africa), the context of this surrogate parenting in sub-Saharan and Southern Africa is perhaps unique within this volume. This is because it is so strongly related to issues of health and conflict. Research on grandparenting in sub-Saharan Africa settings has explored

TABLE 11.1 Summary of Key Studies of Grandparenting in Sub-Saharan Africa

Topic	Author (date)	Country	Type of study (sample size)	Findings
Carer Resourcing	Matshalaga (2004)	Zimbabwe	Cross-sectional qualitative study ($n = 8$)	Grandmothers provided their own resources in carer roles by engaging in contract piecework, cooperative vegetable gardens, poultry projects, and cross-border informal trading. Their social resources included obtaining assistance from social networks, accessing government food facilities, and securing help from the community and NGOs in the studied district.
	Kidman & Thurman (2014)	South Africa	Cross sectional multi-level analysis ($n = 726$)	Grandparent carers reported challenges with food insecurity, income, and AIDS-related illness, which suggested greater economic vulnerability in their roles.
	Kimemia (2006)	Kenya	Cross sectional quantitative study ($n = 116$)	Social support, hope, acceptance, planning, and personality were important for coping with caregiver roles and were related to caregiver burden. Significant relationships were found between demographics and caregiver burden.
Health related quality of life	Ice et al. (2012)	Kenya	Longitudinal study ($n = 640$) (three waves) 2000, 2008, 2011	Grandparents who provided care reported more health complaints and a lower quality of life than non-carers. Female grandparents were healthier, and health status was similar among carers and non-carers.
	Sabella (2012)	South Africa	Cross sectional mixed method ($n = 324$)	Grandparents reported high satisfaction with health services for selves and their charges despite limited materials resources.
	Reijer (2013)	Zimbabwe	Qualitative ($n > 120$) Quantitative ($n = 200$)	Depression is also common among these households, especially among older caregivers.
	Oburu and Palmerus (2005).	Kenya	Quantitative ($n = 241$)	Grandmothers who provided care for grandchildren alone reported higher levels of stress, relative to those who shared caregiving with at least one of the parents.
Everyday coping	Rutakamwa et al. (2015)	Uganda	Cross sectional qualitative study ($n = 80$)	Relationship tensions between grandparents and their grandchildren revolved around generation gaps. Reciprocity involved meeting basic needs for grandchildren by carers while grandchildren performed menial household tasks (e.g., cleaning, farming, and cooking).
	Shaibu (2013)	Botswana	Cross sectional qualitative study ($n = 12$)	Grandparent caregivers were accepting of their roles even though they had limited material resources.
	Ssengonzi et al. (2009)	Uganda	Cross-sectional qualitative study ($n = 27$)	Grandparent caregivers' burden was increased by caring for the sick parents of their grandchildren and also their grandchildren.

a number of themes: health and wellbeing in Uganda, Kenya, and Botswana (Ice, Sadruddin, Vagedes, Yogo, & Juma, 2012; Kamya & Poindexter, 2009; Kipp, Tindyebwa, Karamagi, & Rubaale, 2007; Shaibu, 2013; Ssengonzi, 2009); resilience resources (Mhaka-Mutepfa et al., 2014); social support rendered to grandparent caregivers in Zimbabwe and South Africa (Howard et al., 2006; Sabella, 2012); stress (Ice et al., 2012; Kipp et al., 2007; Kamya & Poindexter, 2009; Oburu & Palmerus, 2005); coping strategies in Botswana and Kenya (Kipp et al., 2007; Kamya & Poindexter, 2009; Shaibu, 2013); reciprocity in Uganda, South Africa, and Zimbabwe (Rutakamwa, Zalwango, Richards, & Seeley, 2015; Kasedde et al., 2014; Mhaka-Mutepfa et al., 2014); living arrangements in Uganda (Ssengonzi et al., 2009); and needs of carers in South Africa, Zimbabwe, and Kenya (Nyasani et al., 2009; Howard et al., 2006; Nyambedha et al., 2003). Table 11.1 summarizes the results of ten of these studies. We will next discuss the findings on caregiver health and wellbeing, resilience resources, spirituality, personal and social resourcing, and social support.

Health and Wellbeing

A couple of studies have reported high levels of happiness and life satisfaction among grandparents with care of children (Mhaka-Mutepfa et al., 2014), even though they may have unmet needs in their carer roles (e.g., Kidman & Thurman, 2014). Focusing on the deficiencies and unmet needs of carers may cause one to overlook the inherent strengths of grandparent carers (Kolomer, & Himmelheber, Murray, 2013). Caregiving responsibilities have been associated with better health status, greater satisfaction and quality of life, even for caregivers living with HIV, as long as resources were available (Mhaka-Mutepfa et al., 2014; Schatz & Seeley, 2015). Nonetheless, grandparenting with adequate resources (environmental, e.g., housing; social, e.g., social networks; and personal, e.g., self-esteem) was more successful as it was associated with less stress (Musil et al., 2011; Nyirenda et al., 2013; Schatz & Seeley, 2015).

The capabilities of grandparents in their carer roles depend heavily on their physical and mental health (Payne, Mkandawire, & Kohler, 2013; Skovdal et al., 2011). The 2013 Global Burden of Disease database identified cardiovascular and circulatory disease, nutritional deficiencies, cirrhosis of the liver, and diabetes as major causes of disability-adjusted life years in sub-Saharan Africa's older population (Aboderin & Beard, 2014). Their high rates of disease morbidity coincide with a lack of requisite primary health care. For instance, about 96% of elderly with hypertension in Ghana have inadequate treatment (Lloyd-Sherlock, Beard, Minicuci, Ebrahim, & Chatterji, 2014). Good physical health and positive mood are important for carer roles in general and in particular for ageing persons. For example, positive mood allows caregivers to recover more quickly, improves their ability to self-regulate, and it buffers against energy depletion from care provisioning.

Resilience Resources

Self-perceptions of the caregiver role as rewarding and satisfying rather than a burden can have positive effects on health (Kimemia, 2006; Mhaka-Mutepfa et al., 2014). This might be explained by the fact that grandparents with a positive attitude towards life are likely to see caregiving as a challenge rather than a burden (Hughes, Waite, LaPierre, & Luo, 2007). Counselling and support interventions for grandparents in carer roles results in them attaining higher levels of emotional wellbeing than would be the case without such services (Matshalaga, 2004; Nyirenda et al., 2013). Furthermore, personal and social resources cushioned grandparents in their caregiver roles.

In African communities, spirituality is a resource for coping with everyday life (Hodge & Horvath, 2011; Kamya & Poindexter, 2009; Sabella, 2012; Shaibu, 2013). Faith in God was found to be associated with greater satisfaction among grandparents in carer roles (Mhaka-Mutepfa et al., 2014; Mpofu et al., 2014). The emotional supports they receive enable them to adapt to carer roles from a capable and positive perspective. Supportive social relationships with friends and family also lead to greater resilience among grandparents in carer roles (Gerard, Landry-Meyer, & Roe, 2006; Goodman, 2006; Mpofu et al., 2014). These studies have shown that grandparents caring for children were committed to their grandchildren for the sake of the social support they could provide, and they also received care from the children. Social resourcing of carer grandparents in sub-Saharan Africa is premised on the value of social harmony and interdependence of families.

Caregiving and Social Protection

Many grandparent child carers in sub-Saharan Africa have no access to public or social welfare support. Only a few countries in this region have introduced comprehensive social security programmes for the elderly: Botswana, Lesotho, Mauritius, Namibia, Senegal, South Africa, and Swaziland. These countries provide social benefit grants to support grandparents with carer roles. With social security grants, caregivers manage to keep their grandchildren in school, which delays the premature entry of children into the labour force.

Nevertheless, more countries, such as Mozambique (in 2010), Kenya (in 2011), Uganda (in 2010), and Zimbabwe (in 2012) have approved social protection frameworks. Tanzania still has no old age benefits, with nearly two million elderly people living in poverty. However, the Zanzibar government had promised to begin giving pensions of 20,000 shillings (US$9) per month to all older people over 70, beginning in April of 2016. Uganda's development partners had committed another 290 billion shillings (US$30 million) towards expansion of the Senior Citizen Grant established in 2010. However, in sub-Saharan Africa as in many developing countries elsewhere in the world, the elderly rely on non-formal and non-state-regulated forms of social protection, the major source being the support structures of extended family systems, religious and community groups, and other forms of mutual assistance (Shaibu, 2013; Ssengonzi et al., 2009). Social welfare policies to support grandparents in carer roles need to address reduction of material poverty.

Grandparents in sub-Saharan Africa are trusted with childcare provision roles for different reasons, "providing a safe and emotionally nurturing environment that benefits their children" (Jappens & Van Bavel, 2012, p. 87). The elders perceived grandchildren as important resources within the extended family, so that some grandchildren reciprocate the care they receive in practical ways like running errands for their caregivers and doing minor domestic chores (e.g., farming, cooking, and trading; Mhaka-Mutepfa et al., 2014).

Other Effects of Grandparent Caregiving on the Grandparents

Grandparent caregivers also benefit from the company of their grandchildren, when they might ordinarily live alone because their own children have left home to pursue careers elsewhere. Previous studies (Kolomer et al., 2013; Kasedde et al., 2014) have reported mutual benefit between carers and their grandchildren. This mutual exchange of support strengthens family ties and bonds as well as increasing wellbeing (Chen & Feeley, 2012; Kasedde et al., 2014; Kolomer et al., 2013; Rutakamwa et al., 2015) and resilience (Mpofu et al., 2014). Grandparenting also provides a social bridge for children with losses or who are orphans (Castillo, Henderson, & North, 2013; Yancura & Greenwood, 2013). Overall, successful grandparenting adds to the elderly's social value to their family and community.

The extent to which grandchild care affects the health of grandparent caregivers depends on the balance between the demands of caregiving and resources available to the grandparent (Mhaka-Mutepfa et al., 2014). For instance, personal resources (e.g., energy level, self-esteem), social supports (e.g., family and professional support), and environmental resources (e.g., a healthy physical environment) have been associated with the resilience, health, and wellbeing of carer grandparents (Mhaka-Mutepfa et al., 2014). In addition, children's difficult behaviours correlate positively with grandparents' stress levels (Oburu & Palmerus, 2005; Kamya & Poindexter, 2009).

With the exception of Ice et al.'s (2012) longitudinal studies, most of the preceding studies were cross-sectional qualitative and quantitative studies. Cross-sectional studies fail to capture the dynamics of grandparenting over time, and more longitudinal studies are needed. In addition, other people in the household should also be interviewed to reveal different perspectives and to add to the richness of the findings.

Social Policy Issues Related to Grandparenting

Grandparents throughout the nations of sub-Saharan Africa are committed to caring for their grandchildren and are in need of viable policies to enable them to assume caregiving roles from a capable position. As we illustrated in the previous section of this chapter, there is variability between nations in the availability of public or social welfare programmes. It is common that poorly developed or a lack of implementation of social protection systems across sub-Saharan Africa result in neglect of the elderly (Shaibu, 2013; Lloyd-Sherlock et al., 2014), which compromises their carer roles. Most national governments in Africa and the international community who work on the continent place a growing emphasis on social protection to alleviate poverty and achieve the MDG goals of economic development. The social welfare policies need to be formulated with input from the grandparents so that they are appropriately supported. A multi-sectoral approach by stakeholders (NGOs, religious bodies, and public sectors) would help more grandparent caregivers benefit from provision of support (e.g., social services) and avoid duplication of services. Multi-lateral aid agencies working in sub-Saharan Africa will prioritize a set of shorter-term challenges devoted to humanitarian emergencies that affect children rather than the wellbeing of grandparent carers.

Correctly managed and with the appropriate level of healthcare provision and social protection programmes, population ageing can be an unprecedented opportunity for older citizens to enjoy full and active lives far beyond that of previous generations (Nabalamba &Chikoko, 2011). For example, programme implementation should be monitored and evaluated to ensure that support is directed to elderly caregivers. Gathigah and Moyo (2015) stressed the importance of raising awareness among decision makers on the benefits of security grants and social pensions to grandparent caregivers. Advocacy should also include implementations to enable self-sustenance among caregivers. Provision of quality care to caregivers requires a complex set of interventions and actions at both the community and national level.

After providing an extensive review of the literature related to grandparenting or foster childcare in marginal communities in sub-Saharan Africa, we feel obligated to provide a simple framework for a comprehensive social policy development to address the needs of elders as well as children without strong family supports in marginal communities. It is our belief that elder care or childcare cannot be addressed independently in traditional societies without a focus on the family and overall community. A focus on creation of healthy or sustainable communities seems necessary, but what does this mean? Sustainable neighbourhoods or communities require a focus on economic or enterprise development at the micro-level. At the same time, the environment, at both the social and ecological level of the community, must be enhanced or maintained. Two major strategies must be employed to stimulate reform and progress for elders, children, and families in individual communities. Education for sustainability or improved viability must be introduced in all schools and in all informal community educational initiatives. The last dimension involves movement towards local control or the empowerment of elders and children to direct the changes, and take charge of their own communities.

With the growth of communication networks and technologies, sub-Saharan African societies need to stimulate pilot projects across the regions and nations involved. The diffusion of local creative models is much more rapid now in the current social media environment. For example, one non-profit organization called Future Without Poverty has a model labelled the Four E Model of Sustainability Development (www.fwop.org). In another geographical region, the Grameen Bank of Bangladesh has created many programmes that integrate enterprise, environmental, educational, and empowerment dimensions in a single programme (see Chapter 8 for discussions of NGOs in South Asia). That is, a comprehensive strategy is in place to improve the lives of many women, children, and families in Bangladesh (Yunus, 2008). Although the bank's programmes are not geared to help grandparents, many participants in the bank's poverty reduction programmes are grandparents. Therefore, many grandparents are *de facto* beneficiaries of these activities in that they are able to improve their economic conditions, which enables them to provide for their grandchildren. A similar approach to poverty eradication should be considered for the sub-Saharan African region. This step, in turn, could potentially empower grandparents by providing the resources to care for their grandchildren.

Most African countries do not have a caregiver remuneration policy other than natural motivation based on blood relationships and kinship ties (Rutakamwa et al., 2015). In the context of widespread poverty in much of the region, however, the Mozambique government has drawn up an attractive policy to remunerate the caregivers with a package of 60% of the government minimum wage, which is about US$55 per month. African policy makers can find many local and other initiatives to consider as they seek to reduce extreme poverty among elders and children. The need for social policies to support grandparent caregivers must drive stakeholders to contemplate the future of grandparenting.

Recommendations for the Future of Sub-Saharan Grandparenting

Sub-Saharan families place a high premium on planning for the future ("The future requires planning" – *Ramangwana rirongere*, Shona language, Zimbabwe), and grandparenting serves a family care insurance function in that grandparents are default care providers. Unlike the case in many Western countries (e.g., the US and UK, Chapters 3 and 6) where grandparents' involvement in childcare can often be considered elective, the percentage of grandparents who provide care to children in sub-Saharan Africa is quite high (perhaps close to 100%) because extended family childcare is normative and expected. The percentages of grandparents providing care in several countries are as follows: UK (63.0%), Germany (40.3%), Sweden (50.9%), Hungary (55.7%), and the Netherlands (56.9%, Glaser & Dessa, 2012). In the US (see Chapter 3) estimates show that 2.5 million grandparents are main care providers to their grandchildren, while 5.4 million children live in grandparent-headed homes (Scommegna,

2012). These lower proportions of carer grandparents in Western countries compared to sub-Saharan Africa are explained by the better developed public welfare systems for children and families in economically developed countries, as well as by cultural differences in family role expectations for the elderly.

Grandparenting in sub-Saharan Africa would be enabled better if care support interventions matched country-specific circumstances. For instance, grandparent carer support programmes should take into account (1) the demographic situation, trends, and variations (social, political, and health situations of specific countries); (2) the effectiveness of current policies and programmes in reaching older people (management issues); (3) the socioeconomic situation of older people; and (4) the effectiveness of formal and informal social protection systems and older people's requirements. Aboderin and Beard (2014) recommended establishment of a commission on ageing in developing countries. They suggested that the commission should promote the necessary research and operationalization of emerging findings on grandparenthood by policy makers and external drivers of health-system development in sub-Saharan Africa.

There is also a need to monitor and evaluate national experiences in grandparenthood and identify future priorities for implementation (e.g., inclusion in the MDG and prioritization of women). Longitudinal studies such as the WHO Study on Adult Health and Ageing and dementia research are starting to improve our knowledge of priority intervention needs in a small number of sub-Saharan African countries. However, further social and epidemiological investigations are necessary in these and other national contexts.

Interventions may include (1) relief of current suffering among poor older grandparents; (2) implementation of support systems to prepare for increasing numbers of grandparent caregivers; and (3) education of grandfathers about the importance of support for their spouses. In addition, grandparents willing to stay economically active should be supported through policy changes. Furthermore, societies should be encouraged to maintain and uphold traditional familial and community support structures, which have been impacted by modernization, acculturation, migration, and HIV/AIDS. Finally, viable social policies relating to grandparent caregivers should be formulated and implemented.

Conclusions

In conclusion, grandparenting with significant carer responsibility for minor children and also other family with health challenges is a typical role function in the sub-Saharan African context. Grandparenting carer roles are increasingly beginning in early middle age (late 30s) because the HIV/AIDS pandemic is depleting the numbers of people in early adulthood with younger families. The effects of early grandparenting are also multiplied in those sub-Saharan locations with endemic civil wars such as the Democratic Republic of the Congo, Sudan, and Somalia. While grandparenting is a cultural norm in the sub-Saharan Africa region, resource constraints present a major challenge to success in the carer role and in the face of poorly implemented public welfare support programmes by national governments. Nonetheless, despite extreme poverty, grandparents in sub-Saharan Africa are resilient and committed to raising their grandchildren.

It is important for those who formulate and implement national and international policies to adopt grandparent-friendly support programmes so as to enhance their carer roles. Such social policies to aid grandparents with carer roles should address their health and wellbeing as carers, enhancing their resilient caregiving. Grandparents successful in carer roles are an investment in the future generations of sub-Saharan African children who otherwise would have their health and wellbeing compromised. National governments in sub-Saharan Africa and multilateral agencies could do more to support seniors with childcare responsibilities, ensuring that the children's rights to care are protected.

As will be illustrated further in Chapter 12 of this volume, grandparent care is the preferred care option for orphans and vulnerable children, although most grandparent carers are themselves in need of care and need assistance to assume the caregiving role. The re-parenting role introduces a multitude of challenges that can deplete grandparents' coping reserves, and undermine their health and wellbeing. Carers who are optimistic tend to view caregiving as controllable; therefore, they tend to work continuously through challenges by using different active coping strategies. Supportive relationships (e.g., mutual support) keep caregivers united over time, and social support from peers and social networks protect at-risk families because they reduce emotional distress, parental stress, financial difficulties, and workloads. Finally, many caregivers appear to need effective assistance despite their commitment to caregiving, and commitment to caregiving is a result of cultural expectations and practices which must be maintained.

Appendix

Meanings of Proverbs

"Foster them and they will also foster you."

This expresses the reciprocal nature of relationships between the generations.

"One is elderly only to one's significant others (partners)."

This proverb says that age and ageing is subjective so that people carry equal social value regardless of chronological age. That is, being of advanced age does not count for anything and a person is highly valued regardless of age.

Additional Resources

Focuses of grandparenting around the world: www.helpageusa.org/support-us/giving-tuesday-match-her-generosity/

HIV and AIDS and grandparenting: www.heraldextra.com/news/world/kenya-aids-village-orphans-paired-with-grandparents/article_bbf0bd09-0565-55cd-8982-72f65b9fd937.html

Ageing-related issues including grandparenting: www.un.org/en/development/desa/population/publications/pdf/ageing/Dir_Research_Ageing_Africa_%202004–2015.pdf

Discussion Questions

1. Analyse and discuss the different lifestyles, if any, experienced by grandparents living in multi-generational and skipped-generational households.
2. A significant number of older people in sub-Saharan Africa have been impacted by AIDS. Many older Africans have become active providers of care to their grandchildren whose parents have died of AIDS. What policies or policy changes would help improve the situation of these grandparents, especially those with limited resources?
3. Contextual factors such as death, divorce, and emigration may require grandparents to provide care to their grandchildren, grandparenting is inherently expected in African cultures. Do you think this cultural expectation will survive in a rapidly changing world? Why or why not?

References

Aboderin, I. A. G., & Beard, J. R. (2014). Older people's health in sub-Saharan Africa. *The Lancet, 385*(9968), e9–e11.

Alber, E., Martin, J., & Notermans, C. (2013). *Child fostering in West Africa.* Leiden: Brill.

Bogoba, D. (2010). Health and ancestors: The case of South Africa and beyond. *Indo-Pacific Journal of Phenomenology, 10*(1), 1–7.

Carey, G., & Crammond, B. (2015) Systems change for the social determinants of health. *BMC Public Health, 8,* 1–10.

Castillo, K. D., Henderson, C. E., & North, L. W. (2013). The relation between caregiving style, coping, benefit finding, grandchild symptoms and caregiver adjustment among custodial grandparents. In B. Hayslip & G. C. Smith (Eds.), *Resilient grandparent caregivers: A strengths-based perspective* (pp. 25–47). New York: Taylor & Francis.

Chen, Y., & Feeley, T. H. (2012). Enacted support and wellbeing: A test of the mediating role of perceived control. *Communication Studies, 63*(5), 608–625.

Cheng, S., Linda, C. W., & Kwok, T. (2013). The social networks of Hong Kong Chinese family caregivers of Alzheimer's disease: Correlates with positive gains and burden. *The Gerontologist, 53*(6), 998–1008.

Ferreira, M. (2004). *HIV/AIDS and family wellbeing in southern Africa: towards an analysis of policies and responsiveness.* Paper presented at the United Nations Department of Economic and Social Affairs Division for Social Policy and Development Policy Workshop.

Gerard, J. M., Landry-Meyer, L., & Roe, J. G. (2006). Grandparents raising grandchildren: The role of social support in coping with caregiving challenges. *International*

Journal of Aging and Human Development, 62(4), 359–383. Retrieved from www.embase.com/search/results?subaction=viewrecord&from=export&id=L43508773

Goduka, I. N. (2000). Indigenous/African philosophies: Legitimizing spirituality centered wisdoms within academy. In P. Higgs, N. C. G. Vakalisa, T. V. Mda, & N. A. Assie-Lumumba (Eds.), *African voices in education.* Landsdowne: Juta and Co. Ltd.

Goodman, C. C. (2006). Grandmothers raising grandchildren: The vulnerability of advancing age. In B. Hayslip & J. H. Patrick (Ed.), *Custodial grandparenting: Individual, cultural, and ethnic diversity* (pp. 133–150). New York: Springer.

Henderson, T. L., & Cook, J. L. (2005). Grandma's hands: Black grandmothers speak about their experiences rearing grandchildren on TANF. *International journal of aging & human development, 61*(1), 1–19. Retrieved from www.embase.com/search/results?subaction = viewrecord&from=export&id=L41471469

Hodge, D. R., & Horvath, V. E. (2011). Spiritual needs in health care settings: A qualitative meta-synthesis of clients' perspectives. *Social Work, 56*(4), 306–316.

Hosegood, V. (2009). The demographic impact of HIV and AIDS across the family and household life-cycle: Implications for efforts to strengthen families in sub-Saharan Africa. *AIDS Care, 21*(S1), 13–21.

Howard, B. H., Phillips, C. V., Matinhure, N., Goodman, K. J., McCurdy, S. A., & Johnson, C. A. (2006). Barriers and incentives to orphan care in a time of AIDS and economic crisis: A cross-sectional survey of caregivers in rural Zimbabwe. *BMC Public Health, 6*, 11.

Hughes, M. E., Waite, L. J., LaPierre, T. A., & Luo, Y. (2007). All in the family: The impact of caring for grandchildren on grandparents' health. *Journals of Gerontology – Series B Psychological Sciences and Social Sciences, 62*(2), S108–S119. Retrieved from www.embase.com/search/results?subaction = viewrecord&from=export&id=L46917225

Ice, G. H., Heh, V., Yogo, J., & Juma, E. (2011). Caregiving, gender, and nutritional status in Nyanza Province, Kenya: Grandmothers gain, grandfathers lose. *American Journal of Human Biology, 23*(4), 498–508. Retrieved from www.embase.com/search/results?subaction = viewrecord&from=export&id=L51398102

Ice, G. H., Sadruddin, A. F. A., Vagedes, A., Yogo, J., & Juma, E. (2012). Stress associated with caregiving: An examination of the stress process model among Kenyan Luo elders. *Social Science and Medicine, 74.* Retrieved from www.embase.com/search/results?subaction = viewrecord&from=export&id=L51940826

Jappens, M., & Van Bavel, J. (2012). Regional family norms and childcare by grandparents Europe. *Demographic research, 27*, 85–120.

Kamya, H., & Poindexter, C. C. (2009). Mama Jaja: The stresses and strengths of HIV-affected Ugandan grandmothers. *Social Work in Public Health, 24*(1–2), 4–21.

Kasedde, S., Doyle, A. M., Seeley, J. A., & Ross, D. A. (2014). They are not always a burden: Older people and child fostering in Uganda during the HIV epidemic. *Social Science and Medicine, 113*, 161–168.

Kidman, R., & Thurman, T. R. (2014). Caregiver burden among adults caring for orphaned children in rural South Africa. *Vulnerable Children and Youth Studies, 9*(3), 234–246.

Killian, B. (2004). *Vulnerable Children and Security in Southern Africa: A Generation at Risk of HIV/AIDS.* SAFAIDS (Southern African AIDS Trust). Pretoria: South Africa.

Kimemia, M. (2006). *Caregiver burden and coping responses for females who are the primary caregiver for a family member living with HIV/AIDS in Kenya.* (Unpublished thesis). Researchgate.

Kimuna, S. R., & Makiwane, M. (2007). Older people as resources in South Africa: Mpumalanga households. *Journal of Aging and Social Policy, 19*(1), 97–114.

Kipp, W., Tindyebwa, D., Karamagi, E., & Rubaale, T. (2007). How much should we expect? Family caregiving of AIDS patients in rural Uganda. *Journal of Transcultural Nursing,*

18(4), 358–365. Retrieved from www.embase.com/search/results?subaction = viewrec ord&from=export&id=L47501576

Kolomer, S. R., Himmelheber, S. A., & Murray, C. V. (2013). Mutual exchange within skipped generation households. In B. Hayslip & G. C. Smith (Eds.), *Resilient grandparent caregivers: A strengths-based perspective* (pp. 121–133). New York: Taylor & Francis.

Lamb, M. E., & Hewlett, B. (2005). *Hunter-gatherer childhoods: Evolutionary, developmental, and cultural perspectives.* Piscataway, NJ: Aldine Transaction.

Lewis, J., & Meredith, B. (1988). *Daughters caring for mothers.* London: Routledge.

Lloyd-Sherlock, P., Beard, J., Minicuci, N., Ebrahim, S., & Chatterji, S. (2014). Hypertension among older adults in low and middle income countries: Prevalence, awareness and control *International Journal of Epidemiology, 43*, 116–128.

Mackinnon, C. . (2009). Applying feminist, multicultural, and social justice theory to diverse women who function as caregivers in end-of-life and palliative home care. *Palliative and Supportive Care, 7*, 501–512.

Matshalaga, N. (2004). *Grandmothers and orphan care in Zimbabwe.* Harare: SAfAIDS.

Mhaka-Mutepfa, M., Mpofu, E., & Cumming, R. (2014). Impact of protective factors on resilience of grandparent carers fostering orphans and non-orphans in Zimbabwe. *Journal of Aging and Health, 35*, 1–26.

Mpofu, E., Ruhode, N., Mhaka-Mutepfa, M., January, J., & Mapfumo, J. (2014). Resilience among youth with orphanhood. In M. U. L. Theron, and L. Liebenberg (Eds.), *Resilience and culture(s): Commonalities and complexities.* New York: Springer.

Mudavanhu, D., Segalo, P., & Fourie, E. (2008). Grandmothers caring for their grandchildren orphaned by HIV and AIDS. *New Voices in Psychology, 4*(1), 76–97.

Musil, C.M., Gordon, N. L., Warner, C. B., Zauszniewski, J. A., Standing, T., & Wykle, M. (2011). Grandmothers and caregiving to grandchildren: Continuity, change, and outcomes over 24 months. *The Gerontologist, 51*(1), 86–100. Retrieved from www.embase. com/search/results?subaction = viewrecord&from=export&id=L361490716

Nabalamba, A., & Chikoko, M. (2011). Aging population challenges in Africa. *African Development Bank, 1*(1), 1–19.

Nyambedha, E. O., Wandibba, S., & Aagaard-Hansen, J. (2003). "Retirement lost": The new role of the elderly as caretakers for orphans in Western Kenya. *Journal of Cross Cultural Gerontology, 18*(1), 33–52.

Nyasani, E., Sterberg, E., & Smith, H. (2009). Fostering children affected by AIDS in Richards Bay, South Africa: A qualitative study of grandparents' experiences. *African Journal of AIDS Research, 8*(2), 181–192.

Nyirenda, M., Newell, M-L., Mugisha, J., Mutevedzi, P. C., Seeley, J., Scholten, F., & Kowal, P. (2013). Health, wellbeing and disability among older people infected or affected by HIV in Uganda and South Africa. *Global Health Action, 6.* doi:10.3402/gha.v6i0.19201.

Oburu, P. O., & Palmerus, K. (2005). Stress related factors among primary and part-time caregiving grandmothers of Kenyan grandchildren. *International Journal of Aging and Human Development, 60*(4), 273–282. Retrieved from www.embase.com/search/ results?subaction = viewrecord&from=export&id=L40617532

Ogunmefun, C., Gilbert, L., & Schatz, E. (2011). Older female caregivers and HIV/AIDS-related secondary stigma in rural South Africa *Journal of Cross Cultural Gerontology, 26*(1), 85–102. Retrieved from www.embase.com/search/results?subaction = viewrec ord&from=export&id=L361489896

Oppong, C. (2006). Familial roles and social transformations: Older men and women in Sub-Saharan Africa. *Research on Aging,* 28(6), 654–668.

Payne, C. F., Mkandawire, J., & Kohler, H. P. (2013). Disability transitions and health expectancies among adults 45 years and older in Malawi: A cohort-based model. *PLoS Med*, 10, e1001435.

Ramose, M. B. (1999). *A new approach to African philosophy: African philosophy through Ubuntu Harare*: Zimbabwe: Mond Books.

Reijer, D. B. J. (2013). *Grandparents as parents: Skipped-generation households coping with poverty and HIV in rural Zambia*. (PhD thesis). Amsterdam Institute for Social Science Research. Retrieved from http://dare.uva.nl/record/1/398404

Rutakamwa, R., Zalwango, F., Richards, E., & Seeley, J. A. (2015). Exploring the care relationship between grandparent/older carers and children infected with HIV in South-Western Uganda: Implications for care for both the children and their older carers. *International Journal of Environmental Research and Public Health*, *12*(2), 2120–2134.

Sabella, G. P. (2012). Use of a mixed methods approach to investigate the support needs of older caregivers to family members affected by HIV and AIDS in South Africa. *Journal of Mixed Methods Research*, *6*(4), 275–293.

Schatz, E., & Seeley, J. A. (2015). Gender, aging and carework in East and Southern Africa: A review. *Global Public Health*, *45*, 1–16.

Scommegna, P. (2012). *More U.S. children raised by grandparents*. Retrieved from: http://www.prb.org/Publications/Articles/2012/US-children-grandparents.aspx

Shaibu, S. (2013). Experiences of grandmothers caring for orphan grandchildren in Botswana. *Journal of Nursing Scholarship*, *45*(4), 363–370.

Skovdal, M., Campbell, C., Madanhire, C., Nyamukapa, C., & Gregson, S. (2011). Challenges faced by elderly guardians in sustaining the adherence to antiretroviral therapy in HIV-infected children in Zimbabwe. *AIDS Care*, *23*, 957–964.

Ssengonzi, R. (2009). The impact of HIV/AIDS on the living arrangements and wellbeing of elderly caregivers in rural Uganda. *AIDS Care*, *21*(3), 309–314.

UNHCR. (2013). *UNHCR global cost 2013*. Retrieved from www.unhcr.org/5399a5314f5399.html

UNICEF. (2012). *UNICEF annual report 2012*. Retrieved from www.unicef.org/publications/index_69639.html

WHO. (2013). *Good health adds life to years: Global brief for World Health Day 2013*. Geneva: World Health Organization.

World Bank (2016). *GNI atlas index*. Retrieved from http://data.worldbank.org/about/country-and-lending-groups

Yancura, L. A., & Greenwood, H. (2013). Raising grandchildren as an expression of Hawaiian cultural values. In B. Hayslip & G. C. Smith (Eds.), *Resilient grandparent caregivers: A strengths-based perspective* (pp. 105–120). New York: Taylor & Francis.

Yunus, M. (2008). *Creating a world without poverty: Social business and the future of capitalism*. Dhaka, Bangladesh: Subarna.

12

GRANDPARENTING IN SOUTHERN AFRICA

What the Elders See While Sitting the Young Ones Standing on Their Toes Won't See

Monde Makiwane, Ntombizonke A. Gumede, and Mzolisi Makiwane

PROVERBS

1. "Ask those who are ahead about a buffalo." (*inyathi ibuzwa kwabaphambili.*)
2. "Are there no longer any wise elders in this family?" (*akusekho zinkonde na kulomzi?*)

(see pp. 290–291 for interpretations)

CASE STORY: THE RADEBE FAMILY

Were it not for roles played by grandparents, many families in Southern Africa would have weakened much further than is currently the case. This is because the traditional role played by biological parents in raising their children is not as strong as it was in the past. Due to the tumultuous history of Southern Africa, the distinct roles of fathers as breadwinners and mothers as caregivers and home-makers which evolved during the colonial era and the 1948–1994 apartheid era (Townsend, 2013) have progressively deteriorated. The complex case story of the Radebe family (all their names are pseudonyms) reveals the vastly contrasting roles and fortunes of a new generation of grandparents who have come to play a major role in sustaining their grandchildren's generation. We will make additional mention of this family throughout this chapter to illustrate various points.

> *Nozi Radebe, a 78-year-old grandmother, is married to Buya Radebe, a 78-year-old grandfather. They live in Imbali in the Black settlement of Pietermaritzburg, in the KwaZulu-Natal province of South Africa. They were separated and have three daughters (Pretty, Lindiwe, and Nombuso) and three sons (Zola, Zici, and Sboniso).*

At the time of the interview, Zola had already died. Although he had declared to the family that he was a father, no one ever took him seriously. Long after Zola's death a 25-year-old man named Jabu introduced himself as a son of Zola. His physical resemblance to Zola and to other members of the family made it easy for the Radebe family to accept this claim. Grandmother Nozi took care of him after he was adopted into the family, until he left to search for employment opportunities in the city. Their daughter Pretty is married, but unfortunately her only daughter died. Lindiwe is married and has a son. The son resides with his parents but spends most of his time at his maternal grandmother's homestead. This is probably because he is the only child at his home, and he seeks the company of his cousins. Nombuso is not married but has two children from different fathers. These children became the responsibility of their maternal grandmother. Nombuso was a dependent school girl when she gave birth to her children; by tradition such children become the responsibility of the grandmother. One of the fathers never contributed anything towards the support of his child, while the other father sent intermittent remittances for the support of his son. The reason one father could not provide support for his child was because he was a delinquent. As a result, the maternal grandmother also had to take charge of this grandson. The other grandchildren's stories are likewise complex. Many of the children were born to parents who were not married, or married subsequent to their children's births. Overall, the multi-generational Radebe household includes five great-grandchildren from two unmarried granddaughters.

Scope of this Chapter

Historically in the region of Southern Africa (and, as shown in Chapter 11, throughout sub-Saharan Africa overall), younger generations have looked for guidance from the wisdom and the experience of their elders. The strong and caring role played traditionally by families in African societies has been widely documented. However, over time migration and urbanization have contributed to the destabilization of values that bestowed respect and care to older persons, in the context of an age-integrated African society. This is in spite of the fact that older persons now play a bigger role than before to sustain younger generations.

Race, gender, and place of residence remain the most distinctive features of contemporary Southern African societies, because of past discriminatory practices. The majority of the poor Black population in Southern Africa continues to live in multi-generational family units, despite social and political changes in the country and region. It is not so much that traditional foundations of the extended family system which fostered intergenerational solidarity are being eroded, as pundits would suggest. Rather, new types of intergenerational relations are now evolving to meet the needs of contemporary Southern African families. These new relationships are still based on intergenerational solidarity, although expressed differently than in the past. The family remains a central institution in African societies in spite of many challenges, including the HIV/AIDS pandemic. The pandemic has put an unbearable strain on families, and contributes to diminished family capital. Although multi-generational families remain common, they are more fluid than before, as many young adults migrate from rural areas to cities for job opportunities and leave young children behind in the care of grandparents. In addition, the current middle generation (today's parents) is increasingly subject to high rates of morbidity and mortality. As a result, grandparents, typically grandmothers (as we saw in Chapter 11, all across sub-Saharan Africa), have become the main caregivers of orphaned grandchildren. Female-headed households, particularly those headed by older females, have become increasingly common. This is due to high male mortality and mobility, and the fact that more children are being born to parents who are neither married nor living together.

We recently conducted an observational study on practices related to grandparenting in South Africa. For a majority of the Black population, female and unmarried children who struggle to climb the social ladder are more likely to co-reside with their ageing parents or grandparents. Intergenerational co-residence appears to be important for the social and health status of older persons, while struggling members of the younger generation benefit from the support of their elders. On the other hand, grandparents who are financially better off than the younger generation prefer to remain alone. Most would rather maintain regular contacts with their children and grandchildren in the form of short visits, gift-giving, and (especially among more affluent grandparents) regular communication by telephone and email.

The scope of this chapter is limited to the Southern African region (the southernmost region on Figure 11.1, p. 247), with a special focus on South Africa, Botswana, Lesotho, and Swaziland. The main theme of this chapter is how grandparents continue to act as anchors for families in this region. Although the HIV/AIDS epidemic may have exacerbated the situation, it is important to note that care for grandchildren by grandparents and other members of the extended family pre-dates the HIV/AIDS epidemic. As noted above in the case story, grandparents can assume the roles of primary parents, and do not have the luxury and time just to be story-tellers. The current economic climate has meant that numbers of unemployed young adults have increased in the region, and this has resulted in a widened gap between the rich and poor. Seen in this context, the role played by grandparents to sustain families is invaluable.

Theoretical Framework

In the West, longer life expectancy and lower fertility means that people now live longer, and that there are fewer younger people to take care of them. Thus, the problem of generational relations in the West has been linked to the need to care for older persons. In Africa, the problem of intergenerational relations is logically linked to life opportunities that include caregiving for children, guidance and value transmission, safety nets for adults, and ultimately care for older persons.

Intergenerational relations thus provide support for individuals across the lifespan. In spite of the importance of intergenerational relations in African societies, very little has been done to investigate these relations. The recent surge in interest in intergenerational relations has mainly been confined, in our view, to Europe and North America, where valuable studies and theoretical approaches have emerged.

The solidarity model (Kahn & Antonucci, 1980) has been used to describe relationships between generations. As an elaboration of this model, five domains of solidarity were delineated by Silverstein and Bengston (1997): (1) association (social contact, shared activities); (2) affect (feelings, affection); (3) consensus (agreement); (4) function (exchange of aid); and (5) norms (mutual obligation). Solidarity encompasses the use of the vantage point of being outside a particular generation to be of assistance to a generation in need. For instance, the older generation with greater longevity is expected to share its life experiences with the younger generation as it "provides humans with an opportunity to examine their lives in retrospect, to correct some of their mistakes, to get closer to the truth and to achieve a different understanding of the sense and value of their actions" (United Nations, 1982, p. 1B). The main drivers of solidarity between generations have been identified as filial piety and reciprocity. Filial piety (discussed most extensively in Chapter 9 on East Asia) involves respect, reverence, and obedience toward one's elders and is a universal cultural norm, although the extent and its manner of expression differ among societies. Although reciprocal action is an important component of solidarity between generations, it is sometimes found to be weak or non-existent. For example, in a study in Mpumalanga province, South Africa, a strong act of solidarity expressed by older persons in support of younger generations with their pensions elicited little reciprocal support in return (Makiwane, Schneider, & Gopane, 2004). On the other hand, conflict among generations is associated with lower levels of solidarity. In most cases, conflict arises as a result of competition for limited resources, fights over political power, or disagreements about personal autonomy. Recently, some scholars (e.g., Pillemer et al., 2007) described generational relations as best explained by the concept of ambivalence, rather than by outright conflict versus solidarity. Ambivalence presupposes simultaneously positive and negative sentiments between the generations (Pillemer et al., 2007).

This chapter documents generational relations in Southern Africa which oscillate along a continuum of four states: solidarity, conflict, ambivalence, and ambiguity. The state of "ambiguity" was added to describe a weak bond that may exist between generations, or to explain disengagement from intergenerational relations. A Cartesian scale, using the four broad classifications mentioned above, illustrates this broad continuum in Figure 12.1. Two measures are easily identifiable: solidarity and conflict. Ambivalence and ambiguity are synthetic of the two measures, as is also shown in Figure 12.1.

We hypothesize that rapid social changes in Africa are the cause of a generally high level of intergenerational disconnect. These rapid changes are the result of changing mortality patterns, high mobility (e.g., middle generation moves in search for employment), major social epochs dividing generations (e.g., one

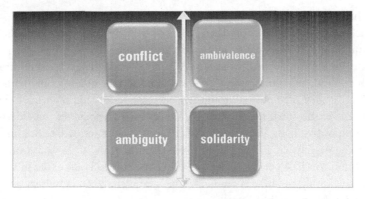

FIGURE 12.1 Intergenerational relations mechanisms

Source: Courtesy of Mandlenkosi Makiwane and Monde Makiwane.

generation grew up in a closed, apartheid society, now children are growing up in a liberal, post-apartheid environment), rapid social advances (high educational attainment of children born of parents who never went to school), changes in childbearing and child-rearing patterns, etc.

While such contextual factors are important determinants of the nature of generational relations, attitudes and values held towards other generational groups are also a key to congenial relations. For instance, *ageism* (a negative view of people belonging to another generation) is not conducive to a positive interaction with people of the other generation. At the same time, *generational imperialism* (imposing agendas, aims, priorities, and goals of one generation on a different generation) in the long run leads to conflict between generations. Biggs (2007) has suggested *generational intelligence* as a key to sustained solidarity between generations.

Generational intelligence refers to consciousness of the self as part of a generation and awareness of both positive and negative elements of another generation as keys to sound intergenerational relations. The significance of intergenerational intelligence is that as a societal quality it enhances the flow of wealth between the generations. Furthermore, a general mood of empathy across generations might reduce the prevalence of such tendencies as neglect and abuse of children and elderly people. An increased consciousness of ourselves as links in a line of descent extending from the past to the future can enhance social cohesion in Southern African families (and in other societies). Social cohesion, in turn, might lead to better cooperation between the generations, and ultimately to better quality of life.

Cultural and Contextual Background: Recognized Roles of Grandparents in Society

Grandparents as elders have always played a key role in Southern African families. The roles of older persons in traditional African societies are considerably different from the roles many play in the West. For example, in Southern Africa they have provided care for sick and/or dying children and orphaned grandchildren, and also much needed financial support for the household (HelpAge International, 2007). In most Southern African societies, grandparents generally were integrated into their family and community. This was done so that older people could share wisdom that they accumulated from their life experiences and offer mature judgements. It is in this spirit that in many Southern African societies the elderly were seen in a positive light and expected to play positive roles in families and communities where their wisdom was revered. Thus, as a way to bestow honour and appreciation to older persons, elders were given a role as counsellors in the community and family, and in many instances they presided over community and family ceremonies (Nhongo, 2004).

> *Although separated, Nozi and Buya still visit one another and share events like Christmas. Nozi is the matriarch of the family and keeps the family tight-knit. Her main concerns have been that the children should be fed, clothed, and schooled. She is also the family's spiritual leader and mentor, and for years has taken the family to church. Now that many in the family have grown up she does not force them to attend, but Nozi believes that she must continue to set an example by conscientiously attending church herself every Sunday. On the home front, she keeps alive the tradition of evening family prayers. Whenever there are challenges in the family or joyful things to share, she is the one who calls family "imbizos" (family gatherings) as either a disciplinary precaution or for a celebration. She is also a community activist who has helped her community to build preschools, and runs small businesses where she sells cheap second-hand clothing to augment her pension grant. Nozi is a very active, agile, and brilliant lady.*
>
> *Buya (Grandfather) is a quiet and an unassuming individual who likes to stay in the background. But in reality he is a warm, engaging, dedicated, and determined individual. Grandchildren turn to him for financial support and pocket money. He is also available to give advice on a variety of issues. He likes to tell stories about how he grew up and his previous workplaces and experiences. He further shows interest in the youngsters' long-term goals. When in a jolly mood he even discusses sports, especially soccer and his young days as a soccer player at amateur clubs.*

This historical honour given to grandparents has been challenged due to societal changes. After the introduction of formal education, grandparents and the elderly were not seen as the family's only repository of history, knowledge, and wisdom. Meanwhile, the rise of non-familial sources of income has in some instances weakened relationships between generations. For instance, a study in West Africa found that the grandparents in rural areas were at particular risk of losing support from their children, particularly when they were poor and their children did not expect sizeable inheritances (Schreider & Knerr, 2000). Thus, there was a general decline in the historical role played by extended families in reciprocal care.

Most Southern African elderly live in rural areas, and many young adults leave for the cities and leave their children with grandparents, because the law prohibits them from bringing their children along. A common pattern is that as they get older more people tend to relocate back to their original rural areas. This is a typical occurrence in Southern African nations, where workers move back to their provincial residences subsequent to reaching pensionable age. They want to reconnect with their extended families to share their meagre annuities. Going beyond the traditional role played by older persons in the pre-colonial era, the elderly continue to play a crucial role in family life.

Older persons filled the void of socialization and care for the children left behind by their parents. In addition, many children born out of wedlock have been taken care of by grandparents. Most recently, the role of elders has become more pronounced, as many take care of sick young adults as well as orphans and vulnerable children left behind as a result of the AIDS pandemic, which was experienced with great severity on the Southern tip of Africa (Spiegel, Watson, & Wilkinson, 1996; Makiwane et al., 2004; see also Chapter 11 on sub-Saharan Africa).

FIGURE 12.2 A 63-year-old grandmother looks after her 4-year-old grandson and 3-month-old granddaughter, in KwaNdaya Reserve, a small rural area in KwaZulu-Natal, South Africa. This photo was taken after the mother went back to work and left the grandmother to take care of the grandchildren. The grandmother's way of looking at her grandchildren projects warmth and love, and instead of watching television she is content to watch the grandchildren.

Source: Courtesy of Ntombizonke Gumede.

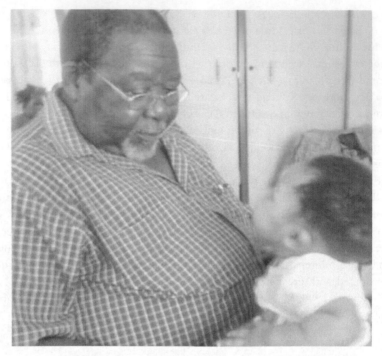

FIGURE 12.3 A 65-year-old grandfather with his 2-month-old grandson in KwaZulu-Natal, South Africa. This photo depicts the first time he held his grandson. He had been waiting to see him for a while, and now that he has arrived he is overwhelmed even though he is not the first grandchild he has held.

Source: Courtesy of Ntombizonke Gumede.

Grandfathers and Grandmothers in Cultural Context

It is apparent that grandfathers and grandmothers play different and somewhat complementary roles in this family context. Grandmothers play a more hands-on, motherly role that seeks to guide grandchildren from the front. Meanwhile, grandfathers remain more in the old-style grandfather mode whereby they are in the background and are comfortable to allow the grandmother the more visible, hands-on approach. The story-telling tradition has created a special bond between grandchildren and grandparents. At the end of the stories children would ask questions about characters, the meanings of stories, and even the expressions used. Grandparents were dramatists and actors; great orators and exceptional linguists would relish opportunities to give a masterly display of their knowledge and skills. Thus they were revered and respected by all at home and especially grandchildren.

Grandparents also played a special role of being buffer and safety zone for children who were facing the anger of their parents. The busy parents, who in many cases were strict disciplinarians, would punish their children, who would turn to their grandparents for refuge. They also knew that these family elders (*iinkonde namathongo eentsapho*, "wise elders who were on the verge of ancestry") were the safest sanctuaries in the family. The grandchildren in particular and other members of the family turned and still turn to these family patriarchs and matriarchs for advice on life issues; hence we cited the African proverb *inyathi ibuzwa kwabaphambili* ("Ask those who are ahead about a buffalo"). Both Townsend (2002, 2013) and Richter and Morrell (2006) identify grandfathers as important influences on the upbringing of grandchildren.

In contrast, modern grandparents play very different roles. The grandchildren we spoke with all concurred that there were no story-telling sessions. Indeed, their grandmothers rarely told stories. Their grandfathers sometimes told stories, but they are stories about the modern world of the workplace, as mentioned above. These stories were few and far between; there were no set times and places or even patterns for these stories. But with an abundant stock of knowledge and life experiences, the elders' multiple roles as listener, adviser, mediator, parent, friend, and provider of support and stability continues nowadays regardless of increased external pressures.

Social and Historical Backgrounds of Grandparenting

The relationship between parents and children in Southern Africa is one of parental power or control and reveals a particularly paternalistic predisposition. Respect is awarded to elders since they are considered a fountain of wisdom. The wisdom of the elders compels young families to keep contact with grandparents with the intent of cultural transmission.

Migrant Labour and Household Dynamics

Southern Africa has a long history of intra-regional migration, dating back to the mid-19th century. With the discovery of gold and diamonds in South Arica there was a shift away from an exclusively agrarian-based economy towards industrialization and the development of urban infrastructure (Holborn & Eddy, 2011, p. 1; Department of Social Development [DSD], 2012, p. 25). Most migrant labourers for these farmers were recruited from former Ciskei and Transkei homelands (which are now part of the Eastern Cape Province), Mozambique, Namibia, and other parts of Southern Africa. As a result most of the males and young people within Southern Africa moved into the cities and mining regions to find jobs (Townsend, 2013; Wilson, 1972), and grandparents played a crucial role in holding families together. Many young adults left for the cities while leaving their children with grandparents because, as we noted earlier, the law did not allow them to bring their children. Older persons filled the gap of socialization and care for children left behind. In addition, many children born out of wedlock were taken care of by grandparents among Southern African Black families (Posel, 2006; Ramphele & Richter, 2006; Murray, 1980).

Empirical studies on matters pertaining to African urbanization highlight the dehumanizing impact of the migrant labour system on the family life of Africans. Jones (1993) has noted the pain endured by children and adolescents from rural areas, who, driven by desire for reunification, embarked on long journeys in search of their parents, who worked and lived in urban centres such as Cape Town. Often these rural children searched for and found their parents in migrant hostels. The evidence from studies of household dynamics in migrant hostels contradicts the claim that modernization or industrialization promoted the development of the nuclear family or household among the African population. Even in urban industrial contexts, among Africans the extended family continues to be the idealized family or household form.

Mamphela Ramphele (1993) documented the conditions of life in the migrant hostels of Cape Town. One of the defining characteristics of the migrant labour system was the separation of spouses, and the subjugation of male workers to a life of state-enforced "bachelorhood," irrespective of the actual marital status of the migrant. Ramphele's work revealed the triumph of the human spirit even in an environment of blight. Many men laboured and sought to normalize their lives, in contexts where both spouse and children were legally barred from co-residence with male migrants. Her work on life in the migrant hostels of Cape Town has relevance for our current understanding of intergenerational relations as well as gender and social power in the household. One of the themes of Ramphele's work concerns social relations between men of different ages, men and women, and youth and adults. According to Ramphele, in a situation characterized by spatial constraints, ritual plays an important role in maintaining a system of social relations typical of "traditional" African settings. For example, customary practices such as the circumcision of male youth served two main purposes: first, these customs helped male youth through a transition from boyhood to manhood; second, they helped to reconnect male youth with their male elders from the countryside. Without a doubt, in the context of the difficulties that characterized life in apartheid South Africa, solidarity between migrant men was crucial in order to survive in a hostile urban environment. As a result of the migration of males to the cities rural women had to rear children on their own, without the support of a male figure in the household. In particular, some scholars have pointed out the economic and social effects on children of growing up in households or families in which the father figure was absent for prolonged periods of time (Richter & Morell, 2006).

Social Policy Issues: State Ideology, Social Security, and the Care of Children

Discussion of the role of the state in shaping intergenerational relations must take account of political and historical shifts. Much of what has been said about the effects of migrant labour on African families or households may be attributed to the apartheid system. In Southern Africa, economic disparities between rural and urban households derived from the apartheid policies of White rule in South Africa, and Cold War rivalries persist unrelentingly in the post-apartheid era. One indicator of this phenomenon is the scarcity of employment opportunities in rural areas, and the subsequent rural-to-urban migration.

Within Southern Africa there are social assistance schemes which enable individuals and families to take care of the destitute. This statement should not only be understood from a purely economic perspective but also within a cultural context, that of the Nguni word *ubuntu* (also discussed in Chapter 11), which represents notions of universal human interdependence, solidarity, and communalism (Roederer & Moellendorf, 2004). In this context, it means that no person should be destitute or without assistance. Limited resources, however, make it difficult at both the individual and family levels to accommodate other needy persons (Olivier, Kaseke, & Mpedi, 2008).

Several governments in the region make provisions for social assistance benefits that enable other individuals to look after the destitute. In South Africa, for example, there is the means-tested Foster Care Grant, which is payable to a foster parent. Mauritius, on the other hand, provides the Basic Orphans Pension to children (up to age 15, or 20 if at school) who have lost both parents. In addition, there is the Guardians Allowance, which is payable to a responsible adult who takes care of orphans, and there are social assistance benefits which enable certain categories of persons to look after themselves. These benefits include old age grants and disability grants (Kaseke, Gumbo, Dhemba, & Kasere, 1998). For instance, after the end of apartheid in South Africa, social grants were equalized for all citizens, and currently the government is extending old age pensions to all citizens who are 60 years and older, for both men and women. Previously, the old age pension was given to women after they reached age 60 and men at age 65. In addition, the state has extended the Child Support Grant to all South Africans. The Child Support Grant was introduced in order to alleviate poverty among mothers from socially deprived backgrounds. The intention of the authorities when they introduced the Child Support Grant was to assist mothers from underprivileged communities with financial resources that would help them meet the basic necessities of the young.

It should be borne in mind that impoverished elderly people and people with disabilities are, in accordance with African values, the responsibility of their next of kin, i.e., their extended families (Nino-Zarazua, Barrientos, Hulme, & Hickey, 2010). This has a profound effect on relations between the generations. For example, old age pensions operate as a very extensive and effective poverty alleviation scheme in Southern Africa. They are essentially distributive in nature, and reach more rural communities than urban and benefit women more than men. The Old Age Grant has helped enhance the status of the elderly, as they have become wage earners and breadwinners. According to Du Toit (1994), pensions have raised the status of the elderly and reduced their drift towards marginalization, which is common in countries in the throes of social and economic change. Some of the main expressions of solidarity between generations in Southern Africa are economic transfers and caregiving. Regrettably, they are also sources of conflict that sometimes lead to detachment between generations.

Contemporary Social/Economic Conditions and Policies that Impact Grandparenting

A number of recent studies place generational issues in the context of socio-political change, high levels of unemployment and poverty, and the incidence of HIV/AIDS among Southern Africans. An emerging literature emphasizes the role of grandparents as they nurture and groom the young. Studies conducted in Southern Africa make two points that are important for this discussion of inter-generational relations. First, historically, grandparents in African communities considered it a duty and an honour to care for their grandchildren. In fact, in the apartheid era grandparents took care of their grandchildren, while the biological parents worked in the cities. Second, in the cities parents go to work during the day, and leave their children behind in the care of the grandparents. In urban areas, imposition of the Group Areas Act since the 1960s has separated families and weakened extended families (Pinnock, 1984; Western, 1981).

Data obtained from the 1996 census and analysed by Rama and Richter (2007) indicate that the child dependency ratio was higher in South Africa among low-income households. Households headed by pensioners were most likely to fall under this category. Their study revealed that most pensioners lived in three-generational households, often female-headed, whereby pensioners took care of and provided for their unmarried children and grandchildren, and possibly even other relatives. Under normal circumstances the aged in African culture regard the younger generation as the ones who will secure the future of the household. But in the face of unemployment and HIV/AIDS, social roles have been reversed. The elders are nowadays increasingly responsible to raise children and grandchildren, and also to provide care and financial support later in life for the younger generations. This is captured by this statement from one elderly women: "I am responsible for the children and grandchildren...instead of getting help from them. They should look after me being an old lady" (Bohman, Van Wyk, & Ekman, 2009, p. 5). From the perspective of the elderly, relations with the younger generations should be reciprocal, and grandchildren and children should be able to provide them with "payback".

From the perspective of the younger cohort, reciprocity entails taking care of parents or grandparents, in return for the care they received when they were young. This might entail caregiving to the aged. Often grandchildren and children take on the responsibility of caregiving for the aged because the aged cater for their financial and emotional needs (Bohman et al., 2009). Here the impact of social distance on care for the elderly cannot be ignored. Social distance between children and parents might be a result of vast differences in educational status between generations, or of being socialized during different social epochs. This is exemplified by parents who grew up in a closed, apartheid society and are responsible for parenting children who are growing up in a more liberal, post-apartheid society. Social distance thus resulted in a growing gap between the younger and older generation (Bohman et al., 2009). According to Clay and Vander Haar (1993), children's support of their parents is dependent on the feelings of loyalty they hold for their parents. The intergenerational relationship can be weakened by various factors such as the education level of children, relationships between parents, and the mass media (Nuget, in Clay & Vander Haar, 1993). Although old age homes have been opened up for all South Africans, the majority of elderly persons in old age homes are Whites. These institutions are generally seen as un-African and as symbols of neglect. At the same time, more African older persons need access to these institutions because of the spread of careerism among the young generation, which has left the aged without any care or support structure. At the same time the aged in most African households have taken on more responsibility to care for their children and grandchildren, due to limited family resources and the spread of HIV/AIDS (Bohman et al., 2009). Fear is expressed by the aged in that they feel that this transition has left them with "less influence, less control and sometimes less respect and care from family members" (Bohman et al., 2009, p. 7). The elderly are not only responsible for the children and grandchildren within a three-generational household; they are also responsible for other than their own siblings and in some cases even friends (Aworolo et al., 2016). Many of the elderly may feel that due to unemployment, modernization, and the HIV/AIDS pandemic, they now have total responsibility for entire households, with little in return for their sacrifices.

Demographic Context: Ageing Trends

As of 2015, the median age of the global population, that is, the age at which half the population is older and half is younger, is 29.6 years. About 26% of the world's people are under 15 years of age, 62% are aged 15–59 years, and 12% are 60 or over (United Nations, 2015). Although African societies are still considered to be "developing", current demographic trends will soon make Africa's population part of a global demographic revolution. As in many parts of the world, the proportion of older people is increasing at a fast pace in Southern Africa. This was shown in a rapid rise in the proportion of elderly between the census years of 1996 and 2011 in South Africa.

The proportion of older persons among both Whites and Indian/Asians in South Africa, who are at an advanced stage of demographic transition, showed a further steep increase of 5.7% (from 14.4% in 1996, to 20.1% in 2011) and 4.8% (from 6.4%

in 1996 to 11.2% in 2011), respectively, from 1996 to 2011. Similarly, the aged population among Coloured and Black Africans, who lag behind Whites and Indian/ Asians in this demographic transition, showed a noticeable rise of 1.9% (from 5.8% in 1996 to 7.7% in 2011) and 0.4% (from 6.2% in 1996 to 6.6% in 2011), respectively. Projections (Aworolo et al., 2016) have shown that the population of the aged will not only continue to grow for a number of decades to come, but this will be at a faster pace than currently. A noteworthy feature of ageing in South Africa is that there are considerably fewer older men compared to older women. This is a result of higher mortality for males compared to females. While this is the case in most parts of the world, mortality differentials by sex are somewhat higher in Southern Africa. As a result, a higher proportion of elderly-headed households are led by females, who traditionally have not been the breadwinners of African families.

As Van Dullemen (2006, p. 101) described this situation,

> Old age is a gendered experience…Women often work in the informal sector, in agricultural environments, or as the main health care givers, and contribute to the household. For women, as for men, the aging world is a working world. Often, there is no retirement for older women until death, dementia, or disability.

Therefore, even though cultural expectancies for old age are emphasized, the roles of the elderly are in flux. Further, old age in years *per se* has not been especially revered, but rather the respect is for the maturity and wisdom born of a lifetime's experience in raising new generations.

Family Structures and Grandparents

Family structures differ significantly from society to society. Globally and especially within Southern Africa, the AIDS epidemic, along with unemployment of young adults and births out of wedlock, have placed grandparents in the position of breadwinners in multi-generational households. Those who live in AIDS-affected households have less working members in relation to non-working members. The elderly, and almost always grandmothers, are the main caregivers in such households, especially when there are pre-teenage children. They carry out not only a significant financial support role, but also have to undertake a large portion of domestic chores and responsibilities. In addition, productive working hours among caregivers are reduced as they divert time away from paid activities to care for ill household members (Makiwane et al., 2004). Consequently, with the disappearance or literal death of the middle generation, research on living arrangements and orphans in Southern Africa indicates that more and more children are growing up without their parents or other middle-aged adults, and increasingly live with their grandparents and other older caregivers (Ferreira, 2013; UNICEF, 2012; Madhavan, Schatz, & Clark, 2009; Schatz, 2007).

One living arrangement that has become increasingly prevalent in Southern Africa as a result of the loss of adults in their prime and the increasing interdependence of young and old is called the "skipped-generation" household. Skipped-generation families, where grandparents live with their grandchildren, have regularly been depicted as fragile on the grounds that the grandparents frequently struggle simultaneously with their own well-being, custodial matters, budgetary limitations and commitments, and also with the psychosocial and behavioural issues they confront with their grandchildren (DSD, 2012). Previous studies have illustrated a positive role of extended kinship for child development, in particular female headship of households and the presence of grandparents (Case & Deaton, 1999). Despite the processes of industrialization and urbanization that may weaken family unity, the weight of evidence makes it clear that Blacks' cultural preference for extended families has persisted (Amoateng, 2004). However, the above-mentioned demographic changes can be taxing and a challenge for the older person as an individual, even beyond their added responsibility of caring for others.

Review of the Grandparenting Literature

Theme 1: Impact of Economic and Financial Conditions

A number of studies have documented the social and economic contributions that older people make to their families (Ferreira, 2005; Nyasani, Sterberg, & Smith, 2009; Tran, 2012; Obioha & T'soeunyane, 2012; Dhemba & Dhemba, 2015). Social pensions are an example of intergenerational redistribution. Social pension programmes in developing countries have been found to facilitate economic and social change and address household vulnerability (e.g., to HIV/AIDS in South Africa, and to informal work in Brazil, see Chapter 4) and are perceived as extremely beneficial (Burman, 1996).

> The grandchildren say their grandmother Nozi is a workaholic who has never been out of work, and who actually was willing to take any type of job. She initiated several self-employment schemes to ensure that money continued to come into the family. They marvel at her endless energy that has benefited such a large family.

South Africa is one of the few African countries that operate a non-contributory social pension system. The Old Age Grant is paid monthly to men and women who are 60 years and older, regardless of whether or not they worked previously. In South Africa, the scheme is "means tested", i.e., given to elderly persons who either do not have any other regular income, or receive a regular income that is below a minimum standard. The Old Age Grant is the primary source of income for the majority of the elderly in South Africa. Furthermore, in many cases the elderly use their old age grants to support their entire household, which is usually multi-generational (Makiwane et al., 2004).

Many of the grandchildren grew up when grandfather Buya was no longer working, and thus have not as such benefited much. But the successful grandchild knows that Buya's money helped her through when she was at a university. Others remember that on paydays grandfather would organize braais (barbecues) for the family. He enjoyed creating a festive and jolly atmosphere whenever possible.

The need to share income across generations stems from high youth mortality and unemployment, which forces many young people to be dependent on their ageing parents. Southern African societies have shown commitment to the care of older persons by sustaining the social pensions in spite of many financial and developmental challenges that the region faces. In Southern Africa, two models of income sharing have been identified in the context of grandparent-headed households. In general terms, the two models differ according to the economic status of families. The first model is common among people of high economic status in South Africa, as it is also common in many developed societies throughout the world. It has been referred to as *unidirectional wealth flow*. The younger generation benefit from the older generation while they are children. When the younger generation reaches adulthood, there is generally a lull in economic exchanges between generations, and most exchanges between the generations during this time are symbolic in nature. This period is usually followed much later by a windfall to the younger generation in the form of inheritances. This model is common among the relatively small portion of the Southern African population that has enjoyed economic prosperity for at least two generations. This is made possible because the older generation, in addition to its support of children, saves enough money to sustain themselves when they reach pensionable age, and also because the majority of children acquire enough skills during childhood to enter the labour market and become economically independent.

The Radebe family used to meet together over Christmas. But that tradition has now weakened because of financial constraints. There have been complaints from some members of the family that some others do not contribute towards these gatherings, which is a financial strain on those who do contribute.

Some of the grandchildren have made remarkable achievements. One granddaughter, who is a university graduate, got a job. In her first year at work, she sent remittances regularly, and she visited the extended family over weekends. But that is now changing. Tamara is not as generous as she used to be. Sometimes she brings little or nothing home. Grandmother Nozi suspects that Tamara now has other commitments.

The second model is the *multidirectional wealth flow*. This model is applicable to people of low economic status in Southern Africa, and is similar to the model found in most of Africa and in developing societies elsewhere. Children benefit from parents when they are young and during times of social and economic crises, and are expected to support parents with remittances during their adulthood.

Traditionally, subsistence farming served as a repository of wealth that was shared between generations. Children would send remittances for investment in the farming and other sectors while the older generation would be custodians of the enterprise. This fostered continuous social contact while different generations reaped the benefits of the enterprise. This continues to be the case in most of sub-Saharan Africa and Southern Africa in particular.

The South African Migration Project has systematically studied the relationship between migration, remittances, and development in Southern Africa for several years. Internal and external migration, especially from rural areas, has been documented as a survival strategy. Abundant evidence exists on the redistributive effects of social pensions beyond just the elderly recipients (Ardington & Lund, 1995; Lund, 1993; Moller & Sotshongaye, 1996; Moller & Fereira, 2003).

> *Nozi describes the job of raising grandchildren and great-grandchildren as very stressful. She complains that it is tough to support them from her meagre pension grant, as she has to feed many of her grandchildren and see to their school needs.*

Typically, migrants (internal and external) send money home to their families to cover basic necessities (Ramsamy, 2014). However, according to Woolard and Klasen (2004), the dependence of rural households on remittances and social pensions places them in an economically precarious situation. In the KwaZulu-Natal Income Dynamics Study (May, Carter, Haddad, & Maluccio, 2000), it was found that even though the addition or loss of a household member was the principal contributor to change in household income, a fall in remittances accounted for 11% of instances where households fell below the poverty line.

For example, according to Cross (2003) almost 80% of Black migrants' remittances accounted for about 30% of the household incomes. In 1993, one in four Black households depended on remittance income in South Africa (Carter & May, 1999). Migration and remittance patterns for groups other than Blacks have not been well studied, presumably because migration represents a survival strategy mainly for Blacks. Among Blacks, the migration rate was higher for rural Blacks and low-income households, although migration among poor urban and suburban Black families was not uncommon (Posel & Casale, 2003).

Furthermore, research based on studies of long-term cash transfer programmes across the global South, from Mexico (see Chapter 2), Indonesia, and South Africa, to India (see Chapter 8), Mongolia, and Namibia, argues that the biggest problem for people in poverty is a basic lack of cash, rather than a lack of motivation or knowledge. Many people have so little money that they simply cannot afford to send children to school, eat better, or find work. Small amounts of money can thereby make a big difference and transform lives. A small guaranteed income provides the foundation that enables poor people to transform their own lives, and cash-transfers provide a ladder to climb out of the poverty trap (Hanlon, Barrientos, & Hulme, 2010).

Theme 2: Intergenerational Relations and Support

Nozi feels that this generation of grandchildren is very hard to raise, due to changes going on in society. She mentions that such grandchildren do not want to be assigned jobs or chores. She feels that they spend most of their time in front of the television or on the phone, and succumb easily to peer pressure. Nozi points to the examples of two of her grandchildren, who she says are troubled because they are also into drugs. She is also often irritated by the children's obsession with loud music. Once she even had to move away and spend time with relatives to escape the noisy music. Nozi thinks of herself as a strict grandmother who demands work and discipline. She says her grandchildren complain that she always wants them to work and always scolds them.

South Africa is one of the most rapidly ageing societies in Africa, and in recent years it has seen a considerable increase in the number of older people. However, we have seen throughout this chapter that among African families the role of the older generation is imperative as they play a socioeconomic and nurturance role for their grandchildren (Stats SA, 2012, p. 2). A key characteristic of African families is the intergenerational provision of support and care, but we have also seen that changes in African family structure has had an impact on intergenerational relationships (Makiwane, 2011, p. 1).

Striking differences are often found between generations. In Southern Africa, the significance of societal interest in the generations concerns implications that such intergenerational disjuncture has for life opportunities. In conservative family cultures such as those common in Southern Africa, the responsibilities ascribed to young girls are often quite broadly distributed across a variety of domestic chores. To fulfil these household chores can be quite time consuming, which significantly compromises the time girls can spend on school work. This is likely to have the cumulative effect of lowering the academic achievement of girls, which in turn has a long-term effect on their life prospects. Thus, conservative norms and values in the parents' and grandparents' generations can work together to undermine the human potential of girls in the grandchildren's generation.

The grandchildren agree, often to their consternation, that grandmother Nozi is very strict. They have always been expected to come straight home from school. In a locale where many children loiter after school, their grandmother's expectations are a constant source of irritation, disagreement, and confrontation. When they were younger, they were all subjected to corporal punishment. After school those still in school are expected to do household chores and attend to their schoolwork. The grandchildren admit that this has always been and still is a challenge that earns them acidic tongue-lashing from their disciplinarian grandmother.

According to Makiwane (2010) the proliferation of intergenerational households can be attributed to changes in sexual and marital norms, with an increase in childbearing out of wedlock that often results in the older generation taking on the roles of caregiver and provider. Furthermore, the rate of internal migration from rural to urban areas, by parents and their children in search of job opportunities, has influenced intergenerational relationships within families. This has affected the everyday activities and responsibilities of parents and children, and resulted in less time spent with the parents, which hinders the transmission of skills and values (Makiwane, 2010). Modernization is another important factor associated with a change in family values and beliefs. As children become more educated, importance is placed on individual economic opportunities and higher wages (Whitehead, Hashim, & Iverson, 2005). With better educational opportunities, children are exposed to new ideas and values which undermine parental knowledge and authority (Henn, 2005). This shift in power balance and authority between children and their parents (Whitehead et al., 2005) leads to greater intergenerational gaps (Makiwane, 2010).

In this context, three issues have become pertinent to older persons throughout sub-Saharan Africa and including Southern Africa. First is the growing inadequacy of the extended family to take care of the aged (Schreider & Knerr, 2000); second is the lack of adequate social security provision in most African countries (United Nations, 2003); and third is the growing burden and responsibility to provide care that is heaped on the aged (Makiwane et al., 2004).

Theme 3: Care for the Grandparents

In the Southern African context, the traditional social security system assumed that children would take care of their elderly parents. However, the reality is that for a number of reasons children are sometimes not able to fulfil their filial obligations. As a result, grandparents and the elderly do not receive remittances, and hence have to care for themselves (Anderson & Kaleeba, 2002). Concomitantly, all these responsibilities and problems occur at a time when the health of the elderly is deteriorating and when their economic status is poor. As is the case throughout the developing societies portrayed in this book, older persons tend to be vulnerable for a number of reasons. For example, with old age come chronic conditions such as mental and physical degeneration (Barrientos, 2000; Heslop & Gorman, 2002; Lloyd-Sherlock, 2002; Davey & Patsios, 1999). Accordingly, as a result of social and psychological problems including grief, guilt, and anger towards their sons and daughters (Wallace, 2001), grandparents and the elderly often depend on service providers such as social workers for support (Sung & Dunkic, 2009).

HelpAge International (2016) contends that poverty and social exclusion are major challenges facing older persons, and that they are consistently among the poorest of the poor. As Ambrosino, Heffernan, Shuttleworth and Ambrosino (2012) observed, many older people have been self-sustaining members of society and have problems with adaptation only at an older age. Loss of a spouse, friends, families, familiar environment, job income, and physical health, and with the added burden of care with grandchildren, cause grandparents' routines, finances, social life, and emotional state to deteriorate radically (Mokone, 2006).

According to the Global Age Watch Index (2015), the quality of life of older people in Africa is very low. South Africa is the highest ranked African nation at number 78 (of 96 countries compared worldwide), followed by Ghana (81), Morocco (84), Nigeria (86), Uganda (88), Rwanda (89), Zambia (90), Tanzania (91), Mozambique (94), and Malawi (95). The report measured well-being of the elderly in terms of health status, income security, capacity, and enabling environment. With South Africa leading in elderly well-being among African nations, this report helps us to unpack the various ways it deals with senior citizens.

In addition to having the second largest (second only to Nigeria) and most developed economy in Africa, South Africa has one of the largest voluntary retirement funding systems in the world (Organisation for Economic Co-operation and Development – OECD, 2014). While South Africa performed moderately well in income security, it ranked low for the elderly's health status (Global Age Watch Index, 2015). There are a number of studies that indicate pensions can have a significant effect on older people's health status (Schatz & Madhavan, 2011; Ardington et al., 2010; Gómez-Olivé, Thorogood, Clark, Kahn, & Tollman, 2010; Collinson et al., 2002; Case & Deaton, 1999). These studies reported a significantly better health status for pensioners than other household members, controlling for age, sex, and other factors, when the pensioner(s) did not pool their resources with the rest of the household. It was also found that within reach of pensionable age, the health status of South African women has improved.

Despite this, some research indicates that a significant proportion of older South Africans make little use of health services. For example, in a rural district in northern South Africa, a survey of older Black South Africans in 2006 found that only 45% had utilized health services in the previous year (Gómez-Olivé, Thorogood, Clark, Kahn, & Tollman, 2013). This indicates that there are substantial barriers to access of services, which raises the question of whether these barriers are modified by receipt of a pension (Ralston, Schatz, Menken, Gómez-Olivé, & Tollman, 2016).

According to Dhemba and Dhemba (2015), there are two reasons that old people in developing countries face challenges. First is an economic environment which is underdeveloped, and second is an awareness that demographic ageing is associated with the affluent countries of America and Western Europe which enjoy an advanced level of economic development and therefore can provide for their needs. Furthermore, in the Southern African context it has always been thought that the strength of tradition and family solidarity would prevent situations whereby older persons experience social and economic insecurity. Dhemba and Dhemba also contend that the new value of individualism that is emergent in African societies has exposed vulnerable populations to social insecurity.

Thus, despite the belief that it is the family's duty to look after their elderly, comprehensive social assistance with the care of the elderly is needed in Southern Africa. There is a consensus that social assistance, whether formal or informal, is critical to survival, that a history of progressive social welfare policies makes a difference, and that it is never too soon to prepare for population ageing. This is important for other African nations, and indeed for all the nations highlighted in this book, because the elderly can be a significant boon for families and societies alike. As Southern African nations, we can do better when we learn from each other and from non-African nations. Our collective goal is to improve the quality of life for the elderly, for present and future generations.

Conclusions, Speculation, and Final Recommendations

Solidarity between the generations in Southern Africa has been demonstrated from time immemorial. Nevertheless, social changes in society have generally produced disruptions in reciprocal solidarity in this region. The Southern African research literature has identified the migrant labour system and modernization as disruptive forces that have upset intergenerational relations. More recent work has tended to emphasize the harmful impact of AIDS and youth unemployment; these two phenomena may be more threatening in sub-Saharan Africa and Southern Africa than in the societal contexts analysed in non-African chapters of this book.

This chapter has clarified the life course trajectories of intergenerational relations in Southern Africa. We have shown that caregiving for children is highly gendered, i.e., relatively few men co-reside with their pre-teenaged children. In cases where the mother is unable to take care of the child, the grandmother has typically taken over this role. After the teenage years, many children who manage to attain financial autonomy are likely to move away from their childhood households, and leave less successful siblings in the care of parents. Meanwhile, Whites are more likely to spend most of their old age lives in one-generational households. This is a result of a delay in childbearing, having fewer children, and later in life seeing their children leave home to seek independence as a mark of the onset of adulthood, trends which are similar to those in the Westernized societies represented in this book. This contrast is important because among Black Southern Africans, older persons generally co-reside with those adult children who are less successful. Many of such children give birth to children, which leaves the grandparents with responsibility for both their children and grandchildren.

As also noted earlier in this chapter, most older persons in Southern Africa are solely dependent on government grants, which they generously share with other generations within their families. Support from children who become successful and may have left their childhood households is miniscule. The old practice by which younger people send monthly remittances to their ageing parents has declined. Indeed, civil society has increasingly relegated the issue of economic support of older persons to the state. There are a number of support systems that can assist older persons in this plight. They include relief of older people from the burden of unemployed young people, and encouragement of younger people who are economically active to give more support to their parents.

Society must take more to heart the plight of older persons in Southern Africa. The proportion of older persons in South African society is expected to increase dramatically in future. Given that future generations of the elderly are likely to be more educated and have better resources than the current generation which grew up under apartheid, we can expect that older persons will play a bigger role in society than the current cohort. Thus, programmes must invest more in older persons, to enhance better intergenerational relations in recognition of the crucial roles played by older people in Southern African families.

Summary

A substantial body of research confirms that were it not for roles played by grandparents, many families in Southern Africa would have weakened much further than is currently the case. This is because the traditional role played by biological parents in raising their children is not as strong as it was in the past. In many cases, grandparents have taken some of the roles usually played by parents. It should be noted though that in spite of its many challenges the family remains a central institution for raising children in Southern Africa. Although multi-generational families remain common, they are more fluid than they were before, for a number of reasons. The HIV pandemic has put a strain on Southern African families, and furthermore, as many young adults migrate from rural areas to cities in search of job opportunities, they leave their children behind in the care of grandparents. The complex life-course relationships that result from fragile family structures were the subject of this chapter. The expression of filial piety, which is culturally entrenched in the region, results in many young people gaining life opportunities from their grandparents' endeavours. The chapter showed that the duty of caregiving to children is highly gendered and skewed towards grandparents. In cases where parents are unable to take care of children, grandmothers have typically taken over this role. While the scope of this chapter covers the entire Southern African region, the main focus has been on grandparents in South Africa.

Appendix

Meaning of Proverbs

> "What the elders see while sitting the young ones standing on their toes won't see."

This chapter sub-title conveyed that with their age and lifelong experiences, the elderly's view of life has a much wider lens than that of younger people, i.e., their experiences engender wisdom.

"Ask those who are ahead about a buffalo."

This means that younger people, especially grandchildren, rely on grandparents for guidance. This proverb has its origin from the days when hunting was common and the elderly had faced such challenges in their past.

"Are there no longer any wise elders in this family?"

This question would be asked when complicated or unfamiliar problems confronted families. This means that the family lacks wise elderly people to guide the family through a difficult problem.

Additional Resources

Grandmothers Against Poverty and AIDS (www.facebook.com/GAPA-Grand mothers-Against-Poverty-and-AIDS-108121155934330/

South African Older Persons Forum (www.saopf.org.za/)
Following a public outcry in 2000, the Minister of Social Development commissioned an investigation into the abuse, neglect, and ill-treatment of older persons. A report was published in 2003: "Mothers and Fathers of the Nation, the Forgotten People". It called for action to make the concerns of older persons a priority and to improve their quality of life.

Families Southern Africa (www.famsapretoria.co.za) – "FAMSA Pretoria"
This is an outreach group that seeks to strengthen families and communities.

Discussion Questions

1. In Southern Africa, the roles of the grandmother and grandfather are quite different. Why do you think grandfathers are more gentle figures compared to the authoritative grandmother?
2. Southern African grandparents are sometimes faced with custody issues with grandchildren for many reasons, e.g., orphanhood, divorce, separation, abuse, and neglect. In such cases, should grandparents have the legal right to custody of a grandchild despite the judicial presumption in favour of the parent?
3. What happens to grandparent–grandchild relations if the grandparents are divorced? Based on this chapter, is the closeness of the grandparent–grandchild affected by grandparents' marital status, e.g., shared activities and contact frequency?

References

Ambrosino, R., Heffernan, J., Shuttleworth, G., & Ambrosino, R. (2012). *Social work and social welfare: An introduction* (7th ed.). Belmont, CA: Brooks/Cole.

Amoateng, A. Y. (2004) *The South African family: Continuity or change?* HSRC ten years of democracy seminar series. Cape Town: HSRC Press.

Anderson, S., & Kaleeba, N., (2002). *Ancient remedies, new disease: Involving traditional healers in increasing access to AIDS care and prevention in East Africa.* UNAIDS. Retrieved from www.unaids.org

Ardington, E., & Lund, F. (1995) Pensions and development: Social security as complementary to programmes of reconstruction and development. *Development Southern Africa, 12*(4), 557–577.

Ardington, C., Case, A., Islam, M., Lam, D., Leibbrandt, M., Menendez, A., & Olgiati, A. (2010). The impact of AIDS on intergenerational support in South Africa: Evidence from the Cape area panel study. *Research on Aging, 32,* 97–121.

Barrientos, A. (2000). Work, retirement and vulnerability of older persons in Latin America. *Journal of International Development, 12*(4), 495–506.

Biggs, S. (2007). Thinking about generations: Conceptual position and policy implications. *Journal of Social Issues, 63*(4), 696–712.

Bohman, D. M., Van Wyk, N. C., & Ekman, S-L. (2009). Tradition in transition – Intergenerational relations with focus on the aged and their family members in a South African context. *Scandinavian Journal of Caring Sciences, 23*(3), 446–455.

Burman, S. (1996). Intergenerational family care: Legacy of the past, implications for the future. *Journal of Southern African Studies, 22*(4), 585–598.

Carter, M., & May, J. (1999). Poverty, livelihood and class in rural South Africa. *World Development, 27*(1), 1–20.

Case, A., & Deaton, A. (1999). School inputs and educational outcomes in South Africa. *Quarterly Journal of Economics. 114*(3), 1047–1084.

Clay, D. C., & Vander Haar, J. E. (1993). Patterns of intergenerational support and childbearing in the Third World. *Population Studies Review, 47*(1), 67–83.

Collinson, M. A., Mokoena, O., Mgiba, N. et al., (2002). Agincourt demographic surveillance system. In O. Sankoh, K. Kahn, E. Mwageni, P. Ngom, & P. Nyarko (Eds.), *Population and health in developing countries, Vol. 1: Population, Health and Survival at INDEPTH sites* (pp. 197–206). Ottawa, Canada: International Development Research Centre.

Cross, C. (2003). *Migrant workers' remittances and micro-finance in South Africa report.* Pretoria, South Africa: Human Sciences Research Council.

Davey, A., & Patsios, D. (1999). Formal and informal community care to older adults: comparative analysis of the United States and Great Britain. *Journal of Family and Economic Issues, 20*(3), 271–300.

Department of Social Development (DSD). (2012). *White paper on South African families.* Pretoria, South Africa.

Dhemba, J., & Dhemba, B. (2015). Ageing and care of older persons in Southern Africa: Lesotho and Zimbabwe compared. *Social Work & Society, 13*(2), 1–16.

Du Toit, B. M. (1994). Does the road get lonelier? Aging in a coloured community in South Africa. *Journal of Aging Studies, 8*(4), 357–374.

Ferreira, M. (2005). Advancing income security in old age in developing countries: Focus on Africa. *Global Ageing, 2*(3), 32–36.

Ferreira, M. (2013, May 22). *Housing for older persons globally: What are best practices?* International Longevity Centre Joint Discussion Paper. Retrieved from www.ilc-alliance.org/index.php/reports/report_details/housing_for_older_people_globally_what_are_the_best_practices_an_ilc_global

Global Age Watch Index. (2015) *Insight report.* HelpAge International. Retrieved from www.who.int/healthinfo/Vol3_Suppl2_GHA2010.pdf#page=23

Gómez-Olivé, F. X., Thorogood, M., Clark, B. D., Kahn, K., & Tollman, S. M. (2013). Assessing health and well-being among older people in rural South Africa. *Global Health Action, 3*, 23–35.

Hanlon, J., Barrientos, A., & Hulme, D. (2010). *Just give money to the poor: The development revolution from the global south.* Sterling, VA: Kumarian Press.

HelpAge International. (2007). *A better deal for older carers in South Africa: How an organisation from the Durban townships adapted its role to tackle the impact of HIV and AIDS.* HAI AIDS briefing. London: HelpAge.

HelpAge International. (2016). End the neglect: *A study of humanitarian financing for older people.* London: HelpAge.

Henn, C. M. (2005). *The relationship between certain family variables and the psychological well-being of Black adolescents.* (PhD thesis). University of the Free State, South Africa.

Heslop, A., & Gorman, M. (2002). *Chronic poverty and older persons in the developing world.* Chronic Poverty Research Center. Working paper No. 10.

Holborn, L., & Eddy, G. (2011). *First steps to healing the South African family.* Johannesburg, South Africa: South African Institute of Race Relations.

Jones, S. (1993). *Assaulting childhood: Children's experiences of migrancy and hostel life in South Africa.* Johannesburg: Witwatersrand University Press.

Kahn, R. L., & Antonucci, T. C. (1980). Convoys over life course: Attachment roles, and social support. In P. B. Baltes & O. G. Brim, Jr. (Eds.), *Life-span, development, and behavior* (pp. 254–283). New York: Academic Press.

Kaseke, E., Gumbo, P., Dhemba, J., & Kasere, C. (1998). The state and dynamics of social policy practice and research in Zimbabwe. *Journal of Social Development in Africa, 13*(2), 21–23.

Lloyd-Sherlock, P. (2002). Population ageing in developed and developing regions: implications for health policy. *Social science & medicine, 51*(6), 887–895.

Lund, F. (1993). State social benefits in South Africa. *International Social Security Review, 46*(1), 5–25.

Madhavan, S., Schatz E. J., & Clark, B. (2009). HIV/AIDS mortality and household dependency ratios in rural South Africa. *Population Studies, 63*(1), 37–51.

Makiwane, M. (2010). *The changing patterns of intergenerational relations in South Africa.* Expert Group Meeting, "Dialogue and Mutual Understanding across Generations", convened in observance of the International Year of Youth (Vol. 2011).

Makiwane, M., Schneider, M., & Gopane, M. (2004). *Experiences and needs of older persons in Mpumalanga.* Pretoria, South Africa: Human Sciences Research Council.

May, J., Carter, M. R., Haddad, L., & Maluccio, J. (2000). *KwaZulu-Natal Income Dynamics Stufy 1993–1998: A longitudinal household database for South African policy analysis.* Centre for Social and Development studies. Working Paper No 2. University of Natal, Durban.

Mokone, J. M. (2006). Challenges experienced by grandparents raising grandchildren: an exploratory study. *Social Work, 42*(2), 187–200.

Moller,V., & Ferreira, M. (2003). *Getting by: Benefits of non-contributory pensions for older South African households.* Cape Town: Institute of Ageing in Africa.

Moller,V., & Sotshongaye, A. (1996). My family eats this money too: Pension-sharing and self-respect among Zulu grandmothers. *South African Journal of Gerontology,* 5(2), 9–19.

Murray, C. (1980). Migrant labour and changing family structure in the rural periphery of Southern Africa. *Journal of Southern African Studies, 6*(2), 139–156.

Nhongo, T. (2004). *The changing role of older people in African households and the impact of ageing on African family structures.* A paper presented at the Ageing in Africa Conference, Johannesburg, August 18–20.

Nino-Zarazua, M., Barrientos A., Hulme D., & Hickey, S. (2010). *Social protection in sub-Saharan Africa: Will the green shoots blossom?* Brooks World Poverty Institute. Working Paper No. 116. University of Manchester, UK.

Nyasani, E., Sterberg, E., & Smith, H. (2009). Fostering children affected by AIDS in Richards Bay, South Africa: A qualitative study of grandparents' experiences. *African Journal of AIDS Research, 8,* 181–192.

Obioha, E. E., & T'soeunyane, P. G. (2012). The roles of the elderly in Sotho family system and society of Lesotho. *Southern Africa Anthropologist, 14*(3), 251–260.

Olivier, M. P., Kaseke, E., & Mpedi, L. G. (2008). *Informal social security in Southern Africa: Developing a framework for policy intervention.* Paper prepared for presentation at the International Conference on Social Security organised by the National Department of Social Department, South Africa, March 10–14, 2008, Cape Town.

Organisation for Economic Co-operation and Development (OECD). (2014). *Pension fund market.* Retrieved from www.oecd.org/daf/fin/private-pensions/Pension-Markets-in-Focus-2014.pdf

Pillemer, K., Suitor, J. J., Mock, S. E., Sabir, M., Pardo, T. B., & Sechrist, J. (2007). Capturing the complexity of intergenerational relations: Exploring ambivalence within later-life families. *Journal of Social Issues, 63*(4), 775–791.

Pinnock, D. (1984). *The brotherhoods: Street gangs and state control in Cape Town.* Cape Town: David Philip.

Posel, D. (2006). Moving on: Patterns of labour migration in post-apartheid South Africa. In M. Tienda, S. Tollman, & E. Preston-Whyte (Eds.), *African migration and urbanisation in comparative perspective* (pp. 217–231). Johannesburg, South Africa: University of the Witwatersrand Press.

Posel, D., & Casale, D. (2003). What has been happening to internal labour migration in South Africa, 1993–1999? *South African Journal of Economics, 71*(3), 455–479.

Ralston, M., Schatz, E., Menken, J., Gómez-Olivé, F. X., & Tollman, S. (2016). Who benefits – or does not – from South Africa's old age pension? Evidence from characteristics of rural pensioners and non-pensioners. *International Journal of Environmental Research and Public Health, 13*(1), 85.

Rama, S., & Richter, L. M. (2007). Children's household work as a contribution to the well-being of the family and household. In A. Y. Amoateng & Heaton, T. B. (Eds.), *Families and households in post-apartheid South Africa: Socio-demographic perspectives* (pp. 135–170). Cape Town: HSRC Press.

Ramphele, M. (1993). *A bed called home: Life in the migrant labour hostels of Cape Town.* Cape Town: David Philips.

Ramphele, M., & Richter, L. (2006). Migrancy, family dissolution and fatherhood. In L. Richter and R. Moreel (Eds.), *Baba: Men and fatherhood in South Africa* (pp. 73–81). Cape Town: HSRC Press.

Ramsamy, P. (2014). *Remittances from South Africa to SADC including effective practices; Financial inclusion in Southern Africa*. Retrieved from www.awepa.org/wp-content/uploads/2014/02/Dr.-Prega-Ramsamy-Making-Financial-Markets-Work-for-the-Poor.pdf

Richter, L., & Morrell, R. (Eds.). (2006). *Baba: Men and fatherhood in South Africa*. Cape Town: HSRC Press.

Roederer, C., & Moellendorf, D. (2004). *Jurisprudence*. Lansdowne, South Africa: Juta.

Schatz, E. (2007). Taking care of my own blood: Older women's relationships to their households in rural South Africa. *Scandinavian Journal of Public Health, 35*(69), 147–154.

Schatz, E., & Madhavan, S. (2011). Headship of older persons in the context of HIV/AIDS in rural South Africa. *Journal of African Population Studies, 25*, 440–456.

Schreider, G., & Knerr, B. (2000). Labour migration as a social security mechanism for smallholder households in Sub-Saharan Africa: The case of Cameroon. *Oxford Development Studies, 28*(2), 223–236.

Silverstein, M. L., & Bengston, V. L. (1997). Intergenerational solidarity and the structure of adult child–parent relationships in American families. *American Journal of Sociology, 103*, 429–460.

Spiegel, A., Watson, V., & Wilkinson, P. (1996). Domestic diversity and fluidity among some African households in Greater Cape Town. *Social Dynamics, 22*(1), 7–30.

Stats SA. (2012). *Library cataloguing-in-publication (CIP): Data social profile of vulnerable groups in South Africa, 2002–2012*. Pretoria: Statistics South Africa.

Sung, K. & Dunkie, R. E. (2009). Respect for the elderly: Implications for human service providers. *Journal of Gerontological Social Work, 52*(3), 250–260.

Townsend, N. W. (2002). *The package deal: Marriage, work, and fatherhood in men's lives*. Philadelphia, PA: Temple University Press.

Townsend, N. W. (2013). The complications of fathering in Southern Africa: Separation, uncertainty, and multiple responsibilities. In D. W. Shwalb, B. J. Shwalb, & M. E. Lamb (Eds.), *Fathers in cultural context* (pp. 173–200). New York: Routledge.

Tran, M. (2012, October 1). UN report calls for action to fulfil potential of ageing global population. *Guardian*. Retrieved from www.guardian.co.uk/global-development/2012/oct/01/un-report-action-need-ageing-population

UNICEF. (2012). *The state of the world's children*. New York: United Nations Children's Fund.

United Nations. (1982). Vienna international plan of action on aging. New York: United Nations.

United Nations. (2003). *The global youth report*. Retrieved from www.un.org/esa/socdev/unyin/documents/worldyouthreport.pdf

United Nations. (2015). *World population prospects: The 2015 revision, Key Findings and Advance Tables*. Department of Economic and Social Affairs Population Division. Working Paper No. ESA/P/WP.241.

Van Dullemen, C. (2006). Older people in Africa: New engines to society? *NWSA Journal, 18*(1), 99–105.

Wallace, G. (2001). Grandparent caregivers: emerging issues in elder law and social work practice. *Journal of Gerontological Social Work, 34*(3), 127–136.

Western, J., (1981). *Outcast Cape Town*. California: University of California Press.

Whitehead, A., Hashim, I. M., & Iversen, V. (2005). *Child migration, child agency and inter-generational relations in Africa and South Asia.* Paper presented to Children and Youth in Emerging and Transforming Societies Childhoods. 29 June–3 July, Oslo.

Wilson, F. (1972). *Migrant labour.* Johannesburg: South African Council of Churches and SPRO.

Woolard I., & Klasen, S. (2004). *Determinants of income mobility and household poverty dynamics in South Africa.* Institute for the Study of Labour (IZA) Discussion Paper. Bonn, Germany.

PART VI
Conclusions

13

CHAPTER THEMES, HIGHLIGHTS, AND RECOMMENDATIONS

David W. Shwalb and Ziarat Hossain

We will first identify six themes from the main chapters of this book.

1. *Several contextual variables are related to diversity among grandparents.* These are illustrated in Table 13.1, which gives examples of each contextual variable from every chapter (see Shwalb & Shwalb, 2015, for a comparable list of international contextual influences on fatherhood). An example of each variable is as follows:

    *   Historical background – changes in life expectancies and absence of men from their families, between the Soviet and post-Soviet eras in Russia (Chapter 7)
    *   Family characteristics – prevalence of multi-generational families gives way to smaller nuclear families throughout East Asia (Chapter 9)
    *   Economic conditions – social class differences in grandparental care in Brazil (Chapter 4)
    *   Employment conditions – youth unemployment as a major reason for grandparents' financial remittances to younger generations in Southern Africa (Chapter 12)
    *   Urban/rural location – differences in grandparents' roles between urban versus rural locations in Central America (Chapter 2)
    *   Ethnicity – diversity in grandparenthood among several ethnic groups in the US (Chapter 3)
    *   Immigration/emigration/migration – immigration from South Asia to UK (Chapter 6) as source of diversity among grandparents

    In addition, the Subject Index (p. 320) lists examples of these and other sources of diversity: age of grandparent, age of grandchild, globalization, HIV/AIDS pandemic, language, race, religion, technology, and war/internal conflicts.

TABLE 13.1 Sources of Diversity in Grandparents, by Chapter

Ch.	Location	History	Geography	Family Characteristics	Economic Factors	Employment Conditions	Norms, Values, Beliefs	Ethnicity	Immigration/ Emigration
2	Mexico/ Central America	Spanish colonization	Cross-national & urban/rural diversity	Large family size; low divorce rates; high birth rate	Agriculture & mining; poverty & inflation	Dependent on children and extended kin; limited pensions	Extended families; respect for elders; familism; class-based societies	Spanish; Indigenous; mixed	Emigration to developed countries
3	USA	European settlers; Mexican–American war	Ethnic minorities concentrated in large cities; rural Black minority in SE region	Nuclear family; high divorce rate; low birth rate	Capitalism; service & manufacturing; affluence & economic inequalities	Retirement and social security; outside employment opportunities	Individualism; competition; democracy; personal choice	Increasing diversity (White, Indigenous, Latino, African, & Asian)	Immigration from developing countries; urbanization
4	Brazil	Portuguese colonization	Rural–urban migrations; regional differences; many mega-cities	Large family size; low but increasing divorce rate	Agriculture & manufacturing; developing economy	Dependent on children and extended kin; limited social welfare; pensions for some	Extended network; class-based society; respect for elders	White, Black, Asian, Indigenous	Emigration to developed countries
5	Germany	Nationalistic movement; post-war reconstruction	Highly urbanized	Nuclear family; low birth rate; high divorce rate	Capitalism; dervice & manufacturing; public welfare; high income	Social welfare; retirement pensions; employment opportunities	Individualism; competition; democracy; personal choice	Germans, Turkish	Immigration from Turkey, etc.
6	UK	Colonization of Asian and African nations	Highly urbanized; regional differences	Nuclear family; low birth rate; high divorce rate	Capitalism; service & manufacturing; public welfare; high income	Social welfare; retirement pensions; employment opportunities	Individualism; competition; democracy; personal choice	White, Asian, African, Caribbean	Immigration from former colonies
7	Russia	Heavy loss of lives in World War II; Soviet/ post-Soviet eras	Asian/European proximity; huge land mass, most of which is unpopulated	Nuclear family; high divorce rate; low birth rate	Large female labor force; Transition from state socialism to capitalism	Retirement pensions; outside employment; limited social welfare	Individualism; matrifocality; hegemonic gender roles; male alcoholism	Russian, Tatar, Chechen, other minorities	Internal migrations

8 S. Asia	Rural–urban migration; diverse landmass; high population density	British colonization; partition of Indian sub-continent	Extended family; high birth rate; low divorce rate; multiple caregiving	Agricultural & manufacturing; poverty; income inequality	Dependent on children and extended kin; limited social welfare; pensions for some	Collectivism; hegemonic gender roles; son preference; class/caste; respect elders; gender/age hierarchies	Indo-Aryan, Dravidian, Sino-Tibetan	Migration to UK, US, & Middle East
9 E. Asia	Urban/rural differences; huge Chinese land mass; Japan island nation; Korean families split between North/South	Confucian heritage; World War II; Chinese influences on Japan & Korea	Extended network; low birth/divorce rates	Agriculture, manufacturing, & service; moderate to high income; capitalism	Retirement and pensions; social welfare; support from extended kin	Collectivism; hegemonic gender roles; filial piety; respect elders; gender & age hierarchies	Han, Yamato, Korean	Urbanization; Chinese male internal migration for employment
10 MENA	Regional migration to oil-rich countries; demographic differences between countries	Tribal & ancient civilization; Roman-Greco, Ottoman, & British influences	Extended family; high birth rate; low divorce rate; polygamy	Capitalism (government ownership); poverty (except oil countries); state welfare; income inequality	Economic disparities; government assistance in oil rich countries; support from extended kin	Collectivism; tribalism; hegemonic gender roles; respect elders; religious values	Arab, Israeli, Baloch, Kurdish, Turkish, Persian	Migrations within region to seek employment
11 Sub-Saharan Africa	Regional migration to mining cities; rural and pastoral; rural–urban (male) migration	Nomadic lifestyles; experience of colonialism	Extended family; high birth & infant mortality rates	Subsistence agriculture & mining; women's employment in agriculture; poverty; health crises	Dependent on children and extended kin; limited retirement pensions	Collectivism; tribalism; respect elders; gender & age hierarchies	Tribes, Arab,	Migration to oil rich countries; urbanization
12 Southern Africa	Urban–rural disparities; mostly urbanized Whites and rural Blacks	Apartheid & British rule; post-colonial society	Extended family; high birth rate	Agriculture & mining; economic disparities	Limited social welfare and pensions; employment opportunities; support from extended kin	Collectivism; tribalism; hegemonic gender roles; respect elders; gender & age hierarchies	Tribes, Whites	Intra-regional migration to mining cities & countries

2.   *Research on grandparents, and particularly that on grandfathers, is unavailable or deficient from many societies; further, the quality and quantity of research on grandparenting varied widely between the 11 main chapters.* In some affluent societies (e.g., Germany, Japan, Korea, UK, US) there is a relatively deeper and wider research literature, whereas for most developing societies there is a lack in depth and breadth of research on grandparents. Extensive reference citations in every chapter of this book fill in some gaps in the worldwide literature, but there are still important scarcities and voids.

3.   *While some societies have adopted social policies and laws that affect the grandparental role, grandparenting has received very limited attention from policy makers in other societies.* In our view, government policies, laws, and state support for grandparents are more typically in place in developed nations with extensive social welfare and pension systems (e.g., US, UK, and Germany), and are just beginning to have an effect in other developed societies (e.g., Japan and Korea). Meanwhile, relations between families and the state in developing nations have had profound effects in places such as China (One Child Policy) and Southern Africa (pension system), but less impact in many other developing societies. The influence of non-governmental organizations and websites, as supplements or alternatives to steps taken by governments, are also noticeable in some societies, as illustrated in the Appendices of the 11 main chapters.

4.   *Economic conditions have a heavy effect on grandparenting in most locations.* Economic conditions and standards of living vary significantly between societies and regions, and economic contexts may influence the lives of children, parents, and grandparents (Albert & Trommsdorff, 2014). Among the countries listed in Table 1.1, per capita income ranges from US$1,097 in Bangladesh to US$55,800 in the US, with every other level of affluence between these extremes also represented in the table. Some societies covered in this book are relatively stable in economic and social terms, while others are unstable. Such stability and instability affects family systems and thereby grandparenthood, and the wholesale transformation of some economies (e.g., Russia in Chapter 7 and China in Chapter 9) may also redefine grandparenthood. As we have also seen, economic disparities between social classes are an important source of diversity of grandparenting within (e.g., Brazil, Chapter 4) and between (e.g., MENA, Chapter 10) societies, and economic hardships can be an impetus for grandparents' positive involvement with their grandchildren (e.g., South Asia, Chapter 8).

5.   *Many grandparents serve as the primary caregivers to their grandchildren, in a wide variety of societies.* Particular attention was paid to this theme in the chapters from the US (Chapter 3), Brazil (Chapter 4), MENA (Chapter 10), sub-Saharan Africa (Chapter 11), and Southern Africa (Chapter 12). This theme appeared in other chapters but was a more critical issue in locations where

"grandparents raising grandchildren" (Hayslip & Golden-Glen, 2000) was by necessity rather than choice.

6. *Changes in grandparents' roles are found everywhere, but the type and degree of change is specific to each location.* There appears to be a strong cultural tradition of grandparents who take a key role within multi-generational families as portrayed in the chapters from Asia and Africa, compared with what we read about in the European or US chapters. The authors of every main chapter predicted changes in future generations of grandparents in their society or region. Some chapters (e.g., Chapter 4 on Brazil; Chapter 8 on South Asia) predicted greater involvement of grandparents with their grandchildren. One result of divergent demographic trends (e.g., zero or negative population growth within Europe, Japan, and Korea, versus current population increases throughout South Asia) is that the future need for grandparental involvement will continue to vary between societies. In our opinion, there will be future diversification of grandparents' roles rather than convergence on one global model of grandparenthood.

Lessons Learned From Each Chapter

The following is a selection of some findings that stood out in each chapter, along with some general comparisons of grandparents within and between chapters.

The Americas: Mexico and Central America, the US, and Brazil

Gibbons and Fanjul (Chapter 2) showed us that grandparental roles have remained significant throughout Mexico and Central America over the centuries, despite social upheavals and economic changes. This theme of historical continuity was based on the cultural practice of *familismo* which promotes the role of grandparents, who foster family unity and togetherness. *Familismo* is now coupled with a new conceptualization of *caballerismo* that emphasizes the positive roles of grandparents in Latino families. A major theme in the chapter from the US, by Hayslip and Fruhauf, was diversity itself. The wide variety of family settings in which American grandparents enact their roles was as noticeable in this chapter as anywhere in this volume, e.g., LGB grandparents, grandparents with incarcerated children, from various immigrant groups, etc. From Brazil (Chapter 4), Dias, Azambuja, Rabinovich, and Bastos emphasized the impact of social class on grandparental roles. For example, the economic hardship and job-related migration of Brazilian parents reportedly invites grandparents in many families to take full responsibility for grandchildren. In addition, life events such as teenage pregnancy, divorce, parental neglect, and disability are apparently major precursors of Brazilian grandparental involvement with children.

Europe (Germany and the UK) and Russia

Chapter 5 from Germany described grandparents as generally important and involved. Mahne, Engstler, and Klaus also emphasized the important influence of immigrant populations (e.g., from Turkey) on their overall portrayal of contemporary grandparenthood. Although most German grandparents reportedly maintain close contact with their grandchildren, the role of grandparents seemed to be even stronger within immigrant families compared with native German families. Buchanan (Chapter 6) made a similar observation about how traditional UK grandparenthood has changed in the context of major waves of immigrants to the UK from former British colonial locations. Finally, the UK and German chapters both made explicit references to "new grandfathers"; it was notable that the expression "new grandfathers" was not used in other chapters. In contrast, Utrata (Chapter 7) focused on Russian grandmothers. In the context of matrifocal families, it was clear that the main story to be told about grandparenthood in post-Soviet Russia focuses on the *babushka* and not on grandfathers. Perhaps absence itself is among the strongest characteristics of Russian men, including grandfathers.

South Asia: Bangladesh, India, and Pakistan

Babu, Hossain, Morales, and Vij (Chapter 8) presented an integrated view of grandparenthood across three diverse nations on the South Asian sub-continent. Although economic, social, and class diversity all influence grandparent–grandchild relations and families in South Asian societies, the carer role and social importance of grandparents appears to be consistent across the region. Grandparents make positive contributions to grandchildren's lives as they inculcate values, share inheritance, and keep the extended family together. However, it was also clear from Chapter 8 that traditional families and the roles of grandparents were in transition to a new model in each society. For example, the increasing modernization of the region also seems to be leading to a hybrid model of childcare that offers both institutional and grandparental resources and care.

East Asia: Japan, Korea, and China

The East Asia chapter (Chapter 9) by Nakazawa, Hyun, Ko, and Shwalb provided three separate portrayals of grandparenthood in a region with a shared ancient Confucian heritage. We expected that because they live in similar economic systems the behavior of Japanese and Korean grandparents would be similar, and that grandparents in these two societies would diverge from Chinese grandparents. In fact, a more negative view of grandparenthood and somewhat stronger emphasis on academic achievement emerged from the Korean than from the Japanese data. Meanwhile, China seemed to have a unique set of social problems and contexts in which grandparents continue to change. These included internal migrations of the middle generation toward big cities which leaves grandchildren and grandparents behind, transformation from a rural agrarian economy to an urban capitalist economy, and the legacy of the One Child Policy.

The MENA Region

The Middle East and North Africa (MENA) chapter by Emam, Abd-Elazeem, and El-Keshk (Chapter 10) mostly focused on societies where Islam is the predominant religion. Given the availability of quality research on Jewish Israeli grandparents, it also included research findings from Israel. However, due to space limitations, their discussion of religious and other contextual influences on families focused on the impact of Islam. Their chapter conveyed that the revered position of grandparents across MENA societies is influenced by collectivism, the centrality of Islamic beliefs in family life, age and gender hierarchy, and the tradition of reciprocal care. One other issue that stood out in their chapter was the impact of war and internal conflicts, and the resulting instability which has led to a transition away from traditional grandparental roles.

Sub-Saharan and Southern Africa

There was some similarity between Chapters 11 and 12, because sub-Saharan Africa overlaps geographically with Southern Africa. One main theme of Chapter 11 by Mutepfa, Mpofu, Moore, and Ingram was that a very large number of sub-Saharan grandparents, mainly grandmothers, have taken over the parenting role of parents due to the middle generation's health problems. Chapter 12 by Makiwane, Gumede, and Makiwane also emphasized health issues, mostly the HIV/AIDS pandemic which has forced grandparents to support both their children and grandchildren. We read in both Chapters 11 and 12 about changes in the relationship between the state and families, and the reciprocal nature of grandparent–grandchild support and care. Despite economic challenges, norms of reciprocity and resilience motivate sub-Saharan African grandparents to care for their grandchildren. Compared to the situation portrayed overall for sub-Saharan Africa, grandparent–grandchild relations in Southern Africa appeared in Chapter 12 to be even more dire because so many South African families have been split apart by economic necessity.

Agenda for Future Research

Szinovacz (1998; Foreword, this volume) has provided a critique of theoretical and methodological issues in the study of grandparenthood, and we will next add some points about international research, because we expect that research on grandparents will become increasingly international in its coverage.

Compare Societies versus Regions, and Grandmothers versus Grandfathers

Where should future studies of grandparents be focused geographically, and what cross-societal and within-societal comparisons would be most beneficial to the overall international literature? Clearly, international data on grandparents are limited in both geographical and cultural coverage. As a consequence of globalization and contemporary political and economic changes such as creation of nation states and cross-national migrations, it is common for multiple cultures and ethnic groups to reside within a single country or region. Most of the chapters of this book showed that geographical coverage of grandparents includes several communities (e.g., ethnic minority groups in the US). It is important for future research to focus on both societies and regions. We recommend that future research on grandparents include more comparisons between different cultural groups that reside within a particular geographic entity. This type of comparison will provide greater details about cultural parameters that often work in conjunction with geographical factors to define and influence grandparenting. Although there were numerous comparisons between chapters throughout this volume, very few studies of grandparents are either cross-cultural or cross-national in design; Georgas, Berry, van de Vijver, Kagitcibasi, and Poortinga (2006) was a notable exception here, but grandparents were not the main focus of their 30-nation study. Because of the lack of comparative data and data from national samples, we cannot answer definitively such important questions as how grandparents compare between regions and societies in the amount of time given to their grandchildren.

In almost every chapter of this book, and in the Foreword, it was mentioned that international "grandparenting" research had mainly focused on grandmothers, and there was a consistent relative lack of data from and about grandfathers in almost every chapter. This may reflect the prominence of grandmothers and mothers in gendered family roles, by which family life is still perceived (sometimes inaccurately) as women's domain and employment outside the home as men's domain. Whatever the traditions, cultural beliefs, stereotypes, or normative behavior may be in each society, we believe that researchers must document the actual behavior of both grandmothers and grandfathers. Only such evidence will test the assumption that grandmothers merit more investigation than grandfathers, and the assumption that grandmothers are more important or influential than grandfathers.

Focus on the Impact of Social Changes on Grandparents

The main chapters of this book emphasized socio-historical and cultural contexts of grandparents and their roles and responsibilities in the family. We envision three other important areas for the future study of grandparenthood. First, we need to look at how demographic shifts continue to influence the population structure of societies. As noted often in this book, increased longevity allows grandparents to spend more years with their children and grandchildren. This trend has implications for the study of intergenerational relationships between grandparents and grandchildren, in the context of shifting values and lifestyles (Trommsdorff, Mayer, & Albert, 2004). Second, future research should focus on aspects of care and support for aged grandparents. As several chapters here have pointed out, national policies and budgets need to address healthcare, housing, physical care, and recreational activities for the growing number of aged grandparents. Finally, research should examine how the global economic market and international labor migrations impact grandparents' roles and life quality.

Build a Multi-Disciplinary Research Literature

Depending on the academic discipline, each of the major social sciences addresses human development vis-à-vis grandparents within its own scope. For example, sociological research on grandparents often emphasizes the influence of demographic and structural variables on the role of grandparents. Psychological research primarily focuses on individual characteristics and cultural variability of grandparents. Research within the fields of anthropology and family studies often highlights community links, group characteristics, and within-culture variations. Meanwhile, medical science tends to consider grandparents as subjects in a bio-medical process, and the field of gerontology is often interested in grandparents in terms of increased longevity and a definition of the process of "successful aging." Although each of these disciplines does important work on grandparents, we see a need to integrate (or at least be more aware of) these different approaches. Especially from an international perspective, future research on grandparents must become more collaborative and inter-disciplinary.

Conduct Longitudinal Research on Grandparents and Their Influence on Children of All Ages

Szinovacz (1998; Foreword, this volume) observed that most of the research data reported in this book, and generally in research on grandparents, is cross-sectional and ignores the fact that grandparents change over the course of adulthood. We therefore recommend that research on adult development study individuals and cohorts of grandparents longitudinally in various societies, as they grow and develop in their dynamic roles. In our opinion, developmental psychology as a field has often limited its view of grandparents to the contexts of aging and adult stages of development, and downplayed grandparents' impact on child development. As stated in Chapter 1 of this volume, this narrow view is understandable because grandparents may be less active in the Western populations that dominate the human development research literature (see also Smith & Wilde, in press). Yet findings in Africa and Asia, home to two-thirds of the world's population, indicate that grandparents frequently raise grandchildren and have profound effects on child development. Therefore, we believe that research on grandparents, and especially cross-cultural studies, belong more in the mainstream of research on child development.

A Final Case Story

Consider this final case story about a retired school teacher, which we were unable to include in a previous chapter due to space limitations.

> "WG" is a mother of four, grandmother of 12, and great-grandmother of three. Along with her husband, she lives beyond driving distance of all of their extended family. What stands out most about this thoroughly child-centered grandmother is that she is able to appreciate the goodness, unique personalities, and current interests of all of these children, over the years and despite the distances. She makes an effort to visit every one of her progeny in person at least once each year, and where possible to stay in touch with them via phone and social media. Although her children long ago became independent, she still counsels her adult children at key junctures in their lives. Helping out in the home after the latest birth of the newest grandchild, taking a grandbaby for a springtime walk in the flower garden, rough-housing or engaging in fantasy play with a preschool-age grandchild, setting up games and crafts projects when grade school grandchildren visit "grandma's house," listening with empathy to her teenage grandchild's stories of problems with her boyfriend, mailing a "care package" to a homesick grandchild at college, and going to the wedding of an adult grandchild, WG is highly involved even though face-to-face reunions are too infrequent and she misses all the children terribly. It never seems to be "about grandma" when she is with her grandchildren; it is always all about the young ones. Some grandchildren describe WG as their "closest" grandparent despite their geographic separation.

Can you identify where WG lives based on the contextual details in her case story, or from aspects of her character, characteristics, or behavior? Or does she seem like the grandparent in several of the other case stories you have read in this book? Looking back over this volume, WG's case story illustrates a problem faced by every chapter contributor: the difficulty of making general statements. On the one hand WG and the other case story grandparents illustrate the high degree of individuality and uniqueness among grandparents everywhere. But on the other hand, they also demonstrate both culture-specific influences on grandparenting and the common humanity of all grandparents. The literature reviews in each chapter of this book, meanwhile, reported various patterns and trends in grandparents' behavior, influence, and roles. Chapter contributors also described complex sets of contextual variables, to clarify the settings and backgrounds of each population group of grandparents. In sum, each chapter painted a different background and portrait of grandparenting. We were reminded each time we read a case story that we must value each grandparent as an individual. Yet much of the research literature consisted of quantitative analyses of self-report data from large samples of grandparents. General statements based on case stories or quantitative research are both problematic, especially when we seek to draw conclusions about grandparents in cultural context.

We hope that the case stories, descriptions of context, and reviews of research literature add to your understanding of and appreciation for grandparents. As we look ahead to the next generation of research, practice, and policy-making, the international field of research on grandparents faces many challenges and opportunities. This book may provide a benchmark of progress in research on grandparents across several geographic regions and societies, as a forerunner of future research. Indeed, the wisdom, sacrifices, dedication, and companionship of grandparents, in settings as diverse as grandparents themselves, connect us to our past heritage and can help us to improve the lives of future families.

Appendix

Discussion Questions

1. This chapter provided a list of contextual influences on grandparenting. Which of these contexts have the most influence on your own family, or on families in your society generally?
2. Which of the "lessons learned" from the book (summarized in this chapter) were most surprising to you when you first read this book, and why?
3. Which case story from earlier chapters in this book was most similar to the Chapter 13 case story about "WG"? Which earlier case story grandparent was most different from "WG"?

References

Albert, I., & Trommsdorff, G. (2014). The role of culture in social development over the life span: An interpersonal relations approach. *Online readings in Psychology and Culture, 6*(2). doi:10.9707/2307-0919.1057

Georgas, J., Berry, J. W., van de Vijver, F. J. R., Kagitcibasi, C., & Poortinga, Y. H. (2006). *Families across cultures: A 30-nation psychological study.* Cambridge, UK: Cambridge University Press.

Hayslip, B., & Goldberg-Glen, J. (2000). *Grandparents raising grandchildren: Theoretical, empirical, and clinical perspectives.* New York: Springer.

Shwalb, D. W., & Shwalb, B. J. (2015). Fathering diversity within societies. In L. A. Jensen (Ed.), *Oxford handbook of human development and culture: An interdisciplinary perspective* (pp. 602–617). New York: Oxford University Press.

Smith, P. K., & Wilde, L. (in press). Grandparenting. In M. Bornstein (Ed.), *Handbook of parenting, Vol. 3: Being and becoming a parent* (3rd ed.), New York: Routledge.

Szinovacz, M. E. (1998). *Handbook on grandparenthood.* New York: Greenwood Press.

Trommsdorff, G., Mayer, B., & Albert, I. (2004). Dimensions of culture in intra-cultural comparisons. Individualism/collectivism and family-related values in three generations. In H. Vinken, J. Soeters, & P. Ester (Eds.), *Comparing cultures: Dimensions of culture in a comparative perspective* (pp. 157–179). Leiden: Brill.

AUTHOR INDEX

SUBJECT INDEX